Python-Powered Excel

Combining the strengths of Python and Excel for deliverables and complex tasks

Dr Nisha Arora

www.bpbonline.com

First Edition 2026

ISBN: 978-93-78543-555

LIMITS OF LIABILITY AND DISCLAIMER OF WARRANTY

Distributors:

BPB PUBLICATIONS
20, Ansari Road, Darya Ganj
New Delhi-110002
Ph: 23254990/23254991

DECCAN AGENCIES
4-3-329, Bank Street,
Hyderabad-500195
Ph: 24756967/24756400

MICRO MEDIA
Shop No. 5, Mahendra Chambers,
150 DN Rd. Next to Capital Cinema,
V.T. (C.S.T.) Station, MUMBAI-400 001
Ph: 22078296/22078297

To View Complete BPB Publications Catalogue Scan the QR Code:

Published by Manish Jain for BPB Publications, 20 Ansari Road, Darya Ganj, New Delhi-110002 and Printed by him at Repro India Ltd., Rewari.

www.bpbonline.com

Dedicated to

My Guruji, with deep gratitude for blessings,
my loving daughter **Navisha**
and
my husband **Gaurav**

About the Author

Dr Nisha Arora is a seasoned trainer, speaker, and data professional known for her ability to simplify complex technical concepts. With deep expertise in data science, applied statistics, and mathematics, she brings clarity and structure to topics that often overwhelm learners.

Her practical experience extends across analytical tool including Python, R, Excel, Power Query, Solver, Data Analysis Toolpak, MegaStat, and Real Statistics, etc. enabling her to bridge the gap between traditional spreadsheet analysis and modern programming-driven workflows. She works to empower professionals with analytics, data science, and data storytelling, along with Excel automation.

She has authored courses on platforms including Udemy and TutorialsPoint and contributed actively on Stack Exchange, ResearchGate, Quora, LinkedIn, and YouTube. Her content has reached more that over 2.3 million users globally. She has also contributed as a technical reviewer for titles published by BPB Publications.

About the Reviewers

- **Abhishake Gupta** is a senior python engineer with extensive experience building scalable backend systems and data-intensive applications, now focused on quantitative development and algorithmic trading. He has deep expertise in Python and its web frameworks viz. Flask, FastAPI, combined with strong proficiency in data and quantitative libraries such as Pandas, NumPy, SciPy, and Scikit-learn, enabling him to design and implement robust, production-grade trading and analytics workflows.

  He has engineered full-stack platforms, architected high-volume e-commerce backends, and integrated complex third-party REST APIs for payments, logistics, and loyalty systems, consistently improving performance and reducing technical debt. Abhishake has also built a Python-based algorithmic trading framework around Interactive Brokers API & ICICI Direct APIs, covering historical data ingestion, strategy backtesting, and live signal generation, reflecting his passion for financial markets and systematic trading.

  Comfortable working with Docker, AWS, and modern CI/CD pipelines, he emphasizes clean architecture, observability, and reliability using tools such as Datadog, ELK Stack, Splunk, and Zabbix. He is driven by a strong curiosity for markets and technology, continuously sharpening his skills through hands-on projects and dedicated trading-related certifications.

- **Dr. Deepika S. Joshi** is an accomplished educator with demonstrated ability to teach, motivate, and direct students while maintaining high interest and achievement. Offering sterling experience of 20+ years, of which 18+ years have been in the field of academics. She is Ph.D. (Management), MCA, MBA with specialization in HR. Presently, designated as an associate professor (Faculty of commerce and business management) at Amrapali University, Haldwani, Uttarakhand.

- **Sagar Nangare** is a versatile software engineer and data science enthusiast with a strong foundation in Python, web development, and DevOps practices. He is currently focused on building intelligent, scalable applications, particularly in the domain of **governance, risk, and compliance** (**GRC**), where he integrates AI and machine learning to enhance automation and decision-making. His work involves developing end-to-end systems using modern technologies such as React, Node.js, Django, and MongoDB, along with implementing secure features like RBAC and multi-factor authentication.

He is also actively expanding his expertise in machine learning, deep learning, and natural language processing, exploring advanced concepts like transfer learning and generative AI. Alongside his technical development, he is preparing for system design challenges and high-level technical interviews, with a focus on backend engineering and scalable architectures. Sagar follows a structured, hands-on learning approach, building real-world projects such as LMS platforms and AI-driven resume analyzers. He is passionate about continuous learning, automation, and creating impactful solutions that solve complex business problems using data and intelligent systems.

Acknowledgement

I want to express my deepest gratitude to my family, friends, and mentors for their unwavering support throughout the writing of this book, especially my husband Gaurav and daughter Navisha, for their utmost patience, understanding, and cooperation, across all phases of developing this manuscript.

I cannot forgo expressing my heartfelt thanks to my reverend parents and in-laws for their blessing, with a special thanks to my mother Mrs. Sushila for her encouragement, cooperation, moral support and care in various ways.

I am also grateful to BPB Publications for their guidance and expertise in bringing this book to fruition. It was a long journey of revising this book, with valuable participation and collaboration of reviewers, technical experts, and editors.

I would also like to acknowledge the valuable contributions of all my learners and clients over the years. Thank you for challenging me, motivating me, and helping me grow as an educator. Some of the use cases stem from scenarios contributed by clients during training.

Finally, I would like to thank all the readers who have taken an interest in my book and for their support in making it a reality. Your encouragement has been invaluable.

Preface

Excel is an indispensable tool for professionals across industries, but as data grows more complex, repetitive tasks and limitations can hinder productivity. Python, a versatile programming language, can help Excel users unlock new levels of efficiency and analytical power. Although Python is a powerful tool for analysis, the final deliverables are commonly required in Excel to meet stakeholder needs.

Microsoft has introduced the Python in Excel feature for Excel 365 users to leverage Python's capabilities in Excel, however, it is constrained. In order to fully utilize the powers of Python and still deliver results in Excel, Python offers several tools.

This book is a practical guide to automate tedious tasks, perform advanced data analyses, and create dynamic reports, all while saving time and increasing productivity. It covers a wide range of topics, including setting up Python, creation of a virtual enviorenment for dependency management, basics of Python programming, analytical concepts data explaration, manipulation and visualization, the use of openpyxl, xlsxwriter, pyxlsb, xlrd, xlwt, and xlwings for automating Excel reports and building robust and scalable solutions.

This book is divided into four sections, catering to readers of all skill levels.

Throughout the book, many practical examples and use cases are discussed to help you understand the concepts and see their applications.

This book serves Excel users seeking to harness Python for efficient automation, analysis, and spreadsheet management, and Python analysts who are required to deliver results in Excel to satisfy stakeholder requirements. While basic Excel knowledge is beneficial, no prior programming experience is necessary. Familiarity with Python is helpful but not required to begin.

Whether you are a seasoned Excel user or a data enthusiast, this book will empower you to harness Python's potential to extend Excel's [NT1.1] functionality, saving time and enhancing productivity like never before. I hope you will find this book informative and helpful.

Let us discuss what you will learn in each chapter:

Chapter 1: Python for Excel Users – This chapter explains the need for automation in Excel workflows and Python's advantages over traditional Excel methods (VBA, Power Query). Additionally, this chapter provides an overview of the libraries that will be used and guide readers on how to approach the book as an Excel user, whether they are new to Python or have some experience with it.

Chapter 2: Setting Up Python – This chapter guides readers through installing Python via Anaconda, setting up Spyder as their primary IDE, and creating a virtual environment to manage dependencies efficiently. The chapter also explains other available options for running Python code like IDEs, code editors, cloud-based platforms.

Chapter 3: Python Fundamentals – This chapter covers the core concepts and building blocks of the language. It introduces readers to Python's syntax and essential topics such as datatypes, operators, data structures, control flow, functions, and exception handling. This chapter is indispensable for non-programmers, as it provides a solid foundation upon which further learning can be built. Several examples are included for practice purposes.

Chapter 4: External Packages and Date-time Handling – This chapter allows the reader to learn using external packages and modules for enhancing Python's functionality. Moreover, this chapter covers working with date and time in Python, which is crucial for Excel users handling datasets with columns such as application dates, order dates, delivery dates, and visit times.

Chapter 5: Automating File Management with Python – This chapter gives special attention to Python's built-in file handling capabilities for automating key file management tasks. This will allow readers to streamline their routine file operations, reducing manual work and minimizing errors. Some automation use cases are demonstrated in the chapter.

Chapter 6: Data Manipulation with Pandas – This focuses on data manipulation using Python's pandas library. It offers a solid understanding of how to clean, transform, merge, and analyze data using pandas, preparing readers for more advanced Excel-Python integration with libraries like openpyxl and xlwings. Numerous examples are included in the chapter.

Chapter 7: Smart Tools for Faster Analysis –This chapter discusses numpy operations, financial calculations and data visualization using pandas. It also shows some auto EDA libraries and GUI-based tools to quickly uncover patterns, summaries, and relationships. Additionally, it explains numpy operations, using pandas to visualize the data. It helps readers answer business questions faster and enable deeper insights with less effort by generating instant summary reports. Libraries discussed in the chapter are numpy, numpy-financial, pandas, y-data profiling (previously known as pandas profiling), sweetviz, and dtale.

Chapter 8: Unlocking Excel with openpyxl – This chapter is dedicated to openpyxl, a Python library designed for working with Excel files, which allows users to automate these tasks efficiently. It shows a comparative analysis of key Python-Excel integration libraries before diving into openpyxl's capabilities, such as read, write, edit, format, protect, merge, and generate charts in Excel files programmatically.

Chapter 9: Core Excel Read-Write Tools in Python – This chapter introduces xlsxwriter, a powerful library for creating and formatting Excel files programmatically. Additionally, this chapter covers pyxlsb for reading binary Excel files (.xlsb) and briefly touches on xlrd for legacy .xls file support. This chapter covers practical examples of automating Excel workflows and create dynamic reports with rich formatting, eliminating tedious manual work.

Chapter 10: Transitioning to xlwings for Excel Automation – This chapter introduces xlwings library that enables seamless interaction between Python and Excel, offering greater flexibility and automation capabilities than traditional Excel methods. It focuses on fundamental xlwings operations, such as reading and writing data, formatting cells, and automating charts. It also allow readers to explore how xlwings compares to openpyxl and other Excel automation libraries, gaining insight into when and why to use it.

Chapter 11: Running Python Code from Excel – This chapter explores multiple ways to integrate and execute Python scripts within Excel, catering to different levels of flexibility and automation needs. It discusses the use of xlwings add-in, VBA integration, and standalone Python scripts to automate tasks efficiently. It will also enable readers to compare various approaches, understand their pros and cons, and gain step-by-step guidance on setting up each method. This will enable readers to choose and implement the best approach based on their workflow requirements.

Chapter 12: Advanced Automation with xlwings –This chapter explains how to create **User-Defined Functions** (**UDFs**) in Python that can be used directly from Excel cells. This makes complex calculations, data retrieval, and API integrations seamless. This chapter provides a variety of worked examples to exhibit a structured approach to writing, testing, and optimizing UDFs, ensuring Excel professionals can extend Excel's functionality beyond built-in formulas. Furthermore, it includes a real-world case study that demonstrates how xlwings can be used in an Excel-driven workflow to automate reporting, or enhance decision-making.

Chapter 13: Python Excel Integration Limits and Vision – This chapter introduces the key challenges, and best practices to make automation workflows more reliable and efficient. This chapter highlights the key takeaways from the book, discusses common pitfalls and performance bottlenecks, and provides insights into the best solution for Excel automation. This chapter also briefly talks about Microsoft 365's Python in Excel feature and co-pilot along with their limitations. This will allow professionals to make informed decisions about the best tools for their specific needs.

Code Bundle and Coloured Images

Please follow the link to download the
Code Bundle and the ***Coloured Images*** of the book:

https://rebrand.ly/127133

The code bundle for the book is also hosted on GitHub at
https://github.com/bpbpublications/Python-Powered-Excel.
In case there's an update to the code, it will be updated on the existing GitHub repository.

We have code bundles from our rich catalogue of books and videos available at **https://github.com/bpbpublications.** Check them out!

Errata

We take immense pride in our work at BPB Publications and follow best practices to ensure the accuracy of our content to provide an indulging reading experience to our subscribers. Our readers are our mirrors, and we use their inputs to reflect and improve upon human errors, if any, that may have occurred during the publishing processes involved. To let us maintain the quality and help us reach out to any readers who might be having difficulties due to any unforeseen errors, please write to us at: **errata@bpbonline.com**

Your support, suggestions and feedback are highly appreciated by the BPB Publications' Family.

Piracy

If you come across any illegal copies of our works in any form on the internet, we would be grateful if you would provide us with the location address or website name. Please contact us at **business@bpbonline.com** with a link to the material.

If you are interested in becoming an author

If there is a topic that you have expertise in, and you are interested in either writing or contributing to a book, please visit **www.bpbonline.com**. We have worked with thousands of developers and tech professionals, just like you, to help them share their insights with the global tech community. You can make a general application, apply for a specific hot topic that we are recruiting an author for, or submit your own idea.

Reviews

Please leave a review. Once you have read and used this book, why not leave a review on the site that you purchased it from? Potential readers can then see and use your unbiased opinion to make purchase decisions. We at BPB can understand what you think about our products, and our authors can see your feedback on their book. Thank you!

For more information about BPB, please visit **www.bpbonline.com**.

Join our Discord space

Join our Discord workspace for latest updates, offers, tech happenings around the world, new releases, and sessions with the authors:

https://discord.bpbonline.com

Table of Contents

CHAPTER 1
Python for Excel Users

Introduction

In this chapter, we will discuss the need for automation in Excel workflows and explain why Python is a powerful tool for enhancing productivity. We will explore Python's advantages over traditional Excel methods (VBA, Power Query) and set the foundation for the rest of the book.

Also, Python analysts are often expected to deliver results within Excel; they will learn about dedicated tools to achieve this directly in Python.

In this chapter, you will also run a ready-made Python project to see what Python-powered Excel automation can do, without writing or understanding any code. This will give you a preview of what you will learn later.

We will guide readers on how to approach the book, whether you are new to Python or already have some experience with it.

Structure

This chapter covers the following topics:

- Excel users, analysts, and their workflow
- Excel's limitations and the need for automation
- Benefits of learning Python for Excel
- Python and Excel versions used in this book
- Delivering value from this book
- Roadmap for different readers

Excel users, analysts, and their workflow

During training and consulting work, we meet many Excel or Python professionals who share their struggles. To streamline their process, we need to understand their current workflow. Let us look at the stories inspired by real-world scenarios commonly faced by a few representative professionals and analysts.

Common roles and challenges

Alex is a sales professional. He relies heavily on Excel to compile sales data such as products, prices, discounts, revenue, etc., to calculate **key performance indicators** (**KPIs**) for sales, and generate dynamic reports for his manager every month. The process is repetitive, time-consuming, and prone to manual errors.

Maya, a content creator, runs a successful YouTube channel. To grow her audience strategically, she analyzes engagement metrics, publication time, duration, views, watch time, subscribers, impressions, and interactions. Every month, she downloads and organizes such datasets in Excel, manually applying formulas and creating charts to identify trends.

Chris is a financial analyst responsible for evaluating financial performance across various sectors, including stock markets, investment portfolios, and corporate finance. His job involves handling extensive datasets, generating insights, and preparing reports, often repeating the same steps.

Although they are working in totally different domains, they all use the same tool for their work, that is Excel, and share the same challenge of repeating manual tasks. Excel's limitations will be examined in the next section. For now, let us meet Joy, who is highly proficient in Python.

He is a data professional who transforms raw business data into clear insights with Python, but his company still wants reports to be delivered in Excel. Every week, he spends hours copy-pasting results, inserting charts and tables, and adding formats that match his brand template manually in Excel.

All of them feel that as workloads grow, valuable time is consumed by repetitive and mundane tasks that steal focus from interpreting data for better decisions.

Python transformed workflow efficiency

Maya realized that automation could save her hours of tedious work each month. She decided to explore Python for Excel automation. She significantly streamlined the process by writing a bit of code to automate data fetching, analysis, and report generation to simplify her workflow.

Let us take a glimpse at a slice of her workflow in action. Her Python script is available on GitHub. (Do not be concerned if it looks overwhelming; you will learn everything step by step in this book). Follow these steps to run the script and see what it does.

1. **Open the book's GitHub repository** by pasting the following link in your web browser:

   https://github.com/bpbpublications/Python-Powered-Excel/tree/main

   You do not need a GitHub account for this.
2. Inside the repository, open the folder for *Chapter 1*.

3. You will see a Python notebook file, named **`Chapter 1_Maya's Python Workflow.ipynb`**. **Click on this notebook** file to view it.

4. Click the **Open in Colab** button displayed on the page, as shown in the following figure:

***Figure 1.1**: Open in Colab option in Python notebook*

This will open the Python notebook in Google Colab in a separate tab. (Google Colab lets you run Python code directly in your browser without installing anything on your computer. You will learn more about this in *Chapter 2, Setting Up Python*.)

5. Sign in with your Google account (Gmail) and press *Ctrl* + *F9* (or ⌘ + *F9* on Mac or Linux) or go to **Runtime** | **Run All** in the menu as shown in the following figure:

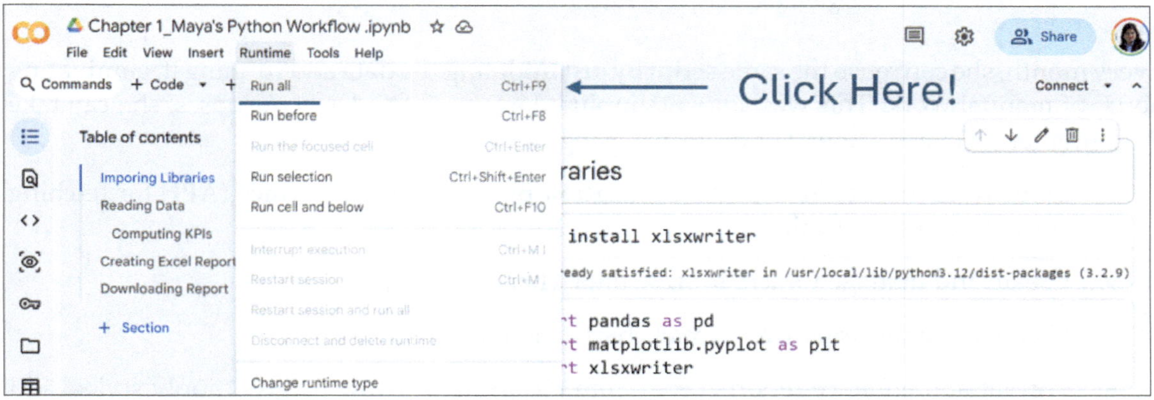

***Figure 1.2**: Run options in Colab*

6. It will show a warning to review the source code before executing the notebook. Click on **Run anyway** as shown in the following figure:

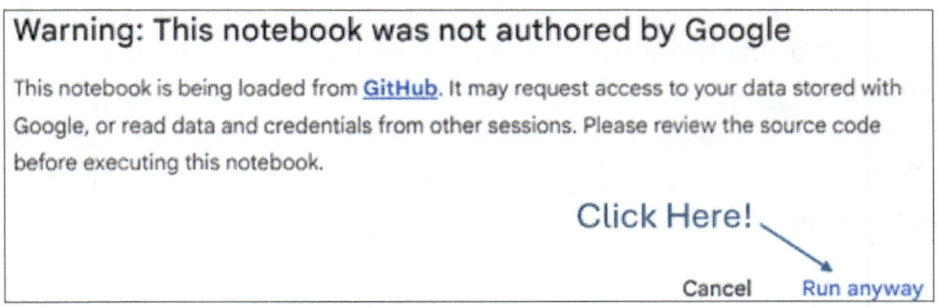

***Figure 1.3**: Colab's authorization warning*

In seconds, a useful report named **`YouTube_Report_upto_June`** is generated and downloaded that combines monthly data, calculates KPIs, and even includes charts in separate sheets. Check your Downloads folder or the location you selected.

The following figure (at a reduced zoom level to fit the page) shows the KPIs sheet of the same:

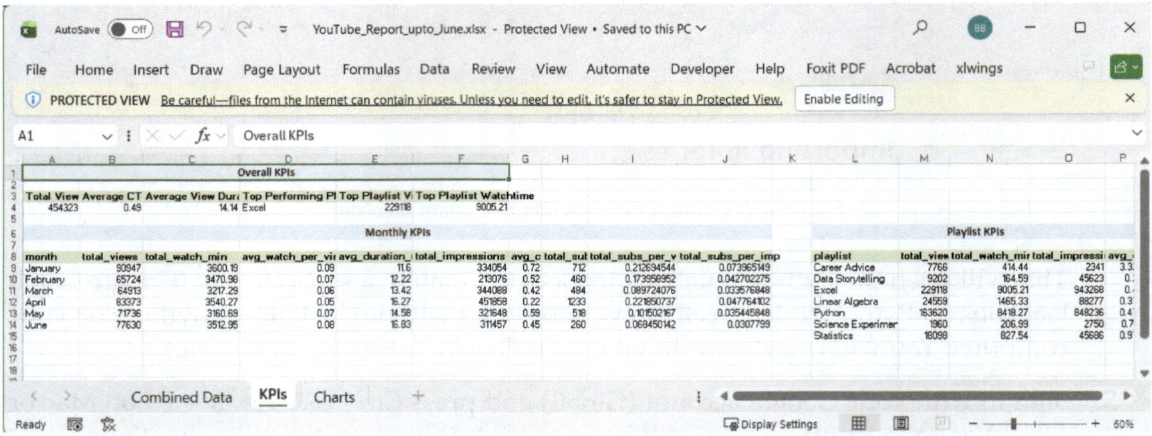

***Figure 1.4**: Glimpse of Excel report generated by Python*

Every month, she can reuse the same script by just updating the data and running it, eliminating hours of manual work. This was an oversimplified example for demo purposes; she can take this automation even further. For example, using Python, she can:

- Directly connect to YouTube's **application programming interface** (**API**) for fetching fresh data automatically.
- Create and manage folders for raw data, charts, and reports.
- Create dynamic, interactive Excel charts and dashboards.
- Format and enhance reports programmatically, adjust row heights, apply styles, add formulas, even protect cells or sheets.

Just like Maya, both Alex and Chris can benefit from automation. Instead of spending hours on repetitive tasks, they could focus on making data-driven decisions and improving their business strategies.

Likewise, Joy can also rebuild the entire workflow in Python. Instead of exporting results to Excel and manually arranging everything, he can write Excel sheets, generate charts, place everything exactly where he needs it, and apply rich formatting as needed using Python. He can even deploy Excel workbooks for his managers, who can get the entire analysis with just one Excel click without needing any Python knowledge.

In later chapters, you will learn how to:

- Create and manage folders for raw data, charts, and reports. Unzipping folders, picking the latest month's data for further analysis, all using simple Python scripts (*Chapter 5, Automating File Management with Python*).
- Transform and analyze data (*Chapter 6, Data Manipulation with Pandas*)
- Create dynamic, interactive Excel charts with Python (*Chapter 7, Smart Tools for Faster Analysis, Chapter 8, Unlocking Excel Automation with openpyxl* and *Chapter 9, Core Excel Read-write Tools in Python*).
- Format and enhance reports programmatically by adjusting row heights, setting tab colors, applying styles, adding Excel formulas, and even protecting sheets (*Chapter 8, Unlocking Excel Automation with openpyxl* and *Chapter 9, Core Excel Read-write Tools in Python* and *Chapter 10, Transitioning to xlwings for Excel Automation*).
- Deploying Python-powered Excel workbook for non-technical end users, who can use Python's capabilities inside Excel (>= 2007) without learning Python (*Chapter 11, Running Python Code from Excel* and *Chapter 12, Advanced Automation with xlwings*)

By the end of this book, you will not only save time but also build a smarter workflow.

Excel's limitations and the need for automation

Excel is an established tool that has been used by academicians, analysts, business professionals, and managers across various industries, and even by households to manage and analyze their data.

However, as the complexity and volume of data grow, many Excel users find themselves grappling with Excel's limitations, leading to frustration and inefficiency. While working with Excel professionals, we often come across common pain points that they encounter. Let us understand the challenges and issues faced by Excel users:

- **Manual copy-paste errors and complex formulas**: Manual copy-pasting data or formulas are error prone. For instance, a misplaced cell reference or incorrect formula can lead to significant discrepancies in the reports.

  Additionally, Excel formulas can become complicated, making them difficult to understand and troubleshoot. Nested formulas and advanced calculations can be intimidating, even for experienced users.

  ```
  =IF(OR(AND(A1>0, B1<100, OR(C1="Yes", D1="Approved")), AND(E1>F1, G1<H1)), IF(SUM(I1:I10)>AVERAGE(J1:J10), ROUND(K1*L1/M1,2), IF(N1="Done", O1+P1-Q1, "")), "")
  ```

  When formulas like fail, it becomes difficult to trace which condition or calculation is causing the error. The sheer number of brackets and nested logic makes troubleshooting slow and frustrating for users. Debugging errors in VBA scripts is also quite irksome.

Creating helper columns to break down a long formula does make debugging easier, but it also clutters the worksheet with extra columns that serve no purpose beyond troubleshooting. This quickly becomes messy and hard to maintain, especially when formulas grow more complex.

- **Scalability issues**: Excel is not well-suited for handling large datasets, as it can show performance degradation or unexpected application crashes during advanced processing tasks for large data.
- **Lack of advanced analytics**: Excel lacks advanced built-in tools for financial analytics, predictive modeling, computer vision, or natural language processing. Even Microsoft 365's built-in **Python in Excel** and AI-powered features like **Copilot** are limited compared to Python's full capabilities in machine learning, artificial intelligence, and automation. We will discuss it in *Chapter 13, Python Excel Integration Limits and Vision.*
- **Version control issues**: Multiple versions of the same file create confusion and data inconsistency. A small, unnoticed change can lead to terrible mistakes or discrepancies in results. Excel lacks robust version control, relying on manual file naming or limited cloud history. As a result, many users end up creating multiple versions of the same file with names such as **`report_final`**, **`report_final_v2`**, or even **`report_final_final`**. This practice quickly becomes confusing and makes version management difficult.

  In Excel 365, version control is handled through version history when files are stored on OneDrive or SharePoint. In older versions of Excel, you need to rely on the auto-recover option (File | Options | Save | AutoRecover every X minute). Excel is not ideal for enterprise-grade version control and collaboration for large-scale projects.
- **Limited integration:** Connecting to APIs, databases, and cloud services requires workarounds.
- **Limited automation**: While **Visual Basic for Applications** (**VBA**) allows for some level of automation, it is not the most user-friendly tool. Learning VBA can be challenging, and it is becoming increasingly outdated in today's times. Additionally, VBA's performance can be sluggish with large datasets. Likewise, Power Query specializes in data import and transformation but remains constrained to its environment.

If you have worked extensively at Excel, you have likely faced some of these challenges and you are certainly not alone. During my PhD, I relied heavily on Excel for calculations because I did not have access to specialized paid software and was not yet familiar with open-source alternatives. Excel helped, but the work often became slow and difficult to manage due to complex formulas and manual debugging. This experience shaped the way I think about automation beyond Excel.

Python, the popular open-source tool, addresses these issues by offering cross-platform automation, handling data retrieval, cleaning, analysis, and reporting end-to-end across systems.

These challenges also impact Python professionals who are expected to deliver final outputs in Excel. Without automation, exporting results often become manual, repetitive, and difficult to reproduce. Python-Excel integration solves this by generating Excel-ready outputs programmatically.

High price of Excel errors

When the limitations of manual spreadsheets lead to errors in critical data, the consequences can be severe. History offers several infamous real-world stories of Excel blunders where seemingly minor mistakes in Excel triggered significant financial losses and operational disruptions across major organizations. These incidents underscore the risks of relying solely on manual processes and highlight the importance of adopting more resilient, automated approaches:

- **JP Morgan Chase (2012)**: A spreadsheet error contributed to a $6 billion trading loss, known as the *London Whale* incident. The error was caused by copying and pasting incorrect data, highlighting the risks of manual data handling (**Source**: **https://www.bloomberg.com/opinion/quicktake/the-london-whale** or **https://www.henricodolfing.com/2024/07/case-study-jp-morgan-chase-london-whale.html**).
- **Fannie Mae (2003)**: A spreadsheet error resulted in a $1.1 billion overstatement of shareholder equity, caused by a simple copying error in an Excel formula (**Source**: **https://www.theguardian.com/technology/2024/oct/28/microsoft-excels-bloopers-reel-40-years-of-spreadsheet-errors#img-1**).
- **TransAlta (2003)**: A misaligned Excel spreadsheet led to a $24 million loss due to an incorrect bid in a power auction (**Source**: **https://www.theguardian.com/technology/2024/oct/28/microsoft-excels-bloopers-reel-40-years-of-spreadsheet-errors#img-1**).

These and many other Excel mishaps (**https://eusprig.org/research-info/horror-stories/**) could have been reduced, detected earlier, or mitigated with better automation practices. **Python-Excel integration** can significantly lower the likelihood of such slip-ups by enforcing structured, repeatable workflows.

Benefits of learning Python for Excel

In today's fast-paced and data-driven world, automation has become a necessity. By automating repetitive, time-consuming, and manual tasks, you can free up valuable time, reduce errors, and focus on strategic activities that drive meaningful outcomes.

Learning to use Python for data transformation, reporting, and analysis will save you time and effort from repetitive manual tasks.

Additionally, using Python can allow you to avoid costly mistakes from manual data entry and writing complex formulas. Complex Excel formulas often break when column positions shift, new columns appear, or existing ones are deleted. Python can replace Excel formulas with reproducible scripts, streamlining analysis and reporting, ensuring accuracy across large datasets, while gracefully managing the changes.

Learning Python set the stage for performing advanced analytics, machine learning, integrating with databases or APIs, and building custom solutions. Python scripts can be scheduled to run automatically, changes can be logged, and reports can be automatically emailed.

Mastering Python alongside Excel can be a revolutionary step for smarter, error-free decision-making.

This book is designed to help Excel users at all levels unlock the power of Python for automation. Whether you are familiar with VBA or have never written a line of code, you will learn everything you need to transform your workflow, step by step.

If you are a Python analyst seeking to deliver results directly in Excel through automation, this book will present a structured guide.

If your goal is to reduce effort, eliminate mistakes, and maximize productivity, now is the perfect moment to get started. The techniques covered in this book, automation, validation, and reproducible workflows, help reduce the kinds of risks that have led to many high-profile Excel failures.

Python's widespread adoption

Python is a programming language that is powerful, fast, and easy to learn. It boasts huge community support, cross-platform compatibility, and seamless integration with other tools. With an extensive collection of libraries and continuous updates, it is at the forefront of programming advancements yet remains free and open source (**https://www.python.org/about/**).

Python has rapidly become one of the most popular programming languages in the world. According to the *TIOBE Index* (**https://www.tiobe.com/tiobe-index/**), Python has consistently held the top spot for the last few years, with its lead over other languages growing ever larger. The *Stack Overflow Developer Survey* (**https://survey.stackoverflow.co/2024/technology#2-programming-scripting-and-markup-languages**) also ranks Python as the most popular language among developers. This surge in popularity is driven by Python's simplicity, versatility, and powerful libraries that make it ideal for data analysis, machine learning, web development, and automation.

Python's popularity in the world of data analysis and automation is undeniable. Guido van Rossum, the creator of Python, has long emphasized the language's ease of use and adaptability, making it a favorite among both beginners and professionals.

Python's integration with Excel has gained significant attention, especially with recent developments in Microsoft 365. As Van Rossum himself stated (**https://techcommunity.

microsoft.com/blog/excelblog/announcing-python-in-excel-combining-the-power-of-python-and-the-flexibility-of-/3893439):

I'm excited that this excellent, tight integration of Python and Excel is now seeing the light of day. I expect that both communities will find interesting new uses in this collaboration, amplifying each partner's abilities.

Similarly, *Peter Wang*, co-founder and *CEO of Anaconda*, highlighted Python's growing role in Excel:

*The integration of Anaconda Distribution for Python into Microsoft Excel is a major breakthrough (***https://techcommunity.microsoft.com/blog/excelblog/announcing-python-in-excel-combining-the-power-of-python-and-the-flexibility-of-/3893439***) that will transform the workflow of millions of Excel users around the world.*

These developments in **Microsoft 365** showcase the growing synergy between Python and Excel. The Python in Excel feature is still restricted and not available for the older versions of Excel.

Python provides a landscape of specific libraries for Excel integration, that too with even greater flexibility and control than what is currently available in Microsoft 365. We will discuss many such tools in detail in the book.

Whether or not you have access to the latest Excel version, learning Python for automation will equip you with powerful, flexible, and scalable solutions to streamline your Excel workflows.

From Excel logic to Python ease

You might think that programming is beyond your reach, but the fact is, if you are using complex Excel formulas, you are already coding.

Excel formulas often involve intricate logic and nested functions that can be harder to understand than Python code, which reads like plain English.

For example, compare the following Excel formula to count unique values in a column (say, range **`B1:B10`**), you need to combine basic functions, for example:

```
=SUMPRODUCT((B1:B10<>"")/COUNTIF(B1:B10, B1:B10&""))
```

If you are using Excel 365, you can achieve the same by using:

```
=COUNTA(UNIQUE(B1:B10))
```

Now, look at the equivalent Python (**`pandas`**) code:

```
data["column_name"].nunique()
```

Another example, an Excel formula to determine whether the sum of values in the range **`A1:A10`** is **`"High"`** or **`"Low"`**:

```
=IF(SUM(A1:A10) > 100, "High", "Low")
```

Also, Python code for the same:

```
values = [10, 15, 20, 25, 30, 5, 10, 10, 10, 5, 10]


if sum(values)> 100:
    print('High')
else:
    print('Low')
```

You might have noticed that the Python code is more readable and easier to understand, even for someone with no programming background. Python is super easy to learn and has a huge community support.

In this book, we will guide you through the fundamentals of Python from the ground up and lead you through the process of integrating it with Excel, empowering you to automate data manipulation, analysis, and reporting. Let us dive in and unlock the full potential of Excel and Python integration. You are now on the path to building faster and more reliable workflows, with the right tools and guidance, whether you primarily use Excel or Python.

Python and Excel versions used in this book

For this book, we have used Python 3.11, the latest stable version at the time of writing this book. You can use any Python 3.9+ version, but it is recommended to use the latest stable release to ensure compatibility with modern libraries and features. If you use an older version, some libraries may not work as expected or may require additional setup. Using a newer Python version is usually not an issue, since commonly used libraries keep pace with Python releases.

We have produced workbooks in both Microsoft Excel 2019 and Microsoft 365 for demonstrations. While version differences exist, the core ideas translate well. Most Python libraries used in this book work reliably with Excel's older versions, too.

We have used a Windows Machine and mentioned notes about Mac or Linux as applicable.

Throughout this book, we will work with various libraries to enhance Excel automation, data analysis, and visualization. While this is not an exhaustive list, some key libraries include **`datetime`**, **`os`**, **`glob`**, **`numpy`**, **`pandas`**, **`matplotlib`**, **`seaborn`**, **`openpyxl`**, **`xlsxwriter`**, **`xlwings`**, and more.

To write and execute Python code, we have used Google Colab and Spyder. However, you can use VS Code, PyCharm, or any other IDE of your choice. Do not worry if you are unfamiliar with these tools; we will cover everything step by step.

In *Chapter 2, Setting Up Python*, you will learn to get the necessary set-up ready with Python and related tools. As we progress, we will introduce additional libraries to expand our capabilities.

Deriving value from this book

Now that you understand why Python can be a smart upgrade for Excel automation, let us talk about how to make the most of this book. Whether you are a beginner or someone with prior programming experience, this guide is designed to help you at every step.

Here we outline the benefits and support you will reliably receive from the book:

- A hands-on, practical approach with real-world Excel automation examples.
- Step-by-step explanations, making Python accessible even if you have never coded before.
- A focus on automation techniques using **`pandas`**, **`openpyxl`**, **`xlsxwriter`**, and **`xlwings`** to integrate Python seamlessly with Excel.
- Best practices, troubleshooting tips, and optimization strategies for efficient workflows.

Prerequisites

Whether you are an Excel user or a Python user, this book is designed for you. Before beginning, review the prerequisites outlined in the following:

- Familiarity with basic Excel interface (**no VBA or Power Query knowledge** is required) is good to have.
- Willingness to learn Python (**no prior programming experience** is needed).
- A problem-solving mindset. Excel automation is about making work easier.

Roadmap for different readers

This book is structured so that you can **start from scratch** or **skip ahead** based on your experience level:

- **Complete beginners (No Python experience)**: You should start from *Chapter 2, Setting Up Python,* and move through every chapter in sequence.
- **Excel users with basic Python knowledge**: You can skim through *Chapters 2 to 4*, learn file management, data analysis, and visualization from *Chapters 5 to 7*, and focus on *Chapters 8 to 13* for Excel automation.
- **Experienced Python analysts**: You can jump directly to *Chapter 8, Unlocking Excel Automation with openpyxl*, or *Chapter 10, Transitioning to xlwings for Excel Automation*, for getting started with Excel integration using the library of your choice. We encourage you to learn about various Excel integration tools in *Chapters 8 to 13* and pick the suitable ones as per your needs.

The accompanying code files contain additional examples beyond those in the book, we recommend consulting these files and practicing alongside them rather than solely reading the code in the text.

Additionally, every chapter includes *Concept check* exercises, which are thought-based exercises, intended to prompt reflection on key concepts without needing to code. They reinforce conceptual learning and strengthen your problem-solving approach, ensuring you build a solid foundation before moving on to practical implementation.

From *Chapter 2* onwards, each chapter includes *Try it yourself* exercises, which are coding exercises aimed at hands-on proficiency and confidence in applying Python to real-world scenarios. Solutions for these exercises are available on the companion GitHub repository.

We recommend you attempt each exercise before proceeding, as this practice reinforces understanding and builds confidence step by step.

Conclusion

Automation is not just about saving time; it is about eliminating repetitive work and focusing on what truly matters.

As the saying by *Abraham Lincoln* goes, *Sharpening the blade before cutting the trees is a good investment of time.* Learning Python is like sharpening your blade; it is an investment that ensures persistent benefits. By dedicating time to mastering Python, you will gain valuable skills and might future-proof your career in data-driven decision-making.

In this chapter, we have discussed how learning Python-Excel integration can help if you come from Excel background or Python. In the next chapter, you will learn to set up Python and required libraries.

By the end of this book, you will have the confidence to build powerful Python-Excel workflows, create automated reports, and optimize your day-to-day tasks.

So, let us get started and unlock Python-powered Excel.

Concept check

Reflect on your experience as an Excel user or Python analyst and answer these questions:

1. From your current work (in Excel or Python), which steps are repetitive (copy-paste, cleaning, formatting, charts, exporting)?
2. Which part of your Excel workflow is most error-prone (data entry, formulas, copy-paste, or formatting)?
3. What would change if your entire workflow could be reproduced and automated and how much time would you save?
4. Do you often analyze data in Python and export results to Excel and then manually adjust formatting, column widths, or charts? Have you ever had to repeat the same export-and-format steps for a new dataset or month?
5. What would change if your Python workflow could generate a polished Excel report automatically, ready to share?

CHAPTER 2
Setting Up Python

Introduction

In this chapter, you will learn how to install Python and the required external packages (with or without setting up a virtual environment) on your machine. You will also learn to work on IDEs such as Spyder, and Jupyter, as well as cloud-based environment, such as Google Colab. Alternatively, you can choose any other IDE of your preference for running Python code. By the end of this chapter, you will be able to run your first Python (Hello World) program using various options.

Structure

This chapter will cover the following topics:

- Google Colab for Python execution without setup
- Python distribution and Anaconda
- Complete installation guide for Anaconda
- Python IDEs and code editors
- Python packages
- Setting up your first virtual environment
- Your first Python program

Google Colab for Python execution without setup

If you want to practice Python without installing anything. You can use Google Colaboratory (Colab in short) (**https://colab.research.google.com/**), a cloud-based platform to write and run your Python code in your browser, just like an online Excel sheet. You will need an internet connection and a Google account for using Google Colab. It can be used for quick tutorials as it allows you to practice or teach Python from anywhere, at home, in an office, or a café, while offering amazing features (we found some features better than Jupyter[1]). It allows users to save, open, and share notebooks directly with Google Drive or GitHub.

Notebooks are files with **.ipynb** extension that not only include code and output but also text, headings, and images, all in one place. These are like an Excel workbook with formulas, charts, and comments explaining the analysis.

Instead of writing all your code at once, you write in small blocks (called cells) and run them one by one. Cells help you test and tweak small parts of your code easily. You see results instantly below the code. In *Chapter 1, Python for Excel Users,* you have used a Colab notebook to run code and generate a report.

Follow these steps to create your first Colab notebook and write some code:

1. Open browser and go to Google Colab (**https://colab.research.google.com/**) and sign-in with your Gmail account.
2. Click **New Notebook**.
3. In the cell (where you see your cursor blinking), type:

```
print("Hello, Excel Users! Welcome to Python!")
```

4. Press *Shift* + *Enter* to run. Your output appears below, and a new cell code is added. If you press *Ctrl* + *Enter*, cell runs but no new cell is added.
5. Explore options to add code or text cells, run code, etc. *Figure 2.1* shows basic navigation:

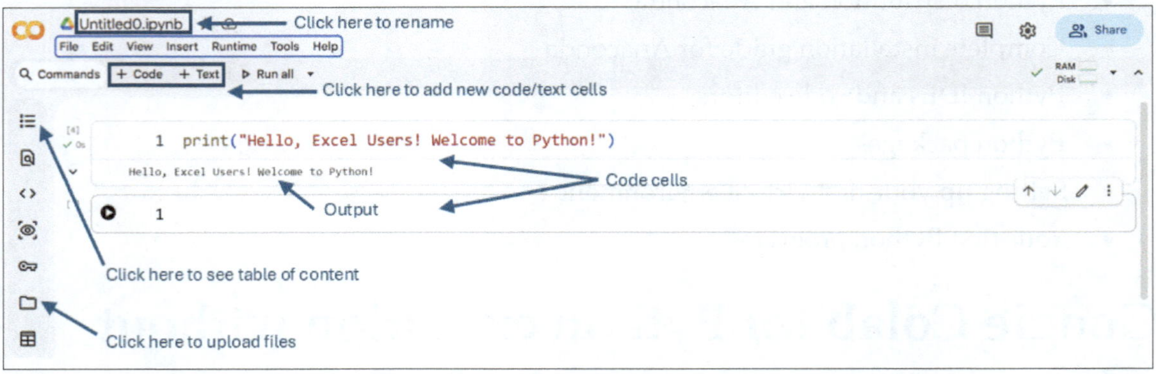

***Figure 2.1**: First look at Colab's interface*

6. Also, Colab comes with generative AI features to assist in coding. We recommend you turn off generative AI features while learning Python. Go to **Tools** | **Settings** | **AI Assistance** and click on **Hide generative AI features** as shown in the following figure:

[1] Jupyter Notebook is similar but runs on your computer, using local Python installation. We will discuss it later.

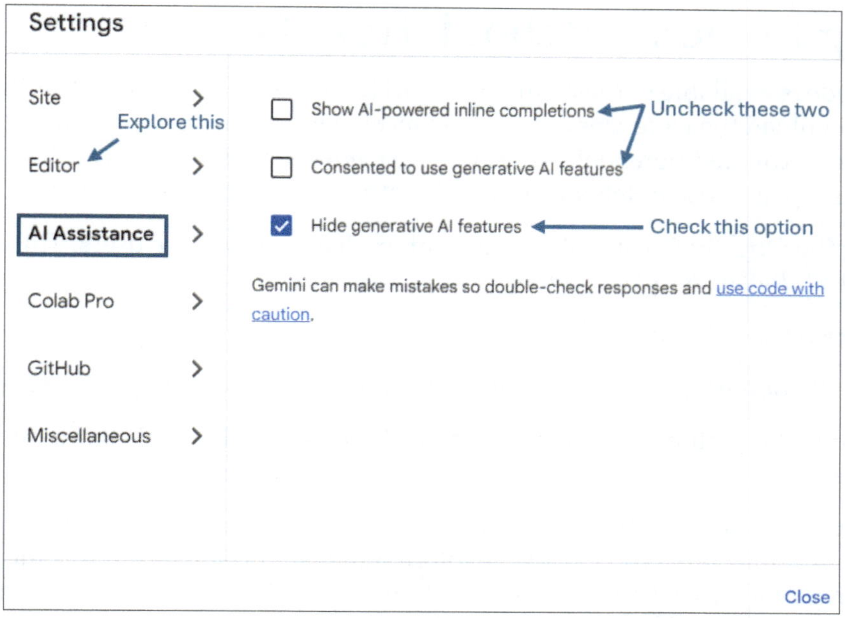

***Figure 2.2**: Turning off Colab's generative AI assistance*

You might also want to look at other settings such as dark mode of editor, font and font size etc. Try it out and make yourself comfortable with the tool.

Opening, saving, and uploading files

To start with, you would need to open, save, rename the notebook, or upload one from your local machine. This is how you can do these tasks:

- To save your work, click on **File** and then **Save**.
- **To rename the file:** your notebook is saved as `Untitled0.ipynb` (or similar) by default. To rename it, either:
    - o Click directly on the filename at the top (where it says `Untitled0`), type a new name (like `Python Basics.ipynb`), and press *Enter*. (Refer *Figure 2.1*)
    - o Or go to **File** | **Rename** and enter the new name there.
- To open an existing notebook, click **File** | **Open notebook**, then choose from Google Drive[2], GitHub[3](public repo), or Upload (from your computer). You might not have any files yet, except for the one you have recently saved or any notebooks you have downloaded from a GitHub repo.

---

[2] To access files outside Google Drive's "Colab Notebooks" folder or save outputs directly to Drive, open the file browser in Google Colab, click "Mount Drive", and complete the authentication steps.

[3] For a private GitHub repository, sign in to GitHub and authorize Colab to access private files.

Running Python notebook from GitHub

This book's code is available in the companion GitHub repo. You can either type the examples yourself or download the code files (`.py` or `.ipynb` extensions) to open on your machine. Also, you can run the provided notebooks (files with `.ipynb` extension) directly in Colab. Here are two easy ways to run those notebooks in Colab without even downloading:

1. Using the Open in Colab button (Recommended for first-time users. This was done in *Chapter 1, Python for Excel Users*):
   a. Open the GitHub repo link of the book.
   b. Look for the Open in Colab button (usually at the top of the notebook or README).
   c. Click the button, the notebook opens directly in Colab and sign-in to your google account.
   d. Go to **Runtime | Run all** (shortcut *Ctrl* + *F9* or *Cmd* + *F9* on macOS) to run the entire notebook. You can also explore other run options from this menu. To run a single cell, use *Ctrl* + *Enter* (*Cmd* + *Enter* on macOS) to execute without moving to the next cell or Shift + Enter to execute and move to the next cell.
2. Using the GitHub Link (Also works for notebooks without the Open in Colab button):
   a. Copy the link to the notebook (`.ipynb` file) from GitHub.
   b. Open **Google Colab**.
   c. Go to **File** | **Open notebook** | **GitHub** tab.
   d. Paste the link and click **Search**.
   e. Choose your notebook from the list and open it.
   f. Execute entire notebook with **Runtime | Run all** or Run cell by cell.
3. For notebooks available in your local machine, you can go to **File | Open notebook | Upload** and browse the file from its location to open in Colab.

Basic markdown guide for notebooks

In notebooks like Colab, you can use markdown to add headings, notes, lists, links, images, videos, and more, helping you create clean, readable, and professional-looking reports. You may have noticed that, along with code cells, there are text cells. This is where you write your notes using Markdown and run them to display nicely formatted text.

Let us add a Text Cell and type:

```
# This is a Heading
Just adding Some Text. Trying out **Bold Text**  and *Italic Text*
```

```
1. Trying to add numbering.
2. As we do in MS Word.
3. I can also see preview here.
```

Now, add another Text Cell and run this:

```
## This is a SubHeading
Trying to add `code chunk` and [link]( https://www.linkedin.com/in/drnishaarora/) here.
• Also adding bullet points.
• You can explore inserting image, emoji or even latex typing here.
```

Figure 2.3 displays Google Colab Notebook with Markdown text and Table of contents:

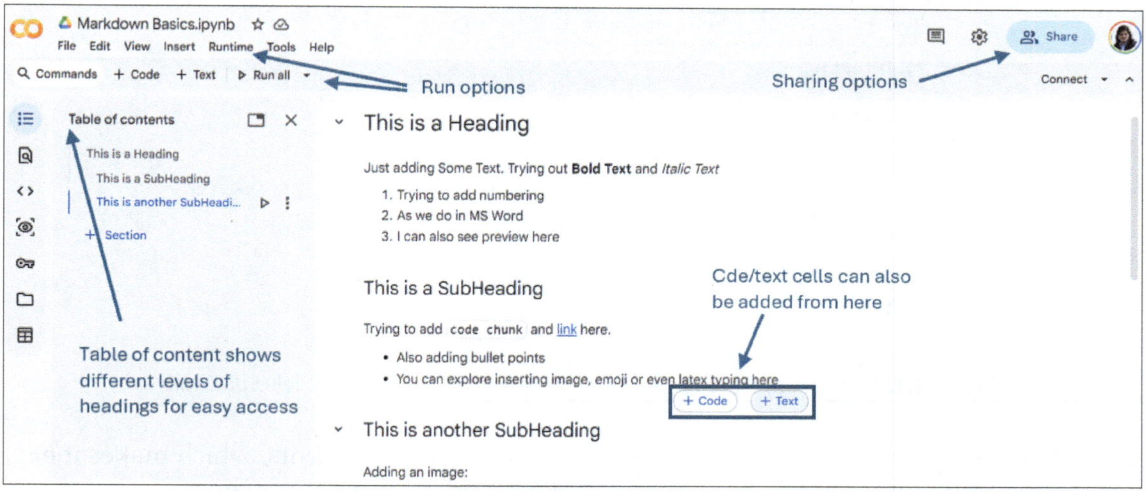

***Figure 2.3:** Google Colab Notebook with Markdown text*

You might have noticed, it is super easy to create documents or reports in Colab using these basic markdown symbols[4]:

What you want	Use this in Colab text cell	Example output
Level 1 heading	`# Heading 1`	Heading 1
Level 2 heading	`## Heading 2`	Heading 2
Level 3 heading	`### Heading 3`	Heading 3
Bold text	`**Bold Text**`	**Bold Text**
Italic text	`*Italic Text*`	*Italic Text*
Numbered list	`1. First item` `2. Second item`	1. First item 2. Second item

[4] **https://www.markdownguide.org/basic-syntax/**

What you want	Use this in Colab text cell	Example output
Bulleted list	`- Item one` `- Item two`	• Item one • Item two
Link	`[Click Here](https://www.example.com)`	Click Here
Inline code	`` `print(x)` ``	`print(x)`

Table 2.1: Markdown basic syntax

You can also do text formatting by clicking on the respective button in a text cell as shown in the figure:

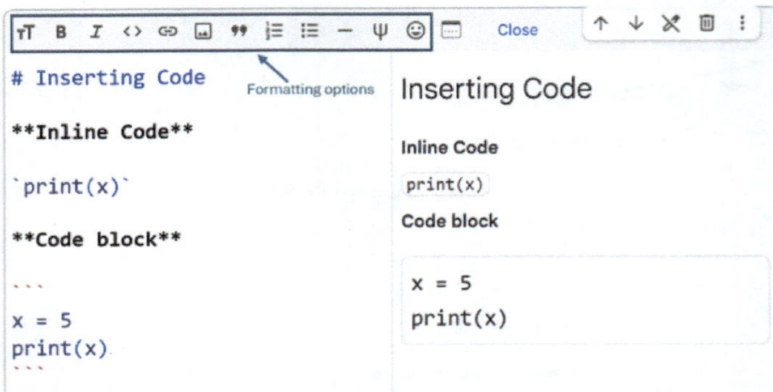

Figure 2.4: Text formatting options (left) and Markdown cell preview (right) in Colab

Colab offers many helpful features, like an automatic Table of Contents, which makes it easy to navigate through your notebook. You can explore more features as you go.

Notebook versus Python script

You can consider notebooks (**.ipynb** file) as interactive documents, like an eBook or a report. They can include your Python code, the output (like results and charts), headings, a table of contents, and even notes, images, videos, links, all in one place. These are perfect for exploration, explanations, and sharing your work in a single file.

However, if you only want to keep just the code, without all the extra explanations and outputs, it is better to use a **Python script**. These are simple text files with a **.py** extension, made purely for writing and saving code. They are like a list of formulas, intended to be reused elsewhere. Python scripts are lightweight and can even be opened and edited using any basic text editor (like Notepad or Notepad++). You can choose to create Python files or notebooks (code remains the same) as per your needs.

In Colab, you can easily download your work as either a Notebook (**.ipynb**) or a Script (**.py**). However, downloading a notebook as a **.py** file is often not very helpful because you will lose the nice structure, headings, and outputs. The comments and markdown notes do not carry over well, and the file may feel messy. Usually, Colab or Jupyter is preferred for working with notebooks and other IDEs such as Spyder are used for Python scripts. We will talk about IDEs soon.

Python distribution and Anaconda

Although you can run and practice Python code in Colab, if you are serious about learning more, you should also install Python on your machine. You can quickly download and install Python from its official website **https://www.python.org/** for free. However, it is better to use a Python distribution to have access to a wide range of pre-installed libraries and maybe other features too.

You might be wondering about Python distribution and what it involves. A Python distribution is a pre-packaged bundle that includes the Python interpreter, standard library, and a collection of additional packages and tools. Anaconda, Miniconda, and WinPython (Windows only) are some popular Python distributions.

Anaconda is perfect for analysts or Excel users who want an easy-to-use Python environment without much setup. It is designed for data tasks and comes with many pre-installed packages, saving you time. Anaconda Navigator make it simple to install, update, and launch tools like JupyterLab and Spyder without using the command line.

Let us understand it using a simple analogy. Imagine you just bought a brand-new smartphone. Before you start using it, you need to:

- Set it up properly.
- Install the essential apps.
- Configure settings to make sure everything runs smoothly.

Now, think of Python as your smartphone, a powerful tool that can do amazing things. But just like a phone without apps and configurations, a plain Python needs some set-up and installations.

This is where **Anaconda Distribution** comes in.

Anaconda is like a fully loaded smartphone that comes with all the essential apps pre-installed. Instead of manually downloading every app (or package) one by one, Anaconda gives you a complete package with Python, useful data analysis tools, and some easy-to-use interfaces (such as Spyder and Jupyter).

Installing vanilla Python (plain Python from Python.org) is like getting a bare-bones phone, you will have to manually install and configure everything yourself. This gives you more control but also leads to more hassle.

Other options like **Miniconda** or **WinPython** are lighter but require you to set things up yourself, which can be confusing for beginners. With Anaconda, you just install and start working, no extra hassle.

System requirement for Anaconda

Anaconda works on all major operating systems like Windows, Mac, and Linux. As of November 2025, you need **Windows 10** version 1809 or later, 64-bit **macOS 12.1**+ (for Apple Silicon), or **Linux**, including Ubuntu 20.04, Red Hat/ AlmaLinux/ Rocky Linux 8+, and others.

If your operating system is older than what is currently supported, you can find older versions of the Anaconda installers in the archive that might work for you.

Anaconda is a full Python toolkit, so it may take up to 5–6 GB after installation. If you create a separate environment for this book (recommended), it may take a few extra GB, depending on operating system, cached downloads, and package dependencies. If you are short on space, you can still follow the book by installing packages directly in the base environment.

Complete installation guide for Anaconda

Now, let us get Anaconda installed. Follow this step-by-step guide, and you will be ready to use Anaconda.

Downloading Anaconda

The steps are as follows:

1. Go to Anaconda Home Page at **https://www.anaconda.com/download** and click on **Skip registration**. Refer to *Figure 2.5*:

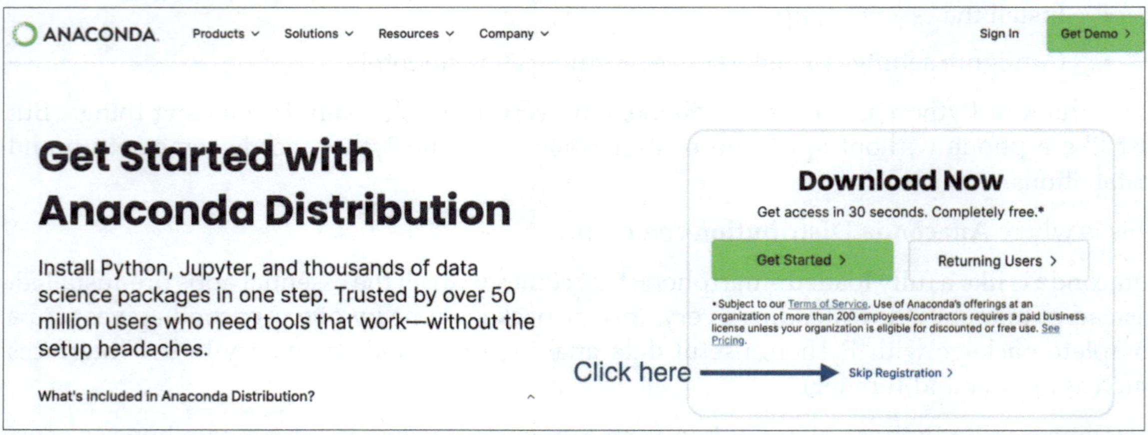

***Figure 2.5**: Anaconda distribution home page*

2. Click the right installer (Refer to *Figure 2.6*) based on your operating system (Windows, MacOS, or Linux) and flavor. For Mac users, we would recommend using a suitable Graphical Installer.

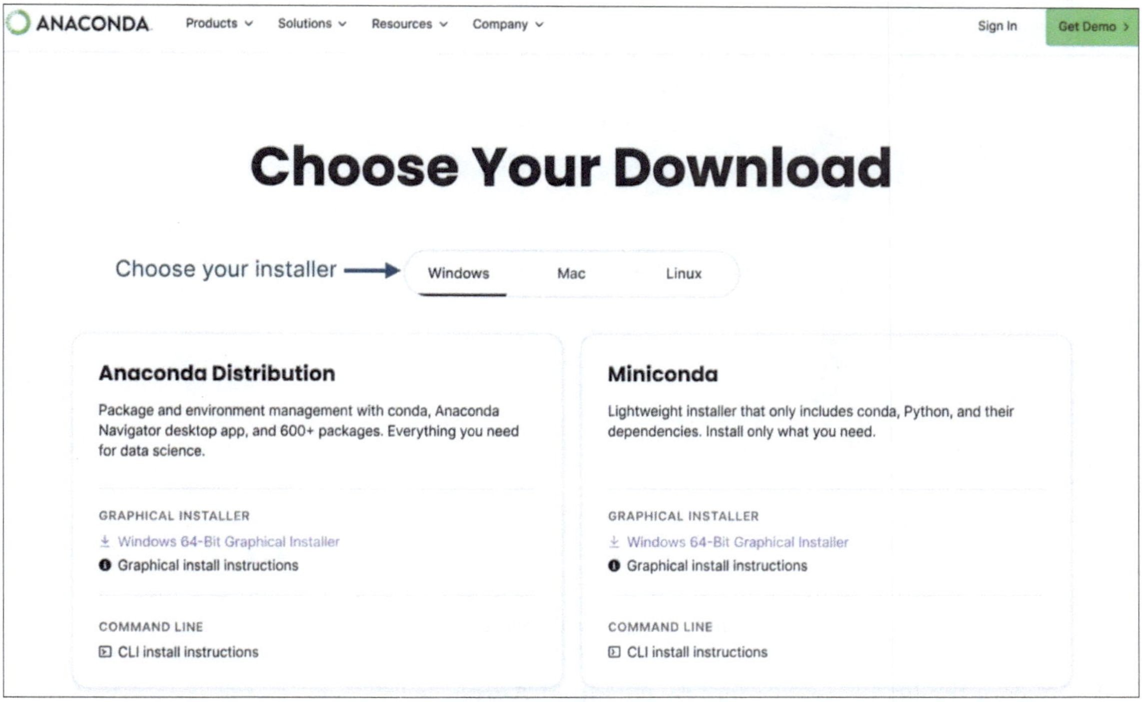

Figure 2.6: Available installers

3. Downloading should start automatically. If it does not, click **Try Again**.

Installing Anaconda

Instructions for Windows users are as follows:

1. Locate the downloaded **.exe** file (usually in the **Downloads** folder).
2. Double-click to run it. The Anaconda Setup Wizard will open.
3. Click **Next** to begin the installation, shown as follows:

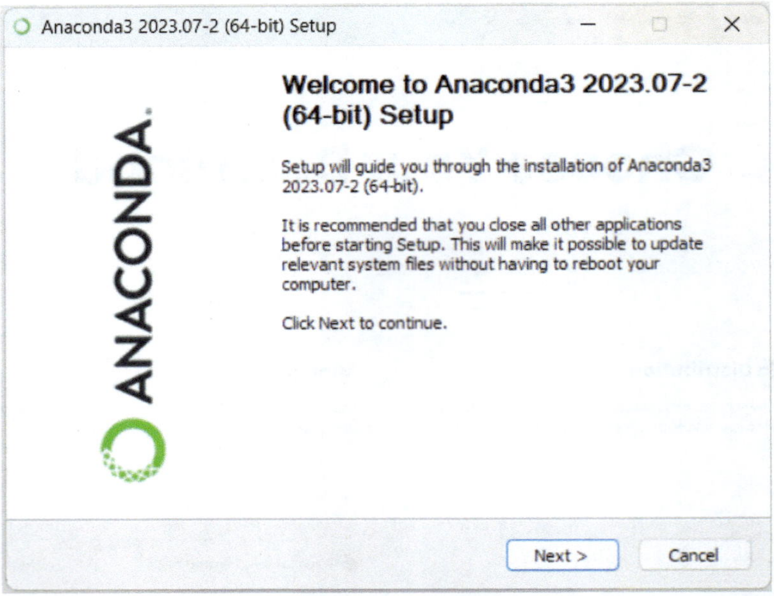

Figure 2.7: Anaconda Setup Wizard

4. Accept the license agreement by clicking **I Agree**, as follows:

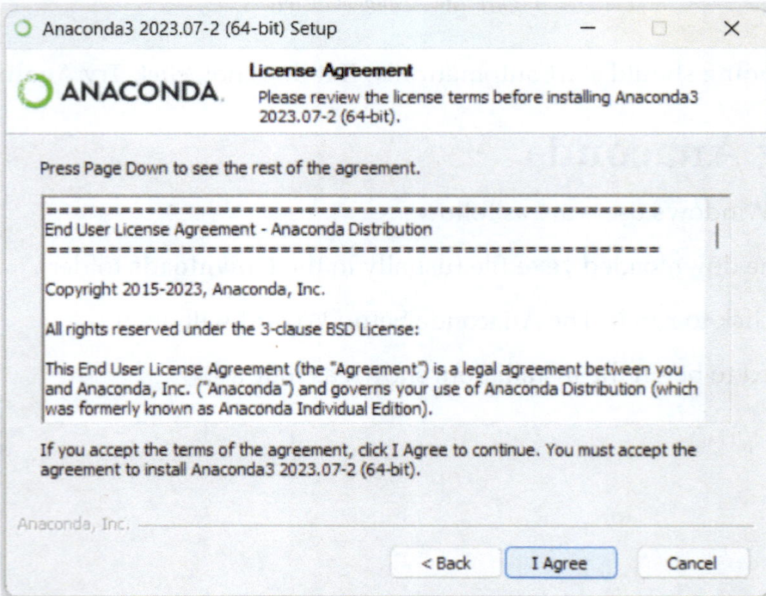

Figure 2.8: License Agreement

5. Choose **Just Me** (unless you want to install it for all users). Click **Next**. Refer to *Figure 2.9*:

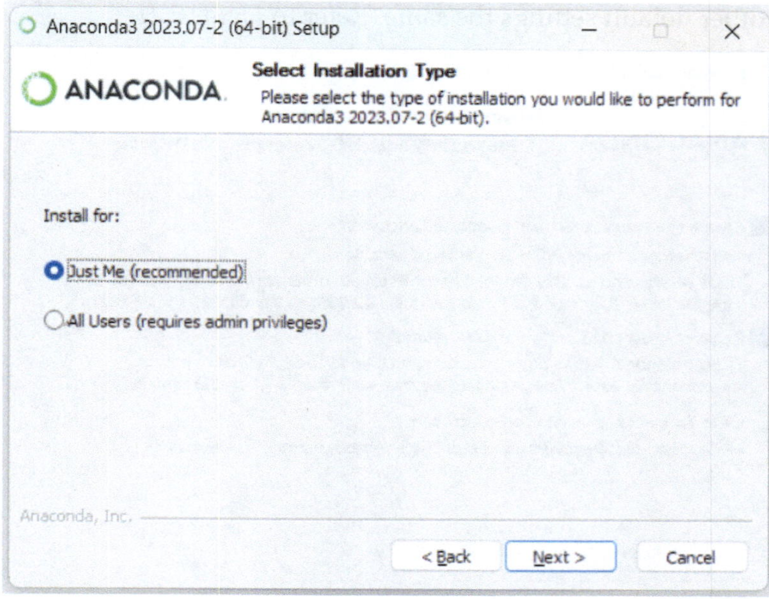

***Figure 2.9**: Installation Type*

6. The default location is fine (e.g., **`C:\Users\UserName\Anaconda3`** for windows and **`~/anaconda3/`** for macOS/Linux). However, if your **C drive is low on space**, you can install Anaconda on the **D drive** or another partition with enough free space. Refer to the following figure:

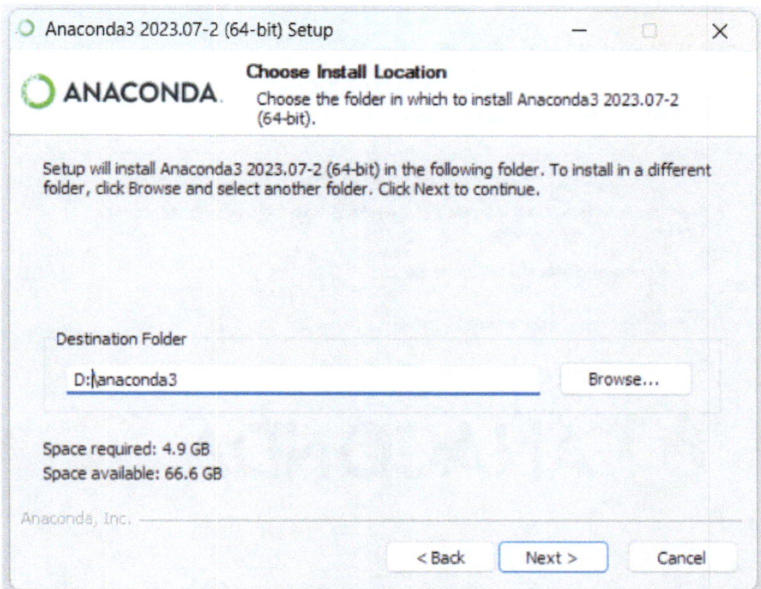

***Figure 2.10**: Choose Install Location*

7. Keep the other default settings the same. Refer to *Figure 2.11*:

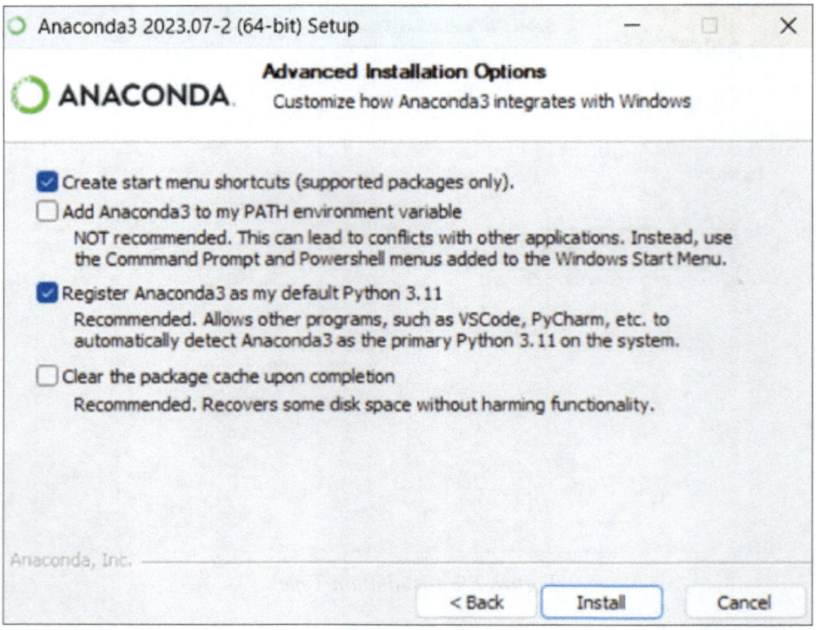

***Figure 2.11**: Advanced Installation Options*

8. Click **Install** and wait for the process to be completed (this may take a few minutes).
9. Once done, click **Next**. Refer to *Figure 2.12*:

***Figure 2.12**: The next step*

10. Once installation is done, click **Finish**, as follows:

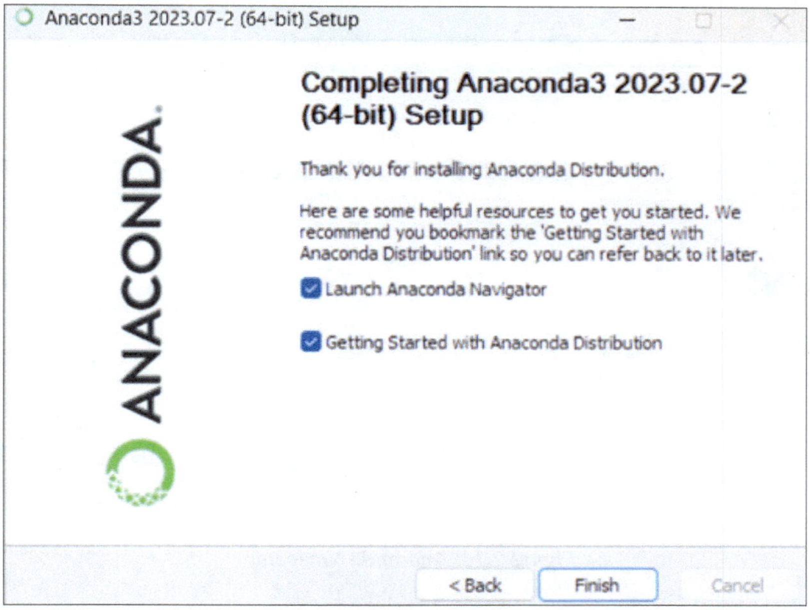

***Figure 2.13**: Completing installation*

After successful installation, it opens Getting Started guide and Anaconda Navigator. If Anaconda Navigator is not launched immediately, you can open it as discussed next.

Verifying the installation

To check if Anaconda was installed correctly:

- **On Windows**: Click on the **Start** menu and search for *Anaconda Navigator* and press *Enter*.
- **Or if you are on macOS or Linux**: Open Terminal, type **`anaconda-navigator`**, and press *Enter*. It takes time to load.

You should see the Anaconda GUI, as shown in *Figure 2.14*, with options like Spyder, Jupyter Notebook, etc. You have now installed Anaconda correctly.

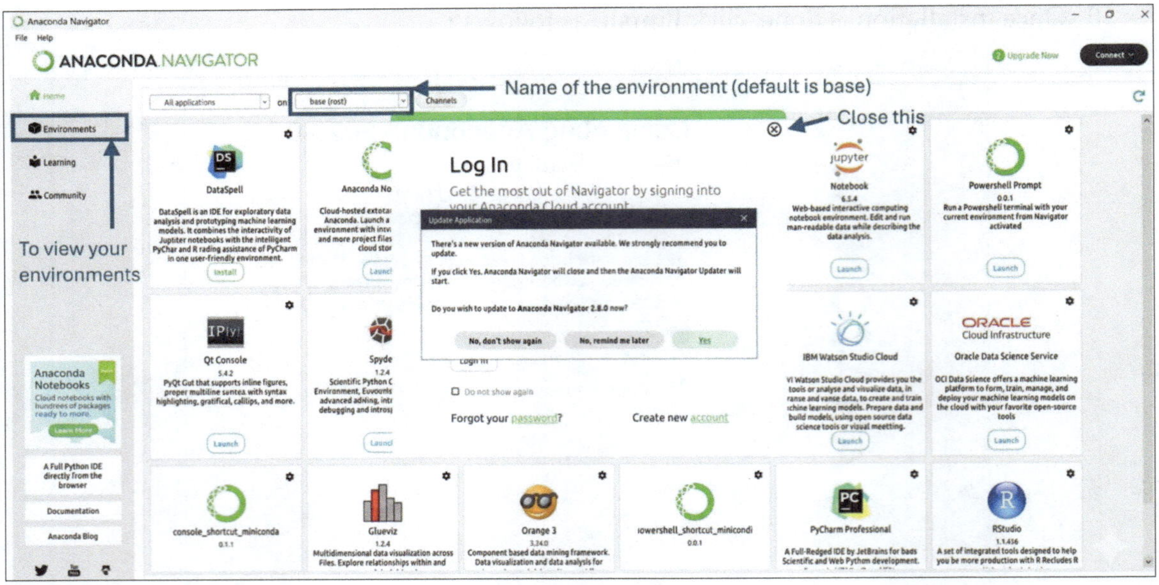

***Figure 2.14**: Anaconda Navigator*

When you install Anaconda, it comes with a default Python setup called the **base environment**, which is the starting workspace that includes core packages and tools.

Alternatively, you can verify by opening Anaconda Prompt[5](on Widows; **`startup menu | type anaconda prompt`**) or Terminal (on macOS or Linux).

Type **`conda --version`** and hit *Enter*. You should see something like **`conda 25.5.1`** (or other similar number). You can also check Python version by running **`python --version`**, and it should return **`Python 3.X.X`**, refer to *Figure 2.15*:

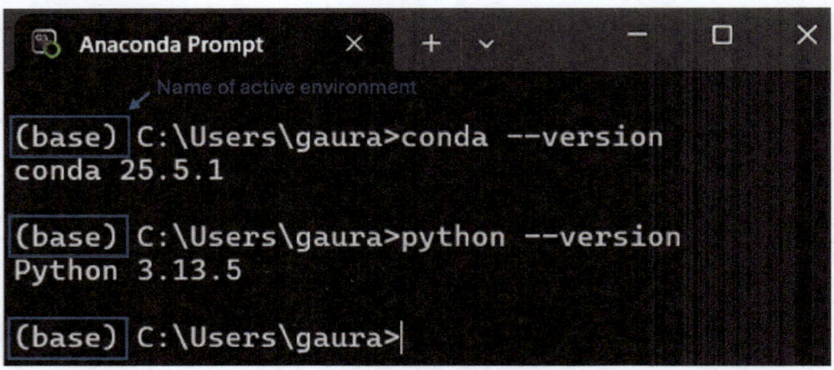

***Figure 2.15**: Anaconda Prompt*

[5]Anaconda Prompt is available only on Windows. macOS and Linux users should use the Terminal to run conda and Python commands.

Python IDEs and code editors

An **integrated development environment** (**IDE**) is a powerful tool that helps you write, test, and debug your code all in one place. It comes with features like auto-suggestions, error highlighting, and debugging tools, making coding easier and more efficient. There are so many Python IDEs available. Spyder (which we recommend), Jupyter Notebook, Jupyter Lab, Visual Studio Code (or VS Code in short) and PyCharm are the popular ones.

You have already seen that you can run your Python code without any installation using Google Colab. You can even write Python code in Notepad and run it from the command line. It is like using Notepad instead of Excel for data analysis. It works, but you would not want to do it.

A text editor like Notepad or Notepad++ is a simpler and lightweight tool focused mainly on writing and editing code. But there is no fun coding like this. Code editors like Atom has been retired and Sublime Text has lost market share to other IDEs, both were once used by many Python developers. However, the best and easiest way to efficiently learn and work on Python projects is to use a full-fledged IDE.

Let us see a few reasons behind recommending Spyder.

Spyder IDE, the best choice for Excel users

Scientific Python Development Environment (**Spyder**) **https://www.spyder-ide.org/** is particularly suited for Excel users transitioning to Python due to its user-friendly interface and powerful features tailored for data analysis and scientific computing.

Here is a comparison table for various features of popular Python IDEs:

Feature	Spyder (Recommended)	Jupyter Notebook	VS Code	PyCharm
Best for	Data analysis, transition from Excel	Data exploration, reports generation, tutorials	General coding, advanced users	Professional development, advanced users
Ease of use	Simple, user-friendly	User-friendly, different style, uses markdown	Moderate, more setup needed	Moderate
Installation requirement	No (Pre-installed with Anaconda, no extra setup needed)	No (Pre-installed with Anaconda, runs in a browser)	Yes	Yes (Bulky installation)
Virtual environments	Uses Anaconda, making it easier to manage dependencies	Uses Anaconda, making it easier to manage dependencies	Managed via terminal, can feel complex to new users	Advanced support but can feel complex to new users

Table 2.2: Comparison of popular Python IDEs

If you are already using another IDE like VS Code, PyCharm or cloud services like Colab, you can still follow along. If you are using cloud platforms like Colab, note that some features such as working with local files or Excel automation may be limited.

Spyder IDE walkthrough

Spyder comes pre-installed with Anaconda Distribution. If you have installed Anaconda, Spyder is ready to use, you just need to launch it. You can launch or open Spyder in any of the following ways:

- **From Anaconda navigator**: Open Anaconda Navigator (search for it in Start menu), Scroll to **Spyder** under **Home**, and click **Launch**.
- **Directly from Start menu (Windows only)**: Click on **Start** menu and type Spyder, click to open.

> Tip **for faster access (Windows only): Next time, pin Spyder to the taskbar or Start menu for quick access!**

Understanding Spyder's interface

After launching Spyder for the first time, you can click on **Start tour** to get a glimpse of its interface, refer to *Figure 2.16*:

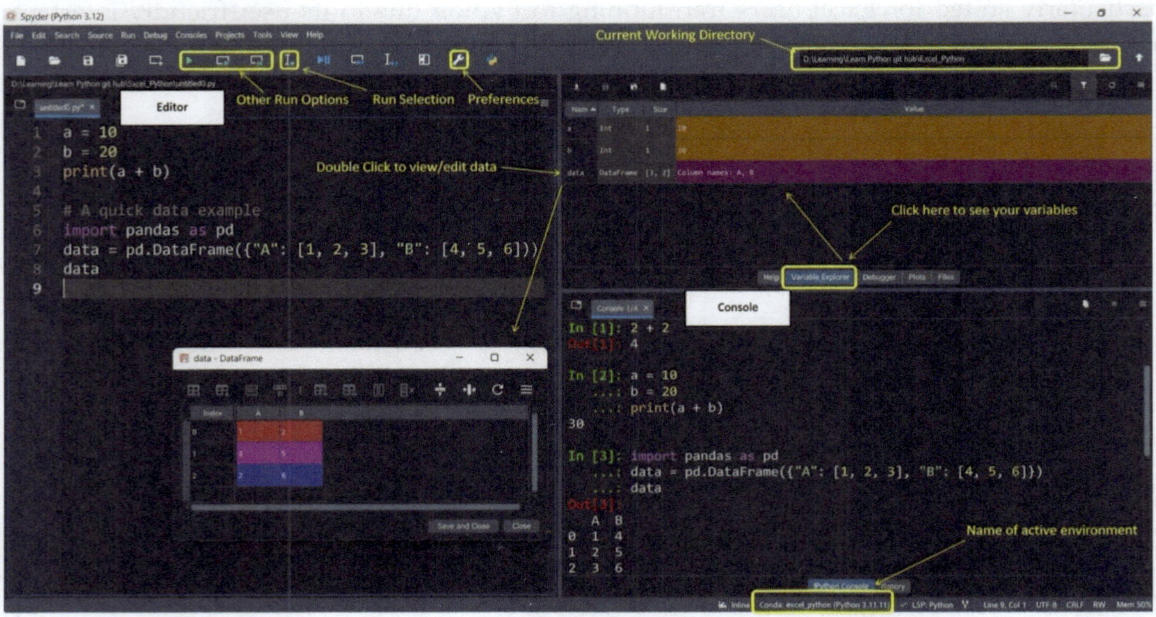

Figure 2.16: Spyder IDE's interface

Spyder is your new *Excel for Python*. Here, instead of cells, formulas, and pivot tables, you will be working with code, variables, and plots. Do not worry, Spyder is designed to be user-friendly. We recommend exploring Spyder a bit before getting started with Python. Let us look at its interface:

- **Console (instant results are shown here):**
  - It is the bottom-right panel, which you can imagine as the output area to display the results of your calculations / code.
  - Type **2+2** and hit *Enter*. You will see the result right there.
- **Editor (your Python Spreadsheet for writing code):**
  - The large area at the top-left creates Python scripts (files) to keep your code saved for future use.
  - Code typed directly in the Console is lost when the session ends, so use a script to store and reuse your work.
  - Type this code in the script area:

```
a = 10
b = 20
print(a + b)
```

To run this code, select these lines and press *F9* or click the **Run Selection button** on the toolbar. The result will appear in the Console. You can **save the file** [6](use *Ctrl* + *S* Windows or *Command (⌘)* + *S* on Mac) by giving it a name like **example.py** (**.py** is the extension for Python files, just like **.xlsx** for Excel files). Please refer to the section titled *Notebook versus Python script* in this chapter.

Later, you can reopen the **.py** file anytime, edit the code, and run it again just like opening and updating an Excel file when needed. Take some time to explore various options, such as creating new files, opening recent ones, editing (cut, copy, paste, and more), using find and replace, running the entire script (*F5*) etc.

- **Variable explorer (your data at a glance)**
  - One of Spyder's best features for Excel users.
  - It automatically shows your variables like an interactive Excel table. If you have run the earlier code, you will see variables like **a** and **b** here. Imported data (like from Excel) will also appear here.
  - Manage your variables easily just like working with ranges in Excel. Think of it as Excel's Name Manager or Power Query preview.

[6] When you create or save a Python file in Spyder, it is usually saved in *C:\Users\<YourUsername>* for Windows users or */Users/<YourUsername>* for Mac users. We can change this location as needed. We will explain how in the next chapter when we talk about the working directory.

- o Let us look at a quick data example. Run this code:

```
import pandas as pd

# Creating a simple table (DataFrame)
data = pd.DataFrame({"A": [1, 2, 3], "B": [4, 5, 6]})
# Show the DataFrame
data
```

Notice, the Variable Explorer shows your table just like Excel. You can double-click on **data** in the Variable Explorer to see it in table format. Refer to *Figure 2.16*).

- **Plots (your Python chart tool)**
    - o Any graph you create appears here. Try running this code:

```
import matplotlib.pyplot as plt
import seaborn as sns
scores = [5,8,6,9,7,6,5,10,8,9,6,8,8,6,5,6]
sns.histplot(scores, kde = True)
plt.show()
```

You got your first Python plot, which appears in the console and in plot window too.

- **Help (your built-in function guide)**
    - o Like Excel's formula tooltips.
    - o You can browse documentations, Spyder shortcuts, tutorial videos etc. here.

To make your experience in Spyder more comfortable, you can adjust settings like **font size** and **theme** (dark or light mode). Just go to **Tools | Preferences | Appearance** to customize how Spyder looks. Also, using **keyboard shortcuts** can save you time while coding. Go to **Tools | Preferences | Keyboard Shortcuts** inside Spyder. There, you can see all available shortcuts and even customize them if you want.

Here are a few helpful ones (for Windows) to get started:

- **Run a line or selection**: *F9*
- **Run all**: *F5*
- **Open variable explorer**: *Ctrl + Shift + V*
- **Cut**: *Ctrl + X*
- **Copy**: *Ctrl + C*
- **Paste**: *Ctrl + V*
- **Undo or Redo**: *Ctrl + Z or Ctrl + Y*

- **Find and replace:** *Ctrl + F*
- **Comment or uncomment lines:** *Ctrl + 1*

Many Spyder shortcuts are the same on both Windows and Mac (especially *F9*, *F5*), but for common actions like copy, paste, or undo, redo, just swap *Ctrl* with *Command* (⌘) on Mac.

By now, you should be comfortable with Spyder. Spyder comes packed with features that make your transition from Excel seamless, e.g., you get auto-completion and help as you type, making coding easier and less prone to errors. Keep exploring and experimenting with simple codes. Assist yourself with the resources available at:

https://docs.spyder-ide.org/current/videos/index.html

Jupyter Notebook

So far, you have been using Google Colab or Spyder to write and run Python code. However, there are other ways[7] too! If you need to create notebook but want to do it locally or do not have active internet connection, Jupyter notebook is what you need.

You can open or launch Jupyter notebook by using any of the following options:

- Open **Anaconda Navigator** | Click **Jupyter Notebook**
- Open **Anaconda Prompt (Windows) or Terminal (Mac)** and type **`jupyter notebook`**

This will also start the notebook server and open Jupyter in your browser, allowing you to create and work with notebooks easily. The interface is quite similar to Colab. Create a new notebook and explore its features. If you are curious, **JupyterLab** is a more advanced version of Jupyter Notebook with extra features like tabs, file browsing, and a cleaner layout, but the basic idea and usage are the same. Shutting down a Jupyter Notebook properly helps free up system resources and prevent unintended code execution. You can do this by going to **File | Close and Shut Down Notebook** or clicking **Running | Shutdown** from the Jupyter Notebook dashboard. To learn more, you can refer to the following:

https://jupyterlab.readthedocs.io/en/stable/user/index.html

Python packages

Now that you have successfully installed Anaconda and explored the Spyder IDE, it is time to talk about packages.

Python packages are like Excel Add-ins, providing extra functionality. They are free and more versatile. Python has some standard built-in packages (no installation needed) and many external packages (which you install separately to add more functionality). Installing any

[7] You can also run your Python code directly from Anaconda Prompt or Command Prompt (Windows), or Terminal (macOS/Linux).

package can be done by running one line of code in the command line, Anaconda Prompt, Terminal, or your IDE like Spyder.

With Anaconda, you already have most essential libraries pre-installed, such as **pandas**, **numpy**, **matplotlib**, **seaborn**, etc. To see the complete list of pre-installed packages, run **conda list** in Anaconda Prompt or **!conda list** in Spyder.

Throughout this book, we will use many packages. Let us understand ways to install packages.

Installing packages

There are two ways to install Python packages: using **conda** or using **pip**. In **Anaconda Prompt** (Windows) or **Terminal** (Mac or Linux), you can run[8] **conda install package name** or **pip install package name**.

To install a specific version, you can use = while using conda commands or == while using pip command:

```
# Using conda
conda install package_name          # Install latest version
conda install package_name=x.y.z # Install specific version

# Or using pip
pip install package_name           # Install latest version
pip install package_name==x.y.z  # Install specific version
```

If you are puzzled about **conda** vs. **pip**, it is best to use Conda when working with Anaconda and only use pip to install those packages that are not available via conda. The reason is conda handles dependencies better and ensures compatibility.

Even if the details feel overwhelming to you, it is to be discussed for realizing the technical nuances.

You can also install multiple packages in one go, for example:

```
conda install numpy-financial xlrd xlwt xlutils pyxlsb xlsxriter
```

Once you confirm the installations, this will install latest possible versions of these packages in base environment.

Warning: If you install updated versions of any package in future, a few outputs may look slightly different. Usually, libraries maintain backward compatibility, but if that is not the case, your code might run into issues.

[8] Adding -y to conda install package_name automatically confirms the installation without prompting, but it is optional. In Spyder, prefixing a command with ! runs it as a terminal (bash) command.
!conda install package -y may not always work as expected in Jupyter. It is recommended to install packages directly from Anaconda Prompt or Terminal for better reliability.

If you are willing to use exact versions of the packages that are used in the book, you can create a separate virtual environment (to be discussed in the next section) and install specific versions of packages in that environment.

Beginners often install packages as and when needed, but that is not the best way to work with packages while building real world projects. We would prefer to tell you the best way to do this to avoid conflicts and dependency issues later. Here is what they mean:

- **Dependencies**: When a package relies on other packages to function correctly.
- **Version conflicts**: Occur when different packages require different versions of the same dependency, causing potential issues.

Tip: **As a beginner, you can learn and practice most of the codes from this book by installing the packages you need as you go. If you are eager to start learning Python right away, you can skip the following section and move to the section Your first Python program and learn about virtual environment, when you are ready. If you have little more patience to get started with learning Python, we recommend learning about creating a virtual environment first. It will be the best investment of your time, saving you hours of effort debugging, searching through Stack Overflow, and managing package conflicts later on in Python journey. Roll up your sleeves to learn about creating a virtual environment.**

Setting up your first virtual environment

Experienced Python users prefer to use separate virtual environments for their projects. If you learn about the same right from the beginning, you are going to derive a significant advantage.

Understanding virtual environment and its importance

A virtual environment in Python is like having separate workspaces for different projects. Imagine you work with different clients, and each client uses a different version of Excel and specific add-ins. If you try to use everything in the same Excel setup, things might break due to version conflicts. In Excel, you cannot easily keep separate setups for different projects.

Python solves this pain with virtual environments, where each project can get its own isolated workspace, with its own packages and versions, so nothing interferes with anything else. Let us understand why is it helpful.

When you follow Python code from different places, it might not work the same on your system because they may use different versions of libraries. Even if your own code works perfectly today, a library update tomorrow could break it if the update is not backward compatible. That is why managing Python environment is so important.

A virtual environment helps you keep things organized by creating an isolated space where only the needed versions of Python and packages exist, as shown in *Figure 2.17*. This way, one project's setup would not mess up another's, and you can easily switch between them when needed.

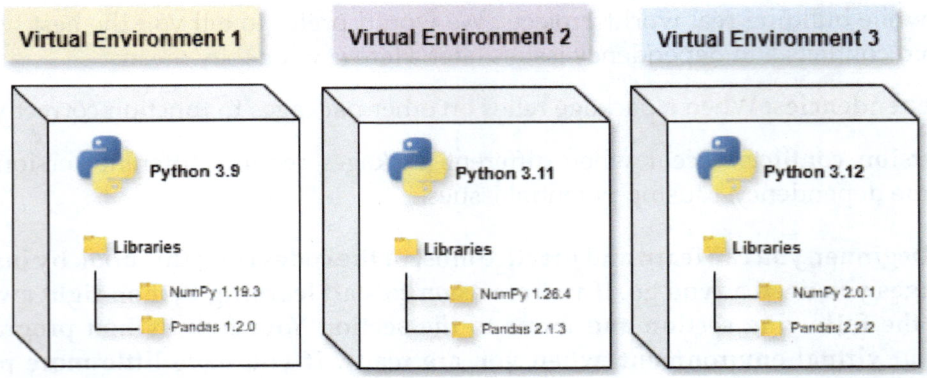

Figure 2.17: Virtual Environments

There are different ways to create a virtual environment, using **conda**, using **pip**, or using Anaconda Navigator (GUI). We recommend creating a conda environment for this book.

Step-by-step guide to creating Conda environment

You can follow these steps to create, activate, or deactivate a conda environment.

Step 1: Creating and activating an environment

1. Open Anaconda Prompt (Windows user) or Terminal (Mac or Linux user) and type:

```
conda create --name excel_python Python=3.11
```

   This creates a clean workspace named **excel_python** with Python 3.11 (same as in this book).

2. To activate it, run:

```
conda activate excel_python
```

   Now, any packages you install will only affect this environment.

Step 2: Installing required packages

Instead of manually installing packages, use the **environment.yml** (download it from the companion repo) file for a smooth setup.

1. Navigate to the folder where **environment.yml** is saved. Run this command to navigate that folder: `cd path\to\folder`

2. Install all necessary libraries using (recommended):

   ```
   conda env update --name excel_python --file environment.yml -prune
   ```

   This ensures you get the exact versions used in the book.

Alternative: The alternative is to directly create and install using **.yml** file

If you **have not created an environment yet**, you can skip *Step 1* and *Step 2* and run just one command to create the environment and install all required packages in one go:

```
conda env create --file environment.yml
```

This will create a new environment (with the name specified inside **environment.yml**) and install all necessary packages. After installation, activate the environment:

```
conda activate excel_python
```

Now, you can perform *Step 3, Verifying installed packages*.

Step 3: Verifying installed packages

1. Check all installed packages with:

   ```
   conda list
   ```

   If everything looks good, you are all set!

2. You can also see the path of your environment by running:

   ```
   where python
   ```

   This will show the location of the **python.exe** file for the currently active environment. This path will be used in Spyder to use the environment.

   If you ever need an exact snapshot of my setup, you can find the complete Conda environment export in **conda_packages_full_export.yml** (includes every dependency with exact versions).

Deactivate, if needed

If you close the terminal or Anaconda Prompt, the environment automatically deactivates. However, if you are running related commands or want to use another environment. The steps are as follows:

1. You should deactivate the conda environment by running **conda deactivate**, and it will take you back to the base environment.

2. If you want to delete the environment completely, run the following command: **conda**

   ```
   conda remove -n excel_python --all
   ```

3. To see the list of all environments, you can run **conda env** list or **conda info -envs**.

To work in this newly created environment in Spyder, you need to change Spyder settings as discussed in the following section.

Using a conda environment in Spyder

There are multiple ways to activate conda environment in Spyder. We would recommend following these steps:

1. Open Spyder, go to **Tools | Preferences | Python Interpreter**.
2. Select **Use the following interpreter**.
3. Browse to **`path\to\anaconda3\envs\excel_python\python.exe`** (Here, you need to paste the full path you got from **`where python`**).
4. Apply and restart Spyder.
5. You can verify this by checking the interpreter displayed at the bottom-right corner of the Spyder interface.

By following these steps, you will have a well-managed Python environment, making it easier to follow along with this book and avoid any dependency conflicts.

Happy coding, and let us continue this exciting journey into Python-powered Excel.

Your first Python program

Now that your Python setup is ready, let us get a feel for writing some real Python code. Do not worry, this is not about memorizing anything yet. Think of it like exploring a new Excel sheet for the first time: clicking around, trying formulas, and getting familiar. The steps are as follows:

1. Open Spyder (or any other IDE you are using) and type this simple line to simply print a welcome message:

   ```
   print("Hello, Excel User!")
   ```

2. Now, run the code and see the result appear, just like pressing *Enter* after writing a formula in Excel.
3. Here, **`print()`** is a **function** that displays text on the screen. Notice the text inside the brackets is in quotes, this is how we tell Python we are working with words (called **strings**). You can use *single* or *double* quotes; both work fine.

Try a few more lines:

```
# Some calculation
print(10 + 20)
```

```
score = 68
# Adding 2
print(score + 2)

# print(20 + 30) # Nothing happens here because this line is commented out
```

You may have noticed that some lines start with **#**. Also, notice that when you run the last line, nothing is printed. That is because lines beginning with **#** are *comments*, and Python completely ignores them when running the code. Comments are needed as they allow users to add notes to explain what the code does, just like leaving a comment on a tricky Excel formula to remind yourself (or others) why it was written that way. Comments are also useful for temporarily turning off lines of code without deleting them.

Quick shortcut to comment or uncomment lines:

Spyder: Ctrl + 1 (Windows) or Cmd + 1 (Mac)

Colab or Jupyter: Ctrl + / (Windows) or Cmd + / (Mac)

Quick tip on best practices

We would recommend you to:

- **Add spaces around operators** like **+** or **-** to make your code easier to read. For example, **`print(10 + 20)`** is much clearer than **`print(10+20)`**.
- **Add comments** whenever something in your code might not be obvious later.

There are plenty more good practices like these. For now, just focus on trying things out and exploring Spyder. Later, we will introduce you to **PEP 8**, Python's style guide, which is like a rulebook for writing clean, professional code.

Conclusion

In this chapter, you have learned different methods to run Python code. You have also learned to set up Python using Anaconda distribution and create a conda environment for isolating your projects.

In the next chapter, you will learn the fundamentals of Python programming. If you already have some programming experience, you will see that the core of programming fundamentals remains similar, only syntax changes.

Try it yourself

1. Just for practice purposes, create a new conda environment named test_env with Python 3.12, install numpy latest version and pandas 2.2.1 on it, verify the installation, and delete the environment again.

   If needed, it will prompt you to confirm downgrading numpy, type y and press Enter to continue.

   You will realize it takes less than five minutes for all this if Anaconda is installed properly.

2. For any newly created conda envionement, try to rename it, create a copy of the same and then delete those.

Concept check

Read and attempt to answer the following questions to check your understanding:

1. What is Google Colab, and what are the benefits of using it?
2. What are some benefits of using Anaconda instead of installing Python manually?
3. What is the difference between an IDE and a code editor?
4. Why is setting up a virtual environment important?
5. What is the difference between .py file and .ipynb file?

Join our Discord space

Join our Discord workspace for latest updates, offers, tech happenings around the world, new releases, and sessions with the authors:

https://discord.bpbonline.com

CHAPTER 3
Python Fundamentals

Introduction

Learning a language always starts with learning the alphabet, small words, basic grammar, and sentence formation before becoming fluent. The same is the case with Python. Learning this programming language starts with numbers, letters, and operators.

In this chapter, we will set the stage for your Python journey by exploring the core concepts and building blocks of the language. Aimed at Excel users with little to no coding background, this chapter will not only make you comfortable with Python but also prepare you for more advanced topics in subsequent chapters. By the end of this chapter, you will have the confidence to write your own functions, handling errors gracefully, and using list and dictionary comprehension to write cleaner and more efficient Python code.

Additional exercises and usecases are provided in the accompanying code files, and readers are encouraged to practice each topic thoroughly before proceeding to the next, as not all examples are included in the chapters to maintain conciseness.

Structure

This chapter will cover the following topics:

- From Excel formulas to Python scripts
- Working directory
- Variables in Python
- Datatypes in Python
- Typecasting in Python
- Operators in Python
- Deep dive on strings
- Python data structures
- Control flow for conditions and repeating actions
- Functions in Python

- Exception handling in Python
- Getting help in Python

From Excel formulas to Python scripts

Excel users have cells, formulas, and logic in their minds, which makes it easier to learn Python. This is because the same logic can be written in Python with super-simple syntax with more power, flexibility, and control.

As Excel formulas work on cell references, in Python, you work with variables, allowing for dynamic calculation. In Excel, functions like `=SUM(A1:A10)` perform operations on ranges, while Python achieves the same with `sum(my_list)`, offering greater flexibility. Conditional logic, used as `=IF(A1>10, "High", "")`, translates effortlessly into Python's `if x > 10: print("High")`, making it equally user-friendly. Another example, merging two data sets in Excel is no fun, but Python can do it so gracefully by `data1.merge(data2)`.

Moreover, Python offers great flexibility in defining custom functions for specific tasks as compared to **Visual Basic for Applications** (**VBA**) or a lambda function (in Excel 365) if you have used those.

While Excel's tables and ranges store data in a grid, Python has many different containers to store data as per the need. Even error handling is analogous. You are familiar with errors like `#VALUE!` or `# DIV/0!`, while Python raises `ValueError`, or `ZeroDivisionError`, both requiring debugging. By observing the resemblances, you will find Python approachable as well as an exciting, powerful extension of your existing skills.

Python as a calculator

You might have used Excel to perform quick calculations like `=A1+B1` or `=A1*10`. You will find Python just as intuitive, if not more flexible. In Excel, calculations are tied to cell references (e.g., A1 and B1), where the formula updates automatically when the referenced cells change. In Python, we achieve the same results using variables instead of cells. For example, assigning `a = 10` and `b = 2` allows us to perform `a+b` or `a*10`. We can print these values by using the in-built `print()` function, as you have seen in *Chapter 2, Setting Up Python*.

Unlike Excel, where operations are confined to a grid, Python calculations work in a free-flowing environment, making it easy to define and reuse values dynamically. By removing the constraints of fixed cell locations, Python enables more complex computations, pushing the envelope of number crunching in Excel.

Here is how Python handles basic arithmetic:

```
# Assigning values to variables
a = 10; b = 3
# Performing operations
print(a + b)   # Addition (10 + 3 = 13)
```

```
print(a - b)    # Subtraction (10 - 3 = 7)
print(a * b)    # Multiplication (10 * 3 = 30)
print(a / b)    # Division (10 / 3 = 3.3333333333333335)
print(a ** b)   # Exponentiation (10^3 = 1000)
print(a // b)   # Floor Division (Quotient part of the division 10/ 3 = 3)
print(a % b)    # Modulus (remainder of 10 / 3 = 1)
```

Except for the exponentiation or power operator, quotient, and remainder operator, all other mathematical operators are the same as in Excel. Before we discuss more about datatypes and operators in Python, we will discuss *variables*. There is one more thing, you need to keep your Python files organized before you start doing more *coding*. Let us look at something useful about using a dedicated folder for all your Python scripts.

Working directory

So far, you might have already created some Python files in Spyder that save to a default folder[1] (`C:\Users\YourUsername` for windows users) and when you try to open, Spyder looks for the file in the same folder. This folder is known as the working directory[2]. You can verify this path by looking at the File Explorer-like bar at the top right of the Spyder Interface. It shows the same folder. You might want to change it. We would recommend creating a folder with a suitable name, like **'Excel_Python'**, for this book and setting it as your permanent working directory.

There are multiple ways to change the working directory in Spyder:

- Click the **folder icon** located in the top-right section of the main Spyder window, as shown in *Figure 3.1* and select a new directory. This option is quick, however, you will need to set the working directory in every Spyder session. Try pressing *Ctr+.* to restart the kernel and you will see it is back to the default folder.

Figure 3.1: Setting working directory in Spyder

- Go to **Tools** | **Preferences** | **Working directory** | **Startup (At startup, the working directory is:)** | **The following directory** (browse here and choose). Click on **Apply** and then **OK**. It will set your desired folder as permanent working directory. You can change it later for your other projects.

---

[1] For Mac and Linux users, the default working directory may be /Users/YourUsername/ and /home/YourUsername/, respectively.

[2] In Colab, the default working directory is /content/, and in Jupyter, the default working directory is the folder where Jupyter was launched.

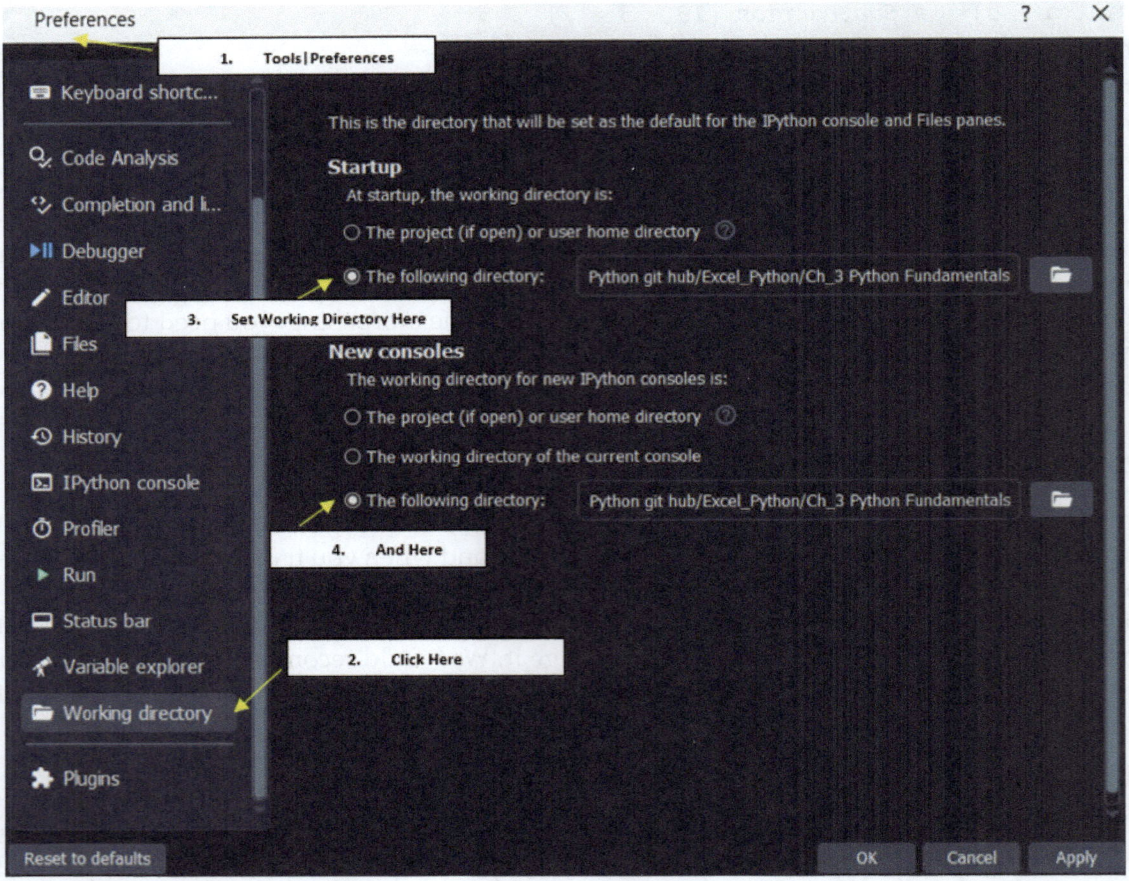

Figure 3.2: *Setting permanent working directory in Spyder*

Many times, you would need to write code for getting or setting working directory and it can be done with **os** module quickly. After importing the module with **import os**, running **os.getcwd()** displays the path of current working directory. Similarly, **os.chdir()** allows you to change working directory to a given path.

```
import os
os.getcwd()                          # Get current directory
os.chdir("D:/Path/That/You Choose")  # Change working directory
```

Note that we have used forward slashes (/) in the folder path as this code is written on a Windows machine.

In Windows, folder paths show up using backslashes (\) while on Mac or Linux it is forward slash (/). Since backslash (\) is also an escape character in Python (e.g., \n, \t), we usually need to replace each backslash (\) with double backslashes (\\) or a forward slash (/) to avoid warnings, errors, or unintended characters. This can be done through the find

and replace feature of the IDE we are using. Alternately, we can use raw strings (r"..."). The r prefix tells Python to treat the string literally, without interpreting backslashes as escape sequences. You will learn more about strings and file paths later. For now, you can refer to the code file for examples.

Now that the working directory is set, you are all set to dive into Python fundamentals.

Variables in Python

In Excel, cells hold some value, and formulas reference those cells for calculations. In Python, variables fit the bill as they store data that can be used and manipulated throughout a script.

A variable in Python is a name given to a value, making it easy to reference (like cell reference in Excel) and reuse. In Python, you can create a variable and assign a value to it using the equals sign (=) as you have done earlier with **`score = 68`**. Here, the variable **`score`** is like a labelled box that stores the value of **`68`**.

Note: **In Python, you do not need to specify the type of data a variable holds (like a number or text). In other words, Python is dynamically typed.**

You should try to give meaningful names to your variables, like **`total_sales`** or **`product_price`**, instead of **`v1`** and **`v2`**. Also, there are some naming rules you need to consider:

- Variable name can include letters, numbers, or underscores, but cannot start with a number.
- It cannot contain space, or any special character such as %, or $ (e.g., names like *marks %* or *total sales* are not allowed). For names containing more than one word, you can use underscore (_), or capitals such as **`total_sales`**, **`MarksPerc`**.
- Unlike VBA, Python is case-sensitive (Revenue and revenue are different in Python).
- Reserved or keywords such as **`if`**, **`next`**, **`for`**, **`while`**, etc. cannot be used as variable names, somewhat similar to Excel, where certain names are restricted or advised to be avoided due to built-in functions or features. (e.g., try to name a sheet as **`History`** and it will show an error).

Here are some examples for defining the variables:

```
age = 40
print(age)              # 40

# Invalid NAMES (You'll get syntax error in these examples):
total sales = 1200      # Spaces are not allowed
discount% = 10          # special characters (like %) are not allowed
1batch = 500            # Variable names cannot start with a number
```

```
# Valid NAMES: (For the examples mentioned above)
total_sales = 1200      # Underscores not spaces(snake_case, recommended)
print(total_sales)      # 1200

discount_perc = 10      # Use descriptive names without special characters
print(discount_perc)

batch1 = 500            # Numbers can be used, but not at the start
print(batch1)

# Different naming conventions
average_price = 550  # snake_case (Recommended for variable names)
AveragePrice = 550   # PascalCase
averagePrice = 550   # camelCase

# Changing data type of a variable (allowed in Python)
x = 10               # x is an integer
print(x)             # 10

x = 'ten'            # Now x is a string/text
print(x)             # ten (Python allows dynamic typing)
```

At this point, it is recommended for you to type and run all the code yourself and try out more examples to get a better understanding of the topic.

For now, you can use Camel Case (**`numberOfGraduates`**), Pascal Case (**`NumberOfGraduates`**), or Snake Case (**`number_of_graduates`**) for variable names. When you grow more comfortable with Python, you can refer to Python's official style guide (PEP 8) **https://peps.python.org/pep-0008/#naming-conventions** or Google's style guide **https://google.github.io/styleguide/pyguide.html** for naming conventions and coding standards.

In Spyder, variables on the last line display their value automatically without needing a **`print()`** command. The same happens in Jupyter or Colab notebooks:

```
x = 10
x # automatically prints the value of x
```

You can use a semicolon (;) to write multiple statements on the same line, like **`score = 68; score + 2`**

Also, Python supports multiple assignments, allowing you to assign values to multiple variables in a single line, e.g., **`a, b = 5, 25`**

Datatypes in Python

In Excel, when you enter data, it can be of different datatypes, such as general, number, currency, short and long dates, text, etc. Broadly, you can store data as numbers (integer, fraction, percentage, scientific, etc.), text, or dates. In Python, broadly, data can be of three types: numbers (integer, floats, or complex), strings (similar to text), and Booleans. In Python, date and time are handled differently using an external module that we will discuss separately in *Chapter 4, External Packages and Date-time Handling*.

Let us understand by creating some variables and checking their datatypes:

- **Integer (int)**: In Python, if you type **`x = 5`**, it is treated as an **integer** (**int**) by default. You can check its datatype by printing **`type(x)`**. Python's **`type()`** function is similar but more powerful than Excel's **`TYPE()`** function. Whole numbers (positive, negative or zero), are referred as integers (int) in Python. More examples:

```
quantity = 10; type(quantity)       #int
score = -5; type(score)             #int
```

Key insight: In Excel, handling large numbers can be a real challenge. For example, entering a value like 123456789123456789123456789123456789 in Excel results in significant loss of precision after 15 digits.

While Python's int type grows dynamically, handling numbers of any size without extra configuration.

```
big_number = 123456789123456789123456789123456789
print(big_number)  # Works seamlessly in Python
```

Note: Excel internally stores all numbers as floating-point values, even if they appear as integers. Unlike Python, which distinguishes between int and float, Excel treats all numbers as floats.

- **Floats**: Now, try running **`10/5`** in your Python IDE, and you will get **`2.0`**, which is basically float (real numbers in math) datatype. Numbers with decimal point are treated as floats in Python, for example, **`3.14, -0.001`**.

```
x = 10/5; x # 2.0
print(type(x)) # float

price = 999.99; print(type(price)) # float
```

Python stores floats like Excel (up to a 15-digit limit) based on IEEE 754 standards. However, higher precision for floating-point numbers can be achieved by using **decimal module** in Python. It is very rare that you might need it, though.

Note: Excel often rounds off or formats float numbers silently, whereas Python exposes the raw floating-point behavior (which is a good thing for transparency and control).

Unlike Excel, Python does not hide tiny floating-point inaccuracies. For example, 0.1 + 0.2 may give 0.30000000000000004 instead of 0.3. This is normal behavior in most programming languages and ensures full precision. For applications requiring exact decimal precision, such as financial calculations, Python provides the built-in decimal module.

- **Boolean (True or False)**: Just like Excel has **`TRUE`** and **`FALSE`**, Python uses **Boolean** (**`bool`**) values to represent logical conditions (we will discuss those shortly):

```
in_stock = True; print(type(in_stock)) # True

10 > 20 # False
```

- **Strings**: In Excel, text entries like Product A are stored as **General** or **Text** format. In Python, text is represented as a **string** (**str**) and must be enclosed in single or double quotes. Inside quotation marks, even if you write any number, that will be treated as a string:

```
product_name = "Laptop"; product_name     #'Laptop'
type(product_name)                        # str


score = 'Twenty'; score                   # 'Twenty'
type(score)                               # str
```

In Python, working with multi-line strings or strings that contain variables is much simpler as compared to VBA:

```
msg = '''Hi, I am Dr Nisha. I welcome you all to learn Python for Excel.
Learning Python is easy and using it with Excel is pure-fun!
Keep learning!'''

print(msg)
```

Output:

```
Hi, I am Dr Nisha. I welcome you all to learn Python for Excel.
Learning Python is easy and using it with Excel is pure-fun!
Keep learning!
```

We will discuss more about strings in the section *Deep dive on string* of this chapter.

- **Dates**: Excel stores dates as serial numbers (e.g., **`1-Jan-2025`** is stored as **`45658`**). While in Python, dates are handled properly using the **`datetime`** module, which allows for date and time manipulation. Refer to *Chapter 4, External Packages and Date-time Handling*, for details on this.

```
from datetime import date
order_date = date(2025, 1, 1) # date() function similar to Excel's
DATE()
print(order_date)              # 2025-01-01

print('current_date: ', date.today())# Similar to Excel's TODAY()
# prints current date in yyyy-mm-dd format
```

- **NoneType in Python**: In **Excel**, an empty cell is simply **blank**, but its behavior depends on how it is used. Some formulas treat it as **`0`**, others as an empty string (`""`). In **Python**, the equivalent concept is **`None`**, which represents the absence of a value. Unlike Excel's blanks, **`None`** is a distinct datatype (**`NoneType`**) and does not behave like **`0`** or an empty string in calculations.

  When you import Excel, text, or CSV data into Python, blank cells or **`#N/A`** values are treated differently depending on the library you use. For example, as **`None`** (No value or empty), **`NaN`** (Not a Number or missing), or empty strings. You will learn all of this in detail later, just know that a few things work differently in Python compared to Excel, especially when it comes to math operations, so a little caution goes a long way.

  Python also supports **complex datatype and fraction datatype from fraction module** you can learn more about these types at: (Python's Official Document here **https://docs.python.org/3/library/stdtypes.html**).

Typecasting in Python

In Excel, datatypes are inferred automatically. For example, entering **`100`**, stores it as a number, while **"`100`"** is treated as text. Excel can also interpret numbers with **/** as dates (this is sometimes annoying). In Excel, you can convert datatypes manually or using some functions like **`VALUE()`** or **`TEXT()`**.

In Python, changing datatype is much more convenient and we call it **typecasting**. Sometimes Python automatically changes data types during operations (implicit typecasting). To deliberately change types (which is known as explicit typecasting), we use the following built-in functions:

- **int()**: Converts to an integer
- **float()**: Converts to a float/ decimal number
- **str()**: Converts to a string (text)
- **bool()**: Converts to a boolean (**`True`** or **`False`**)

Converting to numbers

You can convert text to int or float if the text contains a valid numeric value. While **`VALUE()`** function in Excel can create issues due to hidden characters, formatting inconsistencies, or encoding issues, Python's **`int()`** and **`float()`** work seamlessly:

```
sales = "500" # Stored as a string (text)
type(sales) # str
sales_num = int(sales) # Convert to an integer
type(sales_num) # int
print(sales_num * 2)  # 1000 (works like a number now)


age = "  30  "
type(age) # str
int(age) # 30
float(age) # 30.0
```

You can also convert Boolean to numbers (int or float). It allows you to seamlessly use Boolean values in mathematical operations, logical expressions, and even indexing without extra conversions. In Python, **True** converts to **1**, and **False** converts to **0**:

```
passed = True; int(passed) # 1
present = False; int(present) # 0
```

Converting to Bools

In Excel, **TRUE** and **FALSE** are treated as Boolean values, but if stored as text (**"TRUE"**), you need extra steps to convert them, such as **IF(A1="TRUE", TRUE, FALSE)**. In Python, **bool()** helps in such conversions:

```
status_text = "True" ; bool(status_text)  # True (converted to boolean)
bool("False")      # True as it converts any non-empty string to True
bool("")           # False as only empty string is converted to False
```

Warning: bool("False") still returns True because any non-empty string is considered True in Python. To properly convert "True" or "False" text values, you can use.

```
status_bool = status_text.lower() == "true"
```

In Excel, any nonzero number is treated as **TRUE**. Python follows the same logic but with a simpler implementation:

```
bool(10)    # True
bool(0)     # False
```

You will later see that Python can even convert arrays like list, set, tuple, dictionary, etc., to Boolean. Everything, except empty array converts to **True**. Similarly, **str()** can be used to convert values into text for display, logging, or file output. Now that you are familiar with Python datatypes and conversions, let us explore how to use various operators to manipulate them.

Operators in Python

In Excel, formulas use **operators** to perform calculations, compare values, or apply logic. You have already seen **arithmetic operators** (Refer to the section *From Excel formulas to Python scripts* in this chapter) like `+, -, *,` and `/` in Python, which work similarly to Excel. Let us discuss other common operators and how they work in Python.

Comparison or relationship operators

Just as Excel allows comparisons like `=A1>B1`, Python uses comparison operators to check relationships between values, returning `True` or `False`. Most comparison operators work the same way in Excel and Python, except for equal to (`=`) and not equal to (`<>`) in Excel:

```
price1 = 500; price2 = 700
print(price1 > price2)  # False (500 is not greater than 700)
print(price1 == 500)    # True (equal to 500, similar to A1=500 in Excel)
print(price1 != price2) # True (similar to A1<>B1 in Excel)
```

Logical operators

Excel's `=AND(A1>20, B1<500)` checks whether both conditions are true simultaneously and `=OR(A1>20, B1<500)` checks whether at least one condition is true. In Python, we use logical operators (`and`, `or`, `not`) in the same way. Excel uses `AND()`, `OR()`, and `NOT()` as functions, while Python uses `and`, `or`, and `not` as keywords without parentheses:

```
stock = 50; price = 200
print(stock > 20 and price < 500)  # True (Both conditions met)
print(stock > 100 or price < 500)  # True (At least one condition met)
print(not (price > 500))           # True (Reverses the condition)
```

Key insight: In Python, logical operators use shortcircuit evaluation, meaning they stop checking as soon as the result is determined. This is beneficial because it avoids unnecessary calculations (and even prevents errors, like dividing by zero), unlike Excel, which always evaluates every condition.

```
False and 1/0 # False
True or 1/0 # True
```

In Excel, `=AND(FALSE,1/0)` and `=OR(TRUE, 1/0)` results in `#DIV/0!` error.

Membership operators

In Excel, you might check if a value exists in a column using `COUNTIF(A:A, "Laptop") > 0`. In Python, we use `in` and `not in` to check if a value exists in a list:

```
products = ["Laptop", "Phone", "Tablet"]
print("Laptop" in products)      # True (Found in the list)
print("Camera" not in products)  # True (Not in the list)
```

By understanding these operators, Excel users can easily translate their spreadsheet logic into Python scripts.

Table 3.1 lists Python operators and their Excel equivalents where they differ:

Operator category	Operator name	Python example	Excel equivalent	Description or comment
Arithmetic	Integer division	a // b	=QUOTIENT(A1, B1)	Excel has a function, not an operator
	Modulo (Remainder)	a % b	=MOD(A1, B1)	
	Exponentiation	a ** b	=A1 ^ B1	Raises a to the power of b
Comparison	Equal to	a == b	=A1 = B1	Checks if values are equal
	Not equal to	a != b	=A1 <> B1	Checks if values are not equal
Logical	AND	a and b (supports short circuit evaluation)	AND(A1, B1)	Excel has a function while Python has an operator
	OR	a or b (supports short circuit evaluation)	OR(A1, B1)	
	NOT	not a	NOT(A1)	
Membership	In	a in apple	No direct Excel equivalent	Checks if item exists in a sequence (text or range)
	Not in	a not in apple	No direct Excel equivalent	Checks if item does not exist in the sequence
Assignment	Assignment	x = 10	x = 10 (in VBA only)	Assigns value
	Compound assignment	x += 5	No direct Excel equivalent	Add and assign in one step

Operator category	Operator name	Python example	Excel equivalent	Description or comment
Identity	Is	a is b	Is (in VBA only)	Checks if two variables point to the same object
	Is not	a is not b	IsNot (in VBA only)	Checks if two variables point to the same object
Logical or bitwise equivalence	Eqv	No direct equivalent needed	Expr1 Eqv Expr2 (VBA Only)	Rarely used in practice

***Table 3.1**: Python's operators vs. Excel's operators*

Deep dive on strings

While discussing datatypes, we have introduced Python's strings as text datatype, for example, `'Excel'`, or `'123'`. However, strings in Python can also be considered as a sequence of characters, so *Excel* can be treated as a collection of **5** characters or strings: **`E`**, **`x`**, **`c`**, **`e`**, and **`l`**.

Other basic datatypes that we discussed so far (numbers or bools) represent a single value, hence are called **scalers**, while strings can also be treated as a collection of values, hence are also called **aggregate datatype** or **data structure**. Python's core datatypes are shown in *Figure 3.3*. We will discuss other aggregate datatypes in the next section.

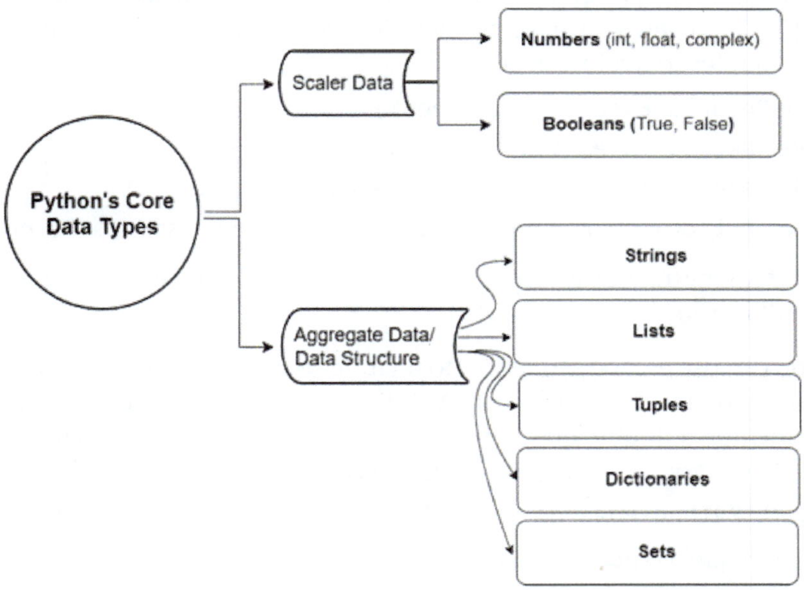

***Figure 3.3**: Python datatypes*

Working with text data in Excel often feels limiting. With Excel's text functions like **LEFT()**, **RIGHT()**, **MID()**, and **TEXT()**, handling complex text manipulation such as splitting full names, cleaning inconsistent data, extracting patterns, or combining text across multiple cells quickly turns unwieldy. Even newer additions in Excel 2021/365 like **TEXTSPLIT()**, **TEXTBEFORE()**, **TEXTAFTER()**, and **TEXTJOIN()** often fall short when tasks become more complex or large-scale.

For advanced text extraction, cleaning up, bulk operations, or conditional string replacement, Excel users switch to VBA. However, the syntax becomes too lengthy and hard to maintain, particularly when you need the functionality across multiple workbooks.

Even Power Query, while powerful, has a learning curve and is not always intuitive for quick one-off tasks. Performance issues also arise with very large text datasets, and there is a stringent cell character limit of 32,767 characters, of which only 1,024 characters are visible directly in the cell grid. This limitation reflects Excel's design as a spreadsheet application, optimized for structured data and calculations rather than large-scale text processing.

By contrast, Python does not impose a practical limit on string length beyond the available system memory. And Python's string handling solves these pain points efficiently. With concise, readable code, you can easily clean, transform, and analyze text data, whether it is standardizing product names, parsing emails, or reformatting dates. Python makes what feels like a workaround in Excel into a smooth, flexible solution, saving time and reducing errors, especially when working with large datasets. This positions Python suitable for handling extensive text datasets, bulk operations, and advanced manipulations such as regular expressions, conditional replacements, and natural language processing.

We have discussed that a Python string is simply text data, enclosed in single quotes (`' '`), double quotes (`" "`). When you need to include quotes within the text itself, you can use different types of quotes to avoid confusion:

```
book = "Python-Powered Excel"; print(book)
book = 'Python-Powered Excel'; print(book)
s1 ='"Python-Powered Excel" is my favorite book.'; print(s1)
s2 = "The book 'Python-Powered Excel' is practical yet simple."; print(s2)
```

To conserve chapter length, many outputs are not shown; run the code stepwise and observe the console for full results.

Additionally, you can use escape sequences to include special characters or quotes within your strings. An escape sequence is a backslash (`\`) followed by the character you want to include. For instance, to include a double quote inside a double-quoted string or a single quote inside a single-quoted string, you can use `\"` or `\'` respectively:

```
s3 = "He said, \"Python-Powered Excel\" is a great book."; print(s3)
s4 = 'It\'s a wonderful book on Excel-Python integration.'; print(s4)
```

The output is:

```
He said, "Python-Powered Excel" is a great book.
It's a wonderful book on Excel-Python integration.
```

Escape sequences can also be used to include special characters like new lines or tabs within strings. E.g., **\n** for a new line and **\t** for a tab:

```
using_tab = 'tool:\tPython'
using_new_line = 'tools:\nPython\nExcel'
```

You should print to see the output. In the next example, we are showing both **\t** and **\n**:

```
info = 'Book:\tPython-Powered Excel\nAuthor:\tDr Nisha Arora\nPublisher:\
tBPB Publications'
print(info)
```

The output is:

```
Book: Python-Powered Excel
Author: Dr Nisha Arora
Publisher: BPB Publications
```

This way, you can include special characters and quotes within your strings without any issues.

Essential string operations

The **len()** function returns the total length of a string, including all characters and spaces. For example, **len('Nisha Arora')** will return **11**, as it counts every character, including the space between **"Nisha"** and **"Arora"**.

Changing case in Python is similar to Excel, as shown in the following code:

```
text = "Hello, Excel Users!"
print(text.upper())      # HELLO, EXCEL USERS!
print(text.title())      # Hello, Excel Users!
print(text.lower())      # hello, excel users!
print(text.capitalize()) # Hello, excel users!
```

Removing extra spaces in Python is easier, even for leading or trailing spaces:

```
text  = "  Learning Python is Fun!  "
print(text.strip()) # Removes both leading and trailing spaces
text.lstrip()       # Removes only leading (left) spaces
text.rstrip()       # Removes only trailing (right) spaces
```

Replacing text, finding the position of a character in the given text are like Excel functions (Refer to the code file for examples). Python directly supports counting occurrences of a character using **count()**. For example:

```
email = "user@example.com"
print(email.count("@"))  # 1
print(email.find("@"))    # 4 (index _ More on this soon!)
```

Splitting strings based on any separator is simpler, as shown in the following code:

```
text = 'Python-Powered Excel'
print(text.split())          # ['Python-Powered', 'Excel']
print(text.split(sep='-')) # ['Python', 'Powered Excel']


text = 'Nisha Arora'
text.split() # Output is a list, can be further sliced. [Refer Next Topic]
text.split()[0] # Nisha
```

In Excel 2021 or 365, you can use **TEXTSPLIT()** for the same, but older versions need a combination of **LEFT()**, **LEN()**, **MID()**, and **FIND()**, etc. The **startswith()** and **endswith()** methods[3] in Python, are great for validating strings. Excel 365 introduced similar functions **TEXTBEFORE**, and **TEXTAFTER**, however, older versions of Excel need a workaround for these tasks:

```
filename = "report.xlsx"
print(filename.endswith(".xlsx"))      # True
print(filename.startswith("report"))  # True
```

String concatenation in Python is more versatile and efficient, compared to Excel, with easier integration of variables and complex expressions:

```
folder = "C:/Documents"
filename = "report.xlsx"
path = folder + "/" + filename
print(path)                     # C:/Documents/report.xlsx
```

While concatenation of strings can be done using the **+** operator, for more dynamic and readable text, especially when mixing variables, numbers, or calculations, Python offers **formatted strings (f-strings)**. These are like having Excel's **TEXT()** and concatenation combined in one smooth step. Inserting a variable or performing calculations inside the string is super easy:

```
cl = 140; imp = 800


print(f"Clicks: {cl}, Impressions: {imp}") # Clicks: 140, Impressions: 800
print(f"Click Through Rate (CTR): {cl/imp:.2%}")
# Click Through Rate (CTR): 17.50%
```

---

[3] The words functions and methods are used interchangeably many times. However, technically, functions are standalone blocks of code, while methods are functions that belong to objects like lists, strings, or dictionaries.

You can even use function calls inside the string. Another much-needed functionality, Python offers to remove prefix or suffix quickly:

```
name = "Ms Nisha Arora, PhD"
print(name.removeprefix("Ms "))   # Nisha Arora, PhD
print(name.removesuffix(", PhD")) # Ms Nisha Arora

# Great thing is you can chain together string methods
cleaned = name.removeprefix("Ms ").removesuffix(", PhD")
print(cleaned)                      #  Nisha Arora
```

Indexing and slicing strings

Another amazing feature of Python's strings is that you can directly access individual characters and substrings using indexing. In Python, indexing refers to accessing an element of a sequence (like a string or list) using its position. Python counts positions from left to right, starting at 0 (Refer to *Figure 3.4*), unlike VBA, where the first character is indexed as *1*:

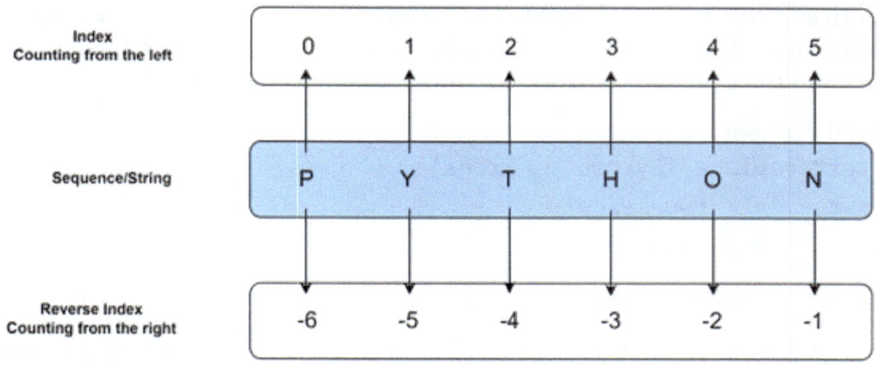

Figure 3.4: *Indexing in Python*

Python also supports negative index to count from right to left, starting from **-1**. So, the last element of the sequence is indexed **-1**. To fetch any character from a string, you need to use square brackets:

```
text = 'Python'
text[0] # first character
text[3] # index 3, i.e., 4th character
text[-1] # last character
text[-2] # index 2 from the end, second last character
```

If you need to extract a substring from a string, it is called slicing, and it can be done using a range of indices. Python goes beyond simple indexing. You can grab slices (ranges) of text easily. Basic syntax is **string[start:stop]** where:

- **Start**: The position where the slice begins (inclusive).
- **Stop**: The position where the slice ends (exclusive).

`string[a:b]` will slice string starting at index **`a`**, and extracting until index **`(b-1)`**:

```
name = "Microsoft Excel"
print(name[0:9])    # Microsoft (characters indexed from 0 to 8)
print(name[:9])     # same as before as it starts from in-
dex '0', if we don't mention explicitly
print(name[10:])    # Excel (from index 10 to end)
print(name[-5:])    # Excel (from 5th last or index -5 till end)
```

You can even skip characters by slicing with step **`string[start:stop:step]`** as shown:

```
print(name[0:9:2]) # Mcoot -> every alternate chracter from index 0 to 8
print(name[::2])    # McootEcl -> every alternate character
print(name[::-1])   # lecxE tfosorciM -> negative step reverses the string
```

In Python, strings are immutable, meaning you cannot change the original string directly. You might have noticed that methods like **`strip()`**, **`replace()`**, and **`removeprefix()`**, etc., do not modify the string itself. Instead, they create and return a new string with the changes applied. If you want to keep the updated version, you must assign it to a variable:

```
text = "I love Python"
new_text = text.replace('Python', 'Excel')
print(new_text)    # I love Excel
print(text)        # I love Python
```

Here, **`text`** remains unchanged unless you reassign it.

With just a few simple string methods (and with the knowledge of control flow that you will learn soon), Python empowers you to handle text far beyond what Excel formulas and VBA can do for data cleaning and file management. Mastering strings is a key step to boost your Excel skills with Python. At this moment, we recommend practicing string methods before reading further. More examples and use-cases are mentioned in the code file.

Python data structures

Strings are powerful, but when you need to store data for multiple people or items like IDs, names, or records, you need something more. Just like you use rows, columns, and tables in Excel, Python uses data structures like lists, tuples, sets, dictionaries, and even strings to organize collections of values. We call them data structures or aggregate datatypes. Let us understand these aggregate datatypes in detail.

Lists

In Excel, you store multiple values, such as the prices of ten products, in a column range like A1:A10. Other options are to create an array in VBA or use Excel's (2021 or 365) dynamic array functionality for better sorting, filtering, etc.

In Python, you can store multiple values in a list (among other options).

A list in Python is:

- **Flexible**: You can include any type of data in it, even a list itself.
- **Mutable**: Modifiable, means it allows you to add, remove, or replace elements.
- **Indexable**: You can fetch elements by indexing or slicing.
- **Ordered**: Elements stay in the same sequence as they were added.

You can create a list by putting different elements (any datatype) separated by commas inside square bracket:

```
products = ['mobile', 'laptop', 'tablet', 'mobile']; products
# ['mobile', 'laptop', 'tablet', 'mobile']
stock = [120, 38, 55]; stock        #[120, 38, 55]
demo = ['Nisha', 40, True]; demo    # ['Nisha', 40, True]
```

In the preceding examples, you must have noticed that a list can include mixed datatypes, and duplicates are also allowed. The following examples show other properties of a list:

```
# Define a list of prices for 4 products
prices = [19.99, 29.95, 9.99, 14.49, 44.99]

# Add a new price to the list
prices.append(34.99); prices # [19.99, 29.95, 9.99, 14.49, 44.99, 34.99]
# Remove a price from the list
prices.remove(14.49); prices # [19.99, 29.95, 9.99, 44.99, 34.99]

# Change the price of the first product
prices[0] = 21.99; prices # [21.99, 29.95, 9.99, 44.99, 34.99]

# Sort the list in ascending/descending order
sorted(prices) # [9.99, 21.99, 29.95, 34.99, 44.99]
sorted(prices, reverse=True) # [44.99, 34.99, 29.95, 21.99, 9.99]
```

In above-mentioned code, we have created a simple list of numbers and performed basic operations to add a new element using **append()** method or remove the existing element using **remove()** method. This is allowed as lists are mutable. We then indexed the list by using square bracket sub-setting (indexing and slicing work the same way it works for strings and tuples). We have also updated the price of the first product, because such operations are feasible with mutable data structures. As a list is an ordered entity, we can sort it (ascending or descending for a list of numbers or alphabetical order for a list of texts) too.

You can join two lists by simply using a **+** sign, which creates a brand new list or **extend()** method, which extends the original list. For more detailed explanation and examples, refer to code file in the GitHub repo:

```
# Merging monthly sales data
jan_sales = [12000, 15000]
feb_sales = [18000, 16000]
mar_sales = [20000, 18000]
q1_sales = jan_sales + feb_sales + mar_sales
q1_sales # [12000, 15000, 18000, 16000, 20000, 18000]

# Appending New Hires to an Existing Employee List
employees = ['Amit', 'Priya', 'John']
new_joinees = ['Sara', 'Leo']
employees.extend(new_joinees)
print(employees) # ['Amit', 'Priya', 'John', 'Sara', 'Leo']
```

Lists also allow you to create a nested data structure for tabular data, as given in the following figure:

Product A	19.99	10
Product B	29.95	5
Product C	9.99	15

Figure 3.5: *Sample data*

In Excel, you use tables, range, or a dynamic array to store 2-dim data like this. Let us create such data in Python using a nested list (list or lists):

```
# A list of lists representing a table of product details
product_details = [
    ["Product A", 19.99, 10],
    ["Product B", 29.95, 5],
    ["Product C", 9.99, 15]
]
```

```
# Accessing elements in the nested list
print(product_details[0])  # ['Product A', 19.99, 10] _ Product A details
print(product_details[1][1])  # 29.95 _ Price of Product B

# Modifying an element in the nested list
product_details[2][2] = 20  # Change the stock of Product C to 20

# Adding a new product to the nested list
product_details.append(["Product D", 14.49, 8])
```

If you are comfortable with Excel's dynamic arrays (Excel 2021 or 365), you will find Python lists even more powerful and flexible.

Tuples

A **tuple** is like a list but is **immutable**, which means once created, it **cannot be modified**. Tuples are useful to protect the data from edits. For example, coordinates, fixed settings, or functions that expect constant values.

You can create a tuple directly, putting elements, and separating values by commas, or you can use parentheses for the same. Indexing is the same as you have done in strings or lists, and there are fewer methods available for tuples, as you can simply not add, remove, or change any element once the tuple is created:

```
# Creating a tuple by using () constructor
coordinates = (10, 20); coordinates        # (10, 20)

# You can also create a tuple directly (sep values by a comma)
coordinates = 10, 20 ; coordinates         # (10, 20)

# Or you can convert a list to tuple
coordinates = tuple([10,20]); coordinates  # (10, 20)
# As tuple is immutable, you can't add/remove or change elements
# However, you indexing/slicing is allowed as it is ordered and indexable

coordinates[0] # 10
coordinates[1] # 20

# append(), remove(), pop(), insert or other similar methods are not avail-
able for tuples
```

You can also create nested tuples (refer to the code file for more examples).

Dictionaries

In Excel, you store structured data in rows and columns, where each column has a header, and data is organized in rows. You use lookup functions, such as **VLOOKUP**, **INDEX**, and **MATCH**, or **XLOOKUP** (Excel 2021/365) to retrieve specific data points based on criteria.

In Python, you can achieve similar functionality using **dictionaries**[4] (**dict**). Dictionaries store data as key-value pairs, which is analogous to how columns and rows are structured in Excel. You can access values corresponding to specific keys via indexing:

```
# Create a dictionary by enclosing a comma-separated key-value pairs in {}.
Use ':' to separate each key from its associated value.

employees = {"E101": "Prateek", "E102": "Pragya"}
employees

# LOOKUP Employee Name by Employee Id
employees.get("E101")

# It safely handles missing keys (You can print a msg as you prefer)
employees.get("E103", "Not Found")
```

Additionally, you can easily merge two or more dictionaries with Python:

```
# Merging two dictionaries (Much easier than Excel) overwrites, if key
repeats

products_prices = {
    "Apple": 120,
    "Banana": 60
}

new_prices = {
    "Mango": 280,
    "Banana": 100
}
```

[4] Python dictionaries are ordered just like Excel tables, preserving the sequence of items as you add them. However, be aware that in Python versions before 3.7, dictionaries did not guarantee order, but since we are using a newer version in this book, you would not face this issue.

```
updated = products_prices | new_prices; updated  # Python 3.9+
# {'Apple': 120, 'Banana': 100, 'Mango': 280}

# |= updates the dictionary in place by merging another dictionary
products_prices |= new_prices; products_prices

# {'Apple': 120, 'Banana': 100, 'Mango': 280}
```

You can also use the unpacking operator for merging dictionaries:

```
updated = {**products_prices, **new_prices}
print(updated) # {'Apple': 120, 'Banana': 100, 'Mango': 280}
```

The above-mentioned methods create new merged dictionary, while update method modifies the original dictionary in place.

Note: Dictionaries require unique keys. When merging dictionaries, duplicate keys are resolved by last-write-wins, i.e., the value from the rightmost dictionary overwrites earlier ones.

Sets

A **set** in Python is an unordered collection of unique values. This is like Excel's **`UNIQUE()`** function, which removes duplicate values from a range:

```
# You can create a set by using curly braces {} or set() function.
numbers = [1, 2, 2, 3, 3, 3]
unique_numbers = set(numbers)
print(unique_numbers)  # {1, 2, 3}

product_id = {'g1001', 'g1002', 'g1002'}
product_id # {'g1001', 'g1002'} # Keeps unique element only
```

Sets are particularly useful for set-theoretic operations such as union, intersection, and difference. In Excel, achieving these operations requires some workarounds.

Warning: Sets are unordered in Python, meaning they do not maintain the original order of values. If the order matters, use a list or a NumPy array (to be discussed later in the book) instead.

Before moving to the next topic, we recommend practicing Python data structures, different methods, and indexing. By understanding Python's data structures in terms of Excel's familiar features, such as dynamic arrays, tables, lookup, etc., learning Python becomes much easier and more intuitive:

Python	Excel equivalent	Description/Use case with simple Python code
List	Vertical or horizontal range, array	Ordered collection of values (can be mixed types) such as [Apple, Banana, 50, 30]
Tuple	Constant range (Locked for edits)	Immutable list (useful for fixed data) such as (Jan, Feb, Mar)
Dictionary	Named range or lookup table	Key-value pairs, e.g., {Apple: 120, Banana: 60}
Set	Not directly available	Unordered collection with unique elements such as {A, B, C}
String	Cell with text	Work as a collection of values, much more powerful e.g., Hello .upper().strip() gives the output HELLO
None	Blank cell or #N/A	Represents missing or no value, e.g., x = None
DataFrame (pandas)[5]	Table or structured range	Table with labeled columns and rows (like Excel table) e.g., pd.DataFrame(products)

Table 3.2: *A quick summary of Python data structures*

Beyond the core datatypes, readers can explore advanced structures such as OrderedDict, frozenset, namedtuple, dataclass, and composite patterns like lists of dictionaries or dictionaries of lists, as these broaden practical understanding.

Control flow for conditions and repeating actions

You must have used `IF()`, `IFS()`, and conditional formatting in Excel to perform logic-based calculations and highlight specific data. You might even use loops and conditions in VBA to automate repetitive tasks. Python takes this idea further with clear, readable structures for decision-making and repetition, what we call **control flow**.

Control flow allows your code to **react** to perform specific tasks based on different conditions, and repeat actions, making your Python script smarter and more dynamic. The three main control flow tools in Python are shown in *Figure 3.6*:

[5] We will talk about dataframes (Tabular data like Excel) *from pandas library in Chapter 6, Data Manipulation with Pandas.*

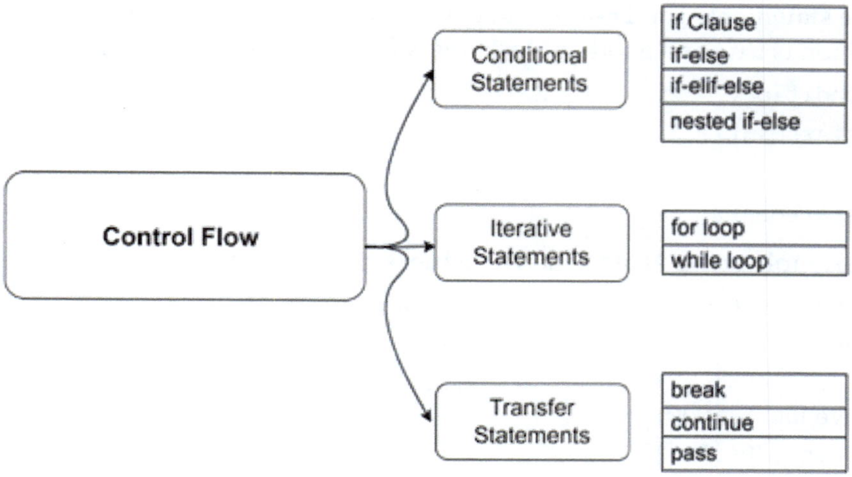

***Figure 3.6**: Control flow in Python*

Conditional statements in Python

To apply logic to your data, such as do something when sales meet the target or inventory reaches a minimum level, you can use Python's **if**, **elif**, and **else** keywords. The details are as follows:

- **if statement**: Python will check if the condition is true. If so, it runs **statement1**. Ensure you add a colon after the condition and indent the next line (your IDE will help). The pseudo-code is:

```
if condition:
  statement1
```

Always use consistent spaces (usually 4) to indent code blocks and never mix spaces and tabs. Incorrect indentation will cause syntax errors, but your IDE usually helps you automatically indenting the code.

```
sales = 1200  # Try changing values of this variable & running the code
again

if sales > 1000:
    print("Eligible for bonus")
```

It is good practice to test the code with different input values to ensure the correctness of the logic. You might notice for lower sales values (upto 1000), no message is printed. This is because we did not include the **else** block in the code. Let us see it in action.

- **if-else statement**: The **`if-else`** statement allows you to execute one block of code if a condition is true and another block if it is false. The pseudo-code is:

```
if condition:
    statement1
else:
    statement2
```

This example prints **`Profit`** when revenue is greater than 1000, otherwise it prints **`Loss`**:

```
revenue = 950       # Try changing values of this variable & notice the
output

if revenue > 1000:
    print("Profit")
else:
    print("Loss")
```

- **if-elif-else statement**: The **`if-elif-else`** statement lets you handle multiple conditions in a readable and efficient way, unlike Excel's nested **`IF()`** functions. You can add multiple conditions using **`elif`** without making it hard on the eyes. The pseudo-code is:

```
if condition1:
    statement1
elif condition2:
    statement2
else:
    statement3
```

For example, to measure the performance of salesmen based on the number of sales they make, you can use multiple **`elif`** blocks as needed:

```
# Example: Sale performance analysis
sales = 1500

if sales > 2000:
    performance = "Excellent"
elif sales > 1500:
    performance = "Good"
elif sales > 1000:
    performance = "Average"
else:
    performance = "Needs Improvement"
```

- **Nested if-else statements**: Nested **`if-else`** statements are used when you need to make multiple layers of decisions. While **`if-elif-else`** is often sufficient, there are scenarios where nested conditions provide better control and precision, especially when you need to check sub-conditions within a primary condition. Here is the pseudo-code:

```
if condition1:
    if condition2:
        statement1
    else:
        statement2
else:
    statement3
```

  For example, for user authentication, if you need to check both username and password to authenticate a user, you can write nested conditions like this:

```
username = "admin"; password = "password123"

if username == "admin":
    if password == "password123":
        print("Access granted.")
    else:
        print("Incorrect password.")
else:
    print("Unknown user.")
```

You can also use shorthand notation, that is one-liner code for simple conditionals, for example:

```
sales = 1200
if sales > 1000: print("Eligible for bonus")       # Eligible for bonus

revenue = 950
"Profit" if revenue > 1000 else "Loss"             # 'Loss'
```

Note: **While shorthand notation is neat, avoid overusing it for complex conditions. It can hamper the readability, just like a messy nested IF formula in Excel.**

Iterative and transfer statements in Python

In Excel, repetitive tasks are often done by dragging formulas, using helper columns or using VBA. Excel 365's **`BYROW()`** and **`BYCOL()`** functions with **`LAMBDA()`** bring loop-like behavior, but Python offers a simpler and more powerful way to handle such tasks.

In Python, there are two types of loops:

- **for** loops
- **while** loops

Use a **for** loop when you know how many times you want to repeat something, like looping **n** times, looping through rows of data or a list of products. Use a **while** loop when you want to repeat an action **until a condition is met**, like checking stock levels until they are all sold out. Examples are a great way to grasp a concept, so let us begin with a few simple ones.

The for loop

You are familiar with Python's core data structures (or aggregate datatypes), such as string, list, tuple, dictionary, or a set that is used to hold multiple data points. Using the **for** loop you can perform a task for each data point of an iterable or collection. An iterable is anything in Python you can go through one item at a time, like aggregate datatypes, or even a range (we have a **range()** function that produces a sequence of numbers), just like dragging down a formula over a range of cells in Excel. There are many other iterables in Python that you will come across while working with Python.

The syntax is similar to conditional statements with a slight change, as you can see:

```
for variable in iterable:
    # Do something with variable
```

If you have a list of scores and you want to give a bonus score (+2) to each participant, you can basically write a **for** loop (as you want to repeat this operation for each score) like this:

```
# Adding Bonus score (+2) for each participant
score_list = [23, 39, 46, 38, 27]
print('After adding Bonus, Scores are: \n')      # Just adding context

for score in score_list:            # Iterating for every element of the list
    print(score + 2)                # performing +2 every iteration
```

For each number in **score_list** (we are referring to those as **score**, but you can call them anything you wish), it prints the sum of that number and 2. You might have understood what it does just by reading the code. Code indentation is something unique to Python that reduces cognitive load by avoiding guesswork, as we can simply see it.

In the following example, the product list has the names of fruits, but in different cases. By iterating through each product, we are converting each item's name to lowercase:

```
# Printing each product name in lower case
products = ["Apple", "banana", "MANGO", "ORANGE"]
print('After text cleaning, product names: \n')
```

```
for item in products:
    print(item.lower())
```

From a product price dictionary, if you want to find products that are priced above 100, you can loop with condition. The code is written by indenting the code block as per logic:

```
# Print products priced above 100
prices = {"Apple": 120, "Banana": 60, "Mango": 280, "Orange": 145}

for product, price in prices.items(): # first iterate through the dictionary
    if price > 100:                              # Then check condition
        print(product, "is premium product") # print if condition is True
```

It will print results for all products for which the price is greater than 100 (*Apple, Mango,* and *Orange*). If there is a requirement to only print the first product that meets the requirement and stop after the first match is found, this can simply be done by using the **break** statement. In Python, **break**, **continue**, and **pass** are known as **transfer statements,** as these keywords transfer the flow within the loop or code block:

```
# Find the first product over ₹100
for product, price in prices.items():
    if price > 100:
        print("Found:", product)# Found: Apple (1st product with price>100
        break  # Stops after first match, basically loop ends
```

The **break** statement allows the loop to exit immediately, while **continue** statement skips the current iteration and moves to the next:

```
# Print only items under ₹150
for product, price in prices.items():
    if price > 150:
        continue  # Skip expensive items (priced > 150)
    print(product, "is affordable")
```

The statement **pass** does nothing and is used as a placeholder when a statement is syntactically required. For example, when we are not sure yet what to write inside a loop or function, but cannot leave it blank, as Python will throw an error, we use **pass** as a proxy:

```
for product, price in prices.items():
    if price > 150:
        pass  # Not Sure what to do yet, will add code Later
```

Similarly, you can also loop through nested lists (or other similar iterables). One such example is:

```
# Looping through rows of a table (nested list)
product_data = [
    ["Apple", 120],
    ["Banana", 60],
    ["Mango", 280]
]

for row in product_data:
    name, price = row
    print(f"{name}: ₹{price}")  # Like reading rows from Excel
```

In all the preceding examples, we have iterated over different data structures. Sometimes, we need to repeat some operation a fixed number of times (say five times). We can do this using the in-built iterable **range(start, stop, step)**. The **range()**[6] function generates a sequence of numbers, commonly used for looping a specific number of times. By default, it creates a sequence of numbers starting from **0** up to one less than the specified stop value. For example, **range(5)** constructs a range object containing numbers **0 to 4**, but it does not display numbers directly, you can convert it to a list to see the values:

```
range(5)            # range(0, 5)
list(range(5))      # [0, 1, 2, 3, 4]

# You can also use it with start and step:
list(range(start=1, stop=10, step=2))  # [1, 3, 5, 7, 9]
```

Using **range()** in loops is as intuitive as using a list:

```
# Send 3 reminder messages
for i in range(1, 4):
    print(f"Reminder {i}: Please submit your report.")
```

You can also refer to code files to explore examples related to other powerful functions, such as **enumerate()** and **zip()**.

We will now discuss the **while** loop. We use it when we do not know in advance how many times an operation is to be repeated.

---

[6] Range object is lazy, i.e., it does not generate all elements at once but can be iterated over. It is memory efficient and faster to use range(1000) rather than use list of 1000 numbers.

The while loop

The **while** loop allows repeated until a condition is no longer **True**. The pseudo-syntax is:

```
while condition:
    # code to run repeatedly
```

The code keeps running if the condition is always **True**, which can basically become an **infinite loop**, good enough to crash your machine or freeze your program. Always ensure the loop condition, in due course, terminates, or use a **break** statement to stop running the loop. If by mistake, you have run an infinite loop, you can manually interrupt the code by using the stop button in Spyder interface (Console) or hitting the *Esc* key in Colab. Some use-cases of while loop are:

```
# Wait for Correct Password_ Try giving different inputs to the prompt
password = ""

while password != "open123":
    password = input("Enter password: ")

print("Access granted!")# This will run when condition is met & loop ends

# Countdown Timer
count = 5
while count > 0:
    print("Countdown:", count)
    count -= 1
print("Go!")
```

List and dictionary comprehension

You have learned to use loops to perform an operation repeatedly. Many times, you can achieve the same by using comprehensions too, often in just one line of code. Once you master loops and conditional statements, you can learn about list and dictionary comprehension. For now, this topic is not mandatory, but it will help you make your code shorter, faster, and easier to read. Feel free to skip and move to the next one if you find it overwhelming.

To create a list of squares of numbers from 1 to 5, we can start with an empty list and then iteratively append the square of each number within the specified range:

```
squares = []
for x in range(1, 6):
    squares.append(x**2)

print(squares)  # Output: [1, 4, 9, 16, 25]
```

This can easily be done using list comprehension in one line. Let us understand how it works.

To create a list using list comprehension, the pseudo-code is:

```
[expression for item in iterable]
```

You already understand **`iterable`** (for example, aggregate datatype or **`range()`**), the line **`for item in iterable`** basically is to iterate over each element of that iterable (as you do in a **`for`** loop). And `expression` means the statement which says what to do with each item (e.g., **`item + 2`**, or **`item.upper()`**, etc.).

Using list comprehension for our example to create a list of squares of numbers from 1 to 5:

```
[x**2 for x in range(1, 6)]       # [1, 4, 9, 16, 25]
```

You might have noticed that using list comprehension is efficient and concise.

When we are to introduce conditions in loops, we can achieve the same by slightly changing the code to accommodate the if condition:

```
[expression for item in iterable if condition]
```

Here again:

- **item**: The current value from the iterable.
- **iterable**: The original list, range or any iterable.
- **condition**: A filter only includes items that meet this.

For example, to create a list of squares of even numbers (numbers that are divisible by 2) from 1 to 10, we can write a loop with the condition:

```
squares_even = []
for x in range(1, 11):
    if x%2 == 0:
        squares_even.append(x**2)

print(squares_even)    # [4, 16, 36, 64, 100]
```

However, this can be done in one line by using list comprehension as shown here:

```
[x**2 for x in range(1, 11) if x % 2 == 0] # [4, 16, 36, 64, 100]
```

Just like list comprehension, **dictionary comprehension** helps create a dictionary (key-value pairs) in a concise one-liner:

```
{key_expr: value_expr for item in iterable if condition}
```

You might have guessed that here, **`key_expr`** indicates what to use as the key, and **`value_expr`** indicates what to use as the value.

```
squares = {x: x**2 for x in range(1, 6)}
print(squares) # {1: 1, 2: 4, 3: 9, 4: 16, 5: 25}
```

To turn a list of products and prices into a dictionary:

```
products = ["Apple", "Banana", "Mango"]
prices = [120, 60, 280]

product_price = {p: pr for p, pr in zip(products, prices)}
print(product_price) #
 {'Apple': 120, 'Banana': 60, 'Mango': 280}
```

Functions in Python

Suppose you have written some code to clean your text data (maybe assume a list of strings for now) using string methods (convert to lower case, remove white spaces, split by a separator, etc.) in a Python script. Later, you came across another text data (another such list), where you need to do the same cleaning process. You would copy-paste the code with the changed name of the data or list, and you are done. Now imagine if you need to do the same process multiple times in the same script, or maybe in different scripts for different data values. You would need something better than copy-pasting. Python reusability comes to rescue and allows you to wrap your logic in a bundle called **function** and re-use anywhere in your script, even in other scripts too. Python functions offer more advanced reusability, readability, debugging, and maintainability compared to Excel 365's LAMBDA functions.

The functions that we create are called user-defined functions, and we are already familiar with built-in functions such as **type(), len(), range()**, etc. You can run **?function_name** to get a sneak peek of what that function can do, the parameters it takes, and how to use it.

Creating simple functions and docstring

Using **def** keyword, you can create a function that takes some input (or no input) and performs a task as needed. The pseudo-syntax is as follows, you can notice the use of colon and indentation as we have used in control structure:

```
def function_name(input):
    # Code block (what the function does)
    return result              # Optional (with a default of None)
```

While writing or creating a function, we should give it a meaningful name so that we can use this name to call the function whenever needed. Let us start by creating a simple welcome function (with no input parameters) that prints a welcome message. Even though this function is not a useful one, but if we want to add a documentation of what it does, we can add a quick explanation (called **docstring**) in triple code inside the body of the function, as shown in the following code:

```
def welcome():
    """"This function prints a welcome msg""" # ← docstring here, It's
Optional
    print("Hello, welcome to Python!")
```

Adding a docstring to your function allows you to use **?function_name** to get a quick document of the same. So, you can add it when you think it might be useful.

```
# A quick way to inspect/get help on a function
?welcome
```

To use this function, you can call it by its name followed by parenthesis:

```
# Calling the function (The Parenthesis is needed, even if there's no input)
welcome() # Hello, welcome to Python
```

Functions with one or more input parameter(s)

In the previous example, the function does not take any input parameter (or argument)[7] and simply prints a message. You can write functions that take input(s) and perform some operations on the same:

```
# Function with one or more inputs
def add_10(a):
    print(a + 10)                 # prints input value + 10
add_10(20)                        # 30

def add_num(a, b):
    return a + b
result = add_num(5, 15); print(result)    # 20
```

The print and return statements

You might have noticed the use of **print** and **return** in different Python functions. Understanding the difference between the two helps clarify how functions work. In fact, it is not **print** vs. **return** as many Python beginners think.

Every Python function gives back something. It returns a specific value, if you use **return** statement or it returns **None**, if no return statement is provided. So, **return** is always there, visible or invisible.

---

[7] The words parameter and arguments are often used interchangeably. Technically speaking, parameter is the variable name used in function definition for input and argument is the actual value you pass when calling the function like a cell reference vs. the value in that cell in Excel. In the example above, add_10() function takes one parameter a and you are passing the argument 20 to it.

You can use **print()** function anytime to show something on the screen, irrespective of whether you have used the **return** statement or not.

For example, the function **add_10()** does not have a **return** statement, so it returns **None**, and because it has a **print** statement, it prints the result every time you call the function with a valid input. You can not store and use the value from **add_10()** function:

```
x = add_10(20); print(x) # None
x+50 # Error
```

While **add_num()** function has an explicit return statement, which allows the function to return the sum, that can be saved in a variable (e.g., result variable here) to be used anywhere in the script.

You should use **print** statement when you only want to show something temporarily or debug what is happening inside your function, e.g., to show (not to save) total revenue generated, you can create **show_total** function which prints **price*qty** but does not return anything:

```
def show_total(price, qty):
    total_rev = price * qty
    print("Total Revenue is:", total_rev) # Only shows it, doesn't save it

show_total(50, 2)                        # It just prints the value
```

If you try to save the result, and print, it displays **None**:

```
result = show_total(50, 2)        # prints again as the function is called
print(result) # None ->there's nothing stored_ func has no return statement
```

If you want to store, reuse, or pass the result elsewhere in your program, you need to use a **return** statement like this:

```
def get_total(price, qty):
    return price * qty          # Can use the result later as it's saved
```

Here, the **get_total** function returns **price*qty**, and it can be saved in a variable, let us say, **total**, which can be used in the script later.

```
total = get_total(50, 2)
print("Total revenue is:", total)        # Reusable
```

Keyword and positional arguments

So far, you have written functions to take some input parameters, and while calling the function, you need to supply exactly those many parameters, such as the preceding two functions need exactly two parameters (for **price** and **qty**), no more, no less.

Also, note that the order of parameters is important. When you supply two inputs, 50 and 2, Python treats the first value, 50, as the first parameter, *price*, and the second value, 2, as the second one, *qty*. While using functions with multiple inputs (imagine a function with more than 10 inputs), the user might not recall or be aware of the order of arguments. In that case, the user can call the function by supplying inputs in any order, but by using the names of the arguments:

```
def balance(income, expense):
    return income - expense

print(balance(5000, 3500))  # 1500 (Profit or balance)
print(balance(3500, 5000))  # -1500 (Loss)
balance(expense = 3500, income = 5000) # 1500 _ you can write in any order
```

You must have noticed that if you specify name of the parameters while calling the function, you can write arguments in any order (known as keyword arguments), and while calling function without mentioning the names of the arguments, you must pass the arguments in the order of the parameters, and these are called positional arguments. Positional and keyword arguments are basically names given to arguments that are defined by their position or key(name).

A function call may include both positional and keyword arguments simultaneously, with the important rule that keyword arguments must always follow positional arguments.

```
balance(5000, expense=3500)  # 1500
balance(expense=3500, 5000)  # SyntaxError
```

Warning: If you use positional arguments after keyword arguments, Python throws an error, 'SyntaxError: positional argument follows keyword argument'.

Function with default value of parameter(s)

You can also set a default value for the parameters like this:

```
def greet(name="friend"):
    print(f"Hello, {name}!")
greet()                     # Hello, friend! -> Uses default
greet("Nisha")              # Hello, Nisha! -> Uses input
```

While defining the function, you must write parameter(s) with default value(s), after parameter(s) without default(s). If you do otherwise, you will get **`'SyntaxError: parameter without a default follows parameter with a default'`**:

```
def balance(expense, income=100):
    return income - expense   # Works fine

def balance(income=100, expense):
    return income - expense   # SyntaxError
```

In short, Python requires that parameters with default values come after those without, and keyword arguments must come after positional arguments.

Functions with an arbitrary number of input(s)

Remember, **add_num** function to add two numbers. Now, if you have a task to add many numbers from an iterable (but you do not know how many) and you want to write a function that works for any number of input parameters, you can use ***args**.

Let us look at an example, followed by reading the details:

```
def total_bill(*items):
    return sum(items)

print(total_bill())                      # 0   Works with no input
print(total_bill(100, 200, 50))          # 350 Works with 3 inputs
print(total_bill(100, 200, 50, 120))     # 470 Also works with 4 inputs
```

Using an asterisk (*) before the parameter name allows the function to work with an arbitrary number of arguments, i.e., you can call the function with any number of input parameters or even with no input. This example may not be particularly useful, but it provides a general idea of writing a function with an arbitrary number of inputs.

Likewise, passing multiple named arguments can be done using ****kwargs**, i.e., putting ** before the argument name:

```
def product_info(**details):
    for key, value in details.items():
        print(f"{key}: {value}")

product_info(name="Laptop", price=50000)
product_info(name="Laptop", price=50000, stock=10)
```

In these examples, ***args** (short for Argument) and ****kwargs** (abbreviated for Key-Word Argument) are the names used by convention. You can use any other name as well, the asterisk operators * and ** do the job of unpacking arguments and keyword arguments.

The powerful Lambda functions

If you have used Excel 365's **LAMBDA** function to write small formulas on the fly, and you are thinking of that functionality in Python. We have got you covered. Let us show you one-liner lambda functions that make our code elegant. Lambda functions are particularly useful when combined with filter, map, reduce, zip, or list comprehension.

To write a **LAMBDA** function in Excel 365 that adds 10 to a number, you run

=LAMBDA(x, x + 10)(5) and it returns 15. Or you can use *Name Manager* to save it and use it anywhere in the same worksheet or workbook. However, its scope does not extend beyond it. In Python, you can save a **lambda** function simply by assigning it to a variable and use it in the same script. You can also share functions in other scripts (you will learn it later).

```
add_10 = lambda x: x + 10
print(add_10(5))                          # 15
```

Lambda functions are also called **anonymous functions** because they can be defined inline without assigning a name. For example:

```
(discount = lambda price: price * 0.9)(100)                          # 90.0
```

If you want to perform some operation (like the preceding one) on each element of the list, you can either write a loop, or use list comprehension, or maybe use a list-map in combination with **lambda** function:

```
prices = [100, 250, 450, 390, 120]
discounted_prices = list(map(lambda p: p * 0.9, prices))
print(discounted_prices)                  # [90.0, 225.0, 405.0, 351.0, 108.0]
```

This is like applying a formula to the entire column in Excel without needing to drag cells. Other powerful use-cases are shared in the code file. E.g., Lambda functions are convenient for filtering data:

```
list(filter(lambda p: p>300, prices)) # [450, 390]
```

Optional Tech Insight: **In Python, everything is an object. This includes the data you use and even the functions you write. That is why you will often see things like `data.method()` (e.g., `name.upper()` or `list.append()`). Behind the scenes, Python organizes these objects using classes. These concepts are taught in object-oriented programming (OOP).**

Exception handling in Python

So far, you might have written a lot of code and probably also solved some of the practice problems. We are sure you might have encountered **errors**. Yes, let us admit, it is unavoidable to get errors when we write code or do math. Even an experienced coder or a math professor gets errors all the time, therefore it might be a little challenging for a beginner.

Let us make this simple for you. Understanding your errors will help you debug your code easily, and catching (that is the term we use for handling the errors that we might encounter beforehand) the errors will allow your script to run smoothly.

In Excel, we often come across different types of errors, and we use functions like **IFERROR()**, **ISNA()**, **ISERR()**, **ISERROR()**, or nested **IF()** functions to manage those. In Python, broadly there are two types of errors: syntax error and exception error. As you must have met both of those, we recommend you figure out what causes a syntax error vs. other type of errors.

When you forget to put a colon in a loop, use wrong indentation, or parenthesis mismatch, you get a **syntax error**. This type of error occurs when the parser detects an incorrect statement.

Many times, your syntax is correct, but still your code runs into an error, for example, you are dividing a number by zero, trying to convert invalid text to a number, printing the variable that does not exist, or fetching the nth element of a sequence that has less than n elements. In such examples, your syntax might be correct, but you are trying to do something that is not feasible. You will get errors such as **`ZeroDivisionError`**, **`ValueError`**, **`NameError`**, **`IndexError`**, respectively. We refer to such errors as **exception errors**.

There is one more type of error, you can observe, **logical error**, which is hard to debug. When the program runs but produces incorrect or unexpected results due to flaws in the program's logic, user need to check and correct the logic, e.g., adding values which should be multiplied.

In Python, exceptions can be caught and handled using **`try-except`** or extended forms like **`try-except-else-finally`**. You can also raise errors with assert or by defining custom exceptions.

For now, let us focus on using **`try-except`** for error handling with these examples:

```
x1 = 100; x2 = 20
try:
    print(x1/x2)
except:
    print('Something went wrong!')
```

In the current example, when **`x1 = 100`** and **`x2 = 20`**, it prints **`x1/x2`** (i.e., **`5.0`**). But if you change **`x2`** to **`0`**, this code will not break, it will simply print a message **`'Something went wrong!'`** (you can and you should write a meaningful message here). Code break is the term we use to refer to any interruption in the flow of code, caused by errors or manual stops.

While performing a division operation, you might already be suspecting **`ZeroDivisionError`**, in that case, you can handle that specific error as:

```
# To catch ZeroDivisionError

try:
    result = 100/0
    print(result)
except ZeroDivisionError:
    print("Oops! Can't divide by zero.")     # Safe fallback
```

While fetching an element from a list, you might get **`IndexError`** if you use the incorrect index, so you can catch that with a useful message:

```
try:
  print(data[3])
except IndexError:
  print("You've supplied wrong index")
```

Also, you got **NameError: name data is not defined**. Actually, you forgot to create a list named **data** in the first place. It happens, sometimes, you run into errors that you could not think of in advance. To safeguard your code for some cases, you can add an additional except block like this:

```
try:
  print(data[3])
except IndexError:
  print("You've supplied wrong index")
except:
    print('Something else went wrong!')
```

Now, if Python does not find the list **data** in the environment, you will simply print **Something else went wrong!** and will not show any error.

You can surely catch multiple errors with additional **except** block(s):

```
data = [0, 1, 2]
del data # Uncomment/comment this line for different results
try:
  print(data[3])
except NameError:
  print('There is no such list in your enviornment')
except IndexError:
  print("You've supplied wrong index")
```

Learning to handle errors elegantly will empower you to write code that does not break. You can write your loops with **try-except** for cleaner and maintainable code that is easier to debug:

```
# Converting text to numbers
data = ["100", "250", "abc", "400"]
for value in data:
    try:
        num = int(value)  # Try converting to integer
        print("Converted:", num)
    except ValueError:
        print(f"Skipped invalid value: {value}")
```

There are a few more examples in the code file that you might want to practice because even in the world of AI, you still need to practice a lot if you are willing to master a subject. AI can assist you, but you do not want to be totally dependent on it for writing simple code. This chapter will help you get comfortable with the various fundamentals and aid you in quickly grasping advanced topics in subsequent chapters.

We would recommend that you attempt practice exercises (available with solutions in the GitHub repo) yourself without looking at the solutions. For that, sometimes, you might need additional help. Let us share different ways to get help in Python.

Getting help in Python

As a beginner, you would often need help to understand a new function, its arguments, or to figure out the logic to get the task done. Python offers multiple ways to get quick help:

- **help()**: To get detailed docstrings such as **`help(len)`** or **`help(str.upper)`**
- **dir()**: See all available methods such as **`dir(str)`**
- **type(obj)**: Know what you are working with, such as **`type(5)`**
- **?function_name or function_name?**: For quick help, such as **`str?`** or **`str.upper?`** or **`?str`** or **`?str.upper`**

If you are using an IDE (like Spyder or others), hover tips and auto-complete are your friends, just like Excel's tooltips. Apart from these quick and easy options, you can always refer **`docs.python.org`**, which is an official Python documentation to understand anything about Python in depth, straight from the source.

Another great assets are Stack Overflow, and other Stack Exchange communities where you can ask or search for answers related to Python, Excel, or anything related to programming, data analysis, and automation. Chances are, someone has already faced a similar problem and found a solution.

Conclusion

In this chapter, we created a solid foundation for your Python journey. Starting from the very basic datatypes and variables, we have covered all key topics like control flow, functions, and exception handling. If you are a complete beginner, we recommend you spend enough time on these fundamentals and solve practice problems before moving to the next topic. The time invested here is like sharpening your tool, it makes everything that follows easier and more effective.

In the next chapter, we will show you how to use external packages in your script for more advanced work you might want to do. Also, we will discuss ways to work with date and time. A dedicated chapter on date and time will help you understand the operations that you might need frequently.

Try it yourself

To deepen your understanding of the concepts presented in this chapter, it is recommended that you undertake the following exercises:

1. For a sample email-id such as "user@example.com", extract the domain name.
2. Repeat the exercise for each email in the given list ["alice@example.com", "bob@company.org", "eve@test.net"]. Do this using different approaches, such as with a loop, list comprehension or lambda function with list-map.
3. To rename a file name "file 1.txt" to "file_1.txt", use the string method. Now, use this method and iterate over a list of such names by using a loop and by using list comprehension too.
4. For security reasons, you want to mask your passwords. Write code to do the same for password "SuperSecret123" by hiding all characters except the last 2. The output should be ************23
5. You run a shop and want to give a 10% discount on all prices given in the following price list. Compute discounted prices for each product. You can simply print those or save them in a list.

   ```
   prices = [100, 250, 450, 89, 120]
   ```
6. From the following dictionary, extract only those products that are priced above ₹100:

   ```
   product_prices = {'Apple': 120, 'Banana': 60, 'Mango': 280}
   ```
7. Write a function that accepts any number of inputs and returns their average.
8. You have a list of file names:

   ```
   files = ["report.csv", "data.xlsx", "summary.docx", "sales.csv"]
   ```

   Collect the names of only the CSV files in a new list. Such practice will help you with file management tasks that you will explore later in this book.
9. You have imported a list of file names from an Excel sheet. Each name has the prefix Report_. Prepare the file names for display by removing the prefix and showing only the unique part.

   ```
   files = ["Report_Sales.xlsx", "Report_Inventory.xlsx", "Report_Expenses.
   xlsx"]
   ```

   Your output should be:

   ```
   Sales.xlsx
   Inventory.xlsx
   Expenses.xlsx
   ```

10. You are cleaning a customer database and want to flag entries where a certain field (like phone number, customer ID or password) is filled with repeated characters (all characters same such as 000000, aaaaaa, or 11111). This may indicate bad data. Write a code to detect such cases.

11. You have a list of LinkedIn profile URLs as given here:

```
urls = [
    'https://www.linkedin.com/in/nishaarora/',
    'https://www.linkedin.com/in/johndoe/',
    'https://www.linkedin.com/in/pragyasharma/'
]
```

    You need to:

    a. Extract the profile name from each URL.

    b. Ensure no extra / at the end.

    c. Return a clean list of profile names.

    Your output should be ['nishaarora', 'johndoe', 'pragyasharma']

12. Customer Purchase Summary Report: For a raw list of transactions.

```
transactions = [
    {"customer": "Alice", "product": "Laptop", "amount": 1200},
    {"customer": "Bob", "product": "Mouse", "amount": 25},
    {"customer": "Alice", "product": "Headphones", "amount": 150},
    {"customer": "Bob", "product": "Keyboard", "amount": 75},
    {"customer": "Charlie", "product": "Monitor", "amount": 300},
]
```

    a. Calculate the total amount spent by each customer.

    b. Display the result in a clean format.

13. Stock Portfolio Tracker: For your current stock holdings, given as follows:

```
portfolio = {
    "AAPL": {"shares": 10, "price": 165.3},
    "GOOGL": {"shares": 5, "price": 2800.5},
    "TSLA": {"shares": 8, "price": 190.1}
}
```

    Calculate the current portfolio value using these steps:

    a. Multiply shares × price for each stock.

    b. Calculate the total value of the portfolio.

    c. Optionally, print the individual stock values too.

Concept check

The following thought-based exercises are designed to help you reflect on common Excel-based tasks and explore how similar challenges can be addressed using Python:

1. Explain how Python strings are a game-changer for Excel users. Can you think of some case examples where using Python string methods is smoother than Excel text functions?

2. You are storing monthly sales targets for a team that does not change. Would you use a list or a tuple? Why?

3. You want to extract all even numbers from a list of 100 integers. How would you do that, and what concepts would you need for the task that are discussed in this chapter?

4. Note down your everyday lookup tasks: searching prices, matching IDs, pulling names from lists, etc. Try to reimagine how you would solve them in Python using dictionaries. If it starts to feel limiting or repetitive, that is your cue; you are ready for something more powerful: Python's pandas. We will cover the same in detail later in the book.

5. Have you ever worked on a task in Excel where you drag a formula across a column and the formula pulls input from different cells, maybe even from other sheets or files?

   Now think:

   a. Have you accidentally changed one of the input cells, and suddenly your whole formula breaks?

   b. Did you spend time figuring out what went wrong?

   c. Can Python help in such situations? If yes, how do you think it might reduce these errors or make your workflow more reliable?

6. Excel functions are mostly positional, meaning you must enter values in a specific order. Python gives you flexibility with keyword arguments and default values. How could this help in making your code more readable and forgiving?

7. For now, just read the description about read.csv() method from the pandas library mentioned here https://pandas.pydata.org/docs/reference/api/pandas.read_csv.html and figure out which arguments have default values. (It is okay if you do not understand the function yet, as that is to be covered later in the book.)

8. Have you ever seen errors like #DIV/0!, #N/A, or #VALUE! in Excel and had no clue why they appeared? Think of times you wished Excel explained *why* a cell went wrong. How would catching errors help?

CHAPTER 4
External Packages and Date-time Handling

Introduction

As you are well-equipped with Python fundamentals, now, it is the right time to dive into using external packages, which are essential for enhancing Python's functionality. In *Chapter 2, Setting Up Python,* we have discussed ways to install any package you might need. This chapter presents various methods to import and utilize modules, based on your requirements.

We will also cover date and time handling in Python (using libraries like datetime and dateutil), which is crucial for Excel users analyzing datasets with columns such as application dates, order dates, delivery dates, and visit times.

By the end of this chapter, you will be equipped with the knowledge to leverage external packages, unlock new capabilities, and comfortably do date-time arithmetic in Python.

Structure

In this chapter, we will discuss the following topics:

- Modules and packages
- Methods for importing modules or packages
- Foundation of dates and times in Python
- Creating dates and times values
- Working with dates and time values

Modules and packages

In Excel, you might have seen or used **add-ins or macros** for additional functionality. Similarly, in Python, we use **modules and packages**[1] for specific tasks. These are basically collections of ready-made tools created by other people, so we can conveniently use their functions without needing to code everything from scratch.

[1]You can also create your own modules and packages.

For example, if you want **to interact with your operating system**, such as creating, deleting, renaming, or moving folders or files, joining, splitting, or checking file paths, you can use the **os** module. **To work with dates and times**, perform date arithmetic, manage calendars, and handle time zones, you can use the **datetime** module.

While it is not essential to comprehend the taxonomy of terms modules, packages and libraries, it is useful to know how to use these. Still, if you are curious about the difference between the three names which you come across commonly in Python books, let me simplify it for you:

Module is simply a Python script (**.py** file) that contains variables, functions, or classes (templates for creating things like dates) designed to be imported and used in other files.

Package is basically a collection of related modules that work together to provide specific functionality.

A **library** is a broader term that can include multiple individual modules that can provide a wide range of functionality. Python users use these names interchangeably but now, you understand that module is a single Python file while package is a folder of modules. The following figure shows the structure of package 1, which contains two modules and a sub package along with a **_ _ init_ _.py** file[2].

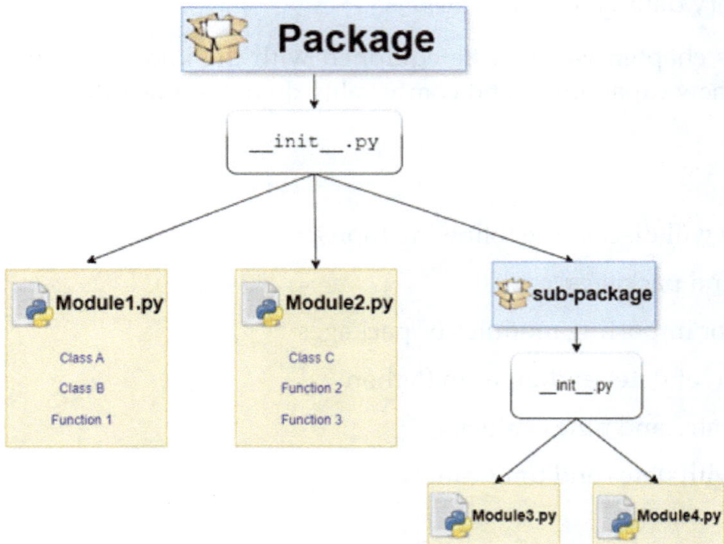

***Figure 4.1**: Modules and packages*

In the second chapter, we have discussed that Anaconda gives you many pre-installed packages and you can install other packages using **pip** or **conda**. Once installed, the package is available to use but you **need to import** it in your session. There are various ways to import a module or a package. Let us understand these in the next section.

[2] A collection of modules is simply a directory/folder unless it has a file named _ _ init_ _.py in it.

Methods for importing modules or packages

In Python, you can use **import** keyword to import modules. You might have seen codes like **import datetime**, **import datetime as dt**, or **from datetime import datetime** at different places and might be wondering what is the difference. It would not be a nuisance anymore, you will understand the use cases of various methods to import modules and packages.

Basic import

You can import a module by running **import module_name** and to call a function from this module, you need to use **module_name.method_name(argument)**. For example:

```
import math

# Calling different methods from 'math' module
math.sqrt(16) # 4.0
math.log(10) # 2.302585092994046
math.sin(2)# 0.9092974268256817
```

You have used this method in the previous chapter to set and check your current working directory using **os** module. This method imports the entire module, making all functions and classes available through the module name allowing us to easily identify where each function and class comes from. However, we will need to type **module_name.method_name** everytime, which is a bit more effort.

Note: This method is recommended in many cases for small libraries but for large modular libraries, selective imports are the norm and better practice as discussed next.

Import specific parts

If you do not want to type the **module_name** every time you use a function, you can import specific functions or classes that you intend to use in your code, such as **from module_name import method_name**.

This method is helpful when you need to use only a few things from the module as it requires less typing and avoid importing entire module. For example:

```
from math import sqrt, log

# Calling method names directly

sqrt(16) # 4.0
log(10)# 2.302585092994046
```

For large libraries like **sklearn** or **tensorflow**, importing the **whole module is impractical** as they are massive and organized into submodules, so selectively importing only what you need is the standard and accepted practice.

Wildcard import

Python also allows you to import everything (all the functions, classes and values) from a module by using **from module_name import *** However, it is often considered as a bad practice because it can create name conflicts. Generally, you should avoid using this method unless you are sure there will not be any conflicts.

```
from math import *

sqrt(16) # 4.0
log(10)# 2.302585092994046
```

Just like you avoid using **SELECT ALL** in a large Excel sheet without knowing what is in every column, avoid using wildcard imports unless you are 100% sure of what is being imported, and there is no risk of conflicts.

Importing a module with an alias

This is a commonly used method with some of the popular libraries to shorten its name for convenience or by convention. For example, importing the popular library **numpy** as **np**:

```
import numpy as np

array_1d = np.array([1, 2, 3, 4, 5])
print("1D Array:", array_1d)      # 1D Array: [1 2 3 4 5]
```

Or importing the mighty **pandas** library as **pd**:

```
import pandas as pd

data = pd.DataFrame({"A": [1, 2, 3], "B": [4, 5, 6]})
```

Quick summary

Here is the guideline for selecting the appropriate import method:

- Use **import package** when you want clarity, and you are using multiple parts of a package (safest and most common).
- Use **from package import item** when you only need specific parts and want shorter code.

- Use **`import package as alias`** when the package name is long and commonly abbreviated (like **`import pandas as pd`**).
- Avoid from package **`import *`** as it is unclear, risky, and rarely needed outside of quick experiments.

Foundation of dates and times in Python

If you have worked with dates and times in Excel, you know how important it is to convert text to dates, format dates, calculate differences between dates, and work with time zones. Python offers powerful capabilities for these and similar tasks using specific packages. Understanding date and datetime in python is essential for tasks such as aging calculations, trend analysis, sorting data by date, calculating durations, grouping data by month or year and time-based comparisons.

In Python, **`datetime`** module provides classes for working with date and time values. The core classes of **`datetime`** module are:

- **The date class**: It works with calendar (Gregorian calendar) dates with attributes year, month and day.
- **The time class**: It represents hours, minutes, seconds, microseconds, and optional time zone information independent of a date.
- **The datetime class**: It combines both date and time.
- **The timedelta class**: It represents durations or differences between date or datetime instances for arithmetic operations.
- **The timezone class**: It manages time zone data.

Creating dates and time values

Let us start using the **`datetime`** package by importing it. The **`datetime`** library provides three classes that make up the high-level interface that most people will use: **datetime.date** (for dates), **`datetime.time`** (for times), and **`datetime.datetime`** (for date and time combination).

Displaying current date and time

We can use **`today()`** function from date class of datetime module to display current local date. It displays the date in **year-month-day** format:

```
from datetime import date


current_date = date.today()
print(current_date) # 2025-03-05 (it will print current date)
```

Else, we can use **now()** function from the datetime class of the same module to capture exact moment. It returns the current local date and time, including hours, minutes, seconds, and microseconds:

```
from datetime import datetime

current_datetime = datetime.now()
print(current_datetime) # 2025-03-05 12:17:20.503186
# (it will print current date and time)
```

The exact output of these functions will vary depending on when you execute the code, the examples shown here reflect the results at the time of my execution.

You can access individual components such as year, month, day or hours, minutes, seconds, etc. by using dot notation.

```
year = current_datetime.year
month = current_datetime.month
day = current_datetime.day

current_hour = current_datetime.hour
current_minute = current_datetime.minute
current_second = current_datetime.second
current_microsecond = current_datetime.microsecond
```

Creating date-time objects

You can create specific **date** objects by supplying the year, month, and day in the **datetime.date(year, month, day)** format. You need to ensure that months and days are valid numbers (e.g., there is no month 13 or day 35). For single-digit days or months, do not use **0** at the beginning.

The great thing is, it supports a wide range of years from **1** to **9999**, as opposed to Excel, where you need a workaround for dates prior to 1/1/1900.

```
from datetime import date

# Creating a date object for October 30, 2025

specific_date = date(2025, 10, 30)
print(specific_date) # 2025-10-30 (Human-readable format)
```

Warning: When creating dates with Python's date() function, always use the full 4-digit year. Unlike Excel, Python does not assume 25 means 2025. Instead, it will literally use year 25 AD. Try it out yourself with some experiments.

```
# Using two-digit years is discouraged to prevent confusion

incorrect_date = date(25, 10, 30)
print(incorrect_date) # Output: 0025-10-30
print(incorrect_date.year) # Output: 25
```

You can also create a time object for applications such as scheduling events or setting a notification at a specific time, where the date is irrelevant by importing the time class.

```
from datetime import time
specific_time = time(13, 45, 5, 23)
print(specific_time)
```

For creating a combined date-time instance, you can use the datetime class. Here, you need to supply valid integers as arguments. Time-related arguments are optional:

```
from datetime import datetime

dt = datetime(year=2025, month=3, day=31,
              hour=13, minute=14, second=31)
print(dt)                   # 2025-03-31 13:14:31
```

Working with date and time values

While working with data and creating reports, many times we need to either format dates as text in desired format or convert dates written as text into date or datetime object for further processing. We also need to add or subtract time periods or manage time zones. All of these can be done smoothly in Python. Let us discuss basics of how these tasks can be done, which will lay the groundwork for analysing date-based datasets using **pandas** library (to be introduced in *Chapter 6, Data Manipulation with Pandas*.

Formatting date-time as strings

If you need to convert dates to nicely formatted strings for use in reports, filenames, or to display user-friendly date information, you can use the **strftime()** function from the **datetime** library. Using **str()** will also help convert it to a string as is, but **strftime()** is powerful because you can get any format of date or datetime you want.

The **strftime()** function takes one parameter, **format**, to specify the format of the returned string. To display the date/datetime in a specific format, you need to use format codes (refer to *Table 4.1*), such as **%d/%m/%Y** for **day/month number/four-digit year**. Let us see it in practice.

```
my_date = datetime(2025, 10, 30, 4, 30)
print(my_date) # 2025-10-30 04:30:00
print(type(my_date)) # <class 'datetime.datetime'>
```

```
short_date = my_date.strftime("%d/%m/%Y")
print(short_date) # 30/10/2025
print(type(short_date)) # <class 'str'>

long_date = my_date.strftime("%A, %B %d, %Y")
print(long_date) # Thursday, October 30, 2025
```

When using **strftime()**, you must provide a string containing special directives/format codes that define the formatting. Some of those are mentioned here:

Description	Format code	Sample value
Year (as four-digit integer)	%Y	2025
Year (as short-digit integer)	%y	47 (for year 1947)
Month (as 0-padded decimal)	%m	08 (for August)
Month Name (Abbreviated)	%b	Aug
Month Name (Full Version)	%B	August
Date (as 0-padded decimal)	%d	03
Hour (as 0-padded decimal with 24-hours clock)	%H	14
Minute (as 0-padded decimal)	%M	50
Second (as 0-padded decimal)	%S	35

***Table 4.1**: Format codes for date-time formatting*

For more format codes, you can refer to **https://strftime.org/** or_**https://docs.Python.org/3/library/datetime.html# strftime-and-strptime-format-codes.**

Converting strings to date or date-time objects

While working with datasets, you will often need to convert text such as application dates, birthdates, time of signing an application, etc. into **datetime** objects. This allows you to validate dates or, even more importantly, perform date and time arithmetic, such as finding the difference between dates or adding days to a given date.

Converting strings to **datetime** objects is simplified using the **strptime()** function from the **datetime** module.

The function **datetime.strptime(string, format)** takes :

- A string (the one you want to convert) and
- A format code (that specifies the format of this string)

And returns a datetime object from the given string **only** if the string is in a certain format. If the string (first argument) and the format code (second argument) passed to **strptime()** do not match, you will get a **ValueError**. In the following example, date string is in **day-month-year** format while the format we are supplying in **strptime()** is **month-day-year**, so we get an error.

```
date_string = "31-01-2020 14:45:37"
format_string = "%m-%d-%Y %H:%M:%S"

datetime.strptime(date_string, format_string)   # ValueError
```

To fix this, we need to change **format_string** accordingly, and it will successfully parse the string into a datetime object:

```
format_string = "%d-%m-%Y %H:%M:%S"
datetime.strptime(date_string, format_string) # 2020-01-31 14:45:37
```

Difference between strftime() and strptime()

You might have noticed that **strptime()** does the reverse of **strftime()**, though they conveniently use the same format codes. And the function names are self-explanatory, in **strptime()**, **p** denotes *parse*, while in **strftime()**, **f** denotes *format*.

```
date_string = "27 Mar, 2025"
print(date_string)                   # 27 Mar, 2025
print(type(date_string))             # <class 'str'>

date_object = datetime.strptime(date_string, "%d %b, %Y")
print(date_object)                   # 2025-03-27 00:00:00
print(type(date_object))             # <class 'datetime.datetime'>

# Converting datetime object to a string again (in a new format)
datetime.strftime(date_object, "%d/%m/%y") # '27/03/25'
```

Date-time arithmetic

Adding/subtracting days or time components can be done with **timedelta()** from **datetime** module easily.

```
from datetime import date, datetime, timedelta

# Add or subtract days
today = date.today()
```

```
next_week = today + timedelta(days=7)
yesterday = today - timedelta(days=1)
print(f'Today: {today}, Yesterday: {yesterday}, Next_week: {next_week}')
# Today: 2025-03-05, Yesterday: 2025-03-04, Next_week: 2025-03-12

# Add or subtract time components
now = datetime.now()
after3hours = now + timedelta(hours = 3)

print(now.strftime('%H: %M: %S')) # 04: 44: 18
print(after3hours.strftime('%H: %M: %S')) # 07: 44: 18
print(after3hours - now) # 3:00:00
```

For adding/subtracting months or years, we can use **dateutil.relativedelta** from **dateutils** library as **timedelta** does not handle months and years.

```
from dateutil.relativedelta import relativedelta

next_month = today + relativedelta(months=1)
last_year = today - relativedelta(years=1)
print(f'Today: {today}, Next Month: {next_month}, Last Year: {last_year}')
# Today: 2025-03-06, Next Month: 2025-04-06, Last Year: 2024-03-06
```

As compared to Excel's EOMONTH, **relativedelta** can shift by years, months, and days simultaneously, snap to month-end, and handle leap years, all in a single expression.

To find the difference between date or datetime instances, you can simply use the subtraction operator:

```
start = date(2024, 3, 1)
end = date(2025, 6, 15)

difference = end - start
print("Difference in Days:", difference.days) # Difference in Days: 471
```

For a human-readable breakdown of differences like 1 year, 3 months, and 14 days, you can use **relativedelta**, which is much more convenient than Excel's **DATEDIF** function. If you need to change a specific part of a date or a date-time object, for example, setting all times to midnight or adjusting dates for reporting, you can use the **replace()** method. A few examples are shown here:

```
# Create a date object
d = date(2025, 3, 15)
```

```
print("Original date:", d) # Original date: 2025-03-15

# Replace year and month
d_replaced = d.replace(year=2026, month=12) # Replaced date: 2026-12-15
print("Replaced date:", d_replaced)

# Create a time object
t = time(14, 30, 45)
print("Original time:", t) # Original time: 14:30:45

# Replace hour and minute
t_replaced = t.replace(hour=9, minute=0)
print("Replaced time:", t_replaced) # Replaced time: 09:00:45

# Create a datetime object
dt = datetime(2025, 3, 15, 14, 30, 45)
print("Original datetime:", dt) # Original datetime: 2025-03-15 14:30:45

# Replace day and hour
dt_replaced = dt.replace(day=20, hour=8)
print("Replaced datetime:", dt_replaced) # Replaced datetime: 2025-03-
20 08:30:45
```

Time zones manipulations

Excel lacks support for time zones, which is a **significant limitation** for global business data involving multiple regions, time-sensitive transactions, or cross-timezone scheduling. Let us discuss what Python offers for dealing with time zones.

So far, we have created and printed date-time objects that do not include information about the time zone; we call them **naive** objects. They contain date and time components, yet do not include time zone context. Naive datetimes are fine for simple calculations.

When working with global data, scheduling, reports, or logs where time zones matter, we need **aware** datetime objects. Aware datetimes mean objects that include time zone information.

To create time zone-aware objects, you use the time zone class from the **`datetime`** module.

```
from datetime import datetime, timezone


naive_time = datetime.now()
```

```
print(f'Naive Time: {naive_time}, TimeZone: {naive_time.tzname()}')
# Naive Time: 2025-03-06 08:37:36.510722, TimeZone: None

aware_time = datetime.now(tz = timezone.utc)# in UTC timezone
print(f'Aware Time: {aware_time}, TimeZone: {aware_time.tzname()}')
# Aware Time: 2025-03-06 03:07:39.108157+00:00, TimeZone: UTC
```

In **datetime.now()**, the **tz** argument specifies the timezone in which the current date and time should be returned. By passing **timezone.utc**, the result is an aware datetime object representing the current time in **Coordinated Universal Time** (**UTC**). With **timezone** class from **datetime** module, you can get time zone info and handle fixed offsets such as UTC-5:30, etc. However, for more realistic time zone manipulations such as *Asia/Kolkata* to *America/New_York*, you need libraries like **dateutil**, **arrows** or **pytz**.

As you are familiar with **dateutil**, let us see how to handle time zones with same. Later, you can explore **arrows** or **pytz** if the need arises. To create naive and aware current datetime instances using **dateutil** library:

```
from dateutil import tz
from datetime import datetime

naive_time = datetime.now()
print(f'Naive Time: {naive_time}, TimeZone: {naive_time.tzname()}')
# Naive Time: 2025-03-06 0.5:55:25.512249, TimeZone: None

aware_time  = datetime.now(tz=tz.tzlocal()))# in Local timezone
print(f'Aware Time: {aware_time}, TimeZone: {aware_time.tzname()}')
# Aware Time: 2025-03-06 05:55:40.571098+05:30, TimeZone: India Standard Time
```

Here, **tz.tzlocal()** sets time zone to your machine's local[3] timezone (for the author, it is India Standard Time).

To create the date-time aware object, you can use **datetime** class by providing time zone info in **tzinfo** argument. Refer to **https://timezonedb.com/time-zones** for names of all time zones:

```
local_time = datetime(2025, 3, 4, 15, 0, 0, tzinfo = tz.tzlocal())
utc_time = datetime(2025, 3, 4, 15, 0, 0, tzinfo = tz.UTC)

# Australia time (Sydney)
aus_tz = tz.gettz("Australia/Sydney")
aus_time = datetime(2025, 3, 4, 15, 0, 0, tzinfo = aus_tz)
```

[3]As tz.tzlocal() returns the local timezone of the system where the code is running, so in Colab, it reflects the server's timezone rather than your own machine's

```
print(local_time) # 2025-03-04 15:00:00+05:30
print(utc_time)   # 2025-03-04 15:00:00+00:00
print(aus_time)   # 2025-03-04 15:00:00+11:00
```

For converting time zones, you can use **dateutil** module's **astimezone()** function as:

```
local_time = datetime(2025, 3, 4, 10, 0, 0, tzinfo= tz.tzlocal())
print("Local Time:", local_time) # Local Time: 2025-03-04 10:00:00+05:30

# Convert to America/New_York time
ny_zone = tz.gettz("America/New_York")
ny_time = local_time.astimezone(ny_zone)
print("New York Time:", ny_time) # New York Time: 2025-03-03 23:30:00-05:00
```

You have got a great understanding of dealing with date and time objects. If you work with time series data frequently, **pandas** provides suitable features for computing time-based aggregations (for example, upsample from monthly to daily frequency or downsample from monthly to quarterly frequency), rolling or moving averages, and much more. Such **pandas** functions with suitable charts are discussed in the *Appendix, Python Charts for Business Analysis*.

Now, it is time to practice what you have learned so far. Get your hands dirty with the practice exercise to test your learning from the chapter.

Conclusion

In this chapter, you have learned different methods to import a module or a package. You have also learned to use datetime and dateutil module to display or create date-time instances, perform arithmetic's on such objects, formatting date-times as per your requirement and time zone manipulation.

In the next chapter, you will learn to use other modules manage files conveniently. Learning file operations using Python will enable you to organize, back-up and automate your file handling tasks.

Try it yourself

The following practice exercises will help you reinforce the learning from this chapter:

1. You are processing employee joining dates. One person joined on 12th August 2023 at 9:30 AM. Create a date-time object for this.
2. Your boss wants the joining date from Exercise 1 formatted as 12-Aug-2023 09:30 AM for the report. Format the joining date accordingly.

3. You have imported some data from Excel where the application date is stored as the string "04/03/2025 14:45" (DD/MM/YYYY HH:MM). Convert this string into a Python datetime object.
4. A customer signed up on 1st March 2025. Calculate in Python to answer:
    a. When is their 30-day free trial ending?
    b. How many days have passed by 4th March 2025?
5. Your company operates in India (Asia/Kolkata), but your manager in New York (America/New_York) wants to know what time a meeting scheduled at 4 PM IST on 4th March 2025 will be in their time zone. Convert the time accordingly.
6. You need to schedule a report to be sent at 9 AM local time in Sydney, Australia on 10th March 2025. You also need to know what time that will be in UTC. Create a datetime for Sydney time and convert it to UTC.

Concept check

Answer the following questions to check your understanding:

1. What is the difference between strftime() and strptime()?
2. What is the difference between naive and aware datetime objects?
3. What are the different ways to import a package or a module in Python? When would you use which method?
4. Why is it not recommended to use wildcard imports (from module_name import *)?

Join our Discord space

Join our Discord workspace for latest updates, offers, tech happenings around the world, new releases, and sessions with the authors:

https://discord.bpbonline.com

CHAPTER 5
Automating File Management with Python

Introduction

Managing files efficiently is crucial for Excel professionals working in any domain, whether they are handling financial reports, sales data, or operational records. In this chapter, we will explore Python's built-in file handling capabilities and automate key file management tasks using libraries such as os, shutil, and glob.

We will cover how to read, write, move, copy, rename, and archive files dynamically, ensuring efficient workflow automation. This learning will help readers in implementing logging and scheduling mechanisms to track file changes and automate recurring tasks later. By the end of this chapter, readers will be able to streamline their file operations, reducing manual work and minimizing errors.

Back in *Chapter 1, Python for Excel Users*, you saw how Maya could generate a YouTube analytics report with a single click. Every month, she manually updates the data and reruns the same script to get her latest report. But what if she did not have to do this manually at all? With just a few extra lines of Python code written once, she can automatically rename and timestamp her downloaded YouTube data files, organize files into monthly folders, sort files by timestamp, or automatically identify to load the most recent file for analysis without any manual effort.

In this chapter, we will learn how to make this a reality, turning repetitive tasks into effortless automation. For that to happen, let us start with the basics of file paths.

Structure

This chapter covers the following topics:

- Absolute and relative file paths
- File and directory operations
- Advanced file search with pattern-matching

- Reading and writing files
- Automation use cases

Absolute and relative file paths

In *Chapter 3, Python Fundamentals*, you have learned about the working directory. Apart from that, for several file handling tasks, such as moving files from one folder to another based on file names, extension, or date of creation, you need to understand how file paths work and what differentiates an absolute path from a relative path.

You might have already guessed it, as the terms are simple to translate from English. Relative path means **related**, i.e., with reference to the current directory or older. For example, `./test.py` is a relative path that means a file named `test.py` in the current directory.

And the full file path starting from the root directory is called the **absolute** path. For example, `D:/Excel_Python/test.py` is an absolute path. While opening and saving files, you can mention the absolute path, making it explicit, or the relative path, making it shorter.

As an absolute path contains full path information starting from the root, you can access files from any location (irrespective of your current working directly). This practice seems more convenient to beginners if they are okay with typing a little more.

However, a script using an absolute path is not portable. This means that if your file[1] The location is `D:/Excel_Python/test.py;` it would not work on another PC where the file is in a different location (imagine you are buying a new laptop in the future, and the code breaks). If you move your file to another folder or you want to share your script with others, it will cause issues.

We would recommend starting to use the relative path early on, and you can always generate an absolute path whenever needed using `os` module as follows:

```
import os

# Relative path (uncomment these relative paths one by one to notice the diff)

relative_path = 'test.py' # File in the current directory
# relative_path = 'scripts/test.py' # File inside a subfolder 'scripts'

# If file is outside the current directory,(../ indicates one level up)
# relative_path = "../test.py"
# relative_path = "../../test.py"
```

[1] In windows folder path is written using backslashes (\) while on Mac or Linux it is forward slash (/). Since backslash (\) is also an escape character in Python (e.g., \n, \t), you often need to replace it with forward slash (/), double backslashes (\\) or raw strings (r"...") to avoid warnings/errors or unintended characters.

```
# Convert to absolute path
absolute_path = os.path.abspath(relative_path)
print("Absolute Path:", absolute_path)  # Now it's a full path

# Again, Getting Relative Path from absolute path
rel_path = os.path.relpath(absolute_path)
print('\nAgain Getting Relative Path:', rel_path)
```

The path you create using absolute or relative methods does not necessarily have to exist, its existence can be checked using functions like **os.path.exists()** that we will discuss soon.

More about file paths

Python can help you check if a particular path exists or not, if a given path is a file or a directory, by using simple functions that are easy to remember, as the names are self-explanatory. This is something great about Python, just by reading function names, you can guess what it does. We recommend you try out some staple exercises on each of these functions. Run this code and observe what it does:

```
filename = 'test.py'


if os.path.exists(filename):
    print(f"The file '{filename}' exists in the current working directory.")
else:
    print(f"The file '{filename}' does not exist in the current working directory.")
```

You might have realized **os.path.exists(test.py)** checks if the file **test.py** exists in the current working directory or not and returns True or False accordingly. Similarly, **os.path.exists('path/to/file.txt')** checks if the specified path exists.

Many times, you will need to verify if the given path is a file or not, and the same for a directory; you can achieve this readily by:

```
os.path.isfile('path/to/file.txt') # True for files
os.path.isdir('path/to/directory')  # True for directories
```

Likewise, **os.path.join(current_folder, file_name)** concatenates path segments using the correct directory separator (**** on windows and **/** on macOS or linux). Instead of manually concatenating directory names with separators, **os.path.join()** ensures paths are constructed in a crossplatform manner without worrying about the correct slash or delimiter. Note that it is not compulsory that the path you create using **os.path.join()** actually exists.

```
current_folder = os.getcwd()  # 'D:\\Excel_Python' on windows machine
file_name = "test.py"

full_path = os.path.join(current_folder, filename)
print(full_path)  # D:\Excel_Python\test.py
```

If your file is nested in a subfolder of any folder, you can still get the absolute file path by using the same function. **`os.path.join('folder', 'subfolder', 'file.txt')`** joins the path components into a single path:

```
current_folder = os.getcwd()
subfolder = "scripts"
filename = "test.py"

full_path = os.path.join(current_folder, subfolder, filename)
print(full_path) # D:\Excel_Python\scripts\test.py on windows
```

If you pass an empty string to **`os.path.join()`**, it simply ignores it. If a path segment is on a different drive or is an absolute path, all previous segments are ignored, and the drive is reset.

```
os.path.join("folder", "")  # 'folder\\'
os.path.join('C:\\scripts', 'D:\\Excel_Python\\test.py') # 'D:\\Excel_Python\\
test.py'
```

Warning: **Avoid using a leading slash (`/filename` or `\filename`) in `os.path.join()`, as it treats a path with a slash as an absolute path and then all previous path segments are ignored.**

```
os.path.join('D:\\Excel_Python', '\scripts\\test.py') # 'D:\\scripts\\test.py'
```

If you are working with user input paths, or reading paths from config files, databases, or APIs, or want to write cross-platform scripts, you would prefer to ensure a consistent format of file paths. As **Windows uses \ (backslash) while Linux and macOS use / (forward slash)**, running the same code on different machines can format paths differently. Leave the worry to Python as the function **`os.path.normpath()`** has you covered. For example, this script asks the user to submit file path (**`input()`** function comes handy for user input) and the user copy-pastes **`D:/Excel_Python`** (from documentation or some other source) as file path, running the following code on my Windows machine will result in a path with mixed slashes potentially causing issues (notice the output):

```
folder = input('Enter File Path: ') # Type to the prompt_ D:/Excel_Python
filename = "test.py"

full_path = os.path.join(folder, filename)
print(full_path) # D:/Excel_Python\test.py on windows machine
```

We can clean the mess by running **`os.path.normpath(full_path)`**, as it gives a path based on the operating system.

```
os.path.normpath(full_path) # 'D:\\Excel_Python\\test.py' on windows machine
```

Note: It is best practice to use `os.path.normpath()` or similar function while performing automated file operations where paths are generated dynamically.

If you want to fetch a file name from a full file path like above, you can use **`os.path.basename()`**:

```
file_path = "D:/Projects/Reports/marketing_data.xlsx"
os.path.basename(file_path) # Output: marketing_data.xlsx
```

Using **`os.path.splitext(file_name)`** helps you remove the extension (refer to the code file or try it yourself).

Apart from dealing with working directory and file paths, **`os`** module also offers great functions to interact with the operating system in a portable way. Along with this module, **`shutil`**, **`glob`**, **`zipfile`**, **`fnmatch`**, and **`pathlib`** modules[2] open doors for amazing automation functionalities. Let us explore some of these if you are excited to automate your file management tasks with Python.

File and directory operations

As you are now familiar with file paths, you can now create, move, rename, and delete files or folders[3] to start with. For such operations, we have created test files and folders (provided in **`Chapter 05`** folder of the companion repo). We would recommend you set **`Chapter 05`** folder as your working directory. Otherwise, you can always use **`os.path.join()`** to get inside the chapter folder from your current working directory **`D:/Excel_Python`**.

To get a list of all available files and subfolders in any folder, you can use **`os.scandir()`**[4]:

```
os.scandir() # An iterator containing all files/folders in current directory
list(os.scandir())# list of files from your current working directory

folder = 'D:\\Excel_Python' # write path of any folder on your machine
list(os.scandir(folder))# list of files/folders from that path3.
```

You might be thinking of getting files of a specific type, e.g., all Excel files. Explore it if you are super excited, or we will cover it soon. For now, you know how many total files there are in a folder (hope you remember the **`len()`** function!).

[2] Modules like os, shutil, glob, zipfile, fnmatch, and pathlib are all built into Python's standard library, so you can use them without needing to install.

[3] *Folder* and *directory* are often used interchangeably; *directory* is the technical term used in programming.

[4] listdir: os.listdir(path) works similarly, but os.scandir() is faster and more efficient since its DirEntry objects provide file type (is_file(), is_dir()) and size (stat().st_size) without extra os.path calls

Try to create, remove, or delete folders using these simple commands:

```
# create a folder/directory in current working directory
os.mkdir('test')

# rename folder
os.rename('test', 'test_backup')

# Delete the folder (only if it’s empty, otherwise it raises an error)
os.rmdir('test_backup')

# rename any file (We have kept an excel file ‘empty.xlsx’ in Chapter 05)


os.rename(‘empty.xlsx’, ‘no_data.xlsx’)

# delete any file
os.remove('no_data.xlsx')
```

You can also create nested folders using **os.makedirs()** (notice the spelling change and extra **s**) and delete using **shutil.rmtree()** from **shutil** module (refer to the code file for detailed examples), which is another standard module for high-level file operations such as move, copy, zip, and unzip folders/files.

For example, **shutil.copy('source.txt', 'destination.txt')** copies the source file to the destination, while **shutil.move('source.txt', 'destination_folder')** moves the source file to the destination folder (refer to the code file). Also, let us see how to zip and unzip a folder:

```
base_path = os.getcwd()
folder_to_compress = 'Back-upFiles' # Folder (in current dir) to compress
zip_location = os.path.join(base_path, 'Back-upFiles')

format = 'zip' # Archive format such as 'tar', 'gztar', 'bztar', 'xztar'

# Create the archive
shutil.make_archive(zip_location, format, folder_to_compress)
Creates a compressed archive of the specified folder

# To unzip a folder
archive_path = os.path.join(base_path, 'Back-upFiles.zip')
extract_to = os.path.join(base_path, 'restored_oldFiles')
```

```
# Unpack the archive
shutil.unpack_archive(archive_path, extract_to)
```

For now, these tasks might feel trivial to do with Python, but this is needed to give you a stepping stone for file organization and automation, as you will see later in this chapter. Renaming files based on dates or departments, consolidating and transferring files to different folders, and archiving old reports, many such tasks can be done with these basics.

As a next step, you might want to explore if there is any way to traverse nested folders and search for files (that will help you in searching files in large folders or organizing files even if those are deeply nested) without even opening your file explorer (Windows) or Finder (macOS).

The **`os.walk()`** function in Python is used to traverse directories and get a list of all folders, subfolders, and files inside a given path. This function **walks** through the folder structure and returns a generator[5] that creates a tuple of 3 values (**`current_folder`**, sub-folder in this, files in the same). You can either use **`next()`** or a for loop to traverse the path. Every time the generator is called, it will follow each folder recursively until no further sub-folders are available from the initial folder that the walk was called upon.

To illustrate, we have created a folder named **`Reports`** with a structure as given in *Figure 5.1* in the **`Chapter 05`** folder.

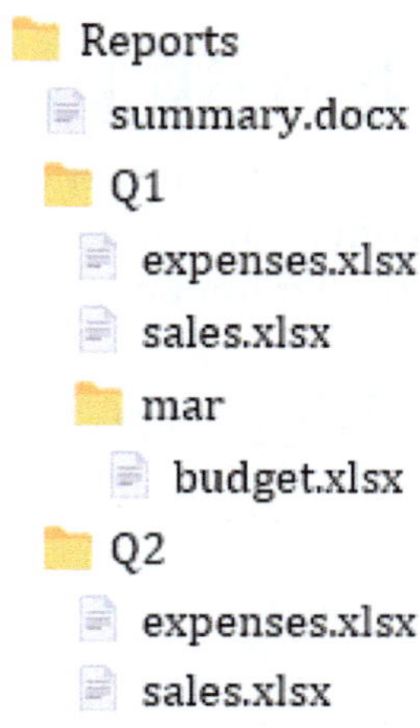

***Figure 5.1**: Folder structure of Reports folder*

You can also use the same to replicate the code example or try out the functions on any other folder on your machine, and your output would vary accordingly:

[5] In Python, a generator is a special type of object that produces values one at a time instead of returning them all at once. It is memoryefficient because it generates items on demand, making them useful for handling large datasets or streams of data.

```
reports_folder = os.path.join(os.getcwd(), "Reports")
# Change this to your actual folder

for root, dirs, files in os.walk(reports_folder):
    print(f"🗀 Root Directory: {root}")  # Prints each scanned directory
    print(f" Subfolders: {dirs}")  # Prints list of subfolders
    print(f" Files: {files}")  # Prints list of files
    print("-" * 40)  # Just a separator for clarity
```

This will print the root directory, its subfolders, and all files iteratively. Else, you can use **next()** keyword to fetch the 3-tuple:

```
my_gen = os.walk(reports_folder)
next(my_gen) # Keep doing it until it covers all subfolders
```

You can do a lot more with this function, like searching, sorting, and organizing files or folders across multiple folders, identifying old files for cleanup, or excluding folders from your search, etc. This is just the beginning, and there is a lot that can be achieved further.

At this point, we have already discussed a lot. Take a pause, and experiment with your own files and folders to fully grasp what is covered so far, and then start fresh for learning powerful pattern-matching with the **glob** module.

Advanced file search with pattern-matching

On Linux and Unix systems, the shell uses **glob** methods for matching files with a specific pattern. Inspired by the same, Python offers such functionalities in the **glob** module. It is like searching for files or folders in Windows Explorer or macOS Finder, but using Python.

Get all the files and folders in a specified folder

If you have created a **Reports** folder as discussed in the previous section, you will get the same output:

```
import glob

reports_folder = os.path.join(os.getcwd(), 'Reports')
content = glob.glob(f"{reports_folder}/*")# * means "everything"
print(content)
['D:\\ Excel_Python\\Chapter 05\\Reports\\Q1', 'D:\\ Excel_Python\\Chapter
05\\Reports \\Q2', 'D:\\ Excel_Python\\Chapter 05\\Reports\\summary.docx']
```

As you noticed, **glob.glob(f"{reports_folder}/*")** returns a list of all files and folders inside the **reports_folder** directory. A subtle difference, you might have noticed that **glob.**

`glob()` returns full paths while **`os.listdir()`** and **`os.scandir()`** which gives file names such as summary.docx.

Get specific types of files

You can also fetch a specific type of files, such as Word, Excel, PDF, images, or more:

```
docx_files = glob.glob(f"{reports_folder}/*.docx")
print(docx_files) # *.docx means all docx files


xlsx_files = glob.glob(os.path.join(reports_folder, 'Q1', '*.xlsx'))
print(xlsx_files) # *.xlsx means all xlsx files
```

Here, to find **`.xlsx`** files in the subfolder Q1, we have mentioned the specific path manually. You can search for files inside the current folder, and its subfolders with **`recursive=True`** using **`**`**

```
xlsx_files = glob.glob(os.path.join(reports_folder, '**', '*.xlsx'), recursive=
True)# Finds all .xlsx files inside " Reports" and all its subfolders, regardless
of depth


print(xlsx_files)
```

Get files by prefix, suffix, and more

During the curation of this book, Word files were created and kept in a folder called *Book Writing* inside the ongoing working directory. However, soon we realized the need to organize that folder. Many Word files were preliminary chapter drafts, and the names were like *ch_1 Intro, ch_2 setup version2, exercises_ch_3 fundamentals,* etc. However, there were other supporting Word files too. We wanted to collect all chapter drafts (maybe to put in the chapter-wise folders later). Here is what followed next:

```
book = os.path.join(os.getcwd(), 'Book Writing')
chapters = glob.glob(os.path.join(book, '*ch_*.docx'))
print('Chapter Drafts: \n', chapters)
```

You can try out one such example on your own files. To collect all Word files that end with *Python* and to collect all Word files that contain *extra,* we run this code that helped us in further organizing our folder:

```
# finding files with suffix 'Python'
topic_python = glob.glob(os.path.join(book, '*Python.docx'))
print('Files Related to topic Python: \n', topic_python)
```

```
# files that contain 'extras' anywhere
extra_files = glob.glob(os.path.join(book, '*extra*.docx'))
print('Extra stuff for chapters: \n', extra_files)
```

You must have noticed the use of capital **P** in **Python**. What if we write **python** with lowercase letters? It is a good time to warn you that on a Windows machine, glob patterns are case-insensitive, so ***Python.docx** will match both **Excel_Python.docx** and **excel_python.docx.** On Mac and Linux, you would need **lower()** method to make the search case-insensitive. It is recommended that you apply searches on your own files and folders.

So now, we can ask Python to create the required folder structure and segregate files nicely in those folders. It is a quick and error-free process, and we can reuse that Python script with minor changes to do such organization elsewhere too. We would recommend you practice using Python with your own file management tasks.

Once you practice all these, you can be in a state of ease for your automation tasks. Know that there is no expectation to mug it up. You can always come back to this chapter for all your file management-related needs. Soon, we will explore different use cases which you might find useful (or at least related to what you do on a regular basis). One more step before we discuss use cases, it will help you to read or write text and binary files directly using Python. Let us see it in action!

Reading and writing files

To create log files or summary reports, you might need to work with text files. Also, sometimes for automation or exporting reports to web pages, you might need to write json or html files. Python allows you to use **open()** method for working with Text, CSV, JSON, HTML, XML files, etc.

Text files

The preferred way of reading or writing such files is to use the context manager **with**. Let us understand using some examples:

```
# Reading a text file ‘sample_1.txt’ from current working directory
with open(' sample_1.txt', 'r') as file:
    content = file.read()
print(content)# prints the content of the file


# Writing content to a new text file named ‘sample_2.txt'
with open('sample_2.txt', 'w') as file:
    file.write('Hello, I am learning Python')
```

You can also read or write files directly using the **open()** method. However, you would need to close the file after using it. See the following example:

```
# Reading a text file 'sample_1.txt'
file = open(' sample_1.txt', 'r')
content = file.read()
print(content)# prints the content of the file
file.close()
```

CSV files

Likewise, you can also read and write **.csv** files. However, we usually prefer to use **.csv** module (as shown below) or **pandas** library to do so (to be discussed in the next chapter):

```
# Reading a csv file
with open("sample_3.csv", "r") as file:
    content = file.read()  # Works fine
print(content)

# Writing a CSV file
with open("sample_4.csv", "w") as file:
    file.write("Date,Product,Quantity,Revenue\n")  # Header row
    file.write("2024-04-01,Laptop,5,5000\n")
    file.write("2024-04-02,Mouse,15,300\n")
```

JSON file

You might also need to use a JSON file to import data from APIs or web services and to create structured log files for automation use cases. A **JavaScript Object Notation** (**JSON**)[6] file is a simple text file used to store structured data, in a key-value format, similar to a Python dictionary. To write or read json file, you can use **json** module:

```
# Writing JSON file using json module
import json
data = {"name": "Alice", "age": 25}
with open("sample_5.json", "w") as f:
    json.dump(data, f)

# Reading JSON file using json module
with open("sample_5.json", "r") as f:
    loaded_data = json.load(f)
print(loaded_data)
```

[6] You can open a JSON file in Notepad, any text editor or web browser.

From json module, **json.dump()** saves (writes) data to a JSON file and **json.load()** reads data from a JSON file back into Python. More examples of working with **html** or **xml** files, etc., are mentioned in the code file.

Automation use cases

Whether you are doing automation testing, software development, or analysis and reporting, you perform various file management tasks, such as organizing or sorting files and folders, managing reports, log files, consolidating multiple CSV or Excel files for analysis, or renaming files based on date, department, or something else.

You can allow Python to assist you with repetitive and manual tasks while you get all the praise for efficiency. Some simple yet powerful use-cases will help you connect the dots and mechanize boring stuff.

Batch renaming files

In case you are planning to rename multiple files, you basically need to locate the file folder and then loop through the files to rename (including or excluding the subfolders).

For the purpose of the demo, you can use a folder named **testfiles** given in **Chapter 05** folder of the companion repo. This folder contains some files and a subfolder. The following code will add a prefix **Jan_** to all filenames (skipping the subfolder):

```
folder_path = os.path.join(os.getcwd(), 'testfiles')
prefix = "Jan_" # Prefix to add to filenames

# Loop through all files in the directory to add prefix to all file names
(skipping sub-folders)
for entry in os.scandir(folder_path):
    if entry.is_file():  # Skip directories, process only files
        old_path = entry.path  # Directly get full path
        new_filename = prefix + entry.name  # Add prefix
        new_path = os.path.join(folder_path, new_filename)
        os.rename(old_path, new_path)  # Rename file
        print(f"Renamed: {entry.name} → {new_filename}")
```

If you need to undo the renaming of files, you can do that with basic string methods such as **startswith()** and **slicing** (refer to the code file). However, it is recommended to create a log file (that saves original names before renaming) and use it to revert anytime you need.

The following code does exactly the same:

```
prefix = "Jan_" # Prefix to add to filenames
log_file = os.path.join(folder_path, "rename_log.
json") # To store original names

# Task 1: To save original filenames before renaming
rename_log = {}
for entry in os.scandir(folder_path):
    if entry.is_file() and not entry.name.startswith(prefix):
        old_path = entry.path
        new_filename = prefix + entry.name
        new_path = os.path.join(folder_path, new_filename)
        os.rename(old_path, new_path)
        rename_log[new_filename] = entry.name  # Store mapping in dict
        print(f"Renamed: {entry.name} → {new_filename}")
# Save the mapping to a JSON log file
with open(log_file, "w") as f:
    json.dump(rename_log, f)
print("✅ Batch renaming complete! Original names saved in rename_log.json»)

# Task 2: To load the log file and revert names

with open(log_file, "r") as f:
    rename_log = json.load(f)
current_files = [entry.name for entry in os.scandir(folder_
path)]# Get current files in directory
for new_name, old_name in rename_log.items():
    old_path = os.path.join(folder_path, new_name)
    new_path = os.path.join(folder_path, old_name)
    if new_name in current_files:
        os.rename(old_path, new_path)
        print(f"Reverted: {new_name} → {old_name}")
    # os.remove(log_file) # Remove log file after reverting
print("✅ Undo complete! All files restored to original names.»)
```

Python even allows you to create a simple GUI where you can do this all with a button click. Possibilities are unlimited, you can explore the creation of such applications on your own later, if you are interested in GUI application development.

Categorizing files by extension

As we have mentioned earlier, in the initial phase of writing this book, we had created a folder *Book Writing* and kept all related work there, be it a word file, image, data, or code. When we planned a proper structure of the directory, we wrote a few lines of Python code to isolate all word files (mostly chapter drafts) from code files and images (that we are creating for the book). To give you an idea, here is the sample code (you can modify as per your requirements):

```
import os, shutil


folder_path = 'path/to/directory/you want to/organize'
# or
folder_path = os.path.join(os.getcwd(), 'testfiles')


# Categorizing files by extension
file_extensions = {
    '.docx': 'WordFiles',
    '.jpg': 'Images',
    '.py': 'CodeFiles',
    '.ipynb': 'CodeFiles' # Notebooks
}
for entry in os.scandir(folder_path):
    if entry.is_file():
        file_ext = os.path.splitext(entry.name)[1]
        if file_ext in file_extensions:
            sub_folder_name = file_extensions[file_ext] # Creating sub-
folders with names by file types
            sub_folder = os.path.join(folder_path, sub_folder_name)
            os.makedirs(sub_folder, exist_ok=True)
            # Moving files to respective folder
            source = entry.path
            destination = os.path.join(sub_folder, entry.name)
            shutil.move(source, destination)
            print(f"Moved {entry.name} → {sub_folder_name}")
```

Deleting older Excel files

To comply with the company policy of data retention, you are to delete all the older Excel files and free up storage. You can do it by running a short Python script like the one given here.

Warning: Running this script on any folder will permanently delete Excel files older than three years. We suggest creating a copy of the demo folder to safely test this code.

```
# This script removes all .xlsx and .
xls files that haven't been modified in over 3 years.
import os, time

folder_path = os.path.join(os.getcwd(), 'demo') # Change to your folder path
three_years_ago = time.
time() - (3 * 365 * 24 * 60 * 60)  # Convert years to seconds
for entry in os.scandir(folder_path):
    file_path = entry.path
    if entry.is_file() and entry.name.endswith(('.xlsx', '.xls')):
        mod_time = os.path.getmtime(file_path)  # Last modified time
        if mod_time < three_years_ago:  # Check if older than 3 years
            os.remove(file_path)  # Delete file
            print(f"Deleted old file: {entry.name}")
```

If you need to send files or folders to the trash (or Recycle Bin), you can use the third-party library **`send2trash`** rather than **`os.remove()`** or **`shutil.rmtree()`**, which deletes files permanently. These files can be restored from the Recycle Bin. **`send2trash`** works across all platforms (Windows, macOS, Linux) and provides a safer alternative.

Timestamp and organize by month

Remember, Maya from *Chapter 1, Python for Excel Users*. She uses a Python script to automatically timestamp her downloaded data and organize it in month-wise folders for consistency and better structure of her work.

Sample code she might be using:

```
import os, shutil, time

source_folder = os.path.join(os.getcwd(), 'organizeByTimeStamp_
Case') # Change to your folder path
destination_root = os.path.join(current_dir, 'Organized_
Reports')  # Where to organize files

os.makedirs(destination_root, exist_ok=True)
```

```
for entry in os.scandir(source_folder):
  if entry.is_file():  # Ensure it's a file
        mod_time = os.path.getmtime(entry.
path) # Get file's last modified timestamp
        formatted_time = time.strftime("%Y-%m-%d", time.localtime(mod_
time))  # YYYY-MM-DD

        # Extract year and month for folder organization
        year_month = time.strftime("%Y-%m", time.localtime(mod_time))  # YYYY-
MM

        # Create destination folder for that year and month
        destination_folder = os.path.join(destination_root, year_month)
        os.makedirs(destination_folder, exist_ok=True)
        # New file name with timestamp
        name, ext = os.path.splitext(entry.name)
        new_filename = f"{name}_{formatted_time}{ext}"
        new_path = os.path.join(destination_folder, new_filename)
        # shutil.move(entry.path, new_path) # Move and rename file
        shutil.copy(entry.path, new_path)  # Copy and rename file
        print(f"Moved/Copied: {entry.name} → {new_filename} in {destination_
folder}")
```

There can be many more such use cases that you can explore now, for example, try moving all Excel files from multiple folders into one master folder.

Conclusion

If you have come this far, you might have realized that learning Python is a good investment of your time, and it can do things that many other modern Excel-related tools cannot. In summary, this chapter covered file and directory operations, working with file paths, and reading or writing text files, along with some automation use cases. We have used Python standard modules such as os, shutil (abbreviated for shell utility), and glob in this chapter. If you are experienced Python users, you can also explore the pathlib module, which provides an object-oriented approach to handling filesystem paths.

In the subsequent chapters, you will see how Python can do the heavy lifting, analyzing data through summaries, charts, and pivots. Once that is done, you will likely want to write those reports back to files on your machine. The learnings from this chapter will aid you in organizing those files.

Try it yourself

The following hands-on challenges will allow you to gain first-hand experience in managing documents and directories. While solving these problems, ensure that your script works regardless of OS (Windows, Mac, or Linux).

1. Rename all files and folders from a specific location to add the prefix 2026_. You should create a log file and use it to undo the rename again.

2. If you have a folder with many project-related files, how would you rename only Word files to replace the word draft with final, such as:

   project_draft.docx to project_final.docx

   notes_draft.docx to notes_final.docx

   Create a folder for this question and try renaming.

3. In the previous exercise, create a log file and use that to undo rename.

4. Extend this exercise to all subfolders too. Do it recursively.

5. Add timestamps, such as filename_yyyy-mm-dd, to file names in a test folder. E.g., Report.xlsx should be renamed as Report_2025-02-04.xlsx in this folder.

6. Using Python, create a folder Finance_Reports in the D drive or your current directory. And replicate the folder structure as shown in *Figure 5.2:*

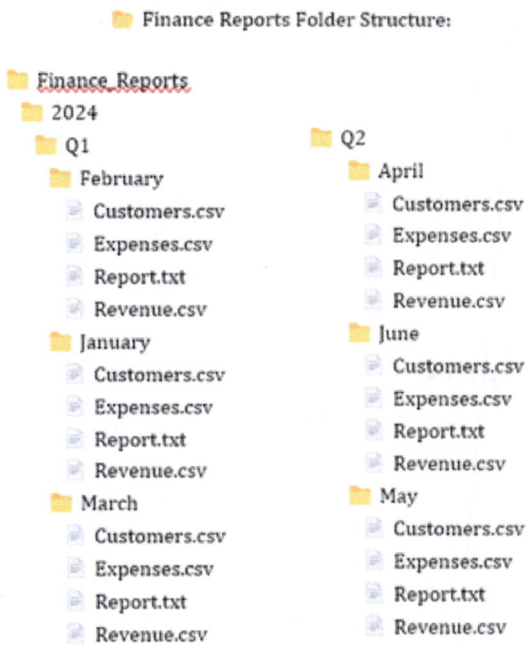

Figure 5.2: *Folder structure to be created*

You need to use open method to create all these dummy files inside sub-folders. Then print the folder structure nicely arranged, similar to the image in *Figure 5.2* [**Hint**: Use os.walk() method].

7. You have many zipped files saved in your Downloads folder. Write a Python script to:
   a. Find all .zip files in the Downloads folder.
   b. Unpack them into a single folder named restored_old_files inside your current working directory.

Concept check

Read the following questions and explain how you will approach the problem. You do not need to write the code.

1. You have thousands of customer invoices stored in different subfolders. How can you use Python to quickly find all invoices related to a specific client?
2. Your script works perfectly on Windows, but when run on Mac or Linux, it fails due to incorrect file paths. How can you modify it to work across different operating systems?
3. What are some possible errors when renaming or moving files using Python, and how can you handle them to prevent script failures?
4. If you are a cybersecurity professional, how would you use Python to monitor a folder for unauthorized file modifications?

Join our Discord space

CHAPTER 6
Data Manipulation with Pandas

Introduction

In this chapter, we will focus on data manipulation using the mighty pandas library of Python. It is designed for data analysis, offering functionalities similar to Excel but with greater efficiency and scalability. You will learn to import data and perform operations such as handling missing values, filtering, aggregating, pivoting, or other complex transformations.

By the end of this chapter, you will have a solid understanding of how to clean, transform, and analyze data using pandas, preparing you for more advanced Excel-Python integration with libraries like openpyxl and xlwings.

Structure

In this chapter, we will discuss the following topics:

- Introducing the mighty pandas library
- DataFrames and Series
- Data import and export
- Datatypes in pandas
- Filtering, selecting, and querying data
- Data cleaning and handling missing values
- Column calculations and quick statistics
- Advanced data transformation
- Grouping and pivoting data
- Combining data sets

Introducing the mighty pandas library

Python's **pandas** library is designed to make your workflow faster, scalable, automation-friendly, even for messy or large datasets. This library has the broader goal of becoming the most powerful and flexible open-source data analysis or manipulation tool available in any language.

Unlike Excel, where copying formulas or updating pivot tables can become tedious and error-prone, `pandas` workflows are **scripted once and reused endlessly**, ensuring both consistency and speed. For advanced users relying on **Power Query**, **Power Pivot**, or even **VBA**, pandas offers a unified environment where importing data, merging files, cleaning columns, and summarizing insights can all be done in one place. Even common Excel pain points, like dealing with slow workbooks, broken formulas, or lookup errors across multiple files, are easily addressed in `pandas` through intuitive, scalable code.

Let us start looking into a concise preview of what we can do with `pandas`, each topic is explained in detail in the following sections.

If you are using Anaconda, `pandas` is already included. You do not need to install it again. If you have created a `conda` environment for the book (as explained in *Chapter 2, Setting Up Python)*, `pandas` is installed there already.

For plain Python users (`python.org`), If `pandas` is not installed, install it by running the following command in Anaconda Prompt or Terminal:

```
pip install pandas==3.0.0
```

Once you have the library installed, you can import it using alias `pd` (refer to *Chapter 4, External Packages and Date-time Handling*).

If you are unsure whether `pandas` is already installed, you can try importing it before installing anything. If it runs without error, `pandas` is already available and no installation is required.

```
import pandas as pd
print(pd.__version__)
```

Expected output:

```
3.0.0
```

This library gives you the ability to import data files from various sources and different formats. For now, use `read_excel()` to read an excel file `employees.xlsx` containing employee records. Data files are available in `Data` folder of the GitHub repo. To import data sets from there, you can use `os.path.join()` method (recommended) or hardcode file path as discussed in *Chapter 5, Automating File Management with Python*:

```
import pandas as pd
import os
DATA_PATH = os.path.join(os.getcwd(), 'Data')
data = pd.read_excel(os.path.join(DATA_PATH, 'employees.xlsx'))
print(data)
```

This will display data in Excel-like table:

```
   emp_id      name            job_title   dept     sal      loc churn
0    E001     Alice      Sales Executive  Sales   72000       NY    No
1    E002      Mark    Software Engineer   Engg   95000      SFO    No
2    E003     Linda           HR Manager     HR   86000  Chicago   Yes
3    E004     David      DevOps Engineer   Engg   91000   Austin    No
4    E005     Susan      Account Manager  Sales   80000   Boston   Yes
5    E006       Tom    Software Engineer   Engg   98000       NY    No
6    E007    Angela            Recruiter     HR   67000  Chicago    No
7    E008     James       Data Scientist   Engg  105000      SFO    No
8    E009      Nina      Sales Executive  Sales   73000   Boston   Yes
9    E010    Robert    Software Engineer   Engg   94000   Austin    No
10   E011      Emma    Marketing Analyst   Mktg   71000       NY    No
11   E012      Liam    Marketing Manager   Mktg   88000  Chicago   Yes
12   E013    Olivia         HR Assistant     HR   62000   Boston   Yes
13   E014      Noah      Account Manager  Sales   82000       NY   Yes
14   E015       Mia         Data Analyst   Engg   89000      SFO   Yes
15   E016     Jacob   Content Strategist   Mktg   76000   Austin    No
16   E017  Isabella      DevOps Engineer   Engg   92000       NY    No
17   E018     Ethan       SEO Specialist   Mktg   73000  Chicago   Yes
18   E019    Sophia      Sales Executive  Sales   71000   Boston   Yes
19   E020   Michael           HR Manager     HR   87000  Chicago    No
```

In Colab or Jupyter, DataFrame will appear as a nicely formatted HTML table. If you are working in Spyder, you can double click on **data** from **Variable Explorer** to open an editor which allows you to format and edit data (you can explore but do not save changes, if any). This is a toy data set, so you can print or view all the rows. If your data set is too big to print, you can have a quick glance at it using **data.head()** (prints the first five rows by default) or **data.tail()** (prints the last five rows by default):

```
print(data.head())
```

The expected output is:

```
  emp_id   name          job_title   dept    sal      loc churn
0   E001  Alice    Sales Executive  Sales  72000       NY    No
1   E002   Mark  Software Engineer   Engg  95000      SFO    No
2   E003  Linda         HR Manager     HR  86000  Chicago   Yes
3   E004  David    DevOps Engineer   Engg  91000   Austin    No
4   E005  Susan    Account Manager  Sales  80000   Boston   Yes
```

To print last 2 rows only, you can run **data.tail(2)** and it will show:

```
   emp_id     name          job_title   dept    sal      loc is_churn
18   E019   Sophia  Sales Executive  Sales  71000   Boston      Yes
19   E020  Michael         HR Manager     HR  87000  Chicago       No
```

A simple **data.shape** command reveals the number of rows and columns **(20, 7)** and **data.columns** will fetch you all column names, which is especially useful when you have too many columns. Moreover, quick information about the size of data, column name, column types, missing values, etc., can be fetched by a simple command **data.info()**, which shows the following output:

```
<class 'pandas.DataFrame'>
RangeIndex: 20 entries, 0 to 19
Data columns (total 7 columns):
 #   Column     Non-Null Count  Dtype
---  ------     --------------  -----
 0   emp_id     20 non-null     str
 1   name       20 non-null     str
 2   job_title  20 non-null     str
 3   dept       20 non-null     str
 4   sal        20 non-null     int64
 5   loc        20 non-null     str
 6   left       20 non-null     str
dtypes: int64(1), str(6)
memory usage: 1.2 KB
```

It tells us that data is basically a **pandas** DataFrame (this is how **pandas** store tables). 20 entries means that there are twenty rows, indexed as 0 to 19 (as the index starts from 0), and a total of seven columns. For each column, it tells us the index (starting from 0), column name, number of non-null or non-missing values, and datatype of that column.

In this data set, there are no missing or null values, as we can see (all 20 values are non-null for each column). The column **sal** is a numerical column, while the rest are **str** (string) datatypes. We will discuss more about DataFrames and datatypes in the next section. For now, let us do some quick analysis of this data.

The function, **data.describe()** provides a summary of all numerical columns by default. You can customize it to include or exclude specific columns, such as non-numeric columns, date columns, or columns by name.

As you can guess, **data['dept']** will fetch you **dept** column of the data, allowing you to perform operations on it. If you are curious to see how many unique values there are in this column and names of different departments in the **data**, you can chain **nunique()** and **unique()** methods to this column shown as follows:

```
data['dept'].nunique() # 4 _ Counts unique values
data['dept'].unique() # ['Sales', 'Engg', 'HR', 'Mktg']
```

To get a count of employees in each department, you can use **value_counts()** function, and with an additional argument, it can also generate percentages without needing to manually write the formula:

```
data['dept'].value_counts()
```

It shows:

```
dept
Engg     7
Sales    5
HR       4
Mktg     4
Name: count, dtype: int64
```

To get the relative frequency (proportion) of each department:

```
data['dept'].value_counts(normalize = True) # Percentage Table
```

The output tells us that most employees, 35%, are from the engineering department:

```
dept
Engg     0.35
Sales    0.25
HR       0.20
Mktg     0.20
Name: proportion, dtype: float64
```

The column **left** indicates if an employee has left the job (yes or no). If you want to get pivot-style count table of how many employees have left from each department, use a simple function:

```
pd.crosstab(data["dept"], data["left"])
```

To add a column and row of totals, **margin** argument can be used:

```
pd.crosstab(data["dept"], data["left"], margins=True)
```

The output is:

```
left    No  Yes  All
dept
Engg     6    1    7
HR       2    2    4
Mktg     2    2    4
```

```
Sales    1    4    5
All     11    9   20
```

Also, to show values as a percentage of row, column, or overall total, the **normalize** argument can be used with or without using the **margin** argument. You can chain together more methods, such as **multiply(100)** or **round(2)**, to display the numbers conveniently:

```
pd.crosstab(data["dept"], data["left"],
            normalize='columns').round(2)                    # % w.r.t. 'left' variable
```

The output is:

```
left      No    Yes
dept
Engg    0.55   0.11
HR      0.18   0.22
Mktg    0.18   0.22
Sales   0.09   0.44
```

It shows that 44% of those who left the job were from the Sales department. To find percentages with respect to index or department, we can use **normalize='index'**:

```
pd.crosstab(data["dept"], data["left"],
             normalize='index').multiply(100).round(2)     # % by 'dept' variable
```

The output is:

```
left       No     Yes
dept
Engg    85.71   14.29
HR      50.00   50.00
Mktg    50.00   50.00
Sales   20.00   80.00
```

It shows, for example, that in the sales department, 80% of employees have left. So far, we have created simple pivot tables[1].

If you are looking at department-wise mean salary, you can use **groupby()**:

```
data.groupby('dept')['sal'].mean().astype(int)
```

The output is:

```
dept
Engg      94857
HR        75500
```

[1] pd.crosstab() is not a full pivot table, it quickly summarizes categorical variables (like Excel's COUNTIFS), but for full pivoting with custom aggregations, we will discuss pivot_table() in detail later in the chapter.

```
Mktg        77000
Sales       75600
Name: sal, dtype: int32
```

Here, **astype(int)** has been chained to convert numbers into integers, or you can choose to round them. To calculate multiple statistics, such as mean, minimum, and maximum, for each department, you can use **agg** along with **groupby()**. (refer to the code file).

If employee names are to be cleaned for lower case and removing white spaces, you can chain together string methods such as **str.lower()** and **str.strip()**. Let us look at the first three entries after cleaning using **head(3)**:

```
data["name"].str.lower().str.strip().head(3)
```

The output is:

```
0     alice
1      mark
2     linda
Name: name, dtype: object
```

You might be wondering about writing **.str** before using string methods, it is needed as the methods like **.lower()**, **.strip()**, or others work on strings, but **data['name']** is not a string itself, it is a column in the dataset. We call it **pandas** Series. The **.str** accessor allows us to apply string methods elementwise to each value in the column.

pandas is not just for data manipulation, it can plot charts too! By chaining **.plot()** to your data or table, you can quickly visualize trends without needing extra libraries. You will explore this in detail later, but even now, see how effortlessly it integrates visuals:

```
pd.crosstab(data['dept'], data['left']).plot(kind='bar')        # Refer figure 6.1a
data.boxplot(column='sal', by='dept')                           # Refer figure 6.1b
```

Chart title, subtitle, grid lines, size, and colour can all be customized easily, for now the charts created by the above-mentioned code are as shown in *Figure 6.1*:

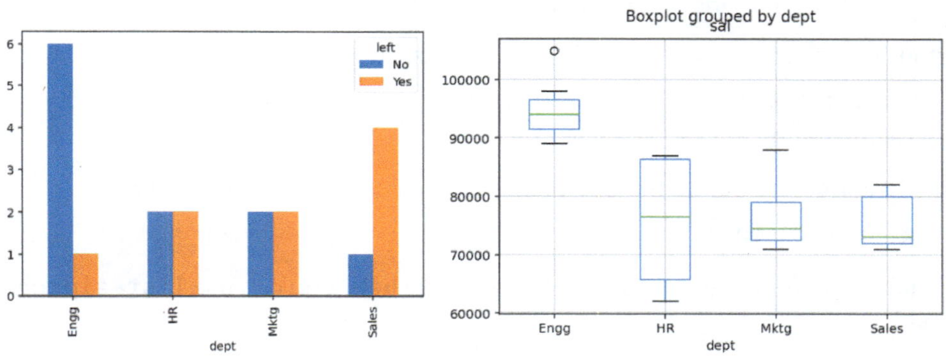

***Figure 6.1**: (a) Grouped bar chart, (b) Side-by-side Box plot*

In this section, you have also seen method chaining, i.e., calling multiple methods in sequence without creating temporary variables. This streamlines code, making it more efficient and readable. This gives you a glimpse of the wide range of possibilities with **pandas**. Before diving deep into the library for analytics, let us first formally introduce DataFrames and Series.

DataFrames and Series

You might have noticed that DataFrames allow you to see the data the way you see it in Excel, letting you explore and analyze it much like in Excel.

Dataframes are 2-dimensional arrays, which means that it has rows and columns where each column can be of a different datatype. We have already worked with 2-dimensional data in the form of a list of lists, a dictionary of lists, or a list of dictionaries, etc., and you will agree that pandas DataFrames make working with such data extremely convenient and efficient. You can convert nested data structures into a DataFrame by using **pd.DataFrame()**:

```
users = [['Excel', 10], ['R', 15], ['Python', 14]]                # List of
lists
df = pd.DataFrame(users, columns=['Tool', 'User_Count'])          # DataFrame
print(df)
```

Here, **columns** argument specifies the labels for the DataFrame's columns. The output is:

```
     Tool  User_Count
0   Excel          10
1       R          15
2  Python          14
```

You might sometimes get JSON data from a web API, which is usually a list of dictionaries such as:

```
users = [{'Tool': 'Excel', 'User_Count': 10},
         {'Tool': 'R', 'User_Count': 15},
         {'Tool': 'Python', 'User_Count': 14}]
```

Or if a certain function results in a dictionary of lists, such as:

```
users = {'Tool': ['Excel', 'R', 'Python'],
         'User_count': [10, 15, 14]}
```

You can easily convert these dictionary-based data structures into a DataFrame:

```
df = pd.DataFrame(users)
```

When you have data for different columns in separate lists, you can use **list-zip** combination as mentioned:

```
tool = ['Excel', 'R', 'Python']
user_count = [10, 15, 14]

df = pd.DataFrame(list(zip(tool, user_count)), columns=['Tool', 'User_Count'])
```

When you import external data using **pandas**, it is usually loaded as a DataFrame. Also, you have seen in the previous section that a single column of a DataFrame works as a 1-dimensional homogeneous array, we call it a **Series**. Refer to *Figure 6.2*:

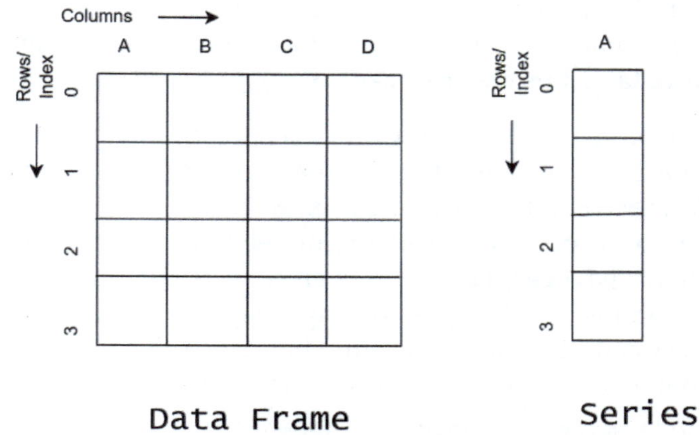

Figure 6.2*: pandas Series and DataFrame*

DataFrames and Series are two core data structures specific to **pandas**. You can create a **pandas** Series using any 1-d data structure, such as a list, a tuple, a dictionary, or even using **range()**:

```
# From List
s_list = pd.Series([10, 20, 30])
# From Tuple
s_tuple = pd.Series((10, 20, 30))
# From Dictionary (keys become index)
s_dict = pd.Series({'0': 10, '1': 20, '2': 30})
# From range()
s_range = pd.Series(range(10, 40, 10))
```

Data import and export

For analyzing your data, you might need to frequently import data from text, CSV, Excel, or JSON files, among other file types. In *Chapter 5, Automating File Management with Python*, you have learnt about reading data from text or a CSV file using **open()** method with or without using the **csv** module. Here, you will learn to use **pandas** to import data from files of different types.

The **pandas** input-output API provides a set of top-level reader functions like **pandas.read_excel()** that you have seen so far. Refer to the official document at **https://pandas.pydata.org/docs/user_guide/io.html** to check the file types it supports. In the Data folder, sample files are provided. Try reading those using **pandas** functions after setting the path:

```
csv_data = pd.read_csv('employees.csv')
json_data = pd.read_json('employees.json')
html_data = pd.read_html('employees.html')
```

Note that **read_html()** always returns a list even if there is only one table, using index [0] extracts it as a DataFrame. Each of these functions has many useful arguments to control how you want to read your data. Let us discuss **read_csv()** and **read_excel()** in detail.

To read text files with tab, semicolon, or any other separator, you can use the **sep** argument. Excel might not auto-parse exotic delimiters, such as caret (^), double colon (::), tilde (~), or custom strings (such as, **@@@** or **###**), which are used when other delimiters conflict or content has standard punctuation inside. Excel users might need to import manually or with Power Query. However, Python's **pd.read_csv()** offers an elegant and unified way to read all text-based delimited files, you just need to pass the right **sep** (separator) argument. It is always recommended to inspect your data once to ensure that it is loaded correctly. Spyder's Variable Explorer helps with that. Read sample data files yourself to verify:

```
df_sc = pd.read_csv("semicolon_sep.csv", sep=';'); df_sc.shape #(20, 7)
df_t = pd.read_csv("tab_sep.tsv", sep="\t"); df_t.shape        # (20, 7)
df_c = pd.read_csv("caret_sep.txt", sep='^'); df_c.shape       #(20, 7)
```

You can also choose to read only specific columns of your data using **usecols** argument and read fewer rows using **nrow** argument, which is perfect for quickly previewing large files or working with just the needed data. It saves memory and reduces processing time, unlike Excel, which loads everything by default unless you perform extra steps in Power Query or VBA:

```
df_sample = pd.read_csv('employees.csv',
                        nrows=10,  usecols=[0,1,4]); df_sample.shape   # (10, 3)
```

If your file contains metadata, extra headers, notes, or inconsistent formatting at the top of a file, before the actual data starts, the **skiprows** argument comes in handy. It allows you to specify line numbers (0-indexed) or the number of lines to skip (int) at the start of the file.

With **pd.read_csv()**, we can also load data directly from a URL, if the link points directly to a **raw CSV file** (i.e., it ends with **.csv** and does not require login or redirects):

```
url = 'https://archive.ics.uci.edu/ml/machine-learning-databases/iris/iris.data'
df = pd.read_csv(url)
```

We can use the **index_col** argument in the **read_csv()** function to set a column as the index column. Alternatively, after loading the data, we can also choose to use a column as the index (row labels) by using the **set_index()** method and reset it again using the **reset_index()** method:

```
df = pd.read_csv('employees.csv')
# Using 'emp_id' as the row-index
df_indexed = pd.read_csv(url, index_col='emp_id')

# Alternately, set 'emp_id' as the new index after reading the data
df_indexed = df.set_index('emp_id')
df_indexed.head(2)
```

The output shows that **`emp_id`** column is now treated as row-labels:

```
        name   job_title          dept    sal   loc   left
emp_id
E001    Alice Sales Executive     Sales  72000   NY    No
E002    Mark  Software Engineer    Engg  95000  SFO    No


# Reset index (bring 'emp_id' back as a column)
df_reset = df_indexed.reset_index()
df_reset.head(2)
```

The output is:

```
 emp_id    name          job_title  dept    sal  loc left
0   E001   Alice    Sales Executive  Sales  72000   NY   No
1   E002    Mark  Software Engineer   Engg  95000  SFO   No
```

Many arguments we have explained for **`read_csv()`** also apply to **`read_excel()`**, as you can see in *Figure 6.3* (Official documentation of **`read_excel()`** function):

pandas.read_excel

`pandas.read_excel(io, sheet_name=0, *, header=0, names=None, index_col=None, usecols=None, dtype=None, engine=None, converters=None, true_values=None, false_values=None, skiprows=None, nrows=None, na_values=None, keep_default_na=True, na_filter=True, verbose=False, parse_dates=False, date_format=None, thousands=None, decimal='.', comment=None, skipfooter=0, storage_options=None, dtype_backend=<no_default>, engine_kwargs=None)` [source]

Read an Excel file into a `DataFrame`.

Supports *xls*, *xlsx*, *xlsm*, *xlsb*, *odf*, *ods* and *odt* file extensions read from a local filesystem or URL. Supports an option to read a single sheet or a list of sheets.

***Figure 6.3**: Arguments of the read_excel() function*

For more options, refer to pandas official documentation (at **https://pandas.pydata.org/docs/reference/api/pandas.read_excel.html**). We would recommend that you try out a few arguments as per your specific needs. Now, let us explore some of the specific features of **read_excel()**:

By default, **read_excel()** function reads first sheet. The **sheet_name()** argument allows you to read a specific sheet by its name or index, or retrieve multiple sheets at once:

```
# By default, it reads first sheet
df_jan = pd.read_excel('finance_data.xlsx')

# To read the first sheet, using index (0-inedxed)
df_jan = pd.read_excel('finance_data.xlsx',sheet_name=0)

# To read the sheet named 'Feb', by specifying sheet name
df_feb = pd.read_excel('finance_data.xlsx',sheet_name="Feb")

# To read the first and second sheets
df_jan_feb = pd.read_excel('finance_data.xlsx',sheet_name=[0, 1])

# To read all the sheets
df_all_sheet = pd.read_excel('finance_data.xlsx',sheet_name=None)
```

When you read multiple sheets, it returns a dictionary, whose length equals the number of sheets read, with sheet names as keys and DataFrames as values.

```
print(df_all_sheet.keys())        # dict_keys(['Jan', 'Feb', 'Mar'])
print(type(df_all_sheet['Jan'])) # <class 'pandas.core.frame.DataFrame'>

# To fetch data from sheet named 'Jan'
df_all_sheet.get('Jan')
```

This function also supports reading xls, xlsb, xlsm, and many other file types. We can also read html data, or connect to databases and read tables. To create the sample files, we have used **pandas** writer functions, such as **to_csv()**, **to_excel()**, **to_json()**, etc. You can also use **pd.ExcelWriter()** with **to_excel()** to write data to multiple sheets. We will cover more on this in *Chapter 9, Core Excel Read-Write Tools in Python.*

Datatypes in pandas

Apart from regular **int**, **float**, **bool** and **str** datatype, **pandas** offer additional datatypes, which makes handling data efficient.

For example, colum ke **Date of Birth**, **Application Date**, or **transaction date** can be considered as the time datatype for smoother manipulation.

Prior to panda 0 (major release dated **January 21, 2026**), columns with text (string) data such as Emp **Employee Name**, etc. were also considered as **object** datatype, which are now infe (string) datatype.

on, **object** datatype is assigned only to non- standard columns or mixed xample, any column like **salary**, **amount** or **approved** contains numeric values So, i nteral string 'missing' (not to be confused with actual missing values like **NaN** dat se columns will be read as **object** columns by default. We can convert it to a a mn either while reading the data or after loading.

y datatype is the **category** datatype, which can be used for qualitative variables categories such as **gender**, **age group**, or **region**. In most cases, it helps save memory.

nize performance and memory usage, we can convert column(s) to more specific pes[2] as needed, depending on the nature of the data. You can either define a datatype e reading data into pandas or change it later.

Defining a datatype while reading the file

If you know the correct datatypes for categorical or datetime columns, you should define the datatype while reading the data. For example, when you print **df.dtypes** for **finance_data.xlsx**, it shows many columns as object datatype, which should be stored as **datetime**, **float** or **category** columns.

```
txn_id          str
txn_date     object
client          str
amount       object
approved     object
region          str
dtype: object
```

You can define an appropriate datatype for one or more columns using the **dtype** argument while reading the data:

```
df = pd.read_excel('finance_data.xlsx', dtype={'region': 'category'})
print(df.dtypes)
```

[2] Other Pandas specific data types include time delta, Interval, Sparse, and BooleanArray, etc. however these are rarely needed for standard analysis.

The output is:

```
txn_id               str
txn_date          object
client               str
amount            object
approved          object
region          category
dtype: object
```

It changes the datatype for the **region** column from **str** to **category**. However, while t to convert the **amount** column to float, it fails.

```
df = pd.read_excel('finance_data.xlsx', dtype={'amount': 'float64'})
# ValueError
```

Inspecting this column tells us that this column has some values stored as **missing** in text format. You might encounter errors when specifying the **dtype** argument if the column contains non-numeric or invalid entries that do not align with the expected type. In such cases, you can import data as-is and later change datatype to suitable ones, or handle missing values while reading the data by using **na_values** argument such as:

```
df = pd.read_excel('finance_data.xlsx', na_values='missing')
print(df.dtypes)
```

We also had values stored as **missing** in text format in the **txn_date** column; all such values are now being treated as missing values. As a result, Python correctly interprets **txn_date** as a datetime column and **amount** as a float column.

```
txn_id                    str
txn_date     datetime64[us]
client                    str
amount                float64
approved               object
region                    str
dtype: object
```

We recommend you inspect the issue with **approved** column as well to read it as float. If the date column is read as an object type, you can also use the **parse_dates** argument in the reader function, which works only if there are no missing or invalid values in that column. Alternatively, you can convert it after reading the file.

Changing datatype after reading the file

Sometimes, after you have imported your dataset, you may need to adjust datatypes if columns are misinterpreted (e.g., numbers as text, dates as objects). For conversion to numeric,

pd.to_numeric() and to datetime, **pd.to_datetime()** methods[3] can be used with the **errors='coerce'** argument to handle invalid or missing values by converting them to **NaN**.

By default, **errors='raise'** is used, which is good when you want strict validation and fail-fast behavior on any non-numeric values, while **errors='coerce'** is useful when working with messy real-world data where invalid entries should be converted into **NaN** instead of stopping execution.

```
df['amount'] = pd.to_numeric(df['amount'], errors='coerce')
df['txn_date'] = pd.to_datetime(df['txn_date'], errors='coerce')
```

For converting column to **category** datatype, you can use **astype()** method:

```
df['region'] = df['region'].astype('category')
```

These functions also allow changing the datatype of multiple columns at once without a loop.

Filtering, selecting, and querying data

So far, you have used **df['column_name']** to fetch a single column. Similarly, you can quickly fetch multiple columns by supplying a list of column names inside **df[]**:

```
df = pd.read_excel('finance_data.xlsx', na_values=['missing', '-'])
df[['client', 'amount']]        # It's a DataFrame
```

Furthermore, pandas offer amazing capabilities to select data you might need for analysis:

- **Selecting data based on datatypes**: Sometimes, you need to get all numeric columns, or all date-based columns, etc., for some analysis. You can do that conveniently with the **df.select_dtypes()** method:

```
# Select only float-type columns (returns full DataFrame slice)
df.select_dtypes('float')

# Get column names of float-type columns only
df.select_dtypes('float').columns

# Select all numeric columns (both int and float)
df.select_dtypes(include='number')

# Select all non-numeric columns (str, object, datetime, category, etc.)
df.select_dtypes(exclude='number')
```

[3] Most of dataframe methods like these create a modified copy (means return a new object) instead of changing the original DataFrame. To apply changes permanently, you must assign the result back to df, like df = df.method().

```
# String datatype
df.select_dtypes('str').columns
```

In older **pandas** versions (< 3.0.0), text columns were treated as **object** datatype. So, for backward compatibility, columns with the new **string** dtype are currently treated as **object** when you call **select_dtypes('object')**. This behaviour is deprecated and will be removed in a future release.

- **Selecting data with row-labels and column names using df.loc**: The preferred way to draw data based on row labels, row index, or conditions and column names is to use **df.loc[row index/label/condition, column_name]**:

```
df.loc[0, :]  # 1st row, all columns

df.loc[0, 'client'] # 1st row, client col
df.loc[:, 'client']  # all the rows, client col

df.loc[:, ['client', 'region']] # all the rows, multiple columns
df.loc[:, 'client' : 'region'] # all the rows, consecutive columns

# NOTE: including 'region' column

df.loc[[0, 2], :] # multiple rows, all columns
df.loc[0:2, :] # consecutive rows (includes row index 2), all columns
```

Note: When using slicing in df.loc, remember that it includes the last element. For example, df.loc[0:2] will include rows 0, 1, and 2, unlike other Python slicing, where the last element is usually excluded.

If you set **txn_id** as the row label (index) in your DataFrame, you can use the same logic, but instead of numeric indices, you would reference the actual **txn_id** values:

```
# Setting 'txn_id' as index/row label
df_index = df.set_index('txn_id')

df_index.loc['T001', :] # row with txn_id T001
df_index.loc['T002', 'client'] # row with txn_id T001, client col
```

- **To filter data based on some condition(s)**: To get data for transactions where amount exceeds 1000, you can mention condition(s) inside square brackets, such as:

```
# Transactions with amount greater than 1000
df.loc[df['amount'] > 1000, :]
```

```
# Amount greater than 1000 and approved transactions
df.loc[(df['amount'] > 1000) & (df['approved'] == 1), :]
```

You can achieve the same results without explicitly using **.loc** (by simply writing **df[condition]**) but using **df.loc[condition]** is safer and preferred for more complex filtering operations.

- **For selecting data strictly based on row-index and column-index**: If your data does not have column headers, or if you are unsure of the names, or simply you prefer numeric indexing instead, you can use **df.iloc[row_index, column_index]** to select data based on the row and column positions. Here, the same indexing principles apply as you have used earlier with lists, tuples, or strings:

```
df.iloc[2, 1]                # third row, second column
df.iloc[0:3, 0]              # first, second, third row _ first column
```

Practicing to subset data the way you need will help you make things easier and faster. We would recommend using **df.loc** whenever possible, unless you specifically need row and column positions, in which case use **df.iloc**.

- **Deleting rows or columns or both**: **df.drop()** can be used to delete rows, columns, or both based on the parameter **axis**, **axis=0** (default) removes rows, and **axis=1** removes columns:

```
# To drop columns
df.drop(['txn_id', 'client'], axis = 1)

# To drop row(s)
df.drop(0)

# To drop row(s) & column(s)
df.drop(index = [0, 1], columns = ['txn_date', 'client'])
```

- **Advanced querying**: Another powerful function, **df.query()**, enables advanced row filtering based on SQL-like string expressions. This makes filtering more dynamic and readable. You can even use Python variables inside queries with **@** or apply complex filtering conditions:

```
# Use variable inside query
threshold = float(input('Enter Min Amount: '))
df.query("amount > @threshold")

# Filter rows where region is in a list
df.query("region in ['East', 'North']")
```

```
# Rows where amount is between 1000 and 1500
df.query("amount.between(1000, 1500)")
```

- **Replicating Excel's COUNT, COUNTIF, COUNTIFS, SUMIF, SUMIFS**: Use the insights gained so far to determine the following: total number of transactions, count of approved transactions, and how many of those were of an amount exceeding 1000, and total amount for approved transactions in the **East** region using the learnings so far. These use cases with solutions are given in the accompanying code file.
- **More filtering functions:** You can also explore **df.filter()**, when you do not want to hard-code column names. It is useful in **extract, transform, and load** (ETL) pipelines where column names vary slightly across files. You can also use **all()** to ensure every element meets a condition, and **any()** to check if at least one element does. Refer to the code files for examples.

Data cleaning and handling missing values

Missing or incomplete data is a common challenge in any analysis, regardless of the tool. Whether working in Excel or Python, unaddressed missing values can lead to incorrect calculations or errors. In Excel, empty cells or cells with **n/a**, **NA**, **NaN**, **#N/A**, **<NA>**, or other similar values often disrupt formulas and may return **#N/A** or **#VALUE!** errors. In pandas, empty cells are stored as **NaN**[4] (stands for Not a Number) for most datatypes and **NaT** (Not a Time) for date-time columns. You can choose to treat missing values carefully before analyzing the data.

Let us start with the same **finance_data.xlsx** that we had used earlier and load the first sheet in pandas. Inspect the data carefully. You will see that pandas automatically identify blank cells (within the data), **n/a**, **NA**, **NaN**, **#N/A**, **<NA>**, or other similar values as missing data and denote them as **nan**. However, this data has some other problematic cells like text written as **missing** (cell B5 and D14) and cell entry as **-** in cell E12, which are kept as is by pandas. You can verify this by using **df.info()** or viewing the data:

```
df = pd.read_excel('finance_data.xlsx')
```

[4] In pandas, NaN (from NumPy) represents missing numerical values, while nan may appear due to display formatting but it refers to the same type.

Figure 6.4 shows the same data in Excel and how it looks in Spyder after reading using pandas:

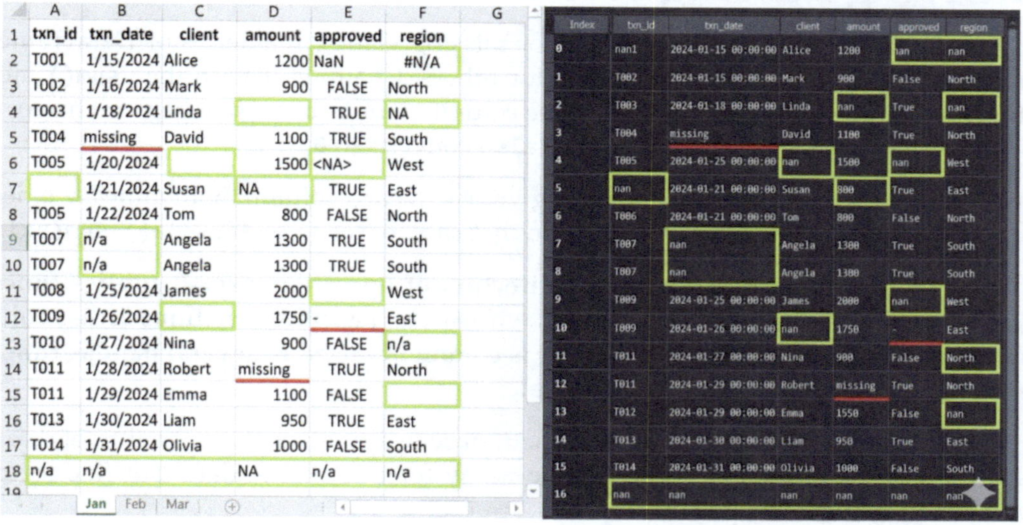

Figure 6.4*: finance_data in Excel and pandas*

To tell pandas to treat any specific value (such as **missing** and **-** in our example) as a missing value, we can use **na_values** argument in the reader function:

```
df = pd.read_excel('finance_data.xlsx', na_values=['missing', '-'])
df.info()
```

You can see in *Figure 6.5* that using **na_values** ensures these values are converted to **nan** or **NaT**, i.e., missing values:

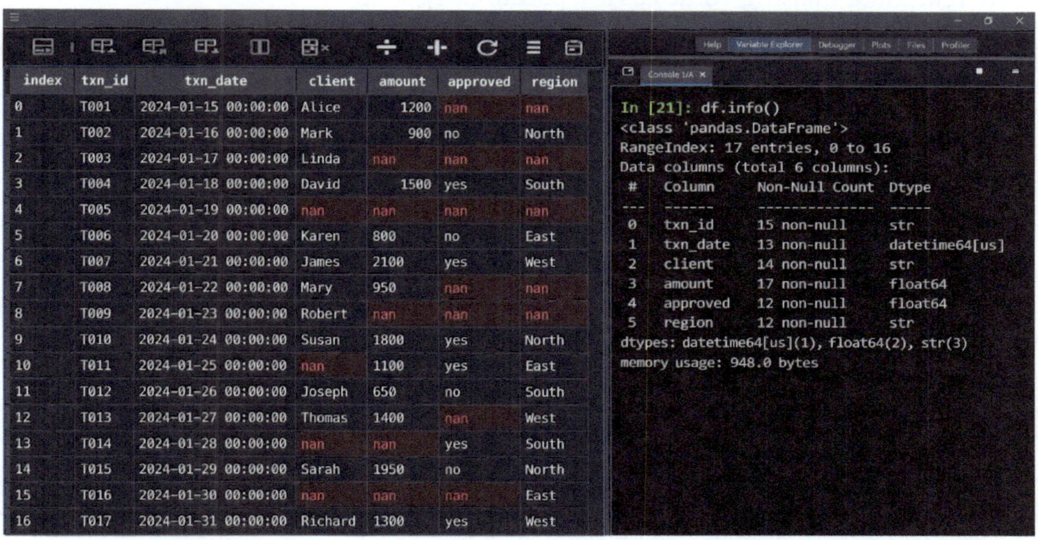

Figure 6.5*: Data view and df.info() after ensuring to read missing values appropriately*

Identifying missing values

The method **`.isna()`** or **`.isnull()`** checks for missing values in a Series or DataFrame and returns **`True`** for missing values and **`False`** for others. Chaining it with the **`.sum()`** method gives the total number of missing values in the column or data, because when you try to apply sum over Booleans, **`True`** converts to **`1`** and **`False`** converts to **`0`**.

`df.isna().sum()` gives the count of missing values in each column. Sometimes, we need to see the count of missing values in each row. In that case, we can use **`df.isna().sum(axis=1)`**.

Note: The axis parameter determines the direction of operation. axis=0 applies functions across rows to produce sum of each column, while axis=1 applies functions across columns to produce sum of each row. This parameter is commonly used in several pandas functions such as `drop()`, `fillna()`, `apply()`, `mean()`, etc.

Chaining any of these with the **`.sum()`** method, once again, gives the overall total. We have a total of 23 missing values in this data (too many for this size of data, but fine for demo purposes):

```
print(df.isna().sum().sum())                    # 23
```

Likewise, the functions **`.notna()`** or **`.notnull()`** check for non-missing values and returns **`True`** where data is present.

Handling missing values

To handle missing values in a data set, it is crucial to understand the data, the reason for non-availability of that value, and the business logic to figure out what to fill in there, or if it is needed to treat those missing values as a separate category.

For this topic, we will show you different ways to fill missing values, which may or may not make sense practically, as we are playing with a toy data set for now.

For now, we would recommend creating a copy of the data so that your original data remains as-is in case you need it later by running this code:

```
df_backup = df.copy() # creating a copy of data
```

Here, the amount column has some missing values, all of these are approved transactions. We can fill them all as a fixed value, say, 500 (assuming that is the minimum order allowed). To fill missing values with a constant, we can use **`fillna()`** method:

```
df['amount'].fillna(500)            # Does not change original data
df['amount']                         # Still it has missing values
```

This code does not change the original data. If you intend to change the same, you can assign the result back to the column or update the whole DataFrame by supplying a dictionary of column name, replacement value, and using the argument **`inplace = True`**:

```
df['amount'] = df['amount'].fillna(500)  # Changes original data
# or
df.fillna({'amount': 500}, inplace=True) # Changes original data
```

Filling missing values using any constant for multiple columns can be done by supplying a dictionary of column name and replacement value in **fillna()**:

```
df = df_backup.copy() # Now again df has missing values in 'amount'

# filling missing values in multiple columns
df.fillna({'amount': 500, 'approved': 1})
```

For the **transaction date** and **client name** column, maybe you can think of filling in the missing values with the previous valid entry, because in a chronological transaction log, a blank date or client usually means **same as the last recorded**, rather than a new, different value. We can use **ffill** method to fill the missing value with the immediate previous value, and **bfill** method to fill the missing data with the immediate next value, if available.

For illustration purposes, we are showing forward fill for **txn_date** and backward fill for the **client** column:

```
df['txn_date'].ffill()
df['client'].bfill()
```

These both methods depend on existing valid values. If the required previous or next value is not available, the missing entry will stay unfilled, which you can fill with a constant value or use other strategies.

You might come across older code using **fillna(method='ffill')**. It worked earlier but is now deprecated.

These were the basic ways to fill up missing values. At times, we need to go beyond the basics. One thing we also do in analytics is to explore the data, other tables and relationship between the variables to take a clue on missing values. For example, some other relationship table gives us information that client **Alice** is from **East** region or the accounts department gave us the info that any transaction that amounts for over 1500 is not approved. We can combine conditional filtering with **fillna()** to fill missing values based on such logic:

```
df.loc[df['client'] =='Alice', 'region'] = 'East'
df.loc[df['amount'] > 1500, 'approved'] = 0
```

Sometimes, we simply replace the missing value by the mean, median, or category-wise statistics for numerical variables and the most frequent value or category-wise mode for categorical variables. Some examples are:

```
# Mean replacement
mean_amt = df['amount'].mean()
```

```
df['amount'].fillna(mean_amt.round(1))

# Median Replacement
df['amount'].fillna(df['amount'].median())

# Mode/ Most Frequent Value Replacement
most_fre_region = df['region'].value_counts().idxmax()
df['region'].fillna(most_fre_region)
```

We can also use advanced options like interpolation for filling up missing values.

```
# Replacement by Interpolation
df['amount'].interpolate()        # Linear Interpolation
```

Data analysts spend a significant portion of their time on data cleaning, with missing value treatment being a major aspect of the process. Library **pandas** provides powerful and flexible functions for handling missing values, enabling efficient data manipulation beyond Excel's limitations.

Beginners often choose to delete rows or columns with missing data for a quick cleanup. This can be done with **dropna()** function (refer to more examples in the code file):

```
df.dropna()  # deletes all the rows with 'any' missing value

df.dropna(how='all') # delete only the row(s) with 'all' missing values

df.dropna(axis = 1) # delete all the columns with 'any' missing value
df.dropna(axis=1, how='all') # delete only the column(s) with 'all' missing values

df          # No change in original data
```

You might have noticed that **dropna()** returns a new object without missing values and does not modify the original DataFrame unless you use **inplace=True**.

Managing duplicates

Sometimes, due to system errors, some transactions get logged twice, and we trust the first entry (based on sort order or timestamp) and want to remove the rest. For example, these two rows of the data contain duplicates:

```
7   T007        NaT  Angela  1300.0     1.0  South
8   T007        NaT  Angela  1300.0     1.0  South
```

You can use the **drop_duplicates()** function to remove duplicate rows from the DataFrame, keeping only the first occurrence of each unique row:

```
df.drop_duplicates()
```

The output is:

```
    txn_id   txn_date  client  amount  approved region
0     T001 2024-01-15   Alice  1200.0       NaN    NaN
1     T002 2024-01-16    Mark   900.0       0.0  North
2     T003 2024-01-18   Linda     NaN       1.0    NaN
3     T004        NaT   David  1100.0       1.0  South
4     T005 2024-01-20     NaN  1500.0       NaN   West
5      NaN 2024-01-21   Susan     NaN       1.0   East
6     T006 2024-01-22     Tom   800.0       0.0  North
7     T007        NaT  Angela  1300.0       1.0  South
9     T008 2024-01-25   James  2000.0       NaN   West
10    T009 2024-01-26     NaN  1750.0       NaN   East
11    T010 2024-01-27    Nina   900.0       0.0    NaN
12    T011 2024-01-28  Robert     NaN       1.0  North
13    T011 2024-01-29    Emma  1100.0       0.0    NaN
14    T013 2024-01-30    Liam   950.0       1.0   East
15    T014 2024-01-31  Olivia  1000.0       0.0  South
16     NaN        NaT     NaN     NaN       NaN    NaN
```

Row index 8 is dropped. You can also remove duplicates based on specific column(s) using a subset argument. Such as removing duplicate payments or records based on transaction ID, i.e., column **txn_id**:

```
df.drop_duplicates(subset=['txn_id'], keep='first') # keep='first' is default
```

If you are doing a data quality audit and want to flag any suspicious duplicate IDs, regardless of which came first, so your team can investigate all instances. To see every row[5] with duplicated **txn_id** values, you can use **df[df['txn_id'].duplicated(keep=False)]**.

Column calculations and quick statistics

In Excel, applying a formula to a column requires copying or dragging, taking care of cell references, while **pandas** allows you to perform operations directly on columns without needing to write a loop. This is called vectorized calculation, and this is one of the reasons **pandas** is fast and powerful.

[5] The keep argument ('first', 'last', False) in duplicated() marks duplicates while keeping the original DataFrame unchanged. keep=first or keep=last marks all duplicates except for the first or last occurrence while keep = False marks all duplicates. In drop_duplicates(), this argument works similarly but removes duplicates instead of marking them. keep=first or keep=last drop duplicates except for the first or last occurrence while keep = False drops all duplicates.

Let us use the same data as before, slightly trimmed for brevity:

```
df = df.head()
df_backup = df.copy()      # Back-up in case we need it
df
```

The output is:

```
  txn_id   txn_date client  amount  approved region
0   T001 2024-01-15  Alice  1200.0       NaN    NaN
1   T002 2024-01-16   Mark   900.0       0.0  North
2   T003 2024-01-18  Linda     NaN       1.0    NaN
3   T004        NaT  David  1100.0       1.0  South
4   T005 2024-01-20    NaN  1500.0       NaN   West
```

Assuming a transaction fee of 5% on all amounts, we are willing to create a column named **fee** that shows this amount. Then, we would prefer to compute the net amount, that is, the difference between **amount** and **fee**. Library **pandas** help us do this neatly with simple code:

```
df['fee'] = df['amount'] * 0.05 # NaNs are produced for missing values
df['net_amount'] = df['amount'] - df['fee']
df
```

The output is:

```
  txn_id   txn_date client  amount  approved region   fee  net_amount
0   T001 2024-01-15  Alice  1200.0       NaN    NaN  60.0      1140.0
1   T002 2024-01-16   Mark   900.0       0.0  North  45.0       855.0
2   T003 2024-01-18  Linda     NaN       1.0    NaN   NaN         NaN
3   T004        NaT  David  1100.0       1.0  South  55.0      1045.0
4   T005 2024-01-20    NaN  1500.0       NaN   West  75.0      1425.0
```

As the amount value was not available for the third row, we got missing values in our newly computed columns too, as expected but we can handle using **fillna()** directly in the current code:

```
df = df_back_up   # Going back to original data

df['fee'] = df['amount'].fillna(0) * 0.05
df['net_amount'] = df['amount'].fillna(0) - df['fee']
```

This code creates a **fee** column by replacing **NaN** values in amount with 0 temporarily and multiplying the result by 0.05. It does not alter the original **amount** column. Alternately, we can use **mul()** or **sub()** functions, as these offer the **fill_value** argument to define a particular value if a data point is missing. This is especially helpful when combining two columns when either one has missing values. With **fill_value=0**, missing values in either column are treated as 0, so **net_amount** will always show a number:

```
df = df_back_up

df.loc[:, 'fee'] = df['amount'].mul(0.05, fill_value = 0)
df.loc[:, 'net_amount'] = df['amount'].sub(df['fee'], fill_value = 0)
df
```

The output is:

```
  txn_id   txn_date client  amount  approved region   fee  net_amount
0   T001 2024-01-15  Alice  1200.0       NaN    NaN  60.0      1140.0
1   T002 2024-01-16   Mark   900.0       0.0  North  45.0       855.0
2   T003 2024-01-18  Linda     NaN       1.0    NaN   0.0         0.0
3   T004        NaT  David  1100.0       1.0  South  55.0      1045.0
4   T005 2024-01-20    NaN  1500.0       NaN   West  75.0      1425.0
```

We have decided to give Rs. 100 cashbacks only for approved transactions, try creating another column for that. In the previously mentioned examples, we have used subtraction and multiplication on columns, and the calculation of the values is done **elementwise**. The following table gives you common operators and their corresponding method names:

Operator	Method
+	.add()
-	.sub()
*	.mul()
/	.div()
//	.floordiv()
%	.mod()
**	.pow()
==	.eq()
!=	.ne()
>	.gt()
>=	.ge()
<	.lt()
<=	.le()

Table 6.1: Common operators and their corresponding method names

For quick computations, you can use operators as you use with numbers, e.g., **df['amount'] += 50**. And when you need more control over missing data or when indexes or column names do not match perfectly, you can use methods such as **add()** or **sub()**.

pandas also provides vectorized versions of common mathematical functions that can be applied on columns, a few are mentioned as follows:

```
df['amount'].min()
df['amount'].max()
df['amount'].mean()
df['amount'].median()
df['amount'].sum()
```

Another powerful function is **df.assign()**, which lets you create new columns dynamically without modifying the original table, ideal for temporary transformations. It works well in method chains (with **df.apply()**, **df.query()**, etc.), improving readability.

> **Note: Method chaining is powerful; however, it can lead to lengthy code. When a line of code becomes too long to fit neatly, Python allows you to break it across multiple lines. You can use a backslash (\) for explicit line continuation, or simply wrap the expression in parentheses (), or brackets [].**

The latter is generally preferred for readability, as it is cleaner and less errorprone. For example:

```
# Using backslash
df_full.assign(net_amount = df_full['amount'] * 0.9) \
       .query("region == 'East'") \
       .sort_values('net_amount', ascending=True)

# Using parenthesis
(df_full.assign(net_amount = df_full['amount'] * 0.9)
        .query("region == 'East'")
        .sort_values('net_amount', ascending=True))
```

The above code computes a **net_amount** as 90% of the amount, filters for rows where **region == 'East'**, and returns the rows sorted by **net_amount** in ascending order.

For advanced logic to compute derived columns, you can use **apply()**, **map()**, or **transform()**. The next section discusses these.

Advanced data transformation

There is a lot you can do with **pandas**, we will cover all key functions that help in efficiently manipulating or analyzing data. For that, start with importing and inspecting a dummy YouTube channel statistic for Maya, the content creator, we referred to in *Chapter 1, Python for Excel Users*. Variable names are self-explanatory. Check the data description for more details:

```
df = pd.read_excel('YT_data.xlsx', index_col='Video Id')
```

This data (150 rows and 15 columns) does not have any missing value. You can check for duplicates as well. Column names are quite lengthy and renaming them would be helpful for analysis. **df.rename()** takes a dictionary to map names:

```
df.rename(columns={
    'Video Title': 'title',
    'Playlist Name': 'playlist',
    'Video Duration (Mins)': 'duration_min',
    'Video_Publish_Date': 'published',
    'Watch Time (Mins)': 'watch_min',
    'Views': 'views',
    'Impressions': 'impressions',
    'Subscribers': 'subs_net',
    'Subscribers Gained': 'subs_gained',
    'Subscribers Lost': 'subs_lost',
    'Average Percentage Viewed': 'avg_view_pct',
    'Likes': 'likes',
    'Comments': 'comments',
    'Shares': 'shares',
    'Dislikes': 'dislikes'
}, inplace=True)
```

The column **playlist** which stores names of playlists, can be converted to category datatype:

```
df['playlist'] = df['playlist'].astype('category')
df.info()
```

The output is:

```
<class 'pandas.DataFrame'>
Index: 150 entries, V_001 to V_150
Data columns (total 15 columns):
 #   Column        Non-Null Count  Dtype
---  ------        --------------  -----
 0   title         150 non-null    str
 1   playlist      150 non-null    category
 2   duration_min  150 non-null    float64
 3   published     150 non-null    datetime64[us]
 4   watch_min     150 non-null    float64
 5   views         150 non-null    int64
 6   impressions   150 non-null    int64
```

```
7   subs_net       150 non-null   int64
8   subs_gained    150 non-null   int64
9   subs_lost      150 non-null   int64
10  avg_view_pct   150 non-null   float64
11  likes          150 non-null   int64
12  comments       150 non-null   int64
13  shares         150 non-null   int64
14  dislikes       150 non-null   int64
dtypes: category(1), datetime64[us](1), float64(3), int64(9), str(1)
memory usage: 17.8+ KB
```

Now, column names are convenient to type, and the playlist is reflected as a category datatype. Feel free to explore unique values and the frequency table for this column. You can also check the summary of the data set for numeric columns, all columns, or selected columns using **`df.describe()`**. We will move to something practically useful.

Applying custom functions to data

To apply a custom function to data, **`pandas`** offer **`apply()`** or **`map()`** functions. For example, to create a column **`video_length`** based on a logic such that if **`duration_min`** is less than 10, label it as **Short**; otherwise, label it as **Long**. There are many ways to do it. Let us do it using both **`map()`** and **`apply()`**:

```
df['video length'] = (
                        df['duration_min']
                        .map(lambda x: 'Short' if x < 10 else 'Long')
                        .astype('category')
                        )

# Or Using apply() function

df['video length'] = (
    df['duration_min']
    .apply(lambda x: 'Short' if x < 10 else 'Long')
    .astype('category')
)
```

We demonstrated the powerful combination of lambda function, combined with **`map()`** or **`apply()`** for column-wise operation. This approach is highly effective for data processing.

The **`apply()`** function can also be used on a DataFrame for applying functions across rows or columns. For instance, suppose we want to create a new column, performance, that categorizes videos (each row) as **High**, **Medium**, or **Low** based on specific criteria involving multiple columns. In this case, defining a function and applying it row-wise is more practical:

```
def tag_performance(row):
    if row['views'] > 5000 and row['watch_min'] > 200:
        return 'High'
    elif row['views'] < 1000:
        return 'Low'
    else:
        return 'Medium'

df['performance'] = df.apply(tag_performance, axis=1)
```

To use **apply()** on a DataFrame, we need to specify **axis = 1** to indicate that the function should be applied to each row rather than each column. This is important because the **tag_performance()** function expects a row.

In short, to transform values in a single column or a Pandas Series, **map()** is often a better choice than **apply()**. For complex row-wise transformations involving multiple columns, **apply()** can be used.

Sorting and ordering the columns

If in any table, you need to sort, reorder, shuffle, or arrange in custom order for improving search, ranking items, or for sampling, all of these can be done with simple code. For example, to sort videos by **views** (highest to lowest), similar to Excel's *Sort Largest to Smallest* feature:

```
# Sort rows by 'views' in descending order
df.sort_values(by='views', ascending=False)
```

You can fetch **title** and **views** columns for information about videos with the highest and lowest views. For further diagnostics, you can either print the first and last few values using **head()** and **tail()** or save the newly created data with a different name.

Next, suppose you are willing to see prioritized videos with playlist names arranged alphabetically (A-Z) and then arranged in descending order of watch time, this is basically sorting using two columns and can be achieved by using a list of column names in **df.sort_values()** method:

```
# Sort by playlist (A-Z), then by watch time (descending)

playlist_watchTime = (df.sort_values(by=['playlist', 'watch_min'],
                                     ascending=[True, False])
                      [['title', 'playlist', 'watch_min']])
```

The first few rows of **`playlist_watchTime`** dataset are as given in *Figure 6.6*:

Video Id	title	playlist	watch_min
V_105	How to Start Data Science Journey | Learn Smartly | Got Less Time, Too Much to Learn | Career Advice	Career Advice	414.44
V_096	Career in Data Science	Career Advice	119.46
V_099	From Campus to Corporate | Get Hired | Data Science Jobs	Career Advice	73.32
V_090	Dr Nisha Arora Talk |Women in Data Science Stanford_2022 | My chart is Lying | Avoiding Chart Lies	Data Storytelling	278.42
V_100	Data Visualizations _ Selecting the appropriate chart | how to select chart? | Types of chart	Data Storytelling	201.47
V_106	Storytelling with Data | Data Visualization | Communicate your analysis effectively	Data Storytelling	164.59
V_101	Why do you need to learn Data Visualization & Story Telling?	Data Storytelling	120.49
V_059	Power BI vs Excel Dashboards	Excel	453.93
V_013	Excel Budget Tracker	Excel	464.39
V_029	Power Pivot made Easy	Excel	452.84
V_043	Top 5 Excel Shortcuts	Excel	450.74
V_012	Top 20 Excel Functions for 80 % of Tasks	Excel	443.11

***Figure 6.6**: Glimpse of playlist_watchTime data set*

This data set does not have missing values, but if you have missing values in some column, you can control the placement of missing values to be at the start or end using the same powerful **`sort_value()`** function. Cumulative sum[6] or a running total of views can be computed easily with **`df['views'].cumsum()`**. Also, **`df.sample()`** allows you to take random samples of data or randomly shuffle the data, and much more, very useful in data science.

Grouping and pivoting data

In Excel, **`COUNTIF`**, **`SUMIF`**, and **`AVERAGEIF`** provide quick conditional summaries while PivotTables and PowerQuery enable interactive groupings, aggregations, and data reshaping for deeper analysis. **`pandas`** offers similar yet more advanced capabilities:

- **`groupby()`**, **`agg()`**, **`transform()`**, and **`filter()`** for summarizing, transforming, and filtering groups (like performing advanced **`COUNTIF`**, **`SUMIF`**, and **`AVERAGEIF`**, etc.).
- **`pivot_table()`** and **`pivot()`** for pivoting and reshaping data (like PivotTables, but with more control).
- **`melt()`**, **`stack()`**, **`unstack()`** for reshaping datasets between wide and long formats (an alternative to PivotTables and PowerQuery).

[6] Similarly, .cumprod() computes cumulative product, useful in compounding or growth calculations

Newer versions of Excel, especially Excel 365, have introduced dynamic arrays, **FILTER**, **UNIQUE**, **LET**, and even **Python integration**, but **pandas** remains unmatched in flexibility for complex data manipulations. Just like Excel, **pandas** provides multiple ways to achieve similar tasks, the key is to choose the most readable and practical option for your needs.

Summarizing, transforming, and filtering groups

Using the same **YT_data**, let us find some key insights using **groupy()**, **agg()**, and **transform()**.

The **groupby()** function in **pandas** is incredibly powerful. It allows you to compute multiple summaries across one or more columns, such as total views and watch time per playlist. You can also generate multiple summaries of a single column (e.g., sum, mean, and max of views) or apply different aggregations to different columns (e.g., sum of views and max of watch time). All of this can be done efficiently without the need for a Pivot Table.

Total views per playlist:

```
df.groupby('playlist')['views'].sum()
```

The output is:

```
playlist
Career Advice            21106
Data Storytelling        33599
Excel                   349088
Linear Algebra           64940
Python                  239396
R Programming            29944
Science Experiments      32514
Statistics               44081
Name: views, dtype: int64
```

The output is a **pandas** Series, you can use **df.groupby('playlist')[['views']].sum()** to get a DataFrame.

Total views and watch time by playlist:

```
df.groupby('playlist')[['views', 'watch_min']].sum()
```

The output is:

```
                      views  watch_min
playlist
Career Advice         21106     607.22
Data Storytelling     33599     754.97
Excel                349088   16064.33
```

```
Linear Algebra         64940    3352.33
Python                239396   12988.73
R Programming          29944    1226.64
Science Experiments    32514    1509.77
Statistics             44081    2604.28
```

Multiple aggregations on a column:

In Excel, applying multiple aggregations requires multiple formulas, manual adjustments, or switching to Pivot Tables or Power Query, while such tasks are as cool as a breeze in Python. You can use **agg()** to perform multiple aggregations, such as computing different statistics on same column or across multiple columns:

```
df.groupby('playlist')['views'].agg(['sum', 'mean', 'max'])
```

The output is:

```
                        sum         mean   max
playlist
Career Advice         21106  7035.333333  8915
Data Storytelling     33599  8399.750000  9489
Excel                349088  5454.500000  9942
Linear Algebra        64940  5411.666667  7949
Python               239396  5093.531915  9837
R Programming         29944  5988.800000  8517
Science Experiments   32514  4644.857143  9365
Statistics            44081  5510.125000  7690
```

To apply multiple aggregations across different columns:

```
df.groupby('playlist').agg({'views': 'sum', 'watch_min': 'mean'})
```

And to give meaningful names to resultant columns. The output is:

```
                     total_views  avg_watch_min
playlist
Career Advice              21106     202.406667
Data Storytelling          33599     188.742500
Excel                     349088     251.005156
Linear Algebra             64940     279.360833
Python                    239396     276.355957
R Programming              29944     245.328000
Science Experiments        32514     215.681429
Statistics                 44081     325.535000
```

You can also perform aggregation with custom functions, which makes it super convenient to perform data tasks on the fly. One such example:

```
# Custom aggregation with lambda with clean custom names

(df
 .groupby('playlist')['views']
 .agg(
    min_views='min',
    max_views='max',
    range_views=lambda x: x.max() - x.min())
.reset_index())
```

The output is:

```
              playlist  min_views  max_views  range_views
0        Career Advice       4425       8915         4490
1    Data Storytelling       7438       9489         2051
2                Excel        633       9942         9309
3       Linear Algebra        755       7949         7194
4               Python        509       9837         9328
5        R Programming       1424       8517         7093
6  Science Experiments       1270       9365         8095
7           Statistics       3824       7690         3866
```

You can also use **df.agg()** to apply aggregation functions on the entire DataFrame (no grouping), or on a single column directly. You can use **df.groupby(col)** without specifying an aggregation immediately. This creates groups, which you can explore or iterate over later. This chapter's code files have many practical, ready-to-use examples, so you do not need to Google common patterns every time!

To broadcast group-level stats back to all rows using **transform()**:

If you need to add group-level stats, such as playlist-average views attached to each row[7], you can use **transform()** instead of **agg()**:

```
df['playlist_avg_views'] = df.groupby('playlist')['views'].transform('mean')
df[['playlist', 'views', 'playlist_avg_views']].tail()
```

[7] agg()reduces groups to one row per group, transform() preserves row count. Also note that agg() is just a shorthand alias for aggregate(), both perform the same task.

The output is:

```
                 playlist  views  playlist_avg_views
Video Id
V_146              Python   5030         5093.531915
V_147       R Programming   7381         5988.800000
V_148       R Programming   7449         5988.800000
V_149          Statistics   6741         5510.125000
V_150       R Programming   8517         5988.800000
```

Yet another powerful function in **pandas** is **filter()** that allows us to refine data dynamically. It can retain or exclude entire groups based on conditions, such as keeping playlists where total views exceed a set threshold. It enables quick selection of rows or columns by matching specific words, like extracting columns containing **min** in their name. With regex-based pattern matching, it provides precise filtering, making complex data extraction effortless, ideal for tasks that would otherwise require tedious manual selection in Excel. Refer code file for impactful examples.

Pivoting and reshaping data

Excel users use PivotTables frequently to summarize and explore the data by dragging fields into Rows, Columns, Values, and sometimes using Slicers or connecting multiple tables with the Data Model. Let us see how this can be done in pandas:

- **Simple Pivot Table**: To fetch playlist-wise total views, you can use **df.pivot_table(values=..., index=..., aggfunc=...)**, where values are like Excel's *Values*, index represents *Rows*, and aggfunc is the *Value Field Settings*:

```
df.pivot_table(values='views',
               index='playlist',
               aggfunc='sum',
               margins = True, # To add a totals
               margins_name = 'Grand Total')
```

As you can see in *Figure 6.7*, the results are the same in Python and Excel:

playlist	views
Career Advice	21106
Data Storytelling	33599
Excel	349088
Linear Algebra	64940
Python	239396
R Programming	29944
Science Experiments	32514
Statistics	44081
Grand Total	814668

	Row Labels	Sum of Views
2		
3	**Row Labels**	**Sum of Views**
4	Career Advice	21106
5	Data Storytelling	33599
6	Excel	349088
7	Linear Algebra	64940
8	Python	239396
9	R Programming	29944
10	Science Experiments	32514
11	Statistics	44081
12	**Grand Total**	**814668**

***Figure 6.7**: Pivot table in Python (left) vs. Excel (right)*

- **Multi-dimensional Pivot Table**: To get **playlist** vs. **published month** with the sum of views, you can create a column for **published_month** in the data and use it as **columns**, while using **'playlist'** as **index** and **'views'** as **values** in **df.pivot_table()**

  Some combinations may not have any values. In Python, these appear as **NaN** (similar to Excel's blank cells). We can replace them with a custom value such as **0** using the **fill_value** argument:

```
df.pivot_table(values='views',
               index='playlist',
               columns='published_month',
               aggfunc='sum',
               fill_value=0)
```

- **Multiple aggregations**: To get the sum and mean of views per playlist, you can pass a list of functions in **aggfunc** argument:

```
df.pivot_table(values='views',
               index='playlist',
               aggfunc=['sum', 'mean'])
```

It is like adding the same field twice to Values (one Sum, one Average) in Excel. Just like **aggfunc**, you can provide multiple values for other arguments, such as **values**, **index**, or **columns** in **df.pivot_table()**.

You can also apply different aggregation functions to different columns, such as:

```
df.pivot_table(values=['views', 'subs_net'],
               index='playlist',
               aggfunc={'subs_net':'sum', 'views':'mean'})
```

Apart from **pivot_table()** for structured summary, you have already seen the use of **groupbby()** for flexible grouping and **crosstab()** for frequency analysis. You can also use **query()**, **loc()**, **assign()**, etc., with **pivot_table()** for dynamic filtering, selecting specific data, and adding computed columns to enable dynamic and efficient analysis[8]. Also, for combining multiple tables in aggregation, you can use pandas merging methods as discussed next.

In addition, you can use **melt()**, **stack()**, and **unstack()** to reshape your data as you need. For complex, multi-step data transformations, you can explore **df.pipe()**. It lets you chain together custom functions cleanly, making long processing pipelines easier to read.

[8] For interactive pivot tables, libraries like pivottablejs can be used

Combining data sets

Excel (even Excel 365) lacks a clean, scalable way to combine datasets. Functions such as **`VLOOKUP`**, **`INDEX-MATCH`**, or the new dynamic array formulas like **`FILTER`** are used to merge data from different tables. However, these tend to be cumbersome and error prone as the volume or complexity of the data grows. Additionally, Excel's built-in functions struggle with multi-key join and advanced merging logic, making it difficult to handle more sophisticated join conditions often required in SQL.

While Power Query supports standard joins, Python allows for more complex merging conditions, such as fuzzy matching, multi-key joins, and conditional joins that go beyond standard inner, left, right, and outer joins. Even experienced Power Query users can benefit from using **`pandas' concat`**, **`join`**, and **`merge`**, especially for large data, automation, complex workflows, and scalability beyond Excel's limitations.

To replicate code examples, load different sheets of **`demo_sales.xlsx`** data with appropriate names and view those to understand how these are related:

```
customers = pd.read_excel('demo_sales.xlsx', sheet_name='Customers')
orders = pd.read_excel('demo_sales.xlsx', sheet_name='Orders')
products = pd.read_excel('demo_sales.xlsx', sheet_name='Products')
sales_jan = pd.read_excel('demo_sales.xlsx', sheet_name='Sales_Jan')
sales_feb = pd.read_excel('demo_sales.xlsx', sheet_name='Sales_Feb')
```

Concatenating

Sometimes, you may need to add rows to an existing table. It is like copying rows from one worksheet and pasting them into another. For example, adding sales for the months Jan and Feb as shown in the following figure:

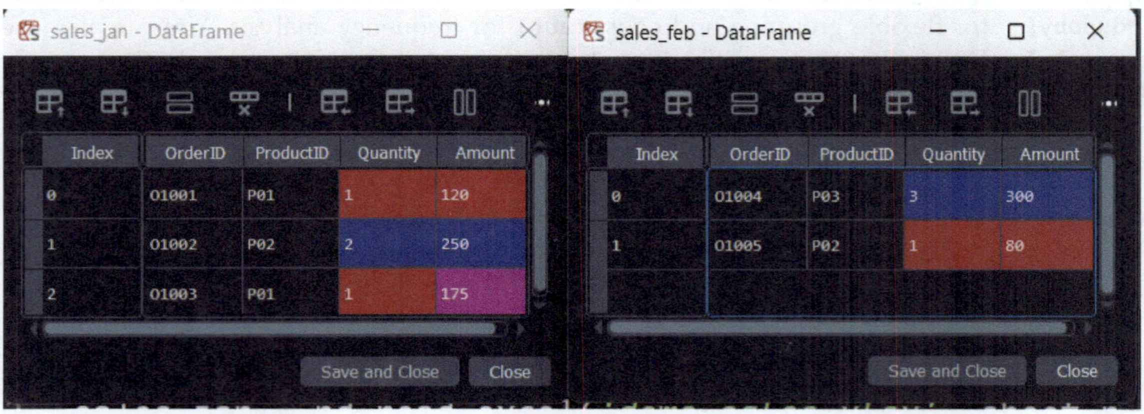

Figure 6.8: sales_jan and sales_feb data

You can do it using the **concat()** function, which joins DataFrames along a particular axis. By default, it stacks data row-wise. The argument **ignore_index=True** resets the index for the new combined DataFrame:

```
sales_jan_feb = pd.concat([sales_jan, sales_feb], ignore_index = True)
print(sales_jan_feb)
```

The output is:

```
  OrderID ProductID  Quantity  Amount
0   O1001       P01         1     120
1   O1002       P02         2     250
2   O1003       P01         1     175
3   O1004       P03         3     300
4   O1005       P02         1      80
```

Also, **axis = 1** can be used to stack data column-wise, if needed. **pd.concat([data1, data2, data3, ...])** lets us stack multiple datasets, enabling us to read multiple Excel files and combine them into a single table for analysis.

Joining and merging like SQL joins

When you want to retrieve data from two or more tables based on logical relationships between the tables, you can perform different types of joins on tables. SQL users might be familiar with these joins. We will join data about orders and customers using **CustomerID** column from both tables, as follows:

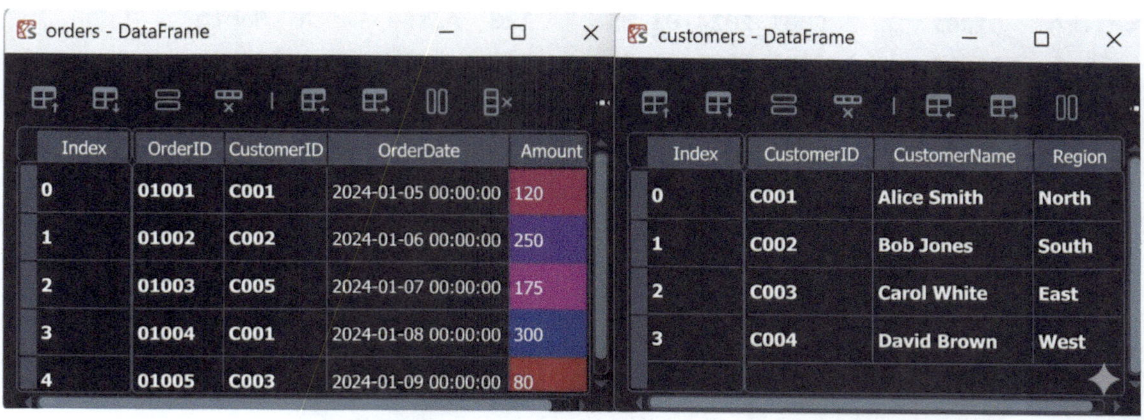

orders - DataFrame

Index	OrderID	CustomerID	OrderDate	Amount
0	O1001	C001	2024-01-05 00:00:00	120
1	O1002	C002	2024-01-06 00:00:00	250
2	O1003	C005	2024-01-07 00:00:00	175
3	O1004	C001	2024-01-08 00:00:00	300
4	O1005	C003	2024-01-09 00:00:00	80

customers - DataFrame

Index	CustomerID	CustomerName	Region
0	C001	Alice Smith	North
1	C002	Bob Jones	South
2	C003	Carol White	East
3	C004	David Brown	West

Figure 6.9: Orders and customers DataFrames

Let us look at different types of joins:

- **Inner join**: It keeps only the matching (common) rows from both datasets. For the given data sets, inner join will keep data for customers with ID C001, C002, and C003:

```
merged_inner = pd.merge(orders, customers,
                        on='CustomerID',
                        how='inner')
print(merged_inner)
# Only Orders where CustomerID exists in both tables
```

The output is:

```
  OrderID CustomerID  OrderDate  Amount CustomerName Region
0   O1001       C001 2024-01-05     120  Alice Smith  North
1   O1002       C002 2024-01-06     250    Bob Jones  South
2   O1004       C001 2024-01-08     300  Alice Smith  North
3   O1005       C003 2024-01-09      80  Carol White   East
```

- **Left join**: It keeps all rows from the first (left) dataset and adds matching data from the second, filling gaps with **NaNs** if no match exists. This might be useful to analyze sales with customers' data to see all orders, while adding customers' details, where available:

```
merged_left = pd.merge(orders, customers,
                       on='CustomerID',
                       how='left')
print(merged_left)   # all Orders, adding customer details if available
```

The output is:

```
  OrderID CustomerID  OrderDate  Amount CustomerName Region
0   O1001       C001 2024-01-05     120  Alice Smith  North
1   O1002       C002 2024-01-06     250    Bob Jones  South
2   O1003       C005 2024-01-07     175          NaN    NaN
3   O1004       C001 2024-01-08     300  Alice Smith  North
4   O1005       C003 2024-01-09      80  Carol White   East
```

- **Right join**: It is the opposite of left join, keeping all rows from the second (right) data and adding matching data from the first. It can help identify customers who have not placed any orders yet:

```
merged_right = pd.merge(orders, customers,
                        on='CustomerID',
                        how='right')
merged_right # all customers, adding order details if available
```

The output is:

```
Out[35]:
  OrderID CustomerID  OrderDate  Amount CustomerName Region
0   O1001       C001 2024-01-05   120.0  Alice Smith  North
1   O1004       C001 2024-01-08   300.0  Alice Smith  North
2   O1002       C002 2024-01-06   250.0    Bob Jones  South
3   O1005       C003 2024-01-09    80.0  Carol White   East
4     NaN       C004        NaT     NaN  David Brown   West
```

- **Outer (full) join**: It keeps all rows from both datasets, filling blanks where matches do not exist. This can be useful if you are auditing mismatches between lists:

```
merged_outer = pd.merge(orders, customers,
                        on='CustomerID',
                        how='outer')
merged_outer # Combining all orders and all customers
```

The output is:

```
Out[37]:
  OrderID CustomerID  OrderDate  Amount CustomerName Region
0   O1001       C001 2024-01-05   120.0  Alice Smith  North
1   O1004       C001 2024-01-08   300.0  Alice Smith  North
2   O1002       C002 2024-01-06   250.0    Bob Jones  South
3   O1005       C003 2024-01-09    80.0  Carol White   East
4     NaN       C004        NaT     NaN  David Brown   West
5   O1003       C005 2024-01-07   175.0          NaN    NaN
```

- **Cross join**: It combines every row from the first dataset with every row from the second, creating all possible pairs (used less often). So, if you want to pair every order with every customer, generating all possible combinations, you can use cross join.

```
pd.merge(orders, customers,  how='cross')
```

Although rare but might be useful for theoretical scenarios like mapping potential product recommendations for each customer.

Also, **`pd.merge()`** accepts column names if multiple columns serve as keys in the datasets.

Similarly, you can use **`df.merge()`**, a chaining style function[9], which makes it easier to chain multiple data sets, from left to right, such as **`df1.merge(df2).merge(df3)`**

[9] Difference between pd.merge() and dataframe.merge() https://stackoverflow.com/a/64101251/5114585

There are many other ways to combine data sets. You can refer to the pandas official guide (**https://pandas.pydata.org/docs/user_guide/merging.html**) for the same. In short, `df.join()` merges DataFrames based on their index, while `pd.merge()` joins them using specific columns, giving more flexibility for complex merges.

Conclusion

This chapter provided a strong foundation in using pandas to clean, filter, pivot, transform, and summarize datasets efficiently. For further depth, the official pandas documentation and tutorials (at **https://pandas.pydata.org/docs/getting_started/overview.html**) offer comprehensive insights.

In the next chapter, we will build on this knowledge by introducing additional libraries and tools that simplify and optimize data analysis and bring advanced insights to your datasets with minimal effort.

Try it yourself

To solidify your understanding, practice the concepts covered and attempt these exercises based on real-world business scenarios.

1. Create a DataFrame to store sales data, columns should be date, customer ID, date, region, products, quantity, sales, etc. Write this data to a CSV file and read it back to pandas. What did you notice about index, and how would you handle that? Try making customer ID as the index column.
2. Download any data set of your choice from **https://datasetsearch.research.google.com/**. Read it in pandas, apply methods learnt in this chapter to summaries, and explore the data. Compute key business KPIs that you understand (you can use aggregation, column statistics, or pivoting).
3. **Project**: Business insights from superstore data

   Imagine you are working as a Data Analyst for a global superstore. Your manager has asked you to analyze sales performance and customer behavior to help optimize strategy. Read the Superstore.csv using pandas. This data set is taken from Kaggle. Understand and analyze the data to answer the following questions:

   - **Part 1: Basic inspection**
     - Are there any missing values in the data?
     - What is the time range of the data (earliest and latest order dates)?
     - Convert Order Date and Ship Date columns to datetime format (if not already).

- **Part 2: Sales overview**
    - o What are the total sales and total profit in the dataset?
    - o Which region has the highest total sales? Which has the highest average profit per order?
    - o For each product category, what are the total sales and average discount?
- **Part 3: Customer insights**
    - o How many unique customers does the store have?
    - o Which three customers brought in the highest total sales?
    - o What is the **average order value** (**AOV**) per customer? (Hint: total sales divided by the number of orders).
- **Part 4: Product performance**
    - o Which sub-category of products has the highest total sales and the highest total profit?
    - o Identify the top three most profitable products overall.
    - o For each region, what is the best-selling sub-category?
- **Part 5: Shipping efficiency (advanced)**
    - o Calculate the average delivery time (days between Order Date and Ship Date).
    - o Which region has the fastest average shipping time?
- **Part 6: Data-driven recommendations**
    - o As you have computed various business KPIs already, based on your findings, list three actionable insights you would report to your manager.

Congratulations on successfully completing an **Exploratory Data Analysis** (**EDA**), a fundamental skill essential for every data analyst to master.

Concept check

1. You filtered rows of a DataFrame using both of the following methods on the same DataFrame:

```
df[df['region'] == 'East']
df.query("region == 'East'")
```

Will both approaches always return the same result? Under what situations could they behave differently? (Hint: Think about special characters, spaces, and column names)

2. For a given dataset, you need to compute the total and average transaction amount for each combination of region and approval status (True or False). Should you:

   a. Keep both region and approved as columns and use **`groupby()`**?

   b. Use a **`pivot_table()`** instead?

   Discuss the advantages and disadvantages of each option.

3. Imagine you manage a retail business and receive daily sales data from multiple branches. Each branch sends its Excel file, but:

   - Some files have missing columns, different formats, or inconsistent headers.
   - Some records do not match exactly due to spelling variations in customer names.
   - You need to merge all files and match customer details from another data set, which contains thousands of records.

   Brainstorm and answer the following questions:

   a. How would you typically combine these data sets in Excel (without Power Query)?

   b. If you use Power Query, how do you handle format inconsistencies and missing values?

   c. Can you easily join data based on multiple keys (e.g., Customer Name and Phone Number)?

   d. What happens when you get millions of rows? Does Excel struggle?

   e. How would Python's Pandas library solve these problems more efficiently?

Chapter 7
Smart Tools for Faster Analysis

Introduction

Once your data is clean, structured, and ready for analysis, the next step is to quickly uncover patterns, summaries, and relationships. This process is known as **Exploratory Data Analysis** (**EDA**). In this chapter, you will learn how to accelerate these familiar tasks using powerful Python tools that extend your pandas skills.

You will discover how numpy offers faster calculations, how Python libraries allow you to visualize the data, how automated profiling libraries generate instant summary reports, and how interactive interfaces simplify data exploration. These tools help you answer business questions faster and enable deeper insights with less effort.

We will start with creating static charts using pandas and interactive ones using plotly. We will also introduce numpy which is building block for many scientific and numerical python libraries followed by numpy-financial for common finance functions. We will then introduce many free tools for automated profiling of data and interactive GUI based analysis before discussing few key points to consider while working with large data files.

By the end of this chapter, you will have a set of efficient techniques to quickly deliver actionable insights and validate your data-driven decisions.

Structure

In this chapter, we will discuss the following topics:

- Data visualization
- NumPy essentials
- Computational finance with numpy-financial
- Automated profiling of datasets
- Interactive analysis with GUI tools
- Working with large data files

Data visualization

As an Excel user, you might have used charts to visualize your data. Python offers robust data visualization capabilities through libraries like **`matplotlib`**, **`seaborn`**, **`plotly`**, **`bokeh`**, etc. Additionally, **`pandas`** integrates well with these tools, allowing users to generate plots directly from data frames.

Quick pandas plotting

As you have worked with the **`pandas`** library, you can start using it to visualize your data. By default, it uses **`matplotlib`** to generate a wide range of charts. For producing **Kernel Density Estimate** (KDE) plots, **`pandas`** relies on the **`scipy`** library to perform the underlying statistical computations. If **`scipy`** is not installed, this specific plot would not work.

Let us import a sample for generating basic charts using pandas:

```
df = pd.read_csv('plotting_data.csv')
```

For simple charts such as a pie chart, bar or column chart, histogram, line chart, or scatterplot, etc. **`df.plot()`** can be used by specifying an appropriate value for the **`kind`** argument. For example, to visualize the sales distribution, let us create a histogram (Refer to *Figure 7.1*):

```
df['Sales'].plot(kind='hist', bins=30, title='Sales Distribution')
```

Depending upon your IDE settings, plot can show up directly inside the console, in a separate plot window, or sometimes not at all unless you explicitly call **`plt.show()`**. In spyder, you can set **`Tools | Preferences | IPython Console | Graphics | Backend`** and set it to **`Inline`**. That way, plots will appear right inside the console. Alternatively, you can add these lines in your code:

```
import matplotlib.pyplot as plt
# Code for your plot here
plt.show()
```

Here, **`plt.show()`** is used to display all currently active figure objects. Depending on the environment you are working in, it can be skipped. For example, Colab and Jupyter notebooks usually automatically show all figures created in a code cell.

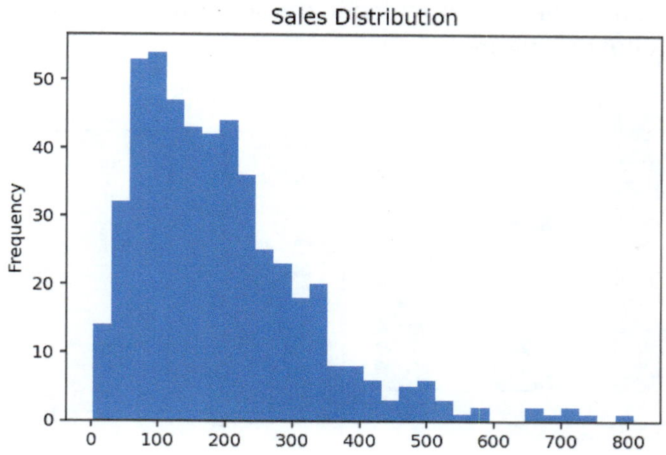

***Figure 7.1**: Histogram generated by pandas (matplotlib backend)*

For creating a scatterplot (shown in *Figure 7.2*), you need to supply two numeric variables and set the argument **kind = 'scatter'** as follows:

```
df.plot(kind = 'scatter', x = 'Sales', y = 'Profit',
        alpha = 0.5, title = 'Sales vs Profit', figsize = (7, 5))
```

Here, the argument **alpha** introduced transparency, and **figsize** sets the figure size (width, height) in inches. You can further customize a chart by tweaking a few parameters to tailor the output more precisely to your data and preferences.

***Figure 7.2**: Scatterplot generated by pandas*

The code for some common charts is provided in the accompanying code file, with illustrative sample charts in the following figure:

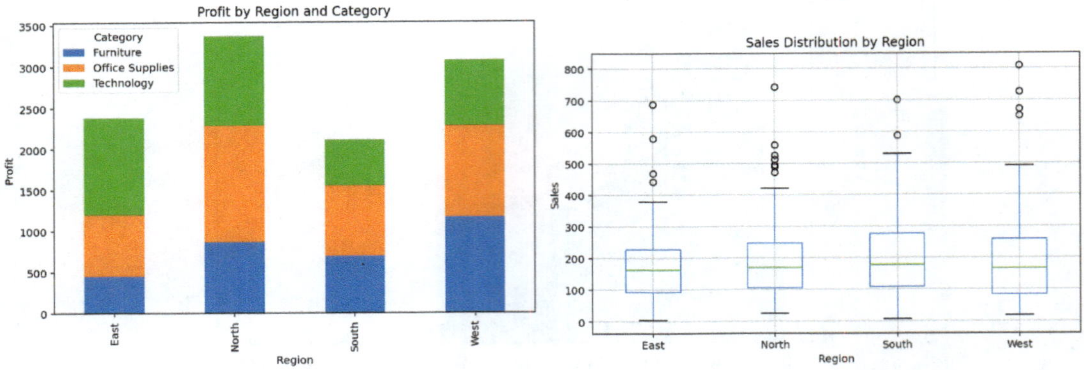

Figure 7.3: *Sample charts created in pandas*

Library **pandas** makes plotting easy by offering built-in functions where you can also customize things like color, layers, labels, grid, subplots, etc.

Running **pd.options.plotting.backend** shows the backend used for plotting, which is by default **matplotlib**. Additionally, you can produce interactive plots directly from a data frame in pandas by using the **plotly** backend, without even needing to import **plotly** explicitly. It enables you to zoom in, select or deselect any category, and view detailed information by pointing to specific data.

To activate this backend, you will need to have **plotly** installed, and then just need to set **pd.options.plotting.backend** to **'plotly'** and call **.plot()** to add interactivity to the **pandas** plot.

In Jupyter and Colab, these charts will display as usual (in notebook), while in Spyder or other IDEs, you might need to export them into an HTML file using **fig.write_html("myplot.html")**. You can open the same by double-clicking the file and it will display in your browser.

plotly also introduced changes in how figures are rendered, setting[1] renderers to **browser** will directly open interactive chart in browser.

```
import plotly.io as pio
pio.renderers.default = 'browser'
```

Using plotly explicitly

If you have created a chart with **plotly** backend, you must have realized that, unlike static plots from Excel or **matplotlib**, **plotly** charts are interactive ones. If you are interested in

[1] This setting works in environment like Spyder and Jupyter, but not in Colab. Because it runs in a hosted environment with restricted access to the local system's browser.

creating impactful charts with animation, faceting, fine-tuned styling, customization, or choosing advanced charts, you can learn about creating charts using **plotly** library explicitly. It is a JavaScript-based library that provides a high-level API **plotly.express** for beginners to quickly create impressive visuals.

Let us recreate the same scatterplot, which we had created with **pandas**, this time with **plotly.express**:

```
import plotly.express as px


px.scatter(df, x='Sales', y='Profit', title='Sales vs Profit', opacity = 0.5)
```

As discussed earlier, Colab or Jupyter shows this chart in output cell without explicitly setting **pio.renderers.default**.

In Spyder, as plotly charts do not automatically show up, either we can set the renderer to browser or we can save the figure as an HTML file named **scatterPlot.html**. This file can be opened manually from the file system or programmatically by running this code:

```
import webbrowser
webbrowser.open("scatterPlot.html")
```

Refer to the following figure to see the Sales vs. Profit distribution visualized by plotly:

***Figure 7.4**: Interactive scatterplot generated by plotly*

Creating a violin chart, that shows **Profit** across **Region** combined with **box=True** and **points='outliers'**:

```
fig = px.violin(df, x='Region', y='Profit',
                box=True, points='outliers',
                title='Profit Distribution by Region')
fig.write_html("Violinplot.html")
```

In the resultant figure, shown as follows, you get a power trio of quartile information, density and outlier points for spotting trends:

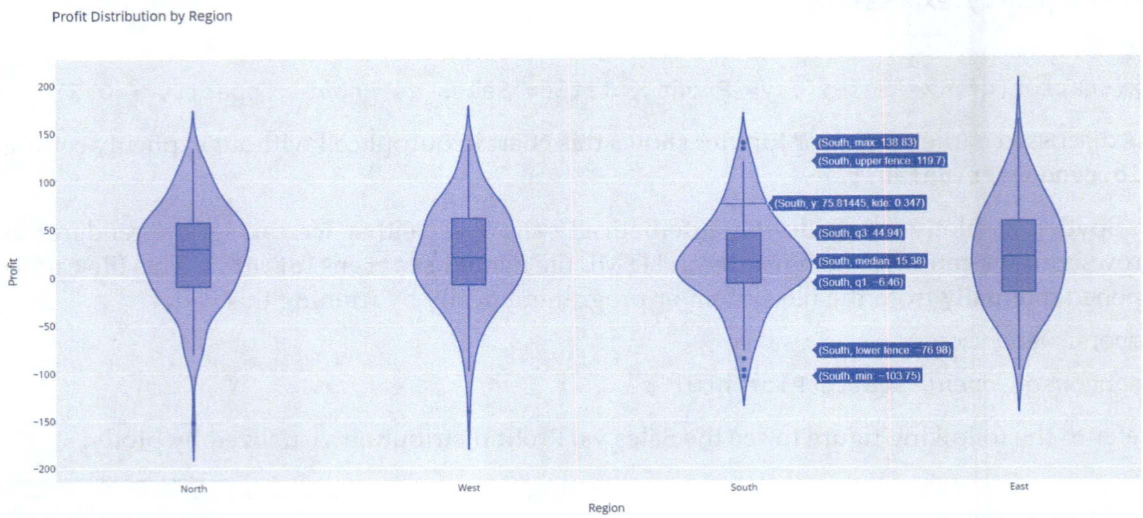

Figure 7.5: Violin chart along with box plot and outliers generated by plotly

To create an animated bar chart, we can use **animation_frame** argument in **px.bar()** after preparing data to summarize monthly sales by region:

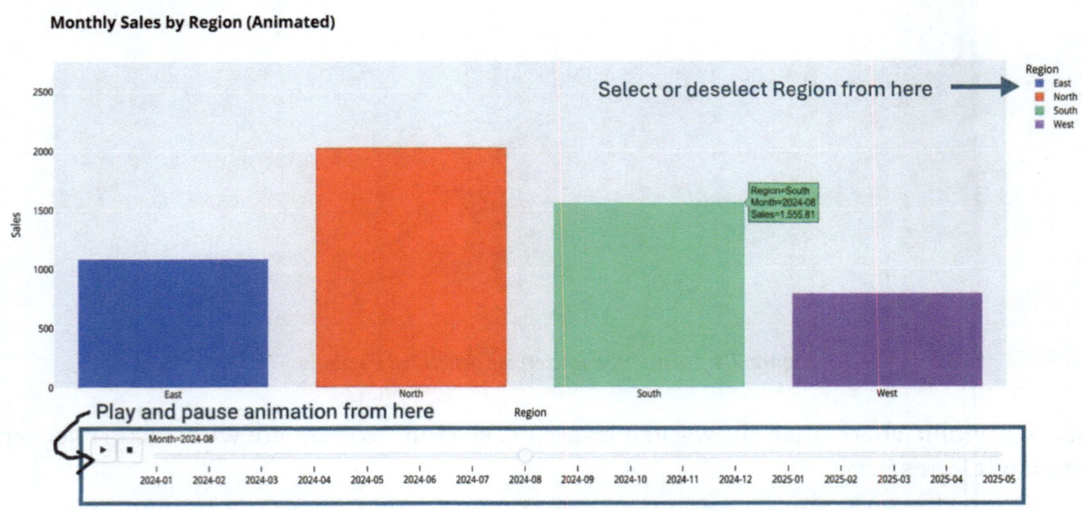

Figure 7.6: Animated barchart generated by plotly

This chart can be played or paused when viewed interactively. Other advanced charts supported by **plotly.express** are area charts, sunburst and treemap diagrams, funnel and funnel area charts, density heatmaps and contour plots, empirical cumulative distribution functions, strip plots, scatterplot matrices, parallel coordinates and categories, as well as icicle charts.

NumPy essentials

Having covered data visualization techniques using **pandas** and **plotly**, we now shift focus to **numpy**, which is the foundation of many libraries, including **pandas**, **matplotlib**, Excel automation tools like **openpyxl** and **xlwings**, etc. We have also used the **numpy** library to create sample datasets throughout this book.

While **pandas** has many built-in operations, **numpy** offers faster, more flexible functions when working with arrays of numbers. If you have worked with MATLAB, you will find **numpy** similar to it for numerical computing and matrix operations. MATLAB is a standalone tool for scientific and engineering workflows, while **numpy** is a Python library that serves as the building block for many advanced Python libraries. A clear understanding of **numpy** strengthens your ability to manipulate data efficiently, both in standalone analyses and when automating Excel tasks.

Once you are comfortable working with **pandas** DataFrames, it helps to understand the core building block underneath them, which is **numpy** array, also known as **ndarray**. Python's built-in data structures, list, tuple, set, and dictionary, are all designed for flexibility so they can store data of different types. In contrast, **numpy** arrays are homogeneous data structures, which means all elements of the array must be of the same datatype. Also, **numpy** array stores data in contiguous blocks of memory, which makes it memory efficient. Another reason **numpy** operations are faster is that they are implemented in optimized, compiled C code.

As an Excel user willing to learn Python, you can learn only the basics for now and dive deep into the library later, if needed.

NumPy arrays

NumPy arrays can be created by using Python sequences or using specific **numpy** functions. We will start by creating some simple arrays. One-dimensional or two-dimensional arrays can be created from a simple list or a nested list, as done here:

```
sales = np.array([1500, 2200, 1850, 2400.])
sales_qtr = np.array([[1500, 1700, 1600],
                      [2200, 2100, 2300]])


sales.dtype     # dtype('float64')
sales_qtr.dtype # dtype('int32')
```

Here, **sales** is a one-dimensional array that can be expressed as a row or a column of data, while **sales_qtr** is a two-dimensional array. Another point to note is that due to one floating-point data in the end, **sales** becomes **float64**[2] array while **sales_qrt** is an **int32** datatype because **numpy** arrays are homogeneous.

Unlike Python's built-in **int** and **float** types, **numpy** provides more specific datatypes, such as **int32**, **int64**, **float32**, and **float64**, allowing for precise control over memory usage and computational performance.

To create an array of ones or zeroes, you can use **np.ones** or **np.zeros**. For the creation of an identity matrix, **np.eye** is a helpful constructor. Many other useful constructors are there for generating pseudorandom numbers, a range of numbers, evenly spaced numbers, or normally distributed numbers in the form of a **numpy** array. Refer to the following:

```
np.zeros(5)                    # an array of 5 zeros
np.ones(3)                     # an array of 3 ones
np.eye(5)                      # 5×5 identity matrix

np.arange(5)                   # an array of numbers 0 to 4 (5 values like range(5))
np.arange(1, 6)                # 1 to 5 (inclusive start, exclusive end)
np.linspace(0, 1, 5)           # 5 evenly spaced values from 0 to 1

np.random.randn(1000)          # 1000 values from a std normal dist
np.random.normal(loc=70, scale=10, size=1000)# normal dist_mean=70, std=10

np.random.rand(5)              # 5 random floats in [0, 1)
np.random.randint(5)           # One random integer from 0 to 4

ids = ['a01', 'a02', 'a03', 'a04', 'a05'] # a list
np.random.choice(ids, size=3) # Randomly select 3 values from the list
```

We can use such functions for creating synthetic data, statistical modeling, and initializing parameters for machine learning models or optimization routines.

[2] In **numpy**, floating-point numbers (for example, **2400.** here) are automatically stored as **float64** by default, not **float32**. This default behavior prioritizes numerical precision, aligning with Python's native floating-point type (which is implemented as a C double). Users can manually specify a lower-precision type like **float32** to reduce memory usage when high precision is not required.

Vectorization

You have seen **pandas** vectorized operations for faster column calculations. It is largely because it builds on top of **numpy**, and internally, many **pandas** operations rely on **numpy** arrays. Let us revisit a simple operation on a **pandas** series:

```
s = pd.Series([1, 2, 3, 4])
s + 10                      # Vectorized addition in pandas
```

Here, **s** is wrapping a **numpy** array under the hood (**s.values** is a **numpy** array). When you add **10** to **s**, **pandas** calls the corresponding **numpy** operation behind the scenes:

```
type(s.values)              # <class 'numpy.ndarray'>
```

You can practice such operations with **numpy** arrays you have created:

```
price = np.array([5, 7.5, 7, 8])
revenue = sales*price
new_sales = np.array([1000, 2000, 3000, 4000])
total_sales = sales + new_sales
```

If you perform arithmetic operations on arrays of different shapes, **numpy** (whenever possible) broadcasts or extends the smaller array over the larger array so that they have compatible shapes:

```
unit_price = 5          # Zero dimensional array or scalar
revenue = sales * unit_price
revenue_qtr = sales_qtr * unit_price
```

You can also apply statistical or mathematical functions[3] as you do on **pandas** series or DataFrame:

```
sales_qtr.sum()             # Sum of all values
sales_qtr.sum(axis=1)       # Sum of each row

sales_qtr.mean()            # Mean of all values
sales_qtr.mean(axis=1)      # Mean of each row
sales_qtr.std()             # Standard deviation of all values

np.argmin(sales_qtr)        # Index of minimum value in array
np.argmax(sales_qtr)        # Index of maximum value in array

np.percentile(sales_qtr, 10)  # 10th percentile of values
np.cumsum(sales_qtr)        # Cumulative sum of values
```

[3] For common statistical functions, numpy offers both methods like arr.sum() and functions like np.sum(arr) that do the same thing. Methods are called on arrays; functions take arrays as input. Functions like np.sqrt() or np.percentile() do not have array methods.

You can also explore functions to reshape, flatten, or stack **numpy** arrays. Refer to the code file.

Computational finance with numpy-financial

Prior to **numpy 1.20** (reference: https://numpy.org/neps/nep-0032-remove-financial-functions.html), it used to offer useful financial functions such as **pmt()**, **npv()**, and **fv()**, etc. in **numpy**. These functions are now available separately as a **numpy-financial** package. It is a lightweight package that is safe to use even in constrained environments. These functions are especially useful for analyzing loan payments, cash flow, investment growth, etc.

This library provides you with Excel-like functions useful for those who work in the finance sector. Just like Excel, it is recommended to use positive values for inflows, and negative for outflows, and to convert annual interest rates to monthly if payments are monthly:

```
import numpy_financial as npf

# 1. Monthly Loan Payment (PMT) or Loan EMI
principal = 500000
monthly_rate = 0.10 / 12     # annual rate = 10%
n_months = 5 * 12            # 5 Years

emi = npf.pmt(rate=monthly_rate, nper=n_months, pv=-principal)
print(f"Monthly Payment: ₹{emi:,.2f}")          # Monthly Payment: ₹10,623.52

# 2. Future Value of Recurring Investment (FV)
monthly_investment = 5000
monthly_rate = 0.08 / 12
n_months = 10 * 12

future_value = npf.fv(rate=monthly_rate, nper=n_months,
                      pmt=-monthly_investment, pv=0)
print(f"Future Value: ₹{future_value:,.2f}")      # Future Value: ₹914,730.18


# Net Present Value (NPV)

# Initial investment = ₹1,00,000
# Returns over 5 years = ₹20k, ₹30k, ₹40k, ₹25k, ₹15k
cashflows = [-100000, 20000, 30000, 40000, 25000, 15000]
rate = 0.10
```

```
npv = npf.npv(rate, cashflows)
print(f"Net Present Value (NPV): ₹{npv:,.2f}") #
Net Present Value (NPV): ₹-583.05


# Present Value (PV)

future_value = 100000
rate = 0.08
n_years = 3

pv = npf.pv(rate=rate, nper=n_years, pmt=0, fv=-future_value)
print(f"Present Value: ₹{pv:,.2f}") # Present Value: ₹79,383.22


# Internal Rate of Return (IRR)

irr = npf.irr(cashflows)
print(f"Internal Rate of Return (IRR): {irr * 100:.2f}%")
# Internal Rate of Return (IRR): 9.77%
```

If you verify the calculations in Excel, you might sometimes notice a discrepancy in the value of IRR. This is because Excel uses a guess-based method and may return **#NUM!** error if it fails to converge. While Python's **npf.irr()** uses a different root-solving algorithm. It may find a root that differs from Excel's. You can always cross-validate with NPV plots or alternative tools, or if you want an aligned result, you can use the custom **scipy.optimize** code example to show IRR more robustly.

Automated profiling of datasets

As an Excel user, you might be spending considerable time exploring and handling data quality issues such as missing values and their position, duplicates in the data, unique values in some column, presence of too many zeros, interaction or correlation between different columns, etc., before you start getting meaningful insights or catching some unusual pattern.

For example, suppose a hospital noticed 20% of cholesterol data was missing. As a beginner analyst, you have done a quick fix by filling the data with the mean. Now, this can be misleading.

By filling in missing values with the mean cholesterol level, you might artificially inflate the cholesterol values of healthy patients. This is risky because doctors will now potentially recommend unnecessary treatments or tests to healthy patients, or the classification model, if used, will classify healthy individuals as high-risk patients.

Later, you decided to dig deeper into the root cause of the issue, after scanning carefully, you noticed that the real reason for the missing values in cholesterol data was something that you had earlier ignored. Patients who had normal vital signs were not tested for cholesterol during routine checkups.

This shows that understanding why data is missing is just as important as the values themselves. Good diagnosis takes patience but prevents bad decisions later.

Before working with any dataset, it is essential to explore and diagnose it carefully by using charts, statistical summaries, correlations, or pivot tables to check for missing values, duplicates, outliers, and unusual correlations.

Let us consider another example. In a logistics firm, duplicate shipment records led to inflated sales figures, causing overstock and financial loss.

Simply cleaning or summarizing data without understanding its structure and data quality issues can lead to serious business mistakes. This is why analysts spend a good amount of time exploring data before arriving at any conclusion.

Even for basic reporting, a detailed diagnosis can uncover hidden inconsistencies and anomalies. As datasets grow larger, manually scanning through rows and columns to understand inconsistent types, skewed distributions, patterns, missing values, or anomalies consumes more time and may not be enjoyable. Although **pandas** offers robust tools for data exploration, you still need to write code for each task.

Python offers a convenient solution through automated data profiling tools, which generate quick overviews, summary statistics, and visualizations of your data by running just one or two lines of code.

These tools are not a replacement for **pandas**, but for a preliminary diagnostic, especially on unfamiliar data, they offer a faster, deeper overview than what most Excel workflows can deliver. Let us discuss some of the popular tools.

Note: Some tools used in this chapter like `dtale` evolve very quickly, while some (like `sweetviz`) are not actively updated and often require specific versions of dependencies. Installing them inside your main book environment can sometimes cause version conflicts with other libraries. So, for this chapter, it is recommended to create a separate experimental environment to explore these tools, while maintaining a clean and stable environment for everyday analysis and automation tasks. Versions used in this book for this chapter are:

Python 3.9

sweetviz 2.3.1

numpy 1.23.5

ydata-profiling 4.16.0

dtale 3.19.1

pandasgui 0.2.15

sweetviz

One very simple and lightweight Python library for automatic **Exploratory Data Analysis (EDA)** is **`sweetviz`**, which quickly generates beautiful visualizations and outputs an HTML application. This library automatically infers datatypes and visualizes each variable and their interactions. Just with two lines of code, you get datatype, missing values, unique values, duplicate rows, and most frequent values, numerical analysis like sum, min, max, range, quartiles, mean, mode, standard deviation, median absolute deviation, coefficient of variation, kurtosis, and skewness for relevant columns. For example:

```
import sweetviz as sv
import pandas as pd

df = pd.read_csv("sales_data.csv")

# To generate the report
report = sv.analyze(df)

# To save and display the report
report.show_html("sales_sweetviz_report.html")
```

It saves an html file in your local machine and opens the same in browser. In Jupyter Notebook, **`report.show_notebook()`** will embed the report inside a Notebook. Here is a glimpse of a report generated for **`sales_data`** in *Figure 7.7*. You can also customize the layout, width, and height of the embedded view.

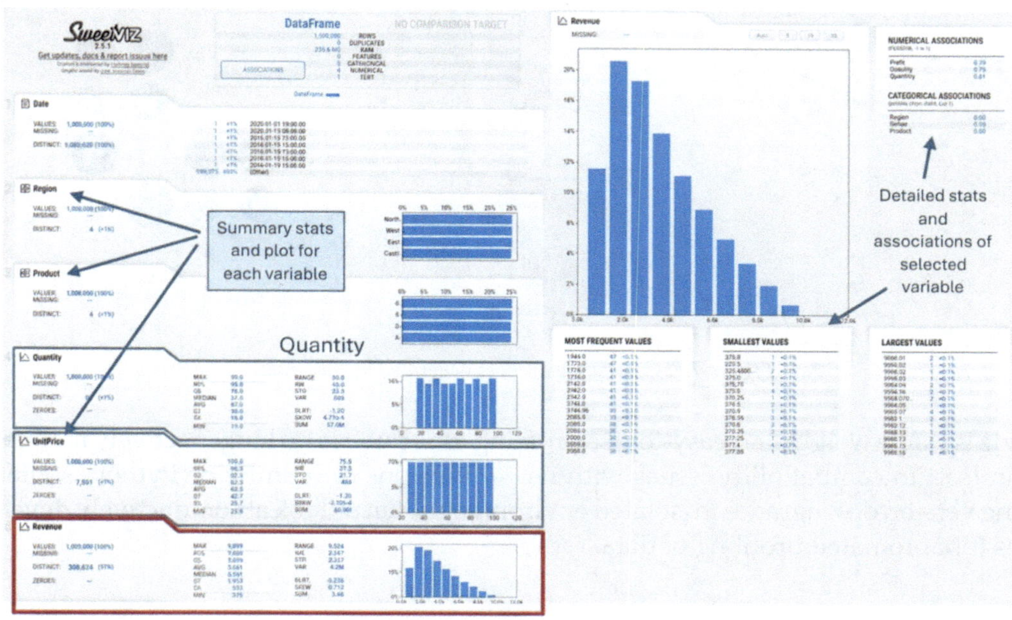

***Figure 7.7**: HTML report generated by sweetviz for sales data*

You can also compare two data sets by using **sv.compare()**. This feature can be extremely useful in comparing the dataset before and after cleaning, allowing you to assess how association, distributions, or data quality indicators change. Other practical use-cases include comparing performance across different geographies, such as sales in the east vs. west region, analyzing relative performance of products A and B to spot the differences in business matrices, or evaluating changes over time, such as January in comparison to February data. In data science or machine learning contexts, it can also be used to compare training and validation datasets to ensure they are representative of each other.

For demonstration purposes, we created a cleaned version of **sales_data** by removing all missing values and compared it with the original **sales_data**:

```
df_cleaned = df.dropna()

# Compare two data sets & generate report
comp_report = sv.compare([df, "Data"], [df_cleaned , "cleaned Data"])
comp_report.show_html("sales_sweetviz_compare_report.html")
```

A glimpse of the comparison report generated can be seen in *Figure 7.8*:

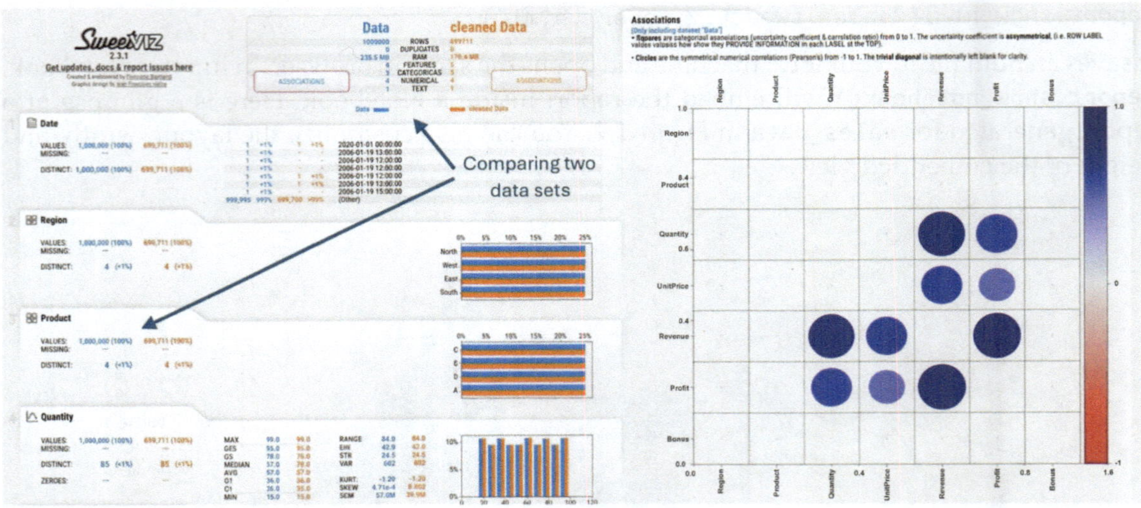

***Figure 7.8:** Comparison report generated by sweetviz*

Sweetviz is a lightweight and easy-to-use profiling tool, but it is no longer actively maintained. This can lead to compatibility issues with newer versions of NumPy or Python, sometimes requiring version downgrades in isolated environments. Let us look at some actively developed libraries for automated profiling of data.

ydata-profiling

This tool was formerly known as **`pandas-profiling`**. With the expansion of its capabilities to support Spark DataFrames, it was renamed to **`ydata-profiling`** to better reflect its broader scope and functionality. It can be used for generating an EDA summary in one line of code that can be exported in different formats such as html and json. In Jupyter or Colab, you can view the report directly within the output cell:

```
from ydata_profiling import ProfileReport

profile = ProfileReport(df, title="Dataset Profile")
profile.to_file("report.html")
```

You can open this **`html`** report from working directory. This profiling report is even more comprehensive and statistically rigorous than the one generated by **`sweetviz`**. Let us have a glimpse of the report for the same data in *Figure 7.9*:

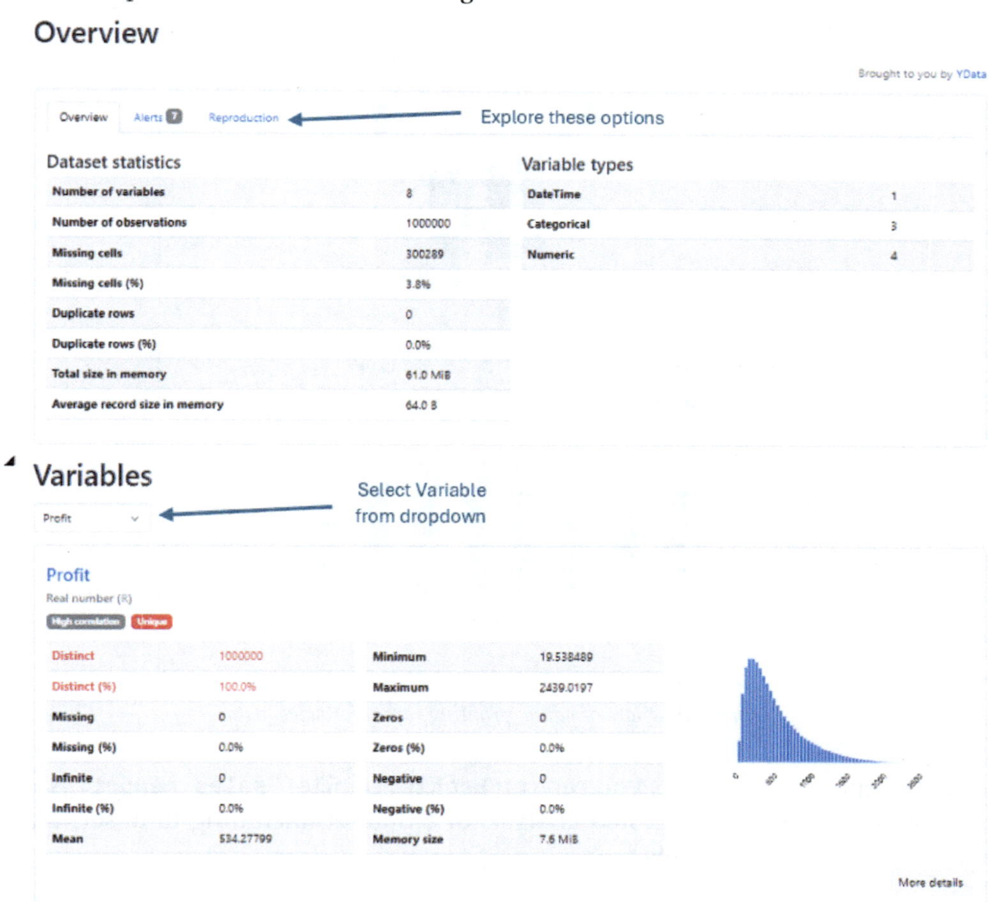

***Figure 7.9**: Part of ydata_profiling report for sales_data*

By clicking on the **Alerts** tab, you can see variables with missing values or high correlation with other variables. On top, you have a tab to browse to different sections of the report, such as interactions, correlations, missing values, or sample data, part of which is shown in *Figure 7.10*:

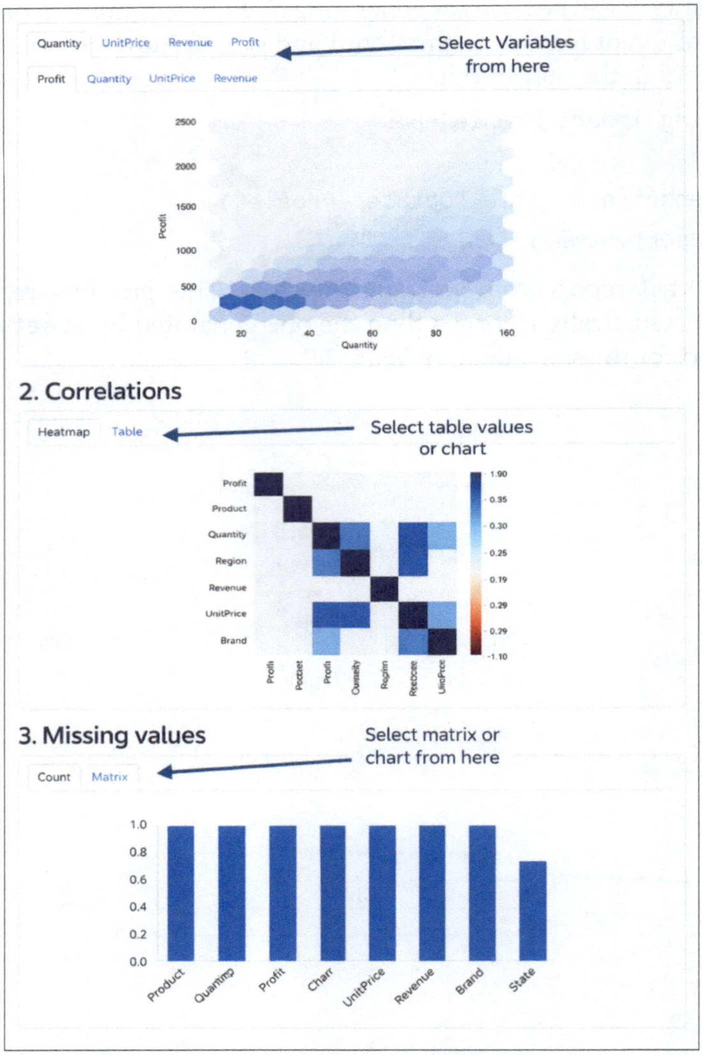

Figure 7.10: *More of ydata_profiling report for sales_data*

To generate the report as a json file, you can run **`profile.to_file("sales_report.json")`**. The package outputs a simple and digested analysis of a dataset, including time-series and text. You can also compare two data sets.

For very large datasets, **`ydata-profiling`** can be memory-intensive, so you can either use a reduced data set, shown as follows, for exploration or switch to **`Spark`**:

```
df_sample = df_full.sample(frac=0.1, random_state=42)

ProfileReport(df_sample).to_file("sample_report.html")
```

You can also create a minimal report or disable expensive computations. The package is actively evolving, and you can check official documentation for the latest features, usage examples, and updates at **https://docs.profiling.ydata.ai/latest/**.

Interactive analysis with GUI tools

Apart from automated profiling tools discussed so far, Python also provides several GUI-based tools for interactive analysis. These tools enable a user to analyze, visualize, and explore data in depth with just a few clicks without writing any code. Many of these tools also generate equivalent pandas code for the actions performed, offering a seamless transition between visual exploration and reproducible scripting.

As an Excel user, you will surely appreciate the intuitive interface and powerful features these tools offer. The following sub-sections highlight some of the most popular options.

dtale

`dtale` is an amazing Python library that allows you to play with and explore your data set using an interactive graphical interface. This library supports various file formats, including csv, xls, xlsx, tsv, and PARQUET. This library would allow you to quickly use editing, filters, pivot tables, slicers, charts, with deeper insights, ease of action, and better performance. **`dtale`** brings a full-featured interactive UI for your **`pandas`** DataFrame, right inside the browser. It feels familiar yet vastly more capable.

`dtale` was inspired by the data exploration capabilities of SAS and translated into Python's open-source world. Hence, it is especially effective for Excel and SAS users who are accustomed to point-and-click interfaces.

Running **`dtale.show(open_browser=True)`** in Spyder[4] will launch the GUI and let you choose your data interactively:

```
import dtale
dtale.show(open_browser=True)
```

[4] dtale works seamlessly in local IDEs like Spyder, and Jupyter but requires minor adjustments when used in Colab environment.

You can explore loading some sample data files in the interface, as shown in the following figure:

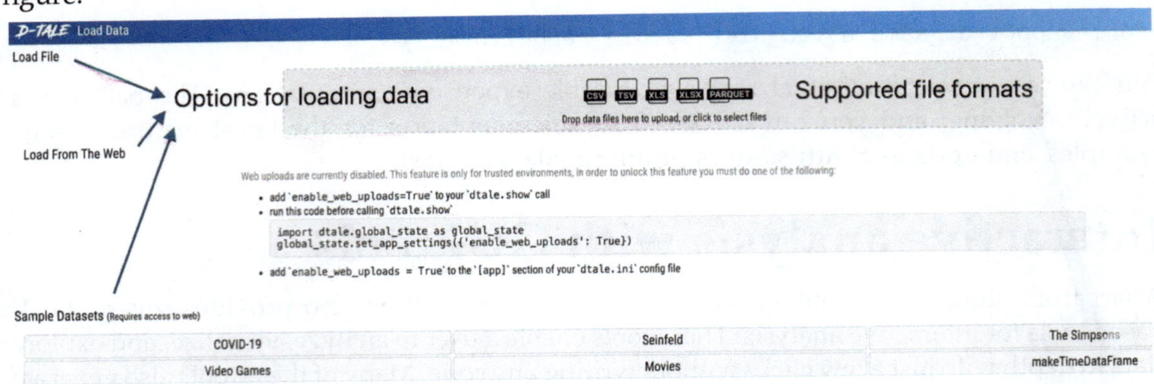

Figure 7.11: Loading sample data files

Alternatively, you can pass the data frame to **dtale.show()** function. It outputs a URL which you can paste in your browser:

```
df = pd.read_csv('sales_data.csv', nrows=1000)
dtale.show(df)
```

This opens a whole new world of possibilities to explore. Here are some game-changing features you can access in just a few clicks:

- **Filter, sort, and rename instantly**: You can click on any particular column and choose to sort, move, duplicate, or rename the column, get a summary, aggregation, format change, and advanced filter options from there.
- **One-click pivot tables**: Action tab at the top allows you to show or hide columns, custom filters, merge or stack DataFrames, feature analysis, and summarize data in the form of pivot tables, as shown in the *Figure 7.12*:

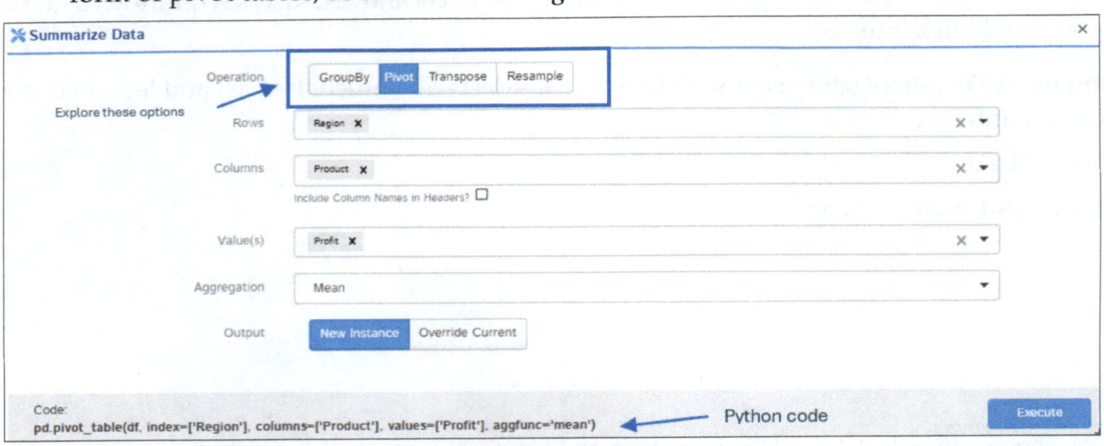

Figure 7.12: Interface for creating a pivot able

You can view the output as a table or as a **pandas** DataFrame. The table view is shown here:

	Region	A	B	C	D
0	East	572.65	507.15	591.57	542.15
1	North	434.97	504.90	450.14	459.14
2	South	505.55	560.89	538.89	567.21
3	West	587.59	547.21	560.92	559.15

***Figure 7.13:** Pivot table generated by dtale*

- **Visualizations built-in**: This tab offers to visualize missing values, analyze correlation, assess predictive power, and generate various types of charts such as line, bar, scatter, pie, histogram, worldcloud, heatmap, 3D scatter, surface, maps, candlestick, treemap, funnel, and pareto chart. The following figure shows a scatterplot between **`Quantity`** and **`Revenue`** grouped by **`Region`** and line fitted by the **`OLS`** method (you can change to **`lowess`** method):

***Figure 7.14:** Scatter plot generated by dtale*

There are many other options that allow you to highlight specific parts of data, edit data, perform string cleaning, handle missing values or duplicates, and even change the look and feel of the interface in the Settings tab with ease, as it requires no coding.

Note: `dtale` handles moderately large datasets well (up to one to two million rows). Beyond that, performance can drop. However, in such cases, you can load less data or consider filtering your data first.

You can also export pandas code for the tasks performed in the GUI. If needed, this code can be copied for running in your IDE. *Figure 7.15* is a screenshot captured after performing basic operations and generating pandas code for the same using the **Code Export** option:

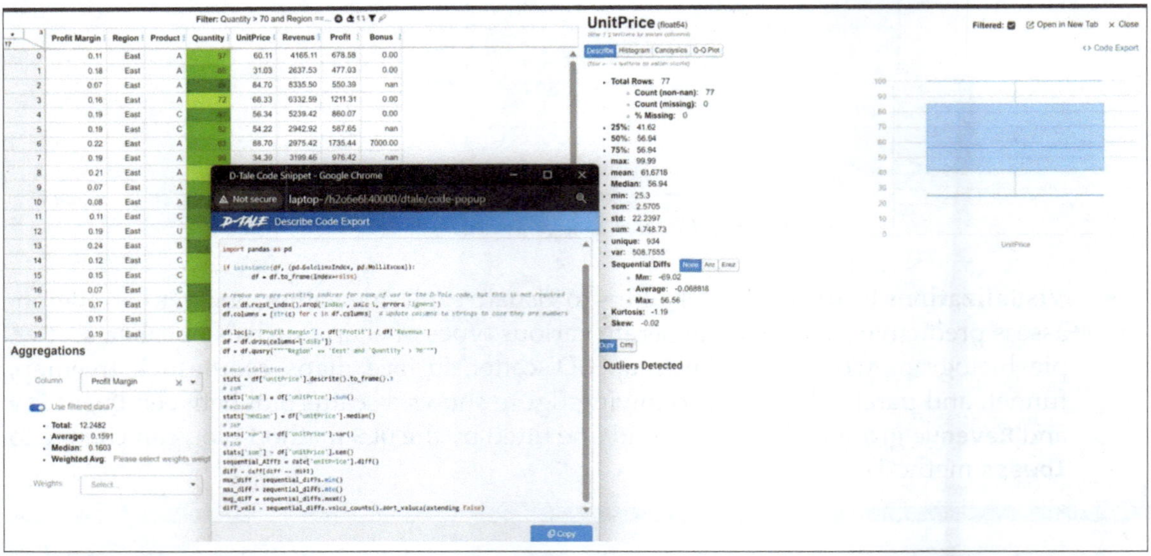

***Figure 7.15**: Python code generated by dtale for various actions performed*

d-tale, while actively developed, relies on a local web server and browser-based interaction, which limits its usability in Colab's cloud-hosted environment.

It internally uses a suite of powerful Python libraries like **dateutil**, **numpy**, **pandas**, **statsmodel**, **matplotlib**, **seaborn**, **plotly**, **scikit-learn**, **missingno**, **dash**, **flask**, and much more. It is like a Swiss Army knife for data exploration, offering an easy-to-use GUI powered by a rich ecosystem of Python libraries. It is not just a viewer, it is a full-fledged data exploration suite.

PandasGUI

PandasGUI is another tool that presents **pandas** DataFrames in a standalone, spreadsheet-like window, enabling users to view, filter, edit, and visualize data without writing code.

You can launch the GUI by running this code:

```
from pandasgui import show
show()
```

It opens a separate window, allowing you to import multiple datasets (if you need) through the import menu in the Edit tab as shown in the following figure:

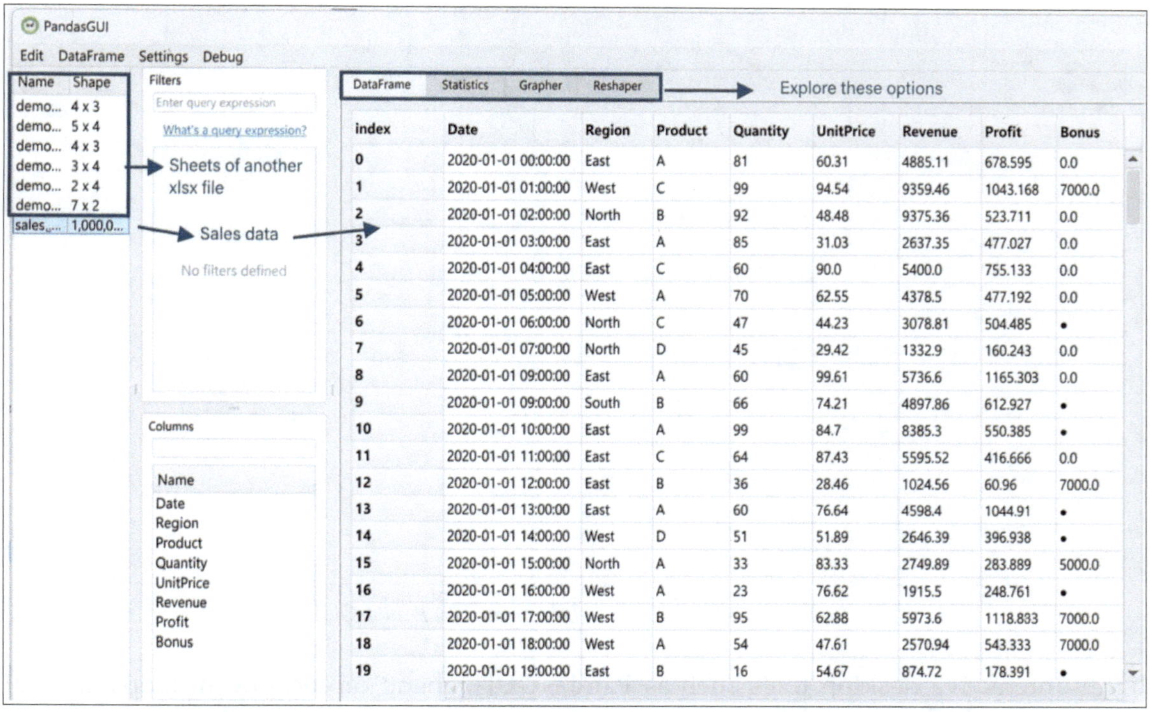

Figure 7.16: Viewing sales_data.csv from multiple DateFrames that are loaded

Alternatively, you can load any **pandas** DataFrame using **`show(df)`** or load one or more sample data set(s) using **`pandasgui.datasets`** module:

```
from pandasgui.datasets import pokemon, titanic
show(titanic)
show(pokemon, titanic)
If you want to load them all in one go, you can run this code:
from pandasgui.datasets import all_datasets
show(**all_datasets)
```

Alternatively, you can import those using the GUI by **`Debug | Browse Sample Datasets`**. If the folder appears empty, run from **`pandasgui.datasets import all_datasets`** once. It initializes and loads all the datasets into memory. Now, reopen the GUI or the **Browse Sample Datasets** menu, and the sample datasets should appear.

You can explore data editing, statistical summary, visualization, interactive filtering, etc. The following figure shows the violin chart backed by plotly created for a sample data set, named **`titanic`**:

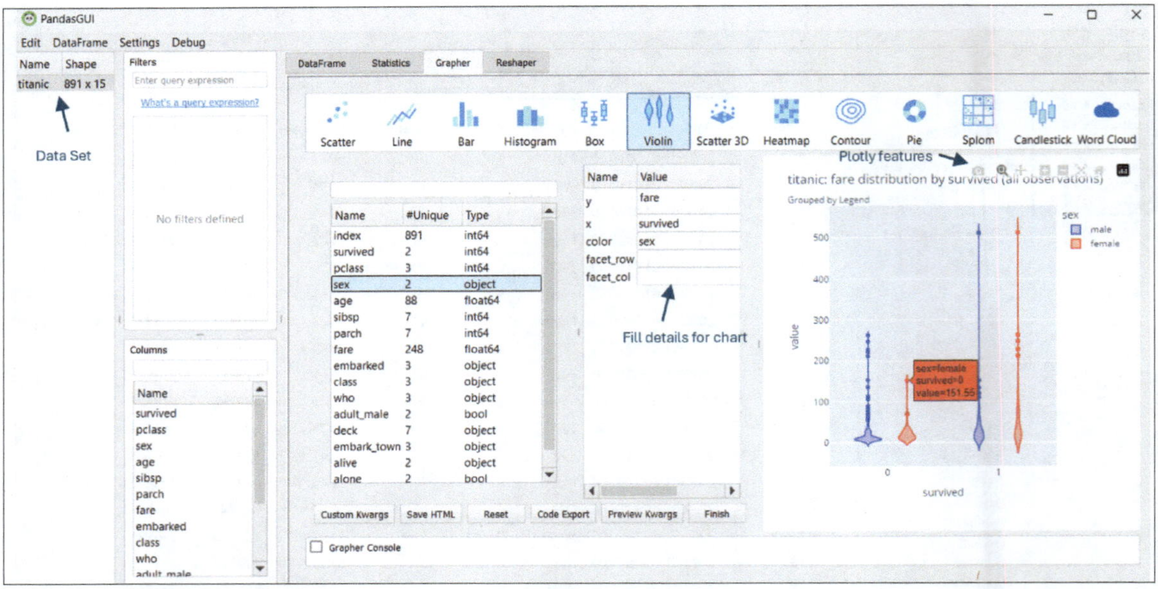

Figure 7.17: Plotly backed chart created by PandasGUI

Highly interactive desktop tools such as **PandasGUI** depend on local event loops, and UI frameworks, which are not fully supported in Colab. As a result, these tools are best used in local Python environments rather than browser-hosted notebooks.

Unlocking conversational AI with PandasAI

`PandasAI` is a promising open-source tool that brings the power of generative AI into your data analysis workflow with pandas. It allows users to ask questions in plain English and get answers, such as summaries, charts, or insights, directly from a DataFrame, much like querying an intelligent assistant built into your data. You can chat with your data with prompts like "**`Which region had the highest total revenue`**", or "**`Plot the bar chart for each region, using different colors`**".

It supports natural language prompts through integration with **large language models (LLMs)** such as OpenAI, Anthropic Claude, Google Gemini, Hugging Face, and more. For example, to use OpenAI's GPT, you only need an API key from **https://platform.openai.com/account/api-keys**.

> **Note: OpenAI's API usage is paid unless you are on a free trial, and charges depend on the model and usage volume.**

`PandasAI` offers two approaches: one through **`SmartDataframe`**, which wraps your DataFrame and lets you interact using **`.chat()`** for conversational exploration, and another through the **`PandasAI.run()`** method, which is more direct and suited for quick, one-off queries. You can also use **SmartDatalake** instead of a **SmartDataframe** for queries with multiple DataFrames and **Agent** to keep track of the state of the conversation and multi-turn conversations

For users familiar with Excel 365's Copilot or other AI-assisted tools, PandasAI offers similar capabilities to interact with data using natural language. While the tool is promising and steadily evolving, it is important to be aware of a few practical considerations. Installing PandasAI within a Conda environment may currently lead to version conflicts or interfere with existing packages, primarily due to dependency constraints. This is not uncommon with fast-developing Python packages that integrate with a range of external libraries and APIs.

For those interested in experimenting with PandasAI, it is advisable to install it in a clean virtual environment using **pip install pandasai**. As development continues and adoption grows, improved compatibility and Conda support can be expected.

Working with large data files

At this point, you have already seen how **numpy** and **pandas** offer a major step up from Excel formulas. It is time to talk about how to optimize performance, reduce memory usage, and work comfortably with large datasets.

While Excel 365 and Power Query allow handling larger files than before, performance can still suffer as file size grows, especially beyond a few hundred thousand rows. Python, using pandas, offers multiple smart ways to work with large files, discussed in the following subsections.

Load only required columns and rows

If you are not analyzing all columns or rows, you can load only specific columns or only a few rows using **usecols** or **nrows** argument of the reader function[5] while loading the data.

For benchmarking, try loading the **sales_data.csv** that has one million rows of sales data that we have created for practice. Then, load the selected columns and fewer rows to compare the time consumed in reading the data and memory usage:

```
# Loading full data
start = time.time()
df_full = pd.read_csv("sales_data.csv")
end = time.time()

print(f"⏱   Time taken: {end - start:.2f} sec») # ⏱   Time taken: 0.72 sec
df_full.info(memory_usage="deep")            # 224.6 MB
```

[5] Most pandas readers for common file types let you pick just the columns and rows. While a few formats have limits, for nearly all everyday tasks, you can load only what matters.

```
# Loading less data
start = time.time()
df_sel = pd.read_csv("sales_data.csv",
                    usecols=["Date", "Region", "Revenue"],
                    nrows=100_000)
end = time.time()

print(f"⏱    Time taken: {end - start:.2f} sec») # ⏱    Time taken: 0.08 sec
df_sel.info(memory_usage="deep")              # 13.9 MB
```

As you can see, the data which we needed was loaded 90% faster and memory usages dropped by almost 95%. For larger datasets, loading the part of data that is needed can drastically reduce memory footprints.

Use efficient datatypes

As discussed in *Chapter 6, Data Manipulation with Pandas,* you can convert a column with just a few unique values to a category column. Similarly, you can downcast numeric columns to their smallest suitable datatype, as **pandas** offers more fine-grained datatypes than base Python. For example, instead of int64 by default, int32 or int16 can be used as space-efficient integers based on their range. This is especially powerful when your data does not need large value ranges.

You can downcast columns using **pd.to_numeric()** or **astype()**. While **astype()** requires you to manually pick the datatype, **pd.to_numeric()** intelligently picks the smallest integer or float type that safely fits your data, making it a smarter option for memory savings. By using more efficient datatypes, you can store larger datasets in memory as shown:

```
df_full.memory_usage(deep=True).sum() # 224.6 MB

df_downcast = df_full.copy()

numeric_cols = ['Quantity', 'UnitPrice', 'Revenue', 'Profit']
df_downcast[numeric_cols] = df_downcast[numeric_cols].apply(pd.to_
numeric, downcast='float')

cat_cols = ['Region', 'Product']
df_downcast[cat_cols] = df_downcast[cat_cols].astype('category')

df_downcast['Date'] = pd.to_datetime(df_downcast['Date'], errors='coerce')

df_downcast.memory_usage(deep=True).sum() # 28.61 MB
```

Here, we have achieved over 87% memory savings after downcasting and conversion. This kind of performance tuning is a game changer when scaling up analysis.

Alternatively, you can use **pandas_downcast** library (**https://pypi.org/project/pandas-downcast/**) to automatically scan and find the minimum viable type for each column for downcasting.

Use chunking

When data is too big to fit into memory, you can read data in smaller chunks and process them in batches. As long as each chunk fits in memory, you can work with datasets that are much larger than memory.

Many key **pandas** readers, like **read_csv()**, **read_table()**, and **read_sql()**, allow you to read large files in memory-friendly batches using the **chunksize** argument. For other file types, **skiprows** and **nrows** arguments would do the job. When you set **chunksize** to some integer, the reader function returns an iterable that you can use in a for loop to get and process only a fragment of the dataset in each iteration. The processed chunks are then concatenated to the processed_data Dataframe.

Let us read **sales_data** in chunks and for each chunk, filter rows where **Revenue > 7000**, without even loading the full dataset into memory. Chunking helps by **processing one piece at a time**, keeping memory usage low, and avoiding full DataFrame loading. This is useful especially if the full file is massive. Refer to the following:

```
# Reading full data
start = time.time()

df_full = pd.read_csv("sales_data.csv")
df_full_filtered = df_full[df_full["Revenue"] > 7000]

end = time.time()
print(f"Total time taken_No chunking: {end - start:.2f} seconds") # 1.35 sec

# Chunked Reading
filtered_data = pd.DataFrame()

start = time.time()
# Reading in chunks and concatenating processed data
for chunk in pd.read_csv("sales_data.csv", chunksize=200_000):
    filtered = chunk[chunk["Revenue"] > 7000]
    filtered_data = pd.concat([filtered_data, filtered])
```

```
end = time.time()
print(f"Total time taken: {end - start:.2f} seconds") # 1.13 sec
```

On small datasets, like the one we have used, chunking might be slower and save little memory. Its real benefit appears with much larger files, when avoiding memory overflow is more important than speed. For example, if you are working with a 1.5 GB CSV file on an 8 GB RAM machine, you can read it in small chunks, say 100,000 rows at a time, the process will be slower, but memory usage will remain low and predictable. You should use chunked reading when you are dealing with huge files and stability is more important than speed. It ensures your system does not freeze, even if it takes a few extra seconds.

> Note: **Chunking is a suitable option for the operations with no or minimal coordination between chunks. For complicated workflows, Python offers other libraries.**

Using Sparse series

If a column has lots of missing values (**NaN**) or zeros, you can use **pandas**'s Sparse format for compressing data. It stores only non-zero or non-missing values, and keeps track of where they are, which reduces memory usage. If you have a column with 10,000 rows, but only 100 have values, Excel still stores the full 10,000. Pandas's Sparse format avoids that. For example:

```
print(df_full["Bonus"].memory_usage(deep=True)/(1024*1024)) # 7.63MB

df_full["Bonus_sparse"] =  (df_full["Bonus"]
                            .astype(pd.SparseDtype("float", fill_value=0.0)))

print(df_full["Bonus_sparse"].memory_usage(deep=True)/(1024*1024)) # 5.72 MB
```

Vectorization and memory clean-up

We would like to remind you about a basic yet important coding practice that can help in general with performance optimization. Using vectorized operations instead of loops, using **numpy** where possible, avoiding creation of temporary variables for chained operations, deleting the objects you no longer need are some habits you should develop early in your coding journey. The following code shows using **numpy** for column calculation:

```
# Slow way_ pandas operation
start = time.time()

def label_profit(val):
    return "High" if val > 500 else "Low"
```

```
df_full["ProfitLabel_map"] = df_full["Profit"].map(label_profit)

end = time.time()
print(f"Mapping a fuction time: {end - start:.2f} seconds») # 0.16

# Fast way _numpy operation
start = time.time()

df_full["ProfitLabel_vec"] = np.where(df_full["Profit"] > 500, "High", "Low")

end = time.time()
print(f"Vectorized time: {end - start:.2f} seconds») # 0.08
```

Although Python automatically manages memory using a built-in **garbage collector** (**GC**), it tracks and reclaims memory when objects are no longer needed. You can still perform a forced garbage collection using **`gc.collect()`** from the **`gc`** module when:

- You are working with large data sets.
- You are inside long-running scripts or notebooks handling multiple large datasets.
- You have explicitly deleted large objects using **`del`**.
- You see memory not being released (e.g. via **`memory_profiler`**, **`psutil`**, etc.).

It is like clearing cache in Excel after large queries.

Other libraries

For very large datasets such as 10M+ rows or multi-GB files (beyond memory limits), Python offers tools[6] like **`dask`** (an extension of **`pandas`**) that mimics **`pandas`** code.

The upcoming chapters will include further insights as we dive into specific reader and writer packages.

Conclusion

In this chapter, you have learned about a wide variety of Python tools that can speed up data exploration and report generation. Many of these tools are evolving, so you can always check official documentation and tutorials when you plan to use them.

We have demonstrated all these tools using Spyder and Jupyter as our development environments. If you are working in Google Colab, some tools may require additional

[6] There are many other tools for working with large data sets in pandas eco-system such as polars, modin, or pyspark, etc.

installations[7], or specific configuration or may simply not work due to dependence on local setup.

Be sure to refer to each library's official documentation for environment-specific instructions, installation commands, or usage tips.

In the upcoming chapters, you will learn about Excel-specific reader and writer packages in detail.

Try it yourself

The following practice exercises will help you reinforce the learning from this chapter:

1. Write code to create synthetic dataset of 2000 rows that contains columns such as [Region, Product Category, Sales, Profit, Date] and perform the following tasks:
   - Create a side-by-side bar chart comparing total Sales and Profit for each product category using Plotly Express.
   - Create a scatter plot between Sales and Profit using pandas with default backend.
   - Create a density plot of Sales using pandas.
   - Create automated profiling of this data using tool(s) of your choice.
2. A user wants to retire in 25 years with a target of ₹2 crore. Use numpy-financial to calculate:
   - The required monthly investment, assuming an 8% annual return, compounded monthly.
   - Simulate the same for 6%, 8%, and 10% returns.
   - Create a simple line plot to show how monthly contribution changes with return rate.

Concept check

1. You are analyzing regional sales performance across multiple product categories using a large dataset.
   - How would you visually compare sales and profit distributions across product categories and regions?

[7] Google Colab comes preinstalled with many commonly used Python libraries. However, tools not included by default must be manually installed using !pip install packagename (with an exclamation mark) and Colab resets installed packages each time a session ends, so you need to reinstall them when reopening your notebook.

- Can you suggest an approach to detect underperforming regions immediately?
- What kind of charts could help management quickly understand trends and outliers?

2. You have received a raw CSV file with 100,000+ rows from the sales team.
    - How would you quickly get an overview of missing values, datatypes, unique values, and top correlations?
    - What tool can help visualize this insight instantly without writing multiple summary formulas?
    - How would this differ from creating pivot tables or charts manually in Excel?
3. You are analyzing a web log file with five million rows to find peak traffic hours and detect anomalies.
    - What limitations would you face using Excel?
    - How would you filter and aggregate data efficiently across millions of records?
    - How would memory management differ when loading this data in Python vs. Excel?

Chapter 8
Unlocking Excel with openpyxl

Introduction

You have gained proficiency with the powerful libraries like pandas and others for exploring, analyzing, and exporting data to various file formats. Now, it is time to learn how to format and style Excel files directly in Python, without requiring Microsoft Excel to be installed.

Most businesses expect reports to be delivered by Excel. After analyzing data using Python, you need to export results (summary, pivot tables and charts) exporting results to Excel for business users. In this chapter, we will discuss practical ways to automate, scale, and enhance Excel-heavy processes using openpyxl.

This chapter begins by discussing the limitations of pandas for Excel file handling, followed by learning openpyxl library for loading or creating Excel files and sheets, populating data, computing, formatting cells, and writing it back to Excel. Everything can be done programmatically without needing Excel installed on your machine. We will also cover multiple use cases for your automation needs.

By the end of this chapter, you will be equipped with skills to automate Excel tasks with confidence and demonstrate efficiency in your work and impress your boss, if any.

Structure

In this chapter, we will discuss the following topics:

- Moving past pandas for Excel work
- Getting started with openpyxl
- Creating and managing workbooks
- Reading data from Excel
- Writing data to Excel
- Advanced sheet operations
- Data validation and conditional formatting
- Creating charts and exporting images

- Working with tables and dynamic named ranges
- Multi-workbook automation use cases
- Excel templates
- Best practices and limitations

Moving past pandas for Excel work

pandas and other libraries work as powerful tools for data analysis workflows to read, write, manipulate, summarize, and plot data with ease. You might not have noticed that while performing Excel I/O operations, **pandas** relies on backend engines like **openpyxl**, **xlsxwriter**, or xlrd. These are separate reader and writer packages in Python.

Python's **openpyxl** library provides fine-grained control over Excel files, allowing us to read, write, format cells, apply styles, manage charts, define formulas, named ranges, and automate workbook-level operations. It is particularly well-suited for generating professional reports, automating repetitive tasks, and customizing workbooks in ways that **pandas** alone cannot. While **pandas** is excellent for data processing and quick exports, **openpyxl** complements it by enabling rich formatting, interactivity, and report generation features essential for Excel professionals. Used together, **pandas** and **openpyxl** offer a powerful combination for end-to-end Excel-based automation to cover both analytical and presentation needs effectively.

Getting started with openpyxl

openpyxl was initially based on and inspired by PHPExcel. It is a powerful Python library to read and write Excel files of various formats, such as xlsx, xlsm, xltx, and xltm files. Actually, it does much more than that. It enables you to create and format sheets, modify values, formulae, styles, insert charts and images, apply custom formatting, and much more, even if you do not have Excel installed on your machine. Such programmatic control allows users to boost productivity by automating repetitive tasks such as generating reports, auditing spreadsheets, building Excel templates, and version control, etc.

Even if you are familiar with **Visual Basic for Applications** (**VBA**), Power Query, or Power Pivot, **openpyxl** offers a smarter choice for automation because it provides greater flexibility, seamless integration with Python's vast ecosystem, and cross-platform support, all while allowing you to handle Excel files without being tied to Excel itself. It is an open-source solution that can streamline complex workflows and provide more powerful customization than Excel's built-in tools.

Before diving into **openpyxl**, it is essential to understand its key terms. These correspond to familiar Excel concepts but are handled programmatically in Python. As an Excel user, you are familiar with the hierarchy of workbooks, worksheets, and individual cells, and **openpyxl** uses the same names. It refers to the currently selected worksheet in a workbook as the active sheet and a group of cells (e.g., A1:D10) that can be manipulated as a single unit as the range. Rows and columns become iterable Python sequences.

Creating and managing workbooks

Let us create an Excel workbook, add some data to it, and save it programmatically:

```
from openpyxl import Workbook
wb = Workbook() # Creating a new Excel Workbook
ws = wb.active  # Accessing active sheet (first sheet here*)
ws.title = 'products' # Giving this sheet a title

ws['A1'] = 'product_id' # Assigning some values to cells
ws['B1'] = 'product_name'
ws['C1'] = 'product_category'
ws['D1'] = 'product_price'
wb.save('business_data.xlsx') # saving as xlsx file
```

This simple code allowed us to create a new Excel file, shown in *Figure 8.1*. Select the active sheet, which means the first sheet here, name it as **'products'**, and write some data to cells A1 up to D1 without even opening the Excel application.

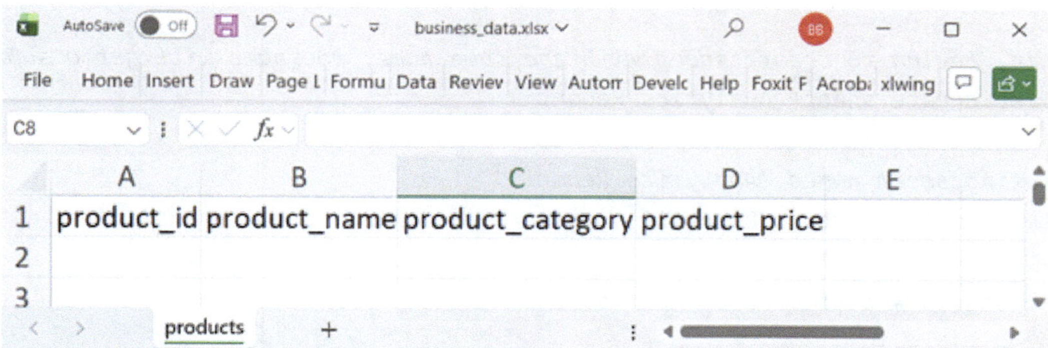

***Figure 8.1:** Excel workbook created by openpyxl*

To access a cell in a worksheet, you can use either A1-style notation, like **`ws['A1']`**, or the index-based approach with the **`.cell()`** method, for example, **`ws.cell(row=1, column=1)`** retrieves cell **`A1`**. Both methods let you read from or write to specific cells, depending on your needs.

Note: When you work with Excel files using `openpyxl`, all changes happen in your computer's memory. To see those changes in Excel, you must save the file using `wb.save()` first. Only then are the updates written to the actual file. This lets you make lots of edits before saving the final version.

Let us make more edits to this file. When we modify a file and save it using the same name and location, it replaces or overwrites the existing version, permanently updating its contents.

After reasonable edits, save the file, open it from the location and check for the updates.

```
wb.create_sheet(title="customers") # Create a second sheet by title
ws2 = wb['customers'] # Accessing the sheet by it's name
ws2['A1'] = 'customer_id' # Adding data
ws2['B1'] = 'region'

wb.create_sheet('delivery') # Creating next sheet
ws3 = wb.worksheets[2] # Accessing 3rd sheet by it's index (in-
dex starts from 0)
ws3.cell(1, 1, 'order_id') # Value assignment to cells at location (row, col)
ws3.cell(1, 2, 'order_date')
ws3.cell(1, 3, 'proposed_delivery_date')
ws3.cell(1, 4, 'actual_delivery_date')

ws4 = wb.create_sheet('Analytics_Report') # Creating another sheet
ws4.sheet_properties.tabColor = '1072BA' # setting the tab color of this sheet

# Again, trying to create sheet with the same name, the name will get a suffix 1
ws5 = wb.create_sheet('Analytics_Report')

# Deleting sheet named 'Analytics_Report1'
wb.remove(wb['Analytics_Report1'])

wb.worksheets # List of all sheet's names

# Insert a sheet named 'marketing' at index 3, i.e., 4th sheet
wb.create_sheet('marketing', 3)

# Move the sheet 'products' to the last position
wb.move_sheet(wb['products'], offset=len(wb.worksheets) - 1)
wb.save('business_data.xlsx')
```

The output Excel file is shown in *Figure 8.2*. As you can see, you can create or insert sheets using **`wb.create_sheet()`**, remove any sheet using **`wb.remove()`**, move or copy a sheet using **`wb.move_worksheet()`** or **`wb.copy_worksheet()`**. Similarly, **`ws.insert_rows()`** inserts rows at a given position, and **`ws.insert_cols()`** does the same for a column.

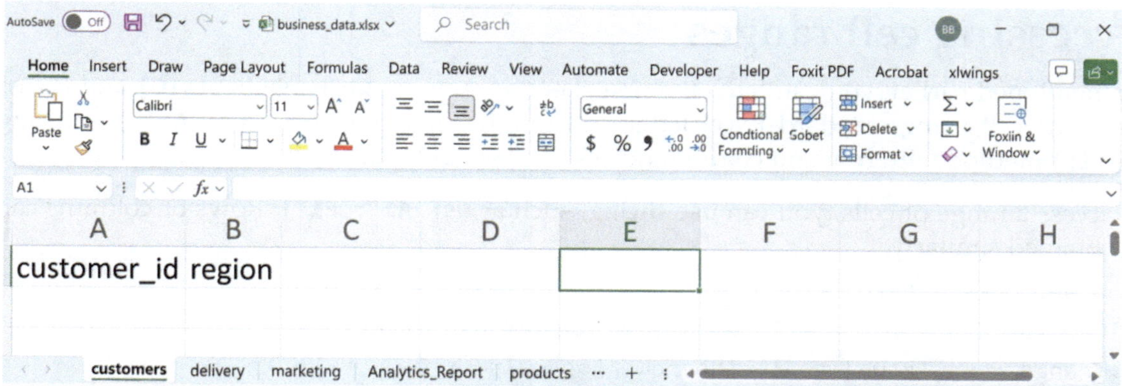

Figure 8.2: Excel workbook with multiple sheets created by openpyxl

Reading data from Excel

Let us import **mydata.xlsx** and print the names of all the sheets:

```
from openpyxl import load_workbook
file = "mydata.xlsx"

wb = load_workbook(file)
wb.sheetnames # All sheets names
```

If you need to read or extract data from massive Excel files without delays, to run fast and lightweight data analysis or reporting scripts without worrying about formatting, charts, and formulas, you can load the workbook in read-only mode:

```
wb = load_workbook(file, read_only=True)
# Do some stuff
wb.close()
```

File opened in **read_only** mode must be explicitly closed with the **close()** method. If your file contains Excel formulas, using **data_only=False** shows the actual formula, if any, for example, **=SUM(B2:B10)** as a string, while using **data_only=True** gets us the calculated values.

Note: When you create a new workbook with `openpyxl`, it automatically includes one sheet by default, called the active sheet. However, when loading an existing file with load_workbook(), active sheet refers to the sheet that was last selected in Excel, not necessarily the first one. You can fetch active sheet by running `wb.active`

However, to ensure code stability and avoid potential errors, it is recommended to access worksheets explicitly by name or index such as `wb['SheetName']` or `wb.worksheets[index]` rather than relying on active sheet. Also, be aware that sheets are zero-indexed, for example, the first sheet is at index 0.

Accessing cell ranges

As mentioned earlier, you can fetch the first sheet by running **`wb.worksheets[0]`** and access a specific cell using standard Excel letter and number notation (e.g., **`ws['A1']`**) or using **`.cell()`** method with row and column indices (e.g., **`ws.cell(1, 1)`** for cell **A1**).

To access a range of cells, you can use slicing, such as **`ws['A1':'E1']`**. Rows or columns can be obtained similarly:

```
ws = wb.worksheets[0]
colC = ws['C']          # Columns are indexed by letters
col_range = ws['B:D'] # All the rows for columns B up till D

row5 = ws[5]          # Rows are indexed by numbers
row_range = ws[5:10]  # All the columns for rows 5 to 10
```

To get row or column boundaries, **`ws.max_row`** and **`ws.max_column`** can be used.

Warning about indexing nuance in `openpyxl`: In `openpyxl`, indexing behaves differently depending on what you are accessing:

- **Rows are indexed by numbers, columns by letters. Hence, `ws[5]` returns a row, not a column, and `ws['C']` returns column C. To fetch a column by its header, you need a workaround.**
- **Worksheet cells use Excel-style 1-based indexing, such as `ws[1]` returns row 1.**
- **Workbook sheets follow Python-style 0-based indexing because wb.worksheets is a (Python's) list of all worksheets in your workbook. So, `wb.worksheets[0]` returns the first sheet, and `wb.worksheets[1]` returns the second.**
- **Iterators like `iter_rows()` and `iter_cols()` return generators that yield tuples of cells. You can access individual cells within these tuples using 0-based indexing.**

Reading structured data

To read the content of a cell **`.value()`** can be applied on a cell, and to get a generator that gives all sheet values row by row, **`ws.values()`** can be used. Let us see this in action.

```
ws['A1'].value # Accessing Data from a single cell

ws_data = ws.values # generator object containing worksheet values

# Preview data by printing each row
for row in ws_data:
    print(row)  # Each row is a tuple of cell values, 1st row has column names
```

You can also use **next()** to extract subsequent values from a generator object, each call resumes the generator's execution and retrieves the next yielded value. If the generator finishes its sequence and is exhausted, **next()** raises a **StopIteration** exception.

```
ws_data = ws.values # Reset the generator
next(ws_data)  # Extract one row at a time
```

If needed, you can save this data in a **pandas** DataFrame (do not forget to reset the generator):

```
data = pd.DataFrame(ws_data, columns = next(ws_data))
```

If you want to read values only from a single column or row, you can iterate through that data as fetching a single row or column results in a tuple:

```
for cell in ws['C']:      # print coordinates and values from Column C
    print(cell.coordinate, cell.value)

for cell in ws[5]:        # print coordinates and values from Row 5
    print(cell.coordinate, cell.value)

# Alternately using list comprehension
[(cell.coordinate, cell.value) for cell in ws[5]]  # Row 5
```

However, while reading data from a range such as **'A1:E1'**, you need to index into the returned tuple correctly, since slices such as **ws['A1':'E1']** return a 2D tuple even for a single row:

```
for cell in ws['A1':'E1'][0]:
    print(cell.value)

for row in ws['B2:D4']:  # 2D tuple of cells
    for cell in row:
        print(cell.coordinate, "=", cell.value)
```

It is better to use **ws.iter_rows()** or **ws.iter_cols()** to avoid the extra indexing required with slicing syntax. Additionally, reading data from dynamic ranges becomes convenient with these functions. Fetching data of all rows except headers from columns **'B:D'**:

```
for row in ws.iter_rows(min_row=2, max_row=max_row,
                        min_col=2, max_col=4,
                        values_only=True):
    print(row)
```

Here, **values_only=True** returns the cell's raw values, while **values_only=False** (default), the method yields Cell objects. To print the same values column-wise:

```
for col in ws.iter_cols(min_row=2, max_row= max_row,
                        min_col=2, max_col=4,
```

```
                                        values_only=True):
    print(col)
```

Writing data to Excel

We will discuss smart ways to add data to this sheet instead of manually writing a value in each cell. Basically, we can use data structures like lists, dictionaries, and even Pandas DataFrames to efficiently populate data to an Excel sheet via **openpyxl**.

Earlier, we had created an Excel file with a sheet named **'products'** that has column headers assigned to cells in the first row. Let us do the same by writing these headers from a Python list and save this file as **products_data.xlsx**:

```
from openpyxl import Workbook
wb = Workbook()
ws = wb.active
ws.title = 'products'

headers = ['product_id', 'product_name', 'product_category', 'product_price']
# Header list
ws.append(headers)
wb.save('products_data.xlsx')
```

Alternatively, we can iterate through the header list and assign those to the cells dynamically:

```
# Populate headers dynamically
for col_num, header in enumerate(headers, start=1):
    cell = ws.cell(row=1, column=col_num)
    cell.value = header
```

This approach gives us more flexibility to apply formatting styles (that we will discuss in the next section, *Advanced sheet operations, Formatting and Styles*), and it also works well when we want to put headers in specific cells, not necessarily the first row.

Writing data from a list of lists

Now that headers are in place, we can add more data from a nested list using **ws.append()** with minimal code:

```
data = [
    [101, 'Wireless Mouse', 'Electronics', 25.99],
    [102, 'Yoga Mat', 'Fitness', 15.50],
    [103, 'Notebook', 'Stationery', 3.99]
]
```

```
for row in data:
    ws.append(row)
```

Append method always appends at the **end of the current data** (the next empty row) starting from column A onward.

Either we can save the file again and launch it to verify the changes, or we can write a function that prints all of the spreadsheet values by just calling it:

```
def print_rows():
    for row in ws.iter_rows(values_only=True):
        print(row)
```

Calling this function **`print_rows()`** shows us the data created so far:

```
('product_id', 'product_name', 'product_category', 'product_price')
(101, 'Wireless Mouse', 'Electronics', 25.99)
(102, 'Yoga Mat', 'Fitness', 15.5)
(103, 'Notebook', 'Stationery', 3.99)
```

If you need more control and flexibility, you can access cells and then write the value as we have done in the following code. This is useful especially when you need to customize formatting, styling, data validation, or track exact cell positions. Let us add more rows by accessing the cells:

```
data = [
    [104, 'Pen', 'Stationery', 10],
    [105, 'USB Cable', 'Electronics', 150]
]

for r_idx, row in enumerate(data, start= ws.max_row + 1):
    for c_idx, val in enumerate(row, start=1):
        ws.cell(row=r_idx, column=c_idx, value=val)
```

Running **`print_rows()`** verifies that the data is added:

```
('product_id', 'product_name', 'product_category', 'product_price')
(101, 'Wireless Mouse', 'Electronics', 25.99)
(102, 'Yoga Mat', 'Fitness', 15.5)
(103, 'Notebook', 'Stationery', 3.99)
(104, 'Pen', 'Stationery', 10)
(105, 'USB Cable', 'Electronics', 150)
```

You can also write data using **`iter_rows()`** or **`iter_cols()`** by leveraging it with **`zip()`**.

Writing data from a list of dictionaries

Sometimes, you get data from JSON or API responses in the form of a dictionary. You can append the same by iterating through dictionary items as done in the following code:

```
products = [
    {'id': 106, 'name': 'Chair', 'category': 'Furniture', 'price': 45.50},
    {'id': 107, 'name': 'Water Bottle', 'category': 'Fitness', 'price': 10.00}
]

for product in products:
    ws.append([
        product['id'],
        product['name'],
        product['category'],
        product['price']
    ])
```

You can run **print_rows()** again to read the rows from the data.

Writing data to a column

You can even write data in a column by looping over a list:

```
ws['E1'] = 'Units Sold'
quantity = [5, 8, 15, 30, 6, 10, 20]

for i, status in enumerate(quantity , start=2):
    ws[f'E{i}'] = status
```

So far, we have added enough data to work with Excel formulas. Now, let us see the Excel file generated after saving it in **openpyxl**:

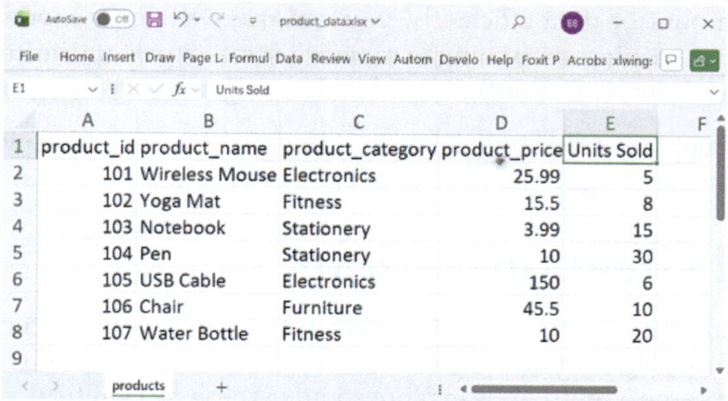

	A	B	C	D	E
1	product_id	product_name	product_category	product_price	Units Sold
2	101	Wireless Mouse	Electronics	25.99	5
3	102	Yoga Mat	Fitness	15.5	8
4	103	Notebook	Stationery	3.99	15
5	104	Pen	Stationery	10	30
6	105	USB Cable	Electronics	150	6
7	106	Chair	Furniture	45.5	10
8	107	Water Bottle	Fitness	10	20

***Figure 8.3:** Excel file with data populated from Python*

You can also create a column that is derived from existing columns. For example, to compute revenue (**`price * units_sold`**) using given columns, you can compute the values in Python and write the result to an Excel cell, shown as follows:

```
ws['F1'] = 'Revenue'

for i in range(2, ws.max_row + 1):
    price = ws[f'D{i}'].value
    units_sold = ws[f'E{i}'].value
    ws[f'F{i}'] = price*units_sold
```

Here, we have used f-strings to insert variable values so they can change dynamically in a loop. This will create a column named revenue that stores values (not formulas) calculated from the **`price`** and **`units_sold`** columns, as shown in *Figure 8.4*. However, as an Excel user, you would prefer to write Excel formulas from **`openpyxl`**, so that the result auto-updates if there is any change in the data. We are discussing this in the next section.

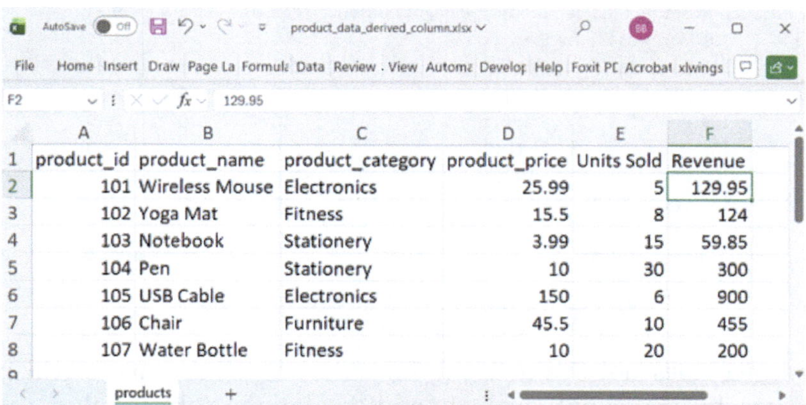

	A	B	C	D	E	F
1	product_id	product_name	product_category	product_price	Units Sold	Revenue
2	101	Wireless Mouse	Electronics	25.99	5	129.95
3	102	Yoga Mat	Fitness	15.5	8	124
4	103	Notebook	Stationery	3.99	15	59.85
5	104	Pen	Stationery	10	30	300
6	105	USB Cable	Electronics	150	6	900
7	106	Chair	Furniture	45.5	10	455
8	107	Water Bottle	Fitness	10	20	200

***Figure 8.4:** Revenue as static calculated values*

To write a huge amount of data efficiently, you can use write-only mode which optimizes memory usage by not keeping everything in memory. It can export **unlimited amount of data** (even more than Excel can handle actually), while keeping **memory usage under 10Mb**.

A write-only workbook can only be saved once, you write data row-by-row sequentially, and it gets flushed to disk as you go.

Advanced sheet operations

Apart from creation and insertion of data, **openpyxl** also offers advanced features such as adding Excel formulas, data validation, conditional formatting, adding charts, images, and styling the sheet, to name a few. Let us explore some of these capabilities.

Excel formulas and calculations

You can write an Excel formula using **openpyxl**, and Excel itself will evaluate the formula and show the correct result in that column (refer to *Figure 8.5*). Creating Excel formula to compute revenue (**price * units_sold**) in column F can be done conveniently as follows:

```
for i in range(2, ws.max_row + 1):
    price = f'D{i}'
    units_sold = f'E{i}'
    ws[f'F{i}'] = f'={price}*{units_sold}'
wb.save('writing_excel_formula.xlsx')
```

You need to start a formula with **=** and write it the same way you do in Excel:

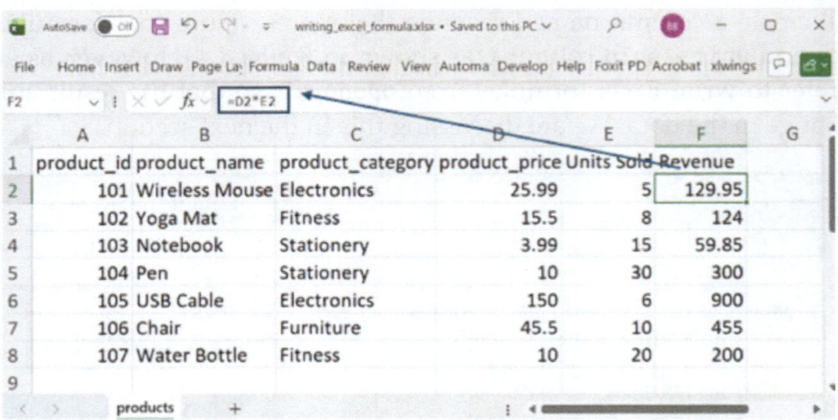

***Figure 8.5**: Revenue using Excel formula syntax*

Note that **openpyxl** does not evaluate the formula, so printing rows will not show you the resultant values, but Excel will evaluate and display the correct value, as shown in the following code. If you want to compute total revenue, you can use Excel's **SUM() function:**

```
ws['H1'] = 'Total Revenue'
ws['H2'] = '=SUM(F2:F7)'
```

This will show total revenue (computed in Excel) in the H2 cell. However, we prefer not to hardcode a data range. This can be done by assigning **ws.max_row** to a new variable and using the same in the code:

```
last_row = ws.max_row
ws[f'E{last_row + 1}'] = 'Total Revenue'
ws[f'F{last_row + 1}'] = f'=SUM(F2:F{last_row})'
sum_formula = f'=SUM(F2:F{last_row})'
```

Similarly, we have also computed the mean revenue by using Excel's **AVERAGE()** formula. The resultant Excel file is shown as follows:

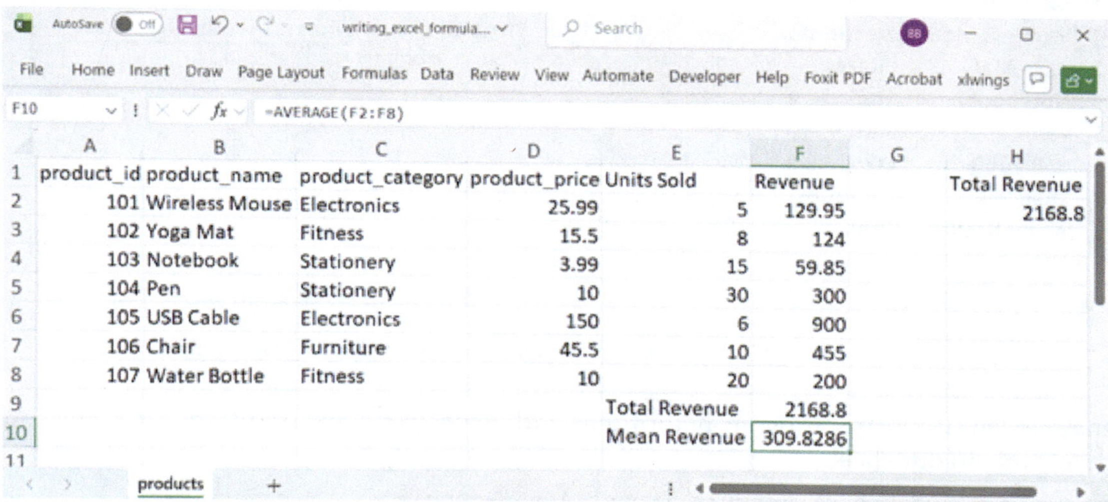

	A	B	C	D	E	F	G	H
1	product_id	product_name	product_category	product_price	Units Sold	Revenue		Total Revenue
2	101	Wireless Mouse	Electronics	25.99	5	129.95		2168.8
3	102	Yoga Mat	Fitness	15.5	8	124		
4	103	Notebook	Stationery	3.99	15	59.85		
5	104	Pen	Stationery	10	30	300		
6	105	USB Cable	Electronics	150	6	900		
7	106	Chair	Furniture	45.5	10	455		
8	107	Water Bottle	Fitness	10	20	200		
9					Total Revenue	2168.8		
10					Mean Revenue	309.8286		

***Figure 8.6:** More Excel formulas written from openpyxl*

To check available Excel formulas supported by **openpyxl**, you can run:

```
from openpyxl.utils import FORMULAE
FORMULAE
```

If **openpyxl** does not recognize a formula (like **XLOOKUP, UNIQUE, SEQUENCE, TEXTJOIN**, etc.), it might show **#NAME** error in Excel. You can check if a formula is supported or not by using **name in FORMULAE**. For example, when you run **'TEXTJOIN' in FORMULAE**, it outputs **False**, indicating that it is not supported by **openpyxl**:

```
ws['I1'] = 'TEXTJOIN() Function'
ws['I2'] = '=TEXTJOIN(": ", TRUE, B2:C2)'  # Shows #NAME error in Excel
```

Trying to use such functions does not throw any error in Python, but Excel fails to evaluate those. We can simply prefix[1] such functions with **_xlfn** and they will work (refer to *Figure 8.7*):

```
ws['J1'] = 'using _xlfn prefix'
ws['J2'] = '=_xlfn.TEXTJOIN(": ", TRUE, B2:C2)'  # Now works
```

In *Figure 8.7*, to show you the output effectively, we have accessed **column_dimensions** attribute of the worksheet and set the hidden property to **True** for hiding some columns:

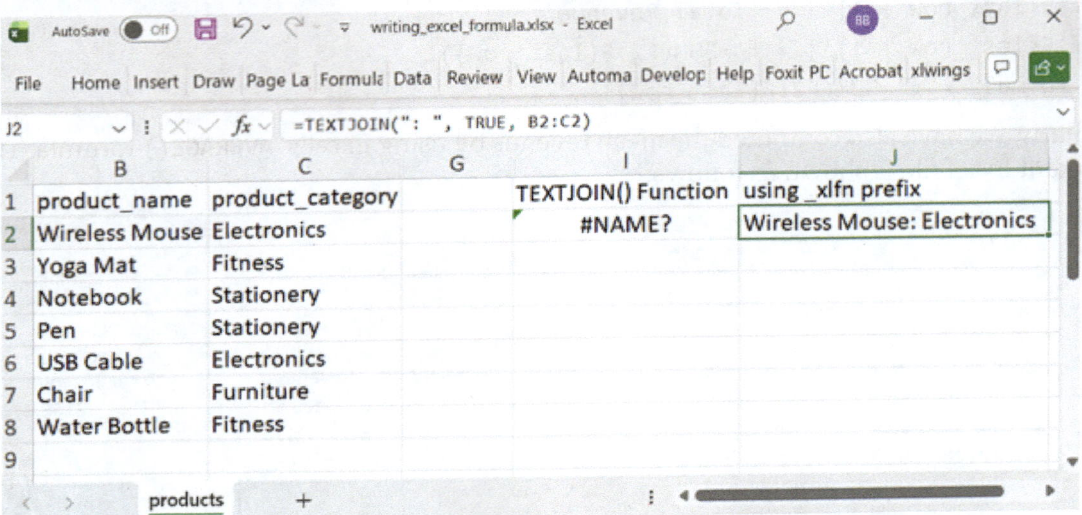

Figure 8.7: Using _xlfn prefix for unsupported Excel functions

openpyxl also supports setting array formulas with **openpyxl.formula** utility. Let us use one such formula in our sheet:

```
from openpyxl.worksheet.formula import ArrayFormula

ws['H4']  = "Transposed Data"
ws['H5'].value = ArrayFormula('H5:I7', '=TRANSPOSE(H1:J2)')
```

[1] This is part of Excel's internal naming for future (unsupported) functions. Excel will show this as a normal formula in the sheet, even if it was saved with _xlfn.FUNCTION_NAME internally.

You can see in the following figure (output Excel file), the data from range H1:J2 is transformed:

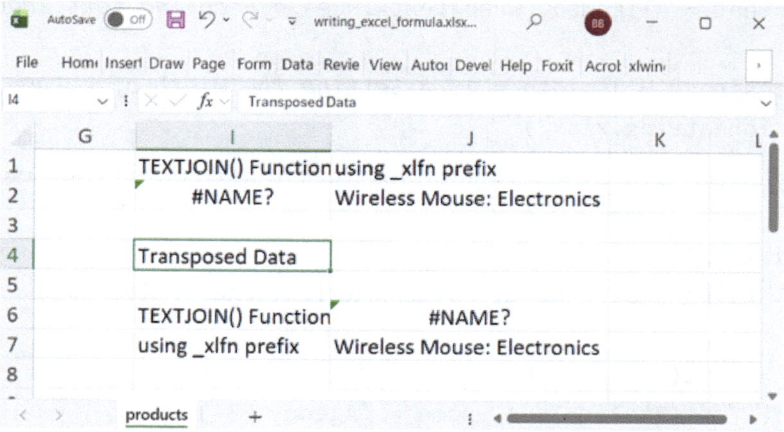

Figure 8.8: Writing an array formula using openpyxl

Formatting and styles

While working with data in Excel, you use many options to make it convenient for you, such as freeze pan, merge cells, wrap text, filter, change row or column dimensions, etc. These can be done smoothly in **openpyxl** as follows:

```
ws.freeze_panes = 'B2' # Freeze top row and first column
ws.freeze_panes = None  # Remove freeze panes

ws.auto_filter.ref = ws.dimensions# Applying filter
ws.auto_filter.ref = None # Removing the filter

ws.insert_rows(1, 2)        # Inserting 2 blank rows on the top
ws['A1'] = 'Sample Data'
ws.row_dimensions[1].height = 20 # increasing row height

# Merge cells
ws.merge_cells('A1:F1')     # Merging cells

# Cell Alignment and Wrap-Text
from openpyxl.styles import Alignment

ws['A1'].alignment = Alignment(horizontal='center', vertical='center')
```

```
ws['H3'] = 'OpenPyXl is an awesome library that helps me automate Excel workflow.'
ws['H3'].alignment = Alignment(wrap_text=True) # Enabling text wrapping

ws.column_dimensions['H'].width = 15 # Setting the width of column
wb.save("data_formatting.xlsx")
```

You can also style your data by setting font, font size, font color, fill color etc. as you do in Excel:

```
# Styling individual cells
from openpyxl.styles import Font, PatternFill, Border, Side

ws['A1'].font = Font(size=16, bold=True, color='FF1F497D')
ws['H3'].font = Font(italic=True, name = 'Agency FB')
wb.save("data_formatting.xlsx")
```

As expected, the output file shown in the following figure shows font (font type, size, color, bold, or italic) and the effect of alignments (wrap text, merge and center):

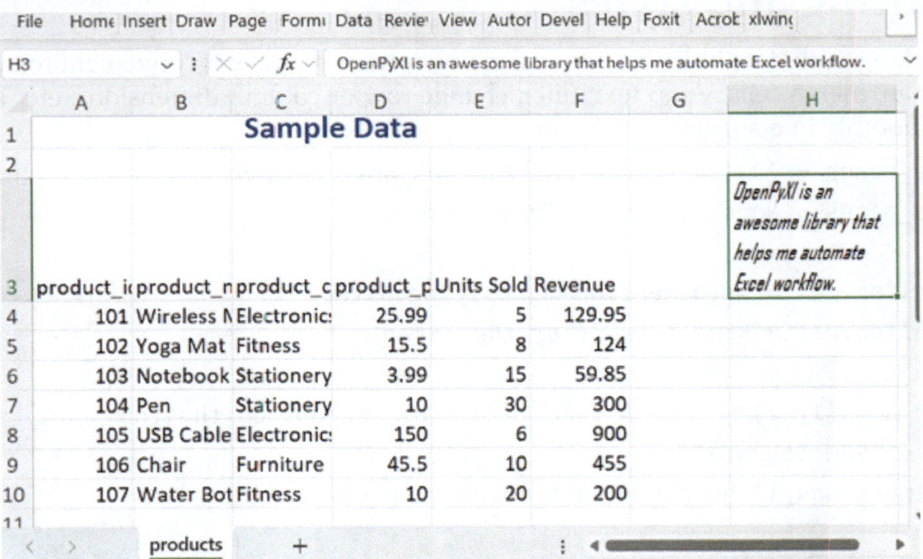

Figure 8.9: Cell dimensions, alignment, and font settings in openpyxl

You can style data at the cell-level or by iterating through a row or a column. However, it helps to use a custom-named style for applying consistent, reusable formatting across multiple cells with a single reference. It is like styling with a shortcut that reflects the visual identity of your brand:

```
# Using a named style to apply anywhere
from openpyxl.styles import NamedStyle, PatternFill, Border, Side
```

```
custom_style = NamedStyle(name="custom_style")
custom_style.font = Font(size=12, bold=True, color="FF0000")
custom_style.fill = PatternFill(start_color="ADD8E6", fill_type="solid")

custom_style.border = Border(
    left=Side(style='medium'),
    right=Side(style='medium'),
    top=Side(style='medium'),
    bottom=Side(style='medium')
)
# Register style to workbook
wb.add_named_style(custom_style)

# Apply style to another cell
ws['B9'].style = "custom_style"

# Save again (We are saving in a different file)
wb.save("styled_named.xlsx")
```

The resultant Excel file is as follows:

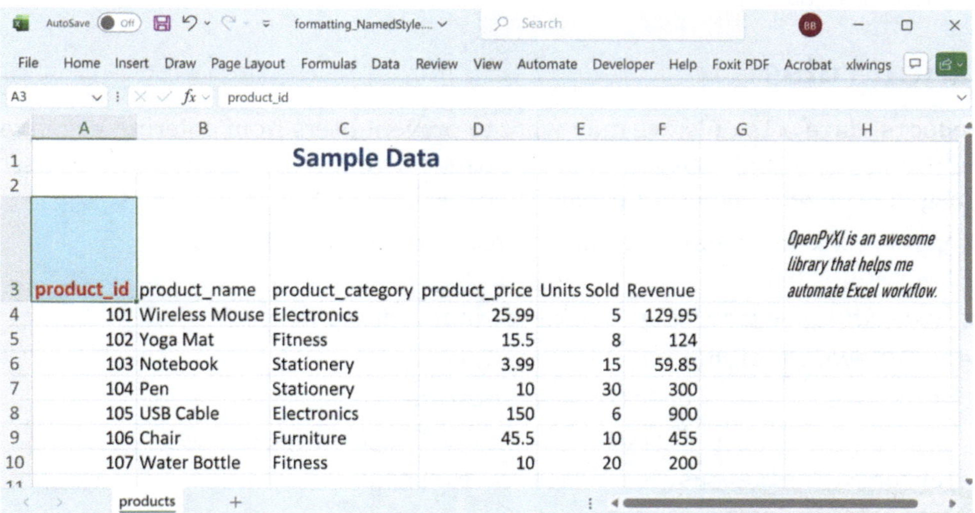

***Figure 8.10**: Excel sheet formatted via openpyxl*

As **openpyxl** works by reading and writing the underlying **Office Open XML** (**OOXML**), invalid or unsupported style assignments may not show, or cause Excel to repair the file. Once you understand a few key rules, you can style cells reliably. If you are facing any errors, we would advise you to apply one style at a time (e.g., just a fill, just a font) to isolate the issue.

A checklist to avoid style errors is given as follows:

- Always use cell attributes such as **`.fill`**, **`.font`**, **`.alignment`**, etc. directly on a cell, never set them to **`.value`**. For example, use **`ws['A1'].font = Font(...)`** and avoid **`ws['A1'] = Font(...)`** as this wrongly sets the cell's value, not its formatting.
- Use a valid **`aRGB`** color using the hex code.
- For merged cells, only apply styles to the top-left cell.
- Avoid using too many unique styles.
- Refer to the official document at **https://openpyxl.readthedocs.io/en/3.1/styles.html** for any more details.

You can also apply text and number formatting, such as currency, percentage, date formats, and more, after importing **`numbers`** from **`openpyxl.styles`**. Apart from this cell, sheet, or workbook protection, etc., can be done.

Data validation and conditional formatting

In advanced Excel workflows, data validation and conditional formatting play pivotal roles in maintaining data integrity and enhancing interpretability. Using **`openpyxl`** library, we can automate these safeguards.

Validation rules

In the **`products_data.xlsx`** file, we may want to prevent users from entering negative prices or highlight unusually high sales figures. Let us set a validation rule to prevent users from entering negative or zero values for **`product_price`**, i.e., column D:

```
from openpyxl.worksheet.datavalidation import DataValidation

# Create validation rule: Only allow decimal values > 0
dv_price = DataValidation(type="decimal",
                          operator="greaterThan",
                          formula1="0", showErrorMessage=True)
dv_price.error = "Price must be a positive number."
dv_price.errorTitle = "Invalid Price"

# Add the validation to the column dynamically
max_excel_rows = 1048576  # Excel's row limit
```

```
dv_price.add(f"D2:D{max_excel_rows}")
ws.add_data_validation(dv_price)
wb.save('products_data_validated.xlsx')
```

This will prevent a user from entering invalid values in column D in Excel.

Note about openpyxl data validation nuance:

Openpyxl's role (manipulation): openpyxl's job is to manipulate the structure of the XLSX file. When you use the DataValidation object and methods, the library simply writes the XML code for the validation rule into the file structure. It has no mechanism to check the values being written by your Python code against that rule. Therefore, you can easily use openpyxl to write an invalid value (e.g., -5 into a cell validated for positive numbers) right next to the rule itself.

Excel's role (enforcement): The validation rules are only activated and enforced when the file is opened by the Excel application (or another compatible spreadsheet software). Excel is the program that interprets that validation XML, prevents the user from manually typing invalid data, and visually flags existing invalid data if the feature (like the "Circle Invalid Data" option) is enabled. In short, openpyxl is a file editor, and Excel is the rule enforcer.

Similarly, for text columns such as **product_name**, we can restrict text length by setting a suitable rule and apply to relevant column:

```
# Create text length validation rule
dv_text = DataValidation(
    type="textLength",
    operator="lessThan",
    formula1="10",
    showErrorMessage=True
)
dv_text.error = "Too long! Text must be under 10 characters."
dv_text.errorTitle = "Text Length Error"

# Apply validation to column B
dv_text.add(f"B2:B{max_excel_rows}")
ws.add_data_validation(dv_text)
```

If you are to choose a dropdown list for **product_category**, you can simply use **type="list"** argument with other related arguments:

```
# Create data validation for a dropdown list
dv_cat = DataValidation(type="list",
                        formula1='"Electronics,Fitness,Stationery"',
```

```
                         allow_blank=False)
dv_cat.prompt = "Choose a value from the list"
dv_cat.error = "Invalid entry. Please choose from the list."

# Apply the data validation to column C
ws.add_data_validation(dv_cat)
dv_cat.add(f"C2:C{max_excel_rows}")
```

This safeguards data integrity by restricting input to predefined options. This is especially useful when handling categories like status fields, department names, or standard responses in forms, anything where variation could cause confusion or reporting issues.

Conditional formatting

For applying conditional formatting, **CellIsRule** class can be used from **openpyxl.formatting.rule** along with style formatting:

```
from openpyxl.formatting.rule import CellIsRule
from openpyxl.styles import PatternFill

# Define formatting rule: highlight with green fill
green_fill = PatternFill(start_color='C6EFCE', end_color='C6EFCE',
                         fill_type='solid')

rule = CellIsRule(operator='greaterThan', formula=['10'],
                  fill=green_fill)
# Apply to "Units Sold" column (column E)
last_row = ws.max_row
E_range_str = f"E2:E{last_row}"
ws.conditional_formatting.add(E_range_str, rule)
```

This rule highlights all cells in column E (Units Sold) with a green fill if their value is greater than 10, helping visually track high-performing entries. Refer to the following figure:

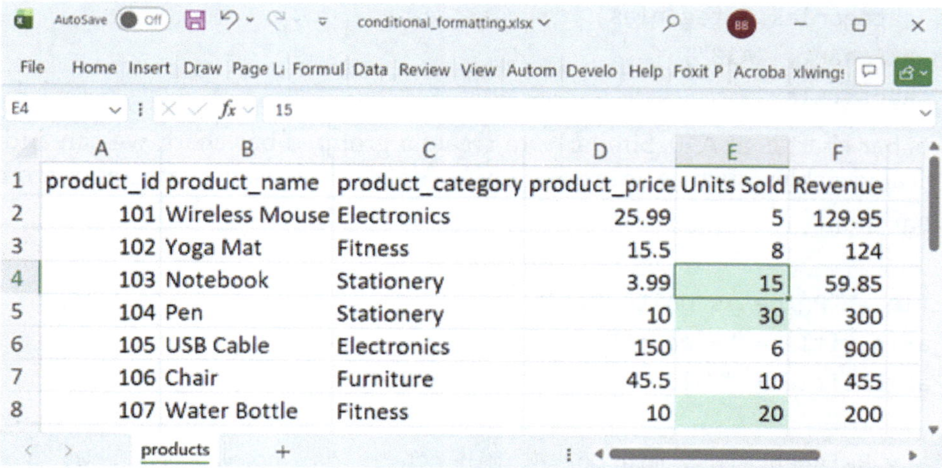

	A	B	C	D	E	F
1	product_id	product_name	product_category	product_price	Units Sold	Revenue
2	101	Wireless Mouse	Electronics	25.99	5	129.95
3	102	Yoga Mat	Fitness	15.5	8	124
4	103	Notebook	Stationery	3.99	15	59.85
5	104	Pen	Stationery	10	30	300
6	105	USB Cable	Electronics	150	6	900
7	106	Chair	Furniture	45.5	10	455
8	107	Water Bottle	Fitness	10	20	200

Figure 8.11: Conditional formatting applied to Units Sold

For conditional formatting, some advanced visual styles are not supported by **openpyxl**, but simple rules based on cell values work reliably. Also, the rules only apply to the range you specify, and they do not auto-extend as new rows are added, so for dynamic data, always apply validation to a generously sized range (like D2:D500).

Creating charts and exporting images

Openpyxl supports many of Excel's core chart types, such as bar chart, line chart, pie chart, area chart, scatterplot, etc. Refer to the official document for more details at **https://openpyxl.pages.heptapod.net/openpyxl/charts/introduction.html**.

To create a bar chart, we need to use the class **BarChart()** and add relevant values and categories (created by the **Reference()** class) to a chart object. Then we can add the chart to any sheet location. We can also set title labels, style, colors, legends, etc., as follows:

```
from openpyxl.chart import BarChart, Reference
chart = BarChart()
chart.title = "Units Sold by Product"
chart.x_axis.title = "Product"
chart.y_axis.title = "Units Sold"

categories = Reference(ws, min_col=2, max_col=2,
                       min_row=1, max_row=ws.max_row)
values = Reference(ws, min_col=5, max_col=5, min_row=1,
                       max_row=ws.max_row)
chart.add_data(values, titles_from_data=True)
```

```
chart.set_categories(categories)
ws.add_chart(chart, "A10")
wb.save("charts.xlsx")
```

This exports bar chart is at A10. Similarly, to create a grouped bar chart, we can add data of two numerical variables, such as **price** and **units_sold**, for the same category reference:

```
chart2 = BarChart()

chart2.title = "Price vs Units Sold"
chart2.x_axis.title = "Product"
chart2.y_axis.title = "Value"

price_data = Reference(ws, min_col=4, min_row=1, max_row=ws.max_row)
units_data = Reference(ws, min_col=5, min_row=1, max_row=ws.max_row)
categories = Reference(ws, min_col=2, min_row=1, max_row=ws.max_row)

chart2.add_data(price_data, titles_from_data=True)
chart2.add_data(units_data, titles_from_data=True)
chart2.set_categories(categories)
ws.add_chart(chart2, "J1")
wb.save("charts.xlsx")
```

The resultant charts are shown in the following figure:

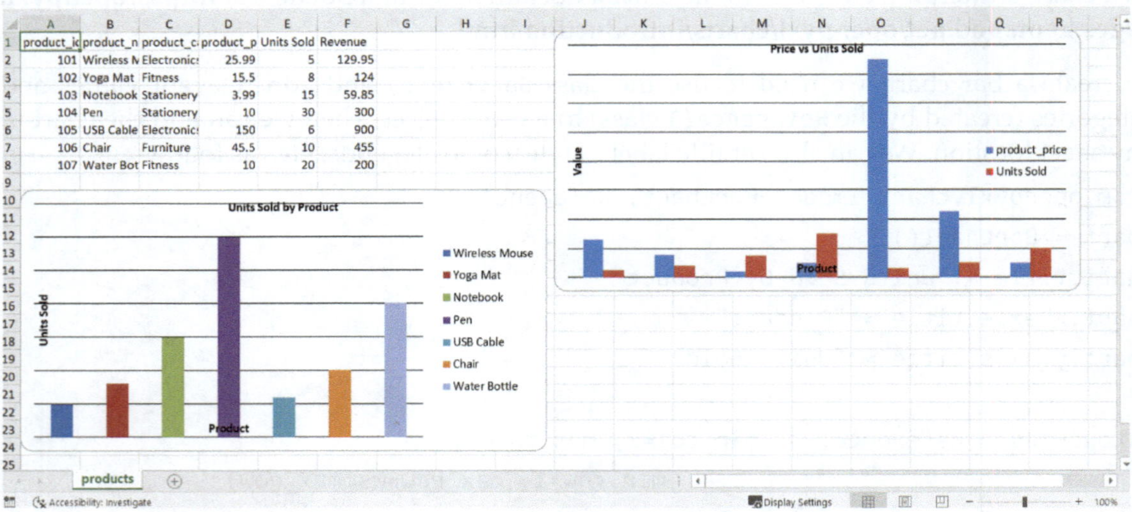

Figure 8.12: Creating Excel charts from openpyxl

You can also create a new sheet and export charts there. If you are willing to use **pandas** (**matplotlib**) or **seaborn** chart, you can export it as an image. Hence, it will not update with the change in data:

```
import pandas as pd
import matplotlib.pyplot as plt
from openpyxl.drawing.image import Image as XLImage

df = pd.read_excel('products_data.xlsx')
df[['product_price', 'Units Sold']].plot(kind='bar', figsize=(8, 5))
plt.title("Price and Units Sold per Product")
plt.ylabel("Value")
plt.xticks(rotation=15)
plt.tight_layout()
plt.savefig("chart.png", bbox_inches="tight")

ws2 = wb.create_sheet(title="pandas chart")
img = XLImage("chart.png")
ws2.add_image(img, "B2")
wb.save("charts.xlsx")
```

This code generates a chart using **pandas**, exports it as an image (see *Figure 8.13*), and inserts it into a new worksheet in the same Excel workbook. You can use **XLImage()** from **openpyxl** to export any image to Excel.

Figure 8.13*: pandas/matplotlib charts are exported as a static image*

Working with tables and dynamic named ranges

You can create Excel tables and defined named ranges using **openpyxl**.

Creating and styling Excel tables

You can create and style an Excel table by using **Table()** or **TableStyleInfo()** class from **openpyxl.worksheet.table**:

```
from openpyxl import load_workbook
from openpyxl.utils import get_column_letter
from openpyxl.worksheet.table import Table, TableStyleInfo
wb = load_workbook('products_data.xlsx')
ws = wb.active

# Define the table range
last_row = ws.max_row
last_col_letter = get_column_letter(ws.max_column)

table_ref = f"A1:{last_col_letter}{last_row}"
table = Table(displayName="ProductsTable", ref=table_ref)

# Optional: add style to table
style = TableStyleInfo(name="TableStyleMedium9",
                       showRowStripes=True)
table.tableStyleInfo = style

# Add table to worksheet
ws.add_table(table)
wb.save('products_with_table.xlsx')
```

This creates an Excel table named **`ProductsTable`** and adds style to the same.

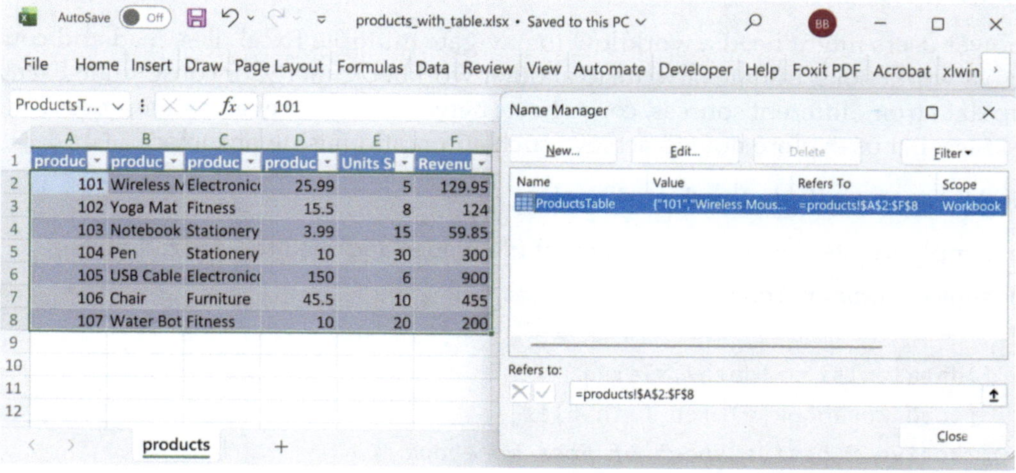

Figure 8.14: Excel table creation

Dynamic named ranges

To define a named range for product prices (D2:D7):

```
from openpyxl.workbook.defined_name import DefinedName
price_range = DefinedName('ProductPrices', attr_text='Sheet1!$D$2:$D$7')
wb.defined_names.add(price_range)
```

You can verify this in Excel through **Formula Tab** | **Name Manager**, shown as follows:

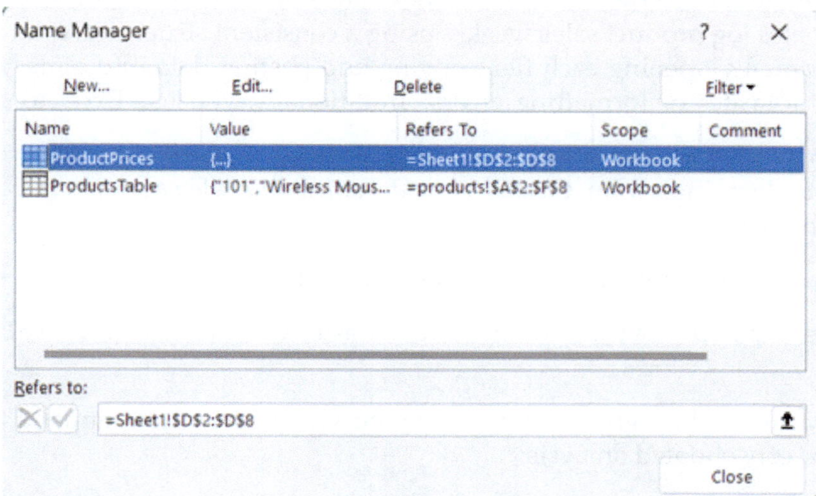

Figure 8.15: Named manager shows the named range and the Excel table

Multi-workbook automation use-cases

Excel power users might need a workflow to navigate multiple Excel files, read and compare data across workbooks, update or write to another workbook, merge or consolidate Excel files, clean up data from different sources, copy sheets between files, or even batch-process a folder of Excel files. Let us explore how to achieve such automation using **openpyxl**.

Load and process multiple Excel workbooks:

You can simply iterate through a collection of file names and read the desired file:

```
from openpyxl import load_workbook

files = ['data1.xlsx', 'data2.xlsx']
books = [load_workbook(f) for f in files]
books[0].active # active sheet of first workbook
books[1].sheetnames # sheet names of second workbook
```

You can use your learnings from *Chapter 5, Automating File Management with Python,* to batch process the files. Using file automation, combining with **datetime** or **re** modules to process files by week or month, backing up originals by renaming before saving, using **NamedStyle** to maintain formatting across files, pave the way for powerful automation. Some use cases are discussed in the following sub-sections.

Automated integration of distributed product logs

Imagine a mid-sized retail company where each department, e.g., Electronics, Fitness, Furniture, etc., maintains its own Excel workbook, say, electronics.xlsx, fitness.xlsx, stationery.xlsx, etc. These files log product sales weekly using a consistent structure. As an analyst, your job includes manually opening each file, copying and pasting data into a master sheet, and watching for duplicates or formatting errors. Traditionally, you use Excel to do this every week.

Combining your learnings from *Chapter 5, Automating File Management with Python,* with insights from the current chapter, to build a script given as follows:

- Loads all departmental files (**.xlsx** files) from a folder
- Extracts and appends their content into a master workbook, e.g., **consolidated_log.xlsx**

You can simply iterate through each row in the individual sheets and append the rows to a master sheet for consolidated analysis:

```
import os
from openpyxl import load_workbook, Workbook

folder = "department_logs"
master_wb = Workbook()
master_ws = master_wb.active
master_ws.title = "All Departments"
master_ws.append(['product_id', 'product_name', 'product_category', 'product_
price', 'Units Sold'])

for file in os.listdir(folder):
    if file.endswith('.xlsx'):
        wb = load_workbook(os.path.join(folder, file))
        ws = wb.active
        for row in ws.iter_rows(min_row=2, values_only=True):
            master_ws.append(row)

master_wb.save("consolidated_log.xlsx")
```

This code can be made efficient by using list comprehension instead of loop. You can also add data validation, conditional formatting, and an automated summary sheet in the workflow. Other similar use-cases are to aggregate product sales from multiple cities or regions, or revenue data from each week or month, etc.

Inventory reconciliation

Sometimes, we need to compare values across sheets or workbooks. For example, **`ERP_Inventory.xlsx`** has **`System-recorded stock levels`**, and **`Warehouse_Count.xlsx`** contains physically counted stock at the warehouse. We need to identify mismatches in item counts. It will help us detect shrinkage, prevent stockouts, overstocking, and update discrepancies or potential fraud. A simple Python script can achieve this:

```
from openpyxl import load_workbook

wb = load_workbook("Inventory_Comparison.xlsx")
ws1 = wb['ERP_Inventory']
ws2 = wb['Warehouse_Count']

for row in range(2, ws1.max_row + 1):
    item_id = ws1[f"A{row}"].value
```

```
    erp = ws1[f"D{row}"].value
    warehouse = ws2[f"D{row}"].value
    if erp != warehouse:
        print(f"Item ID {item_id}:\n System-recorded stock levels={erp},
Physically counted stock at warehouse={warehouse}\n*****")
```

Other such use-cases are to compare two versions of **products_data.xlsx** for discrepancies in units sold, verifying data integrity between master and regional sales files, confirming that all records (IDs, prices, dates) transferred correctly after migrating from a legacy system to the new database, validating vendor billings, quality audits, financial reconciliation, or detecting price discrepancies, etc. Such a quick comparison helps correct accidental overwrites and validate revisions.

Automated deficit detection in department budgets

If you are a financial analyst, accountant, or auditor who is willing to automate financial data, checks across departmental budget spreadsheets. You can write a short script to scan through multiple Excel files in a folder, and identify if any department has overspent (i.e., negative values in budget summaries):

```
import os
from openpyxl import load_workbook
# Folder containing all budget spreadsheets
folder_path = 'department_budgets'
# Column and sheet to scan
target_column = 'C'  # Adjust based on your layout
sheet_name = 'Summary'  # Or use wb.active if sheet names vary
# Scan all files
for filename in os.listdir(folder_path):
    if filename.endswith('.xlsx'):
        file_path = os.path.join(folder_path, filename)
        wb = load_workbook(file_path, data_only=True)
        ws = wb[sheet_name] if sheet_name in wb.sheetnames else wb.active
        for row in range(2, ws.max_row + 1):  # Skip header
            cell = ws[f'{target_column}{row}']
            if isinstance(cell.value, (int, float)) and cell.value < 0:
                print(f"Deficit in {filename} at {cell.coordinate}: {cell.
value}")
                break  # Stop after first deficit found in this file
```

Such automation helps finance teams with budget validation across departments or spot-checking audit anomalies without opening each file manually.

Cleaning and normalizing external files

Incoming workbooks from different sources often have inconsistent formatting. As an Excel professional, you might be manually preparing files for reporting or uploading to ERP systems. For example, to normalize column widths and alignment effortlessly for creating client-facing versions or backups with a consistent appearance:

```
for col in ['A', 'B', 'C', 'D', 'E']:
    src_ws.column_dimensions[col].width = 20
for row in src_ws.iter_rows(min_row=2):
    for cell in row:
        cell.alignment = Alignment(horizontal="center")
```

If you need to standardize inconsistent transaction data by cleaning up messy values like extra spaces, inconsistent casing, improperly formatted dates, and non-numeric prices, etc., to make the data ERP-ready, you can write a short script for the same.

For example, you can create your own version of **clean_text(), clean_price()** and **clean_date()** functions and use those in your script:

```
# Clean each row
for row in ws.iter_rows(min_row=2, values_only=True):
    product_id = row[0] if row[0] else "UNKNOWN"
    product_name = clean_text(row[1])
    category = clean_text(row[2])
    price = clean_price(row[3])
    date_added = clean_date(row[4])

    cleaned_ws.append([product_id, product_name, category, price, date_added])
# Save cleaned file
cleaned_wb.save("Cleaned_Data.xlsx")
```

A sample script is attached in the companion repo for you to modify and use as per your needs. This script will help you write a cleaned version of messy data to a new Excel file.

You have witnessed how managing multiple Excel files programmatically accelerates turnaround time, reduces errors, and liberates analysts from manual repetition. **Openpyxl** allows power users to evolve from passive file consumers to active automation architects.

Excel templates

Excel template files (**.xltx**) are useful for creating reusable, styled workbooks that include predefined layouts, formulas, charts, and formatting. You can also create Excel templates using **openpyxl** by setting:

```
wb.template = True
wb.save("template_file.xltx")
```

This marks the workbook as a template and saves it with the **.xltx** extension. You can also load a template file and save it as a regular **.xlsx** file by setting:

```
wb.template = False
wb.save("new_report.xlsx")
```

Best practices and limitations

Learning **openpyxl** equips you with a deeper control over Excel file structure than what **pandas** alone can offer.

Here are some key takeaways from the chapter:

- **Excel installation not required:** You do not need Microsoft Excel installed; **openpyxl** works independently to read, write, and modify Excel files using pure Python. It means you can create Excel deliverables on any machine without having Excel installation.
- **Workbook control: openpyxl** allows granular access to Excel components, including sheets, cells, styles, merged regions, and formulas.
- **Programmatic reporting: openpyxl** can dynamically generate structured Excel reports, automate sheet population, and modify workbook elements, paving the way for scalable reporting workflows.
- **File support:** It supports loading and saving **xlsx**, **xlsm**, **xltx**, **xltm** files.
- **Integration with pandas and other libraries:** While **openpyxl** can be used alongside **pandas** (via **engine='openpyxl'**), it remains essential when structured formatting or Excel-native behavior is required. You can combine **openpyxl** with other libraries such as **pandas**, **xlsxwriter**, and more to expand functionality.

Let us list down some best practices while working with **openpyxl**:

- It is recommended to always validate workbook structure when loading or writing user-generated files to prevent unexpected exceptions.
- You need to run **workbook.save('filename.xlsx')** to preserve any changes made in **openpyxl**, otherwise, the edits will not show up in the file.

- Changes like Excel formulas, data validation, and conditional formatting only become visible when the file is opened in Excel. You should verify these changes in Excel.
- Use read-only and **`write_only`** mode for large data files.

It is also important to understand the limitations of **`openpyxl`** and proposed solutions as mentioned in the following list:

- **File support**: It does not support legacy **`.xls`** and binary **`.xlsb`** file formats. We will discuss other libraries for such files in *Chapter 9, Core Excel Read-Write Tools in Python*.
- **Limited charting and formatting**: It does not offer support to export **`matplotlib`** and **`seaborn`** charts natively as Excel charts. You can create and export chart using **`openpyxl.`** Advanced styles and themes are not supported by **`openpyxl`**, for that you can refer **`xlsxwriter`** (to be covered in *Chapter 9, Core Excel Read-Write Tools in Python).*
- **Cannot execute Excel macros**: It can read .xlsm files, but it cannot run, trigger, create, or embed VBA code. We will discuss working with VBA code in upcoming chapters.
- **Formula limitations**: Supports writing formulas, e.g., **`=SUM(A1:A10)`**, but it does not evaluate them. You need Excel to open the file to see the calculated results. For live Excel interactions, we will discuss **`xlwings`** in upcoming chapters.
- **No live Excel interaction**: All edits are file-based. Results are visible only when reopened in Excel. As discussed, for live Excel interaction, **`xlwings`** library can be used, which we have discussed in upcoming chapters.
- **No native PDF export**: It can create or manipulate Excel files but cannot render or export them as PDF directly, **`xlwings`** support this.
- **Performance bottlenecks**: For large Excel files, **`openpyxl`** can be memory-intensive compared to binary readers like xlrd or pyxlsb.

  When working with large Excel files in **`openpyxl`**, you should use read-only mode (**`read_only=True`**) to load massive files efficiently without consuming excessive memory through lazy loading. For generating large files, use write-only mode (**`write_only=True`**) to write data sequentially and flush to disk progressively. Avoid normal mode for huge datasets as it loads the entire workbook into memory, which can cause crashes.

Conclusion

In this chapter, we have explored the Python library openpyxl in depth as a powerful interface for reading, writing, and modifying Excel files programmatically. While many of you are already proficient with pandas for tabular data processing, openpyxl offers unique advantages when working directly with Excel workbooks, especially those containing rich formatting, multiple sheets, charts, formulas, and layout-sensitive content.

In the next chapter, you will learn to use pandas' **`ExcelWriter`** class with openpyxl engine to combine pandas' tabular convenience with openpyxl's formatting so you can update DataFrames and retain workbook styles and charts. Also, we will discuss other reader and writer packages that offer alternatives to openpyxl for speed, legacy support, and fine-grained formatting.

Try it yourself

1. In automation use_case Automated integration of distributed product logs, we have used a folder named departmental_log that contains files for different departments with the same structure. Write openpyxl code to replicate this data.
2. Imagine you are a mechanical engineer working in the maintenance team that logs machine failures and repairs. Your task is to track and analyze machine downtime trends and repeat issues. You are exploring openpyxl to automate your workflow. Follow the instructions given as follows to get started:
   a. Create an Excel file using openpyxl and write this data to the first sheet and save it as Maintenance_Log.xlsx, shown as follows:

	A	B	C	D	E	F
1	Date	Machine ID	Issue	Action Taken	Technician	Downtime (hrs)
2	7/1/2025	MX100	Vibration above threshold	Bearing replaced	Anil	2.5
3	7/2/2025	MX101	Overheating	Coolant replaced	Ravi	1.8
4	7/3/2025	MX100	Oil leak	Seal fixed	Anil	1.2
5	7/4/2025	MX102	Sensor failure	Sensor replaced	Priya	2
6	7/5/2025	MX100	Vibration above threshold	Realigned rotor	Karan	2.7
7	7/6/2025	MX100	Vibration above threshold	Bearing replaced	Anil	2.5
8	7/7/2025	MX101	Overheating	Coolant replaced	Ravi	1.8
9	7/8/2025	MX100	Oil leak	Seal fixed	Anil	1.2
10	7/9/2025	MX102	Sensor failure	Sensor replaced	Priya	2
11	7/10/2025	MX100	Vibration above threshold	Realigned rotor	Karan	2.7
12	7/11/2025	MX101	Oil leak	Seal replaced	Ravi	1.5
13	7/12/2025	MX103	Electrical fault	Rewired panel	Priya	2.2
14	7/13/2025	MX100	Overheating	Cleaned radiator	Karan	2
15	7/14/2025	MX101	Sensor failure	Sensor recalibrated	Anil	1.6
16	7/15/2025	MX102	Vibration above threshold	Balanced rotor	Priya	2.1
17	7/16/2025	MX103	Belt slippage	Belt tightened	Ravi	1.3
18	7/17/2025	MX101	Oil leak	Seal replaced	Karan	1.4
19	7/18/2025	MX102	Temperature spike	Coolant flushed	Anil	2.3
20	7/19/2025	MX100	Motor failure	Motor replaced	Priya	3
21	7/20/2025	MX103	Vibration above threshold	Bearing replaced	Karan	2.6

***Figure 8.16:** Maintenance_Log.xlsx to be created*

   b. In a fresh Python session, load this file and loop through rows to extract machine-wise data.
   c. Increase row height of header row.

d. Apply bold, italic, Agency FB font, size 14 to the header row

e. Insert two rows at the top, write 'Sample Data' in A1. Apply merge and center alignment.

f. Color code high-downtime rows.

g. Apply borders to the row of technicians who handled maximum repairs.

h. Create a new sheet named 'Report' and highlight it by using the sheet tab color.

i. Compute aggregate metrics such as total downtime per machine, average downtime per issue or technician, and most frequent issues.

j. Put the KPIs computed above in suitable cells on the 'Reports' sheet.

k. Create a bar chart to show machine downtime and export it to the 'Reports' sheet.

l. Save the resultant file as an Excel template.

Concept check

1. In a mid-sized HR team, monthly payroll is prepared manually using Excel. If the team wants to automate salary slip generation by updating only the variable components (like bonus, leaves, deductions), how could openpyxl help?

2. An internal audit team maintains Excel logs to track financial approvals, vendor onboarding, and exception flags. Auditors manually enter timestamps and reviewer names for each activity. How can openpyxl improve this process?

3. A finance analyst prepares monthly forecasts by updating multiple Excel models with the latest figures from budget, actuals, and revenue projections. Each sheet follows the same structure across months. How can openpyxl assist in this task?

Join our Discord space

Join our Discord workspace for latest updates, offers, tech happenings around the world, new releases, and sessions with the authors:

https://discord.bpbonline.com

CHAPTER 9
Core Excel Read-Write Tools in Python

Introduction

After gaining a working knowledge of Python and libraries like pandas and openpyxl, you also need to learn another library, xlsxwriter, which offers a specialized, high-performance solution for writing .xlsx files with precision and control. Unlike general-purpose libraries that support both reading and writing, xlsxwriter is a write-only engine to generate Excel files from scratch.

While pandas is great for data analysis, but has limitations when it comes to Excel-specific features like formatting, charts, and formulas. This chapter starts with diving deep into pandas I/O tools such as ExcelFile and ExcelWriter class, and then transitions into a detailed guide to xlsxwriter, a powerful library for creating and formatting Excel files programmatically. Additionally, we will explore pyxlsb for reading binary Excel files (.xlsb) and briefly touch on xlrd, xlwt, xlutils for legacy .xls file support.

By the end of this chapter, readers will be able to generate Excel reports with rich formatting, automate file creation, and handle different file formats efficiently.

Structure

In this chapter, we will discuss the following topics:

- Popular libraries for Python Excel integration
- More on Pandas I/O tools
- Comprehensive guide to xlsxwriter
- Working with legacy .xls files
- Reading binary Excel files with pyxlsb
- Mini project: Dashboard automation
- Handling package switching

Popular libraries for Python Excel integration

So far, we have used Python's built-in **open()** function to handle plain text files, the **csv** module to work with comma-separated values, and **pandas** to manage tabular data from both CSV and Excel. While pandas can import or export Excel files, its core strength is in analyzing data. For more advanced Excel operations, such as create, read, modify, insert Excel formulas, formatting, and charts, we turned to **openpyxl**. Many Python users stop there and never look beyond it. However, in practice, you may come across situations where **openpyxl** is not the best or only option. This is where other Excel-related packages come in. Python offers several other libraries that can be useful depending on the type of Excel file you are dealing with, the size of your data, or the level of formatting and automation required.

The selection of a library for Python Excel integration depends on these factors:

- **Compatibility with different Excel formats**: Excel has been around for decades, and not all files follow the modern **.xlsx** format. Older files use the **.xls** format (pre-2007). These cannot be opened with **openpyxl**, but libraries like **xlrd**, **xlutils**, and **xlwt** were designed specifically for them. Some organizations generate or store binary Excel files (.**xlsb**), which are compact and fast to load in Excel but tricky for Python. For those cases, **pyxlsb** provides a reliable reader.

  Thus, if you are dealing with legacy systems, archives, or files created by third-party applications, you may need one of these specialized libraries.

- **Advanced features and special use cases**: Some packages are built with special features in mind. For example, **xlsxwriter** offers highly polished control over formatting, charts, and layout. If you are preparing Excel reports for clients or management, its output can look more professional than what you might achieve with **openpyxl**. Also, for writing large amounts of data efficiently, **xlsxwriter** often outperforms **openpyxl**, especially when generating complex reports with formatting and charts.

  pandas can act as a bridge, allowing you to read and write Excel files seamlessly during data analysis. While you may not control the file format in detail, it is the quickest way to move data between Excel and Python.

- **Filling the gaps**: You might have realized that no single library is perfect for all Excel tasks. While there are many libraries designed for Excel-Python integration, becoming familiar with the most widely used ones can significantly enhance your workflow. Some of these are:

  - **pandas** for seamless data import or export, efficient data analysis or quick plotting.
  - **openpyxl** for reading, writing, and editing **.xlsx**, but not **.xls** or .**xlsb**.
  - **xlrd** for reading legacy **.xls** files.
  - **xlwt** for writing legacy **.xls** files

- o **pyxlsb** for fast reading of binary **.xlsb** workbooks.
- o **xlsxwriter** for creating **.xlsx** files with rich formatting and charts.

Another important library is **xlwings**, which connects Python directly with a running Excel application. Unlike the libraries discussed here, **xlwings** is designed for automation and interactive use, rather than just reading or writing files. We will explore it in detail in subsequent chapters.

By understanding the strengths of each tool, you can select the right one depending on the type of file you encounter and the result you want to achieve. Before we explore these new libraries, let us reinforce our understanding of **pandas** reader and writer functions, building on the concepts introduced in the previous chapter.

More on Pandas I/O tools

We had discussed reading Excel files using **pandas** in *Chapter 6, Data Manipulation with Pandas*. We had explored arguments like **index_col**, **sheet_name**, **na_values**, **header**, **skip_rows**, **use_cols**, etc., and you might have explored a few more arguments as per your requirement. Here, we will explore the engine parameter of **read_excel()** and **to_excel()** functions, the **ExcelFile** class, and the **ExcelWriter** class.

The engine parameter

While reading and writing Excel files using **pandas' read_excel()**, you might have noticed there is a parameter **engine**[1], which can be any of these: **openpyxl**, **calamine**, **odf**, **pyxlsb**, **xlrd** with a default **None**. By default, **pandas** determine the engine based on this logic:

- **engine=odf** is used for OpenDocument format (**.odf, .ods, .odt**).
- **engine=xlrd** is used for **xls** format file.
- **engine=pyxlsb** is used for **xlsb** format file.

So, based on the type of Excel file (**.xls**, **.xlsb**, **.xlsx**, etc.) you are trying to read, **pandas** automatically decides a suitable engine. Otherwise, you can choose an appropriate engine for your file type as shown in *Figure 9.1*:

[1] Other readers, such as read_table() or read_csv(), also allow using engines such as c, python, or pyarrow (added in version 1.4.0). Check documentation for details.

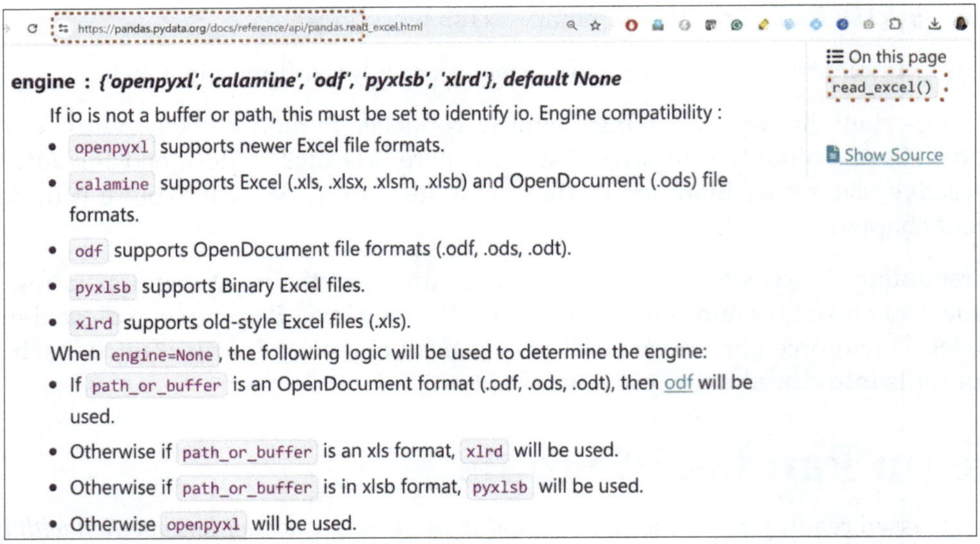

Figure 9.1: Engine parameter of read_excel()

Even though calamine supports many formats, it is not the default as it is newer and still evolving, while **openpyxl** and **xlrd** have been around longer and are more widely used and tested. Another point is that **calamine** is not a pure Python library but a wrapper around a **Rust** library (**rust-calamine**), which adds complexity for some users.

Similarly, **pandas**' writer function **df.to_excel()** allows you to choose the engine parameter. You can use **openpyxl** or **xlsxwriter** for **.xlsx** files and **xlwt** for legacy support for **.xls** files.

You can also set the default engine globally via:

```
pd.options.io.excel.xlsx.writer = 'xlsxwriter'
```

For simple **.xlsx** exports, the engine usually does not matter. However, if you need advanced features like appending to an existing file or adding charts and formatting, you must use **ExcelWriter**, and then the choice of engine becomes important.

The ExcelFile class

We also need to show you an alternative way to read Excel files that **pandas** offers. **ExcelFile** is a class (in **pandas**) that lets you load an Excel file once and then parse multiple sheets efficiently. So, if you are reading multiple sheets from the same file, **ExcelFile** avoids re-parsing the file each time:

```
import pandas as pd
file = pd.ExcelFile("demo_sales.xlsx")
# Read multiple sheets without reloading the file
df1 = file.parse("Customers")
```

```
# Or using sheet index (0-based)

df1 = file.parse(0) # first sheet
df2 = file.parse(1) # second sheet
df3 = file.parse(2) # third sheet
```

To retrieve a list of all sheet names in the workbook, you can use **`xls.sheet_names`**. The following code builds a dictionary where keys are sheet names, and values are the corresponding DataFrames:

```
# Loop through all sheets
dfs = {sheet: xls.parse(sheet) for sheet in xls.sheet_names}
dfs.get('Sales_Jan')
```

This is more efficient than calling **`pd.read_excel()`** repeatedly. You can also use **`ExcelFile`** class as a context manager:

```
# Using context manager
with pd.ExcelFile("demo_sales.xlsx") as file:
    df1 = file.parse("Customers") # with sheet name
    df2 = file.parse(1)        # or with sheet index
    df3 = file.parse(2)
```

Method preference shaped by intended outcome

We have discussed different ways to read multiple Excel sheets; each method has its strengths depending on your use case. Here is a breakdown to help you choose the best one for your scenario:

- Use **`pd.read_excel(sheet_name=[...])`** when you know exactly which sheets you want and prefer a concise, one-liner approach. Best for quick reads of 2 or 3 sheets.
- Use **`ExcelFile.parse()`** in a loop when you need to load **all sheets dynamically**, especially if the sheet names or count may vary. Ideal for automation and scalable workflows such as:

```
with pd.ExcelFile("demo_sales.xlsx") as file:
    all_dfs = []
    for sheet in file.sheet_names:
        if sheet.startswith('Sales'):    # only sales related sheets
            df = file.parse(sheet_name=sheet)
            df["sheet"] = sheet
            all_dfs.append(df)
combined = pd.concat(all_dfs, ignore_index=True)
```

- Use a **`with pd.ExcelFile(...)`** context manager when writing production-grade scripts where resource management matters. It ensures the file is properly closed after reading. This method is efficient for selective reading
- Use **`ExcelFile.parse()`** manually for each sheet when you want fine-grained control over how each sheet is read. For example, applying different parsing options per sheet.

The to_excel() method

Usually, we use the **`to_excel()`** method to write Excel files with a suitable engine type such as **`openpyxl`** or **`xlsxwriter`** (default). You can also specify **`sheet_name`**, **`start_row`**, **`start_col`**, and other arguments as per requirement. A simple example is as follows:

```
import pandas as pd

# Sample DataFrame
df = pd.DataFrame({
    "Flight": ["AI101", "BA202", "LH303"],
    "Passengers": [180, 220, 150]
})

# Write DataFrame to a custom sheet name
df.to_excel("flights.xlsx", sheet_name="Aviation_Report", index=False)
```

By default, **`pandas`** writes to a sheet called *Sheet1*. The **`sheet_name`** argument lets you name the sheet something meaningful. You can start writing in a custom row or column:

```
# Zero-indexed in pandas, so Excel shows it as row 6, col C

df.to_excel("flights_offset.xlsx", sheet_name="Flights",
                startrow=5, startcol=2, index=False)
```

By default, **`to_excel()`** writes a single **`DataFrame`** onto a sheet. If you want to place multiple **`DataFrames`** in the same sheet at different positions, or distribute them across multiple sheets, you need to create an **`ExcelWriter`** object. This allows you to specify the target file and control the placement of each **`DataFrame`** within it.

The ExcelWriter class

As discussed, you need to use **`ExcelWriter`** class explicitly when you need to write data to multiple sheets, place DataFrames at specific cell ranges within the same sheet, append new data, or apply formatting and styles (with engines like **`xlsxwriter`** or **`openpyxl`**).

The writer should be used as a context manager. Otherwise, call **close()** to save and close any opened file handles. You can find the full documentation on **pandas**' official site **https://pandas.pydata.org/docs/reference/api/pandas.DataFrame.to_excel.html**.

Refer to the following:

```
flights = pd.DataFrame({
    "Flight": ["AI101", "BA202", "LH303"],
    "Passengers": [180, 220, 150]
})

cargo = pd.DataFrame({
    "Flight": ["AI101", "BA202", "LH303"],
    "Cargo_Tons": [20, 35, 15]
})

# Use ExcelWriter to control placement

with pd.ExcelWriter("aviation_report.xlsx", engine="openpyxl") as writer:
    flights.to_excel(writer, sheet_
name="Summary", startrow=1, startcol=0, index=False)

    cargo.to_excel(writer, sheet_
name="Summary", startrow=1, startcol=4, index=False)
```

The output file is shown in the following figure:

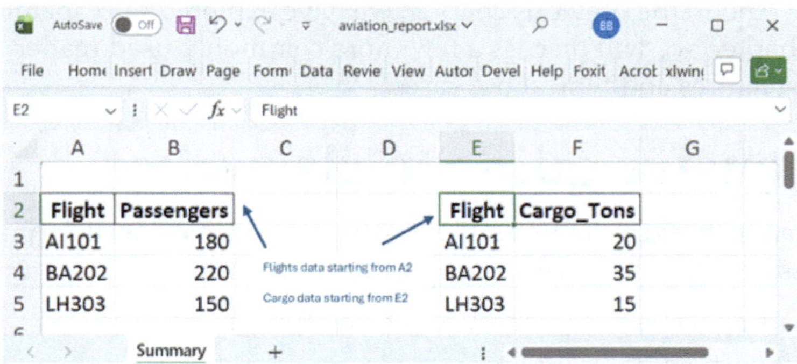

Figure 9.2: Two DataFrames at specific cell ranges within the same sheet

If you received more passenger data that you want to append to the flight data in Excel:

```
new_flights = pd.DataFrame({
    "Flight": ["UA404", "EK505"],
    "Passengers": [190, 210]
```

```
})

# Append data to existing sheet without writing column headers again
with pd.ExcelWriter("aviation_report.xlsx", engine="openpyxl",
                    mode="a", if_sheet_exists="overlay") as writer:
    new_flights.to_excel(writer, sheet_name="Summary",
                         startrow=5, startcol=0, index=False, header=False)
```

The resultant Excel file is shown in *Figure 9.3*. This cannot be done with **xlsxwriter**, because that engine only creates new files. In the next section, we will take a closer look at what **xlsxwriter** has to offer.

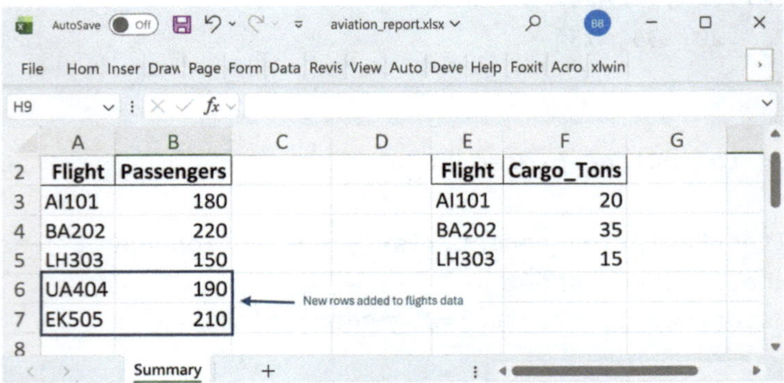

***Figure 9.3**: Appending rows to existing data using openpyxl*

We have seen that **pandas** allows integration with some reader or writer package through its **engine** parameter. And in the previous chapter, we have explored the capabilities of **openpyxl** in detail. In this chapter, we will discuss a few more commonly used reader and writer tools, highlighting their features and typical use cases.

Comprehensive guide to xlsxwriter

Library **xlsxwriter** truly excels in its ability to produce complex, well-formatted workbooks that mirror professional Excel reports. It supports advanced features such as:

- Rich formatting (cell styles, conditional formatting, merged cells)
- Charts, images, and data validation
- Worksheet and cell protection
- Memory-efficient writing of large datasets and much more

Unlike **openpyxl**, which reads and modifies existing Excel files, or **pandas**, which focuses on tabular data export, **xlsxwriter** is ideal when the goal is to generate polished Excel output programmatically, especially for reporting, dashboards, or automated exports.

In summary, **xlsxwriter** is not a replacement for data analysis tools but a powerful complement for those who need to deliver Excel files that look and behave like they were crafted manually.

Creating Excel files and sheets

Let us re-create the same **product_data.xlsx** we had created earlier using **openpyxl**. We will name this file **toy_data.xlsx** to avoid confusion:

```
import xlsxwriter

wb = xlsxwriter.Workbook('toy_data.xlsx')
ws = wb.add_worksheet('products')

header_format = wb.add_format({'bold': True,
                               'bg_color': '#DCE6F1',
                               'font_color': '#223A54'})

headers = ['product_id', 'product_name', 'product_category', 'product_price']

for col_num, header in enumerate(headers):
    ws.write(0, col_num, header, header_format)

wb.close()
```

Here, we have iterated through a list of headers and used **write(row, col, data, cell_format)** method to write data and apply formatting to it. It writes each cell individually, giving you fine-grained control over formatting per column or cell. Finally, we have used **close()** method, which is a required call to close and write the Excel file, unless you are using the with context manager.

We can also write an entire row in one go, applying the same format to all cells with:

```
ws.write_row(row=0, col=0, data=headers, cell_format=header_format)
```

Note: Contrasting openpyxl, which lets you modify existing Excel files and apply formatting after writing, in xlsxwriter, all data and formatting must be applied at the time of writing data, as it does not support editing or reading existing workbooks.

Unlike openpyxl, xlsxwriter doesn't have a separate save() method. The filename is specified when creating the workbook, and close() is what finalizes and writes the file.

Another point to note is xlsxwriter uses are zero-based indices for cell navigation, so row (or column) 0 means the first row (or column) in Excel. While, openpyxl uses one based indices for its cell API and also supports A1 notation

You can also write data to individual columns using **write_column()**, perfect for inserting new variables in data. Sample code is as follows:

```
column_data = ['A001', 'A002', 'A003', 'A004']
ws.write_column('E2', column_data)  # Writes down from cell E2
```

You can add more sheets and set tab color:

```
analytics_ws = wb.add_worksheet('Analytics_Report')
analytics_ws.set_tab_color('#1072BA')
```

However, **xlsxwriter** does not support operations like sheet reordering, copying or deleting sheets, and inserting rows or columns. Worksheets are created strictly in the order they are added. This limitation exists because **xlsxwriter** is a write-only library, designed solely for generating new Excel files, not for reading or modifying existing ones.

Writing data and applying formatting

We will create a **.xlsx** file and populate data from a nested list in the products sheet:

```
import xlsxwriter

wb = xlsxwriter.Workbook('toy_data.xlsx')
ws = wb.add_worksheet('products')

header_format = wb.add_format({'bold': True,
                               'bg_color': '#DCE6F1',
                               'font_color': '#223A54'})

headers = ['product_id', 'product_name', 'product_category', 'product_price']

ws.write_row(0, 0, headers, header_format)

# Sample data (nested list)
data = [
    [101, 'Wireless Mouse', 'Electronics', 25.99],
    [102, 'Yoga Mat', 'Fitness', 15.50],
    [103, 'Notebook', 'Stationery', 3.99],
    [104, 'Pen', 'Stationery', 10.00],
    [105, 'USB Cable', 'Electronics', 150.00],
    [106, 'Chair', 'Furniture', 45.50],
    [107, 'Water Bottle', 'Fitness', 10.00]
```

```
]

# Writing data row-wise from row 1 and col 0 (in excel 2nd row and 1st col)

for row_num, row_data in enumerate(data, start=1):
    ws.write_row(row = row_num, col = 0, data = row_data)

# Adding a new data/variable

units_sold = [5, 8, 15, 30, 6, 10, 20]

ws.write(0, len(headers), 'Units Sold', header_format) # header

# Writing data column-wise (starting row=1 since row=0 is header)
ws.write_column(1, len(headers), units_sold)
ws.set_column('A:E', 15)

wb.close()
```

We have used **write_row()** to add data horizontally (row-wise) and **write_col()** to add data vertically (column-wise). Both methods automatically adjust to the length of the data provided. There is no need to manually specify the number of columns or rows; the methods handle it dynamically. We have also adjusted the column width. The output Excel file is shown in the following figure:

	A	B	C	D	E
1	product_id	product_name	product_category	product_price	Units Sold
2	101	Wireless Mouse	Electronics	25.99	5
3	102	Yoga Mat	Fitness	15.5	8
4	103	Notebook	Stationery	3.99	15
5	104	Pen	Stationery	10	30
6	105	USB Cable	Electronics	150	6
7	106	Chair	Furniture	45.5	10
8	107	Water Bottle	Fitness	10	20
9					
10					

products

Figure 9.4: *Excel file created by xlsxwriter*

As **xlsxwriter** is write-only, every time we add a new column, sheet, or a feature (formatting, charts, validation), we recreate the workbook. To avoid repeating code, from now onwards, we will be providing the code that can be added to existing code, and it will overwrite the same file. If you want to avoid replacing files, you can give a suitable file name while exploring new features (as done in the chapter code scripts).

Modern Excel formula support

Unlike **openpyxl**, which lets you pass a formula string directly to **ws.write()** or **cell.value**, **xlsxwriter** treats formulas as a distinct type and requires its dedicated method, **ws.write_formula()**. Let us add a column revenue based on price and units sold, using **ws.write_formula(row, col, formula)** method:

```
# Add "Revenue" header
ws.write(0, len(headers) + 1, 'Revenue', header_format)

# Write formula row-wise
for row_num in range(1, len(data) + 1):
    price_cell = f'D{row_num + 1}'          # Column D = product_price
    units_cell = f'E{row_num + 1}'          # Column E = Units Sold
    formula = f'={price_cell}*{units_cell}'
    ws.write_formula(row_num, len(headers) + 1, formula)
```

After adding the preceding code to the existing code, we get this Excel:

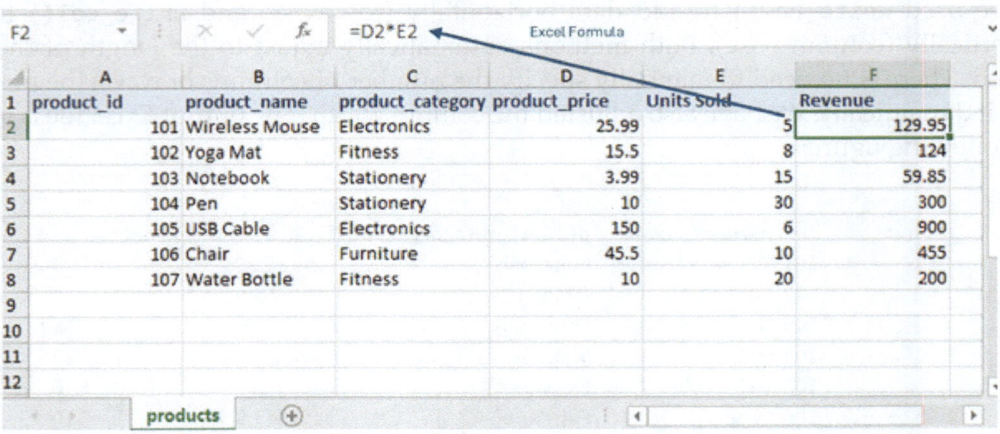

	A	B	C	D	E	F
1	product_id	product_name	product_category	product_price	Units Sold	Revenue
2	101	Wireless Mouse	Electronics	25.99	5	129.95
3	102	Yoga Mat	Fitness	15.5	8	124
4	103	Notebook	Stationery	3.99	15	59.85
5	104	Pen	Stationery	10	30	300
6	105	USB Cable	Electronics	150	6	900
7	106	Chair	Furniture	45.5	10	455
8	107	Water Bottle	Fitness	10	20	200

Figure 9.5: Adding Excel formula using xlsxwriter

Note that Excel stores formulas in the format of the US English version, so all formula function names written using **xlsxwriter** must be in English:

```
ws.write_formula('E9', '{=SUM(E2:E8)}') # Works
ws.write_formula('E9', '{=SOMME(E2:E8)}') # French _ #NAME Error on Load
```

It computes the sum of cells E2 up to E8 and writes the result in E9, as shown in the following figure:

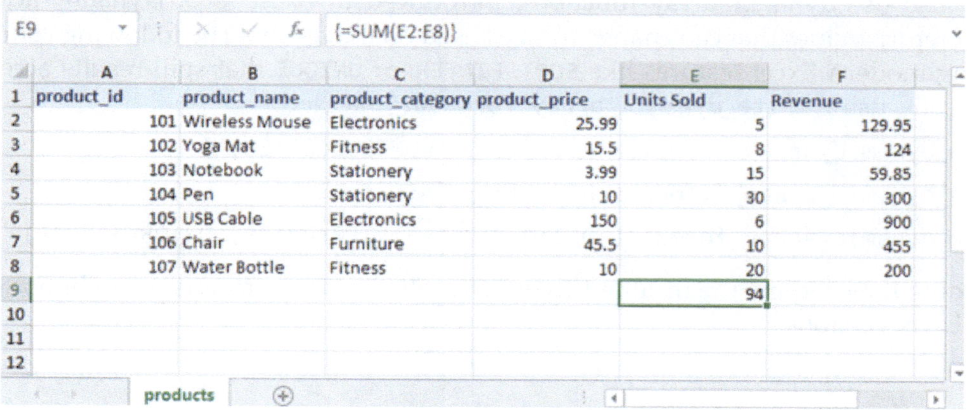

***Figure 9.6**: Formula names must be in English*

Using new functions

Unlike **openpyxl**, **xlsxwriter** does not require you to write the **_xlfn.** prefix for newer Excel functions such as **IFS**, **TEXTJOIN**, or **LET**. These formulas will work as expected in **xlsxwriter**, provided that the version of Excel used to open the file supports them:

```
ws.write_formula('I2', '=TEXTJOIN(": ", TRUE, B2:C2)')
ws.write_formula('H2', '=IFS(F2>500, "High", F2>300, "Medium", F2>0, "Low")')
```

The resultant Excel file is shown in the following figure:

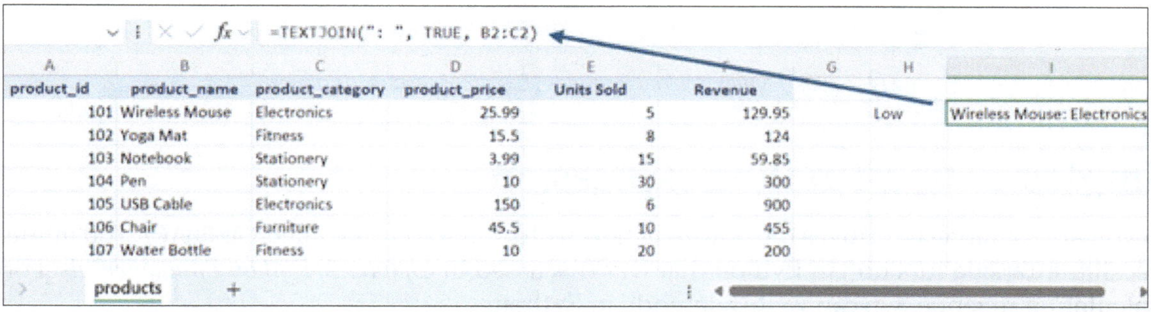

***Figure 9.7**: Adding new Excel formulas and using use_future_functions=True option*

Sometimes, these newer functions, such as **IFS**, **TEXTJOIN** may initially show **#NAME?**. This is not an error. Simply double-click the cell and hit *Enter*, and Excel will compute it correctly. Otherwise, you can simply enable the **use_future_functions=True** option in the **Workbook()** constructor, and **xlsxwriter** will handle the prefixing automatically:

```
wb = xlsxwriter.Workbook('filename.xlsx', {'use_future_functions': True})
```

Working with dynamic array formulas

You can also use dynamic array functions, introduced in Excel 365. Dynamic arrays are ranges of return values that can change in size based on the results. The following code shows leveraging modern Excel features like **SORT**, **FILTER**, or **UNIQUE** that spill results across cells automatically, using **write_dynamic_array_formula()** method:

```
ws.write_dynamic_array_formula('A11:A15', '=UNIQUE(C2:C8)')
ws.write_dynamic_array_formula('B11:B15', '=SORT(B2:B8)')
ws.write_dynamic_array_formula('D11:D20', '=FILTER(B2:D8, D2:D8 > 20)')
```

After adding the heading, the resultant Excel is as follows (These formulas might not work in older Excel versions):

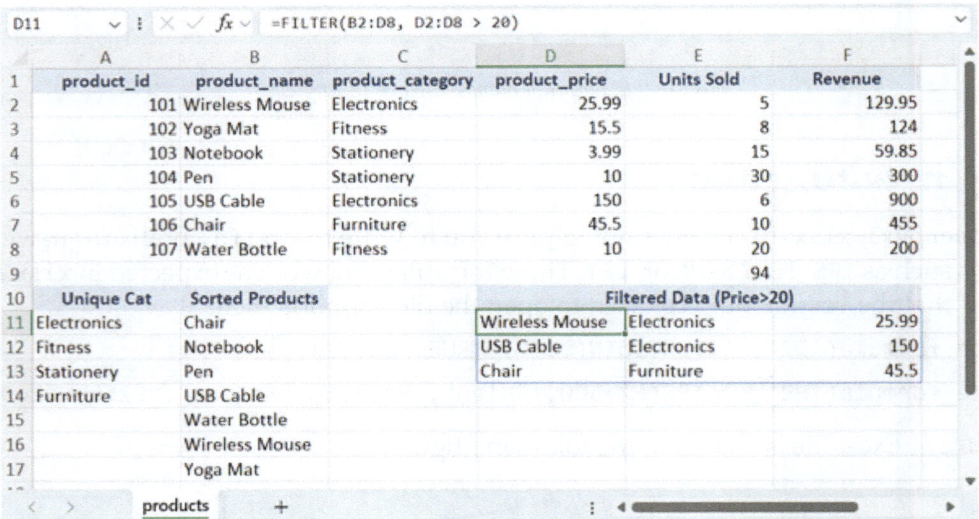

D11 =FILTER(B2:D8, D2:D8 > 20)

	A	B	C	D	E	F
1	product_id	product_name	product_category	product_price	Units Sold	Revenue
2	101	Wireless Mouse	Electronics	25.99	5	129.95
3	102	Yoga Mat	Fitness	15.5	8	124
4	103	Notebook	Stationery	3.99	15	59.85
5	104	Pen	Stationery	10	30	300
6	105	USB Cable	Electronics	150	6	900
7	106	Chair	Furniture	45.5	10	455
8	107	Water Bottle	Fitness	10	20	200
9					94	
10	Unique Cat	Sorted Products		Filtered Data (Price>20)		
11	Electronics	Chair		Wireless Mouse	Electronics	25.99
12	Fitness	Notebook		USB Cable	Electronics	150
13	Stationery	Pen		Chair	Furniture	45.5
14	Furniture	USB Cable				
15		Water Bottle				
16		Wireless Mouse				
17		Yoga Mat				

products

Figure 9.8*: Dynamic array formulas (Excel 365) using xlsxwriter*

Implementing Lambda expressions

If you are someone who loves the powerful new feature of Excel 365 called **LAMBDA()**. You might recall the **lambda** function in Python that was discussed in *Chapter 3, Python Fundamentals*. For calculating revenue, we can write a lambda in Python:

```
Revenue = lambda price, units: price * units
```

In **ws.write_formula()** method, we can use Excel's **LAMBDA()** function, and parameters in the **LAMBDA()** function must have a **_xlpm** prefix for compatibility with how the formulas are stored in Excel. These prefixes would not show up in the formula:

```
ws.write_formula('K2', '=LAMBDA(_xlpm.price, _xlpm.units, _xlpm.price * _xlpm.
units)(D2, E2)')
```

The following figure shows implementation of **lambda** function (in Excel 365) to compute revenue:

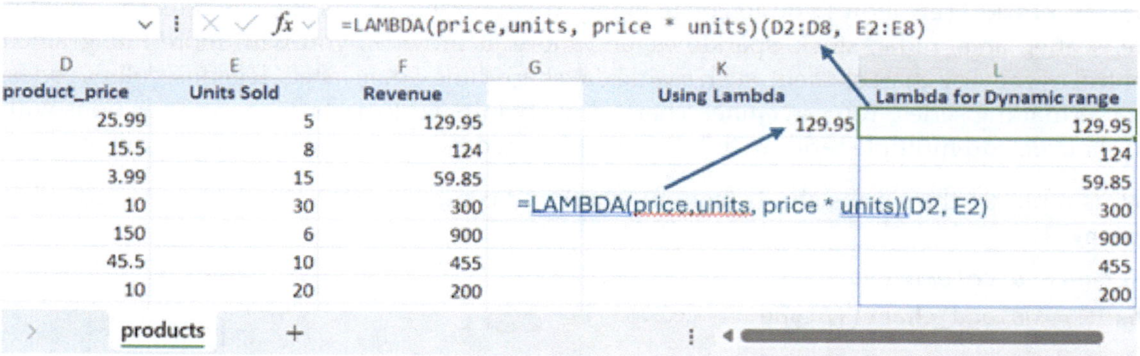

Figure 9.9: Adding Lambda functions

You might have noticed that Excel displays formula without the prefix.

Referencing Excel table

Another powerful feature of **xlsxwriter** is that you can add worksheet tables with **xlsxwriter** using the **add_table()** method. By default, tables are named as Table1, Table2, and so on, in the order that they are added. However, it can also be explicitly set by the user using the name parameter, which is useful when:

- You want to reference the table by name in formulas or VBA.
- You are generating multiple tables and need predictable identifiers.
- You are integrating with other tools or workflows that expect specific table names.

Figure 9.10 shows Excel tables created by **xlsxwriter**:

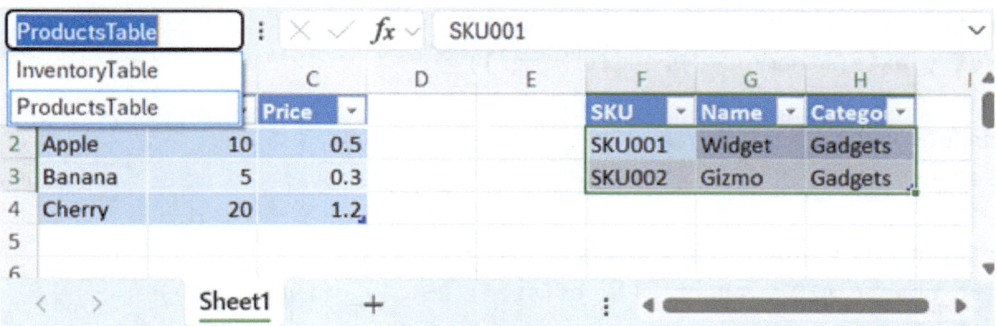

Figure 9.10: Adding Excel tables using xlsxwriter

Charts and images

Library **xlsxwriter** allows you to create highly customizable charts such as column, bar, line, pie, scatter, area, radar, stock, sparklines, and more. It provides you with more fine-grained control over every chart element, such as titles, axes, gridlines, data labels, legends, colors, styles, and formatting series. You can embed charts directly into worksheets at specific positions with pixel offset, add multiple series with full formatting, secondary axes, and even trendlines.

Let us replicate the simple charts (column chart and combo chart) that we had created using **openpyxl**:

```
# Create a column chart
chart = wb.add_chart({'type': 'column'})

# Configure the series
chart.add_series({
    'name':        'Units Sold',
    'categories': f'=products!$B$2:$B${len(data)+1}',  # Product Names
    'values':     f'=products!$E$2:$E${len(data)+1}',  # Units Sold
    'fill':       {'color': '#4F81BD'},
    'border':     {'color': '#1F497D'},
    'trendline':  {'type': 'linear', 'display_equation': True,
                   'line': {'color': '#C00000',
                            'width': 2.25,
                            'dash_type': 'long_dash'}}
})

# Add chart title and axis labels
chart.set_title({'name': 'Units Sold by Products'})
chart.set_x_axis({'name': 'Units Sold'})
chart.set_y_axis({'name': 'Product Name'})

# We can also set chart style
chart.set_style(11)

# Insert the chart into the worksheet
ws.insert_chart('A10', chart, {'x_offset': 25, 'y_offset': 10})

# Another chart
combo_chart = wb.add_chart({'type': 'column'})
```

```
# Revenue series
combo_chart.add_series({
    'name': 'Price',
    'categories': f'=products!$B$2:$B${len(data)+1}',
    'values':     f'=products!$D$2:$D${len(data)+1}',
    'fill':     {'color': '#4472C4'}
})

# Units Sold series
combo_chart.add_series({
    'name': 'Units Sold',
    'categories': f'=products!$B$2:$B${len(data)+1}',
    'values':     f'=products!$E$2:$E${len(data)+1}',
    'fill': {'color': '#ED7D31'}
})

combo_chart.set_title({'name': 'Price vs Units Sold'})
combo_chart.set_x_axis({'name': 'Product'})
combo_chart.set_y_axis({'name': 'values'})

ws.insert_chart('J1', combo_chart)
```

You might have noticed that we have added a nicely formatted trendline to the first chart. The resultant Excel file is shown in *Figure 9.11*. You can also play with the y-axis of the combo chart by slightly changing the code. These charts are embedded as Excel objects; you can also edit them directly in Excel.

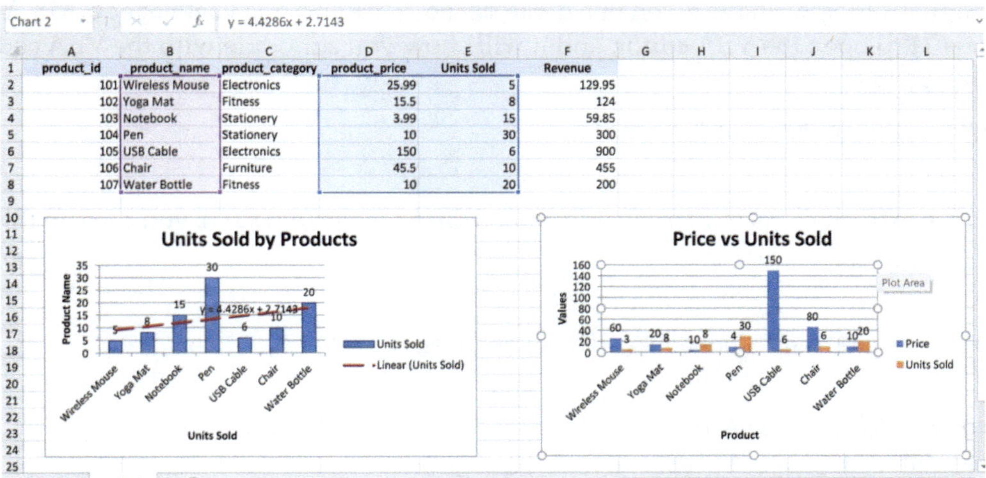

Figure 9.11: *Basic charts created by xlsxwriter*

We recommend that you create other useful charts and play with the chart elements to make them publication-ready. As discussed previously, **matplotlib** or **pandas** charts can be imported as a static image, so they might not be very useful. You can insert any image (in PNG, JPEG, GIF, BMP, WMF or EMF format) and set its position or size by using **worksheet.insert_image(row, col, image, options)**.

You can even embed images into a worksheet cell and have the image automatically scale to the width and height of the cell by using **embed_image(row, col, filename[, options])**.

The X/Y scaling of the image is preserved, but the size of the image is adjusted to fit the largest possible width or height, depending on the cell dimensions. This is the equivalent of Excel's menu option to insert an image using the option to **Place in Cell**, which is only available in Excel 365 versions from 2023 onwards. For older versions of Excel, a **#VALUE!** error is displayed.

Working with VBA macros

Macros are a common way to automate tasks in Excel using **Visual Basic for Applications** (**VBA**). A macro-enabled Excel file (**.xlsm**) is the same as a **xlsx** file except that it contains an additional **vbaProject.bin** file, which contains macros. Using **xlsxwriter**, you can embed an existing macro project into a new workbook. Note that you cannot create or edit VBA code, but you can take an existing compiled macro file (**vbaProject.bin**) and insert it into your **.xlsm** output.

To interact with macros (write, edit, or run VBA) programmatically, you will either need to use COM automation (Windows)/ AppleScript. (MacOS) or you can use Python's **xlwings** library, which lets you control a live Excel session, write and call VBA macros, or even replace VBA with Python functions.

In the chapter folder, we have given one **demo_macro.xlsm** and one **vbaProject.bin**. You can press *Alt+F11* to open the VBA editor, and it will show you a module with the VBA code:

```
Sub HelloWorld()
    MsgBox "Hello from VBA Macro!"
End Sub
```

To attach the extracted macro to a new file named **macro_enabled.xlsm**, you can run this code:

```
import xlsxwriter

workbook = xlsxwriter.Workbook('macro_enabled.xlsm')

# Attach an existing VBA project (compiled as vbaProject.bin)
workbook.add_vba_project('vbaProject.bin')
ws = workbook.add_worksheet('demo')
```

```
# Write some text
ws.write("A1", "This is generated by Python!")
ws.write("A3", "Run the macro 'HelloWorld' from Developer > Macros.")

workbook.close()
```

The **`add_vba_project()`** method can be used to add macros or functions to a workbook using a binary VBA project file that has been extracted from an existing Excel **`xlsm`** file. Only one **`vbaProject.bin`** file can be added per workbook. The name does not have to be vbaProject.bin. Any suitable path or name for an existing VBA bin file will do. You can check **`macro_enabled.xlsm`** file, which has text written in cells A1 and A3. Pressing *Alt+F11* will show you a module with the same VBA code. If you run it from the VBA editor (shortcut *F5*) or from a worksheet control, a modal message box pops up in Excel showing the text **`Hello from VBA Macro!`** (Refer to the following figure):

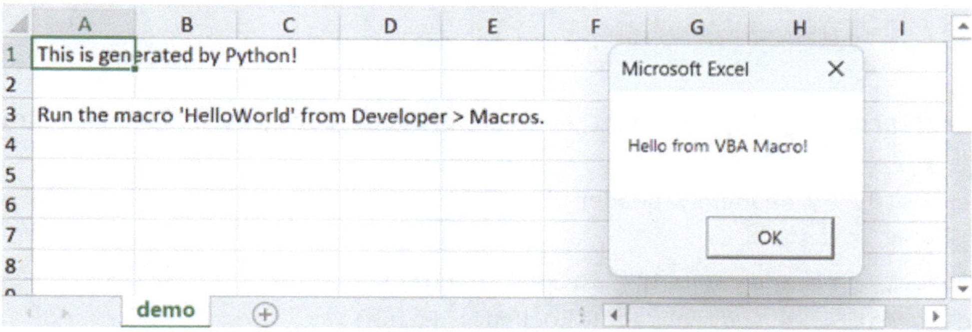

***Figure 9.12**: Inserting and running an existing macro to a new xlsm file*

If you are curious about how to create a compiled macro file (such as **`vbaProject.bin`**) for your macro-enabled Excel file. You can:

- Rename the **`.xlsm`** file to a **`.zip`** file.
- Navigate the **`xl`** folder in the folder structure and find **`vbaProject.bin`** file.
- Copy the **`xl/vbaProject.bin`** file.
- Simply drag it out or copy it to your working directory.
- Use it in your code with **`xlsxwriter`**.

Protecting sheets and cells

If you are generating reports where users should view but not edit certain cells, you can protect worksheets, lock specific cells, and hide formulas or values using **`xlsxwriter`**.

The **protect()** method is used to protect a worksheet from modification, which locks all cells by default. A **locked** cell cannot be edited; you must explicitly unlock cells that might need edits. A **hidden** cell will display the results of a formula but not the formula itself.

The following code protects the products worksheet, locks the header row, and locks and hides formulas in the Revenue column. Meanwhile, it keeps all data cells unlocked, allowing users to edit them freely:

```
import xlsxwriter

wb = xlsxwriter.Workbook('protected.xlsx')
ws = wb.add_worksheet('products')

header_format = wb.add_format({'bold': True,
                               'bg_color': '#DCE6F1',
                               'font_color': '#223A54',
                               'locked': True})

headers = ['product_id', 'product_name', 'product_category', 'product_price']

ws.write_row(0, 0, headers, header_format)

locked_format = wb.add_format({'locked': True})
unlocked_format = wb.add_format({'locked': False})
hidden_formula_format = wb.add_format({'locked': True, 'hidden': True})

data = [
    [101, 'Wireless Mouse', 'Electronics', 25.99],
    [102, 'Yoga Mat', 'Fitness', 15.50],
    [103, 'Notebook', 'Stationery', 3.99],
    [104, 'Pen', 'Stationery', 10.00],
    [105, 'USB Cable', 'Electronics', 150.00],
    [106, 'Chair', 'Furniture', 45.50],
    [107, 'Water Bottle', 'Fitness', 10.00]
]

for row_num, row_data in enumerate(data, start=1):
    ws.write_row(row_num, 0, row_data, unlocked_format)
```

```
units_sold = [5, 8, 15, 30, 6, 10, 20]
ws.write(0, len(headers), 'Units Sold', header_format)
ws.write_column(1, len(headers), units_sold, unlocked_format)

ws.write(0, len(headers) + 1, 'Revenue', header_format)
for row_num in range(1, len(data) + 1):
    price_cell = f'D{row_num + 1}'
    units_cell = f'E{row_num + 1}'
    formula = f'={price_cell}*{units_cell}'
    ws.write_formula(row_num, len(headers) + 1, formula, hidden_formula_
format)

ws.set_column('A:F', 15)

ws.protect()

wb.close()
```

When trying to change the value in the revenue column, it prompted to unprotect the sheet:

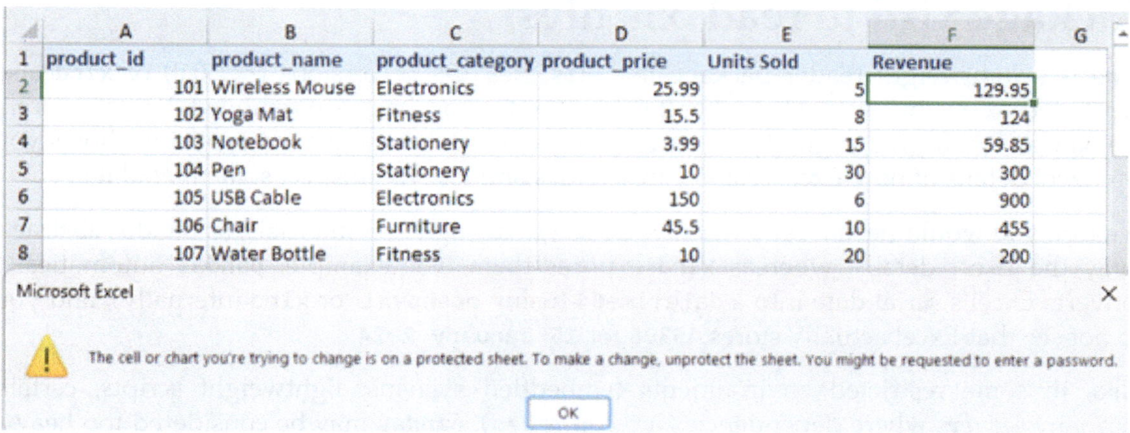

***Figure 9.13**: Protecting, cells and hiding formula using xlsxwriter*

Additional features of xlsxwriter

What we have covered so far are just the basics; you can use **`xlsxwriter`** for writing publication-quality Excel reports (Excel 2007+ .xlsx files). Some of the amazing features supported by **`xlsxwriter`** that you might want to explore are: merge cell, freeze and split pans, autofit, defined names, auto filters, data validation, drop down list, conditional formatting, hyperlinks, inserting text boxes or check boxes, cell comments, headers, footers, outlining and grouping, writing rich strings with multiple formats, working with worksheet tables, set document properties, memory optimization for large datasets, and integration with **pandas** and **polars**.

If you are comfortable with basic Excel and Python, the **xlsxwriter** documentation at **https://xlsxwriter.readthedocs.io/contents.html** is a goldmine, beautifully organized and packed with examples for your favorite Excel feature. You will be amazed at how much you can automate and customize, all from Python[2].

However, **xlsxwriter** is write-only; it cannot read or modify existing files. For that, you will need to explore **xlwings**, which allows live Excel interaction. We will cover this in the upcoming chapters.

You will also need to explore **xlrd**, **xlwt**, **xlutils** for legacy **.xls** formats or **pyxlsb** to read binary **.xlsb** files, if you work with those file formats. Let us discuss these alternative modules for handling such Excel files.

Working with legacy .xls files

If your work requires you to deal with legacy **.xls** files (Excel 97–2003), you might need **xlrd**, **xlwt**, and **xlutils** to read, write, and edit **.xls** files.

Package xlrd to read .xls files

xlrd is a lightweight reader package for **.xls** files. Older versions (< 2.0.0) of **xlrd** also supported **.xlsx**, but since December 2020, **.xlsx** support has been removed. You can surely use **pandas** (with **xlrd** engine) to read **.xls** files; however, using **xlrd** explicitly shows you low-level details of how Excel really stores values and lets you inspect some metadata.

In short, you would need it only when you need to debug Excel internals, as pandas abstracts away the Excel details, whereas **xlrd** exposes them. For example, **pandas** automatically converts Excel's serial date into a **datetime64** (using **openpyxl** or **xlrd** internally), and you do not see that Excel actually stores **45306** for **15 January 2024**.

Also, in some restricted environments (embedded systems, lightweight scripts, certain company servers where dependencies are controlled), **pandas** may be considered too heavy; there, **xlrd** (which is tiny and has no dependencies) can be used to read **.xls** files.

Let us read the same **finance_data.xls** that we had used earlier:

```
import xlrd


# Opening .xls file
```

[2] Advanced users can also explore XlsxPandasFormatter at **https://github.com/webermarcolivier/xlsxpandasformatter**, which is a helper class that wraps the worksheet, workbook, and DataFrame objects written by Pandas to_excel() method using the xlsxwriter engine to allow consistent formatting of cells.

```
wb = xlrd.open_workbook("finance_data.xls")

# Number of all sheets
print(wb.nsheets)
# List of all sheet names
print(wb.sheet_names())

# Get the first sheet by index
sheet = wb.sheet_by_index(0)

# Get a sheet by its name
sheet = wb.sheet_by_name("Jan")

# Sheet metadata
print("Sheet name:", sheet.name)
print("Visibility:", sheet.visibility)
# 0=visible, 1=hidden, 2=very hidden

print("Number of rows:", sheet.nrows)
print("Number of columns:", sheet.ncols)

# Print first row
print(sheet.row_values(0))

# Read a specific cell value
cell_value = sheet.cell_value(rowx=0, colx=0)
print("Cell (0,0):", cell_value)

# Inspecting data type
cell_type = sheet.cell_type(rowx=0, colx=0)
print("Cell (0,0):", cell_type)
```

It gives datatype of specific cell as an integer type code. The type of cells, corresponding integer code and their values are like:

- **XL_CELL_NUMBER (2)**: numbers (General, Number format in Excel)
- **XL_CELL_DATE (3)**: dates (Excel serial numbers)
- **XL_CELL_TEXT (1)**: strings

- **XL_CELL_BOOLEAN (4)**: TRUE or FALSE
- **XL_CELL_EMPTY (0)**: blank
- **XL_CELL_ERROR (5)**: errors (**#DIV/0!**, **#REF!**, etc.)

To read raw values of entire sheet, you can iterate through sheet rows:

```
for r in range(sheet.nrows):
    row_values = sheet.row_values(r)
    print(row_values)
```

The first few rows of the output is:

```
['txn_id', 'txn_date', 'client', 'amount', 'approved', 'region']
[‚T001‘, 45306.0, ‚Alice‘, 1200.0, 1, ‚East‘]
[‚T002‘, 45307.0, ‚Mark‘, 900.0, 0, ‚North‘]
[‚T003‘, 45309.0, ‚Linda‘, ‚‘, 1, ‚NA‘]
[‚T004‘, ‚missing‘, ‚David‘, 1100.0, 1, ‚South‘]
[‚T005‘, 45311.0, ‚‘, 1500.0, 0, ‚West‘]
```

You might have noticed that in **xlrd**, empty cells return **''** (empty string) with cell type reported as **XL_CELL_EMPTY**. This is different from **pandas**, which converts them to **NaN**. So, you must remember that **xlrd** gives you the raw stored value, not the interpreted one.

Also, as you know, Excel stores dates as serial numbers, which represent the number of days since a starting point. When reading date columns using **xlrd**, these values may appear as raw numbers. The **workbook.datemode** attribute shows which date system is used by the Excel workbook:

- **0** indicates the 1900 date system (default on Windows) and
- **1** means the 1904 date system (default on older Mac versions)

Refer to the following code:

```
print("Datemode (0=1900, 1=1904):", wb.datemode) # 0
```

To convert a serial number into a readable date and time format, use **xldate_as_tuple(cell_value, workbook.datemode)**, which returns a tuple **(year, month, day, hour, minute, second)**:

```
# This cell (B2) contains a date
cell_value = sheet.cell_value(rowx=1, colx=1)
date_value = xlrd.xldate_as_tuple(cell_value, wb.datemode)

print(f'Raw Value: {cell_value}\t Date: {date_value}')
# Raw Value: 45306.0  Date: (2024, 1, 15, 0, 0, 0)
```

Let us inspect how Excel has stored data in each cell:

```
# inspecting data type in each cell
for c in range(sheet.ncols):
    print(f"Column {c}:")
    for r in range(sheet.nrows):
        cell = sheet.cell(r, c)
        print(f"  Row {r} - Type: {cell.ctype}, Value: {cell.value}")
```

Note that **xlrd** does not automatically assign a single datatype to an entire column, because Excel columns can contain mixed types such as text, numbers, dates, and blanks, all in the same column. With xlrd package, you do not need to close the workbook in general. If you open a workbook with the **on_demand=True** argument to save memory, the file is not closed automatically and you should call the **release_resources()** method when you are finished with the workbook:

Package xlwt to write .xls files

If you need to send data to legacy systems that still use **.xls**, you can create such files using **xlwt**, which is again a very lightweight and dependency-free library. Sample code for writing **.xls** file is as follows:

```
import xlwt

wb = xlwt.Workbook()
ws = wb.add_sheet("Sales")

# Write some data
ws.write(0, 0, "Product")
ws.write(0, 1, "Quantity")
ws.write(0, 2, "Price")
ws.write(1, 0, "Apples")
ws.write(1, 1, 10)
ws.write(1, 2, 2.5)
ws.write(2, 0, "Bananas")
ws.write(2, 1, 5)
ws.write(2, 2, 1.8)

# Save as legacy .xls
wb.save("sales_report.xls")
```

You can also apply formatting:

```
ws = wb.add_sheet("Report")

# Define a bold style
bold_style = xlwt.easyxf('font: bold on; align: horiz center')

# Define a currency style
currency_style = xlwt.easyxf(num_format_str= "$#,##0.00")

# Header row
ws.write(0, 0, "Item", bold_style)
ws.write(0, 1, "Cost", bold_style)

# Data with formatting
ws.write(1, 0, "Laptop")
ws.write(1, 1, 1200, currency_style)
ws.write(2, 0, "Monitor")
ws.write(2, 1, 300, currency_style)

wb.save("formatted_report.xls")
```

To insert Excel formula:

```
ws = wb.add_sheet("Data")
ws.write(0, 0, "Value1")
ws.write(0, 1, "Value2")
ws.write(0, 2, "Sum")

# Data
ws.write(1, 0, 10)
ws.write(1, 1, 20)

# Formula (calculated by Excel when opened)
ws.write(1, 2, xlwt.Formula("A2+B2"))
wb.save("formula_example.xls")
```

Package xlutils to modify .xls files

xlutils is a small companion library to **xlrd** and **xlwt.** As you know, **xlrd** can only read **.xls**, and **xlwt** can only write new **.xls**. Library **xlutils** bridges the gap, it lets you read an existing **.xls** with **xlrd**, copy it, and then modify it with **xlwt**. It might be useful when you want to update a few cells in an old **.xls** file without rewriting the whole sheet from scratch:

```
import xlrd
from xlutils.copy import copy

rb = xlrd.open_workbook("finance_data.xls")  # read-only
wb = copy(rb)                                 # make a writable copy
ws = wb.get_sheet(0)
ws.write(1, 2, "Updated Value")
wb.save("finance_data_updated.xls")
```

Please note that **xlutils** is not a standalone library, it extends **xlrd** and **xlwt**. It is useful only if you still have **.xls** files and need to read, modify, and save them.

Reading binary Excel files with pyxlsb

An Excel binary workbook file (**.xlsb**) is great for huge workbooks because it is smaller and faster to open in Excel. Some enterprises or finance departments prefer **.xlsb** because it loads faster in Excel with lots of formulas or macros.

If you need to read Excel binary workbook files **.xlsb**, you can use **pandas' read_excel()** with **engine = 'pyxlsb'**.Alternately, you can use **pyxlsb** directly, if you need low-level control such as iterate through rows without loading everything into memory or if you need to process huge **.xlsb** files line by line, instead of pulling them into a **pandas** Data Frame all at once. In both cases, **pyxlsb** needs to be installed:

```
from pyxlsb import open_workbook

wb = open_workbook("finance_data.xlsb")
print("Sheets:", list(wb.sheets))

# Fetching sheet by sheet index or name
sheet = wb.get_sheet(1) # Index is 1-based (1 = first sheet)
# or
sheet = wb.get_sheet('Jan')
# Accessing sheet name
sheet.name

wb.close()
```

Unlike **xlrd** and **openpyxl**, which open Excel files directly and manage resources internally, **pyxlsb** works with binary **.xlsb** files and exposes a file stream that should be explicitly closed. Hence, the preferred way is to use a **with** block to safely manage file access and avoid locking issues:

```
with open_workbook('finance_data.xlsb') as wb:
    with wb.get_sheet(1) as sheet:
        for row in sheet.rows():
            print([item.v for item in row])
```

If you are seeing extra rows or columns filled with **None** values when reading an **.xlsb** file, this is a common quirk. This typically occurs because Excel's used range might extend beyond the actual data, including empty cells that **pyxlsb** interprets as part of the worksheet. To handle this, you can skip empty rows or trim trailing blanks using various filtering techniques, depending on your workflow.

As of now, there is no native open-source Python that writes **.xlsb**. Either you can write .xlsx in Python (**pandas**, **openpyxl**, or **xlsxwriter**) and then manually save as **.xlsb** from Excel, or on Windows, you can use **win32com.client** to automate Excel itself. Another option is to use a commercial, full-featured library, such as **Aspose.Cells**, that supports reading and writing **.xlsb** (refer to the link **https://products.aspose.com/cells/python-java/create/xlsb/**).

pyxlsb is great for fast, lightweight reading of **.xlsb** files, currently extremely limited[3], but functional enough for basic data extraction. In upcoming chapters, we will introduce **xlwings** for full Excel automation, formatting, and macro support when users need deeper integration.

Mini project: Dashboard automation

Suppose you receive data from the aviation industry about flight ID, aircraft type, routes, distances, seats, load factor, delay (in minutes), etc. And you are to prepare a dashboard report. You can read data from some API, database, URL, or a local file and create a dashboard using **xlsxwriter**. For demonstration purposes, we are creating sample data using **xlsxwriter** and then creating a dashboard.

In the following code, we have written raw data in two sheets, where the first sheet, named *Flights*, contains flight-related data and the second sheet, named *Routes*, contains distance data for each route. A glimpse of the Flight data is shown in the following figure:

[3] If you work with binary files, you can also explore pyxlsb2, which offers some changes/improvements in comparison to pyxlsb

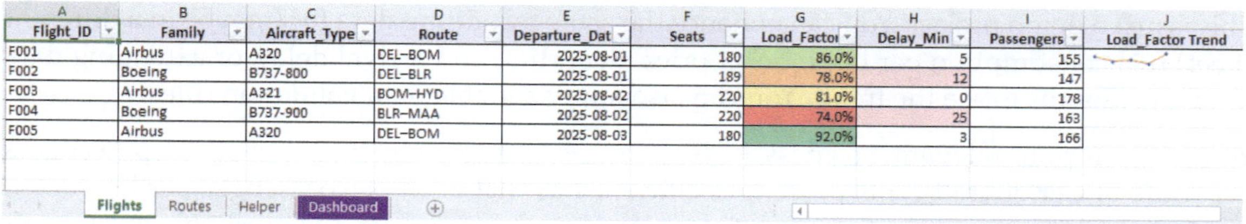

Flight_ID	Family	Aircraft_Type	Route	Departure_Dat	Seats	Load_Factor	Delay_Min	Passengers	Load_Factor Trend
F001	Airbus	A320	DEL-BOM	2025-08-01	180	86.0%	5	155	
F002	Boeing	B737-800	DEL-BLR	2025-08-01	189	78.0%	12	147	
F003	Airbus	A321	BOM-HYD	2025-08-02	220	81.0%	0	178	
F004	Boeing	B737-900	BLR-MAA	2025-08-02	220	74.0%	25	163	
F005	Airbus	A320	DEL-BOM	2025-08-03	180	92.0%	3	166	

***Figure 9.14**: Flights data with color scale, conditional formatting, and a sample sparkline trend*

For creating a dashboard, it is good practice to put your calculations in a separate sheet and keep only what is needed in the dashboard. In the third sheet named **`Helper`**, we have done such calculations, and finally, we have created a minimal dashboard by presenting some aviation KPIs such as average load factor, total fuel burn, route efficiency index, total passengers, and average delay per route.

We used many features of **`xlsxwriter`**, such as auto filter, merge and align cells, format cells, conditional formatting, inserting charts, sparklines, images, etc. You can also protect the dashboard sheet or specific cells that should not change. You can choose to hide sheets as per the requirement. The code is given in the companion repository, we recommend that you play with the code and make changes to include more variations of the data or dashboard. The following figure shows the output dashboard:

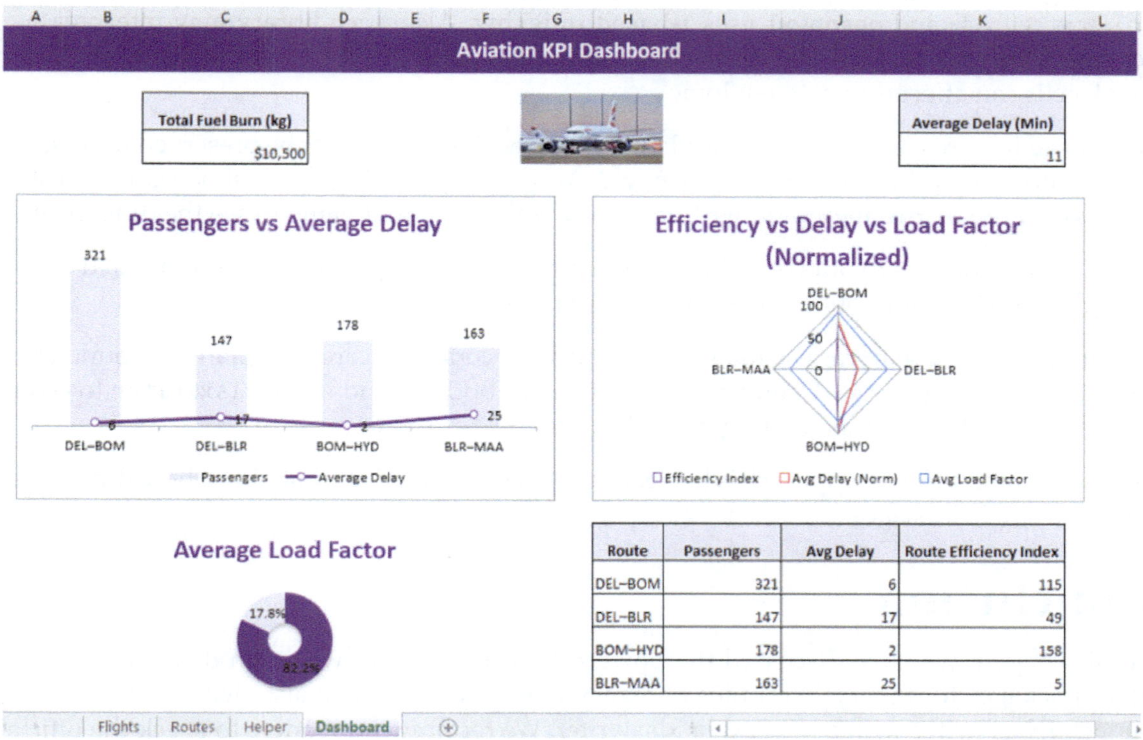

***Figure 9.15**: Aviation dashboard created by xlsxwriter*

This is just a demo project. You can enhance the same by adding data for (maybe in a different sheet) fuel consumption per hour, ticket price, departure and arrival delay, or extending data for a few months to see the trend. You can also apply suitable data validation rules.

You can compute relevant business KPIs as per your objective(s) such as total passengers per route or per aircraft type, passenger efficiency as fuel burn per passenger per kilometer, revenue per kilometer, revenue opportunity loss from empty seats, the most efficient aircraft (fuel vs. range vs. load), the top performing routes based on passenger volume, load factor, and low delays.

You can also add interesting charts, such as a heatmap to show delay by route, a line chart to show load factor trend over time, a scatter plot chart to show route efficiency (distance vs. delay), stacked, or grouped column chart to display passengers by aircraft type and route, or simply a bar chart for top five routes by passenger volume. The possibilities are unlimited; the given code can be a starter for further exploration and development.

Handling package switching

For a project, if you switch between multiple packages such as **`openpyxl`**, **`xlsxwriter`**, or **`pyxlsb`**, you need to be careful about compatibility considerations, namely, indexing, datatype handling, and feature support. For example, **`xlsxwriter`** uses **0-based indexing** (**`row=0, col=0`** is cell A1) and **`openpyxl`** uses **1-based indexing**. Also, each library may interpret and represent empty cells, strings, dates, and formulas differently. For example, **`None`** vs. **`""`** for blank cells can affect downstream logic.

Advanced features (for example, sparklines) of **`xlsxwriter`** might not be preserved if the same file is reopened and modified with **`openpyxl`**. You can try reading the dashboard file created by **`xlsxwriter`** in **`openpyxl`** and writing it back with a different name to see the difference.

To minimize complexity and avoid unintended behavior, it is generally recommended to use a single library throughout a project, whenever possible.

If you must combine libraries, you should adjust the code and carefully plan file boundaries, for example, using **`openpyxl`** and **`pandas`** for iterative updates and using **`xlsxwriter`** to create final dashboards (where no editing is needed later).

For maintainability, one approach is to create a small utility module that hides these differences behind a single interface.

Conclusion

In this chapter, we have discussed the powerful writer tool, xlsxwriter, in detail, along with other packages for binary Excel files or legacy Excel files. We have also demonstrated using pandas ExcelWriter with openpyxl or xlsxwriter. We recommend readers to check the official documentation for more advanced features of the tool(s) discussed.

In addition to the packages we have discussed, there are several other libraries, such as pyexcel, styleframe, pylightxl, pyxll (commercial), and some community-maintained repositories that can offer bug fixes, performance improvements, or niche features not available in the original packages. As your project evolves, you can choose the right tool based on your requirements.

In the next chapter, we will introduce xlwings, which allows seamless interaction between Python and Excel, including running Python code from Excel, calling Excel macros, automating workbooks, and even saving files in various formats including .xlsb through Excel itself.

Try it yourself

The following practice exercises will help you reinforce the learning about reading and writing with different libraries and understanding that the same business problem can be solved in multiple ways.

1. **Working with xlsxwriter and pandas:** In the mini project, we generated aviation operational data and created a KPI dashboard using xlsxwriter. Your task is to:

    a. Save the raw data tables (e.g., Flights and Routes) into an Excel workbook (without charts or formatting).

    b. Read this workbook back into Python using pandas.

    c. Re-compute the same KPIs (total passengers per route, average delay minutes, route efficiency index, average load factor (%), etc.) using pandas operations.

    d. Add more columns for fuel consumption per hour, ticket price, departure and arrival delay, and compute relevant KPIs.

    e. Write the results back into a new Excel workbook (as plain data, not formatted).

    (Hint: Focus on getting the numbers right. Do not worry about formatting or charts here.)

2. **Rebuilding the Dashboard with openpyxl**: We created an aviation KPI dashboard in Excel using xlsxwriter with features like:

    - KPI tables
    - Formulas
    - Charts
    - Formatting

    Your task is to replicate the same dashboard (as much as possible) using openpyxl.

    a. Use openpyxl to create sheets, write data, and apply formulas.

    b. Add basic formatting (headers, bold text, tab color, etc.).

   c. Insert charts using openpyxl's chart module.

   d. Save the workbook as aviation_dashboard_openpyxl.xlsx.

Note: Some formatting features in xlsxwriter may not be available in openpyxl. Focus on replicating the structure and functionality, not pixel-perfect design.

3. **Reading binary Excel data with pyxlsb**: The airline data team sometimes shares large Excel files in binary format (.xlsb) because they load faster and take less disk space. Your task is to:

   a. Convert the raw aviation data workbook you created earlier into .xlsb format (you can use Excel to Save As).

   b. Use pyxlsb to read the .xlsb file.

   c. Extract the flights sheet and print the average delay (minutes).

Concept check

1. In openpyxl, you can update an existing Excel file (add rows, rename sheets, etc.). In xlsxwriter, you cannot. Why?
2. Why can you not use xlrd and xlwt together to read and write modern .xlsx files?
3. If you need to copy a worksheet from one Excel file to another using xlrd/xlwt, why might you also need xlutils?
4. When should you prefer pyxlsb over openpyxl or pandas.read_excel()?
5. We have mentioned many Python libraries for Excel-Python integration so far. Create a summary table, comparing all of those.

Join our Discord space

Join our Discord workspace for latest updates, offers, tech happenings around the world, new releases, and sessions with the authors:

https://discord.bpbonline.com

CHAPTER 10
Transitioning to xlwings for Excel Automation

Introduction

xlwings is a powerful Python library that enables seamless interaction between Python and Excel, offering greater flexibility and automation capabilities than traditional Excel methods. Whether you are an Excel practitioner with no VBA background or a Spreadsheet specialist skilled in VBA programming, but with little Python experience (gained from the previous chapters), now you can learn xlwings as a tool for enhancing productivity and streamlining repetitive tasks.

Libraries like pandas, openpyxl, xlsxwriter, xlrd, xlwt, xlutils, and pyxlsb are tools for working with Excel files, but xlwings is the tool for working with Excel application itself. By allowing Python to talk to Excel, it bridges the gap between the analytical power of Python and the ubiquity of Excel. This library becomes especially valuable at moments your end users live in Excel, you need to automate Excel as an application, and you want to embed Python logic seamlessly into Excel workflows.

This chapter focuses on fundamental xlwings operations, such as reading and writing data, formatting cells, automating charts, running VBA macro, using Excel object model and working with multiple Excel instances. Readers will explore how xlwings compares to other Excel integration. Thereby, gaining insights regarding the usage of the same.

This chapter sets the stage for deeper xlwings integration, with the next chapter covering the methods of calling Python functions directly from Excel using the xlwings add-in.

Structure

In this chapter, we will discuss the following topics:

- Benefits of using xlwings over other tools
- Limitations of xlwings
- Writing data with xlwings
- Reading data with xlwings
- Automating charts with xlwings

- Working with Excel formula
- Formatting ranges
- Managing sheets in xlwings
- Running a VBA macro with xlwings
- Excel object model
- Interacting with Excel in hidden mode
- Working with multiple Excel instances
- Best practices for closing Excel with xlwings

Benefits of using xlwings over other tools

As you have already worked with libraries such as **`pandas`**, **`openpyxl`**, **`xlsxwriter`**, **`xlrd`**, **`xlwt`**, **`xlutils`**, and **`pyxlsb`**, you might be feeling confident about automating Excel tasks with Python. Hence, it is totally natural to think about the advantages of using **`xlwings`** while one already has other tools.

If your goal is server side automation, batch processing, or working in headless environments, then, those libraries are excellent choices.

However, if you already have Excel installed on your machine or have no issues installing it, you must spend a little more time with us to learn **`xlwings`** which occupies a unique and valuable place in the Python–Excel ecosystem. You will soon see, it is absolutely worth spending time with **xlwings**, especially for interactive, desktop-based workflows.

It offers a powerful bridge between Python and Excel, enabling direct control of workbooks, cells, charts, and even VBA macros.

Let us explore what makes it stand out and the key reasons you should learn **`xlwings`**.

Live connection with Excel

Most libraries (**`openpyxl`**, **`xlsxwriter`**, **`xlrd`**, etc.) work on Excel files as static objects. You open, read, write, and save, but the interaction is offline. **`xlwings`** establishes a live **Component Object Model** (**COM**) connection on Windows or AppleScript on Mac with Excel.

It means you can manipulate an already open workbook, and the changes would be reflected immediately in Excel, without saving and reopening. Basically, you can control Excel just like you would always do through formatting, filters, charts, shapes, pivot tables, and even VBA macros, all from Python code interactively in Excel.

Unlike other libraries, which treat Excel as a file format, **`xlwings`** treats Excel as an interactive application.

Richer control beyond data

Library like **pandas** is really good at data processing but lack control over the UI of Excel. Other tools such as **openpyxl** and **xlsxwriter** offer formatting, charting, formulas, etc.

xlwings combines the best of both worlds. It offers full control of the application layer of Excel (menus, ranges, charts, filters, pivot tables, shapes, export to PDF, macro-enabled, or binary format) along with a smooth handoff to **pandas** for advanced data analysis and back into Excel for presentation.

This transforms Excel into a front-end interface for **pandas**. Thereby, opening advanced analytics to Excel users.

Additionally, **xlwings add-in** allows you to call Python directly through buttons, cell formulas, or user-defined functions which means, as an Excel user, you can leverage Python without leaving Excel.

Preserving native Excel behaviors with **xlwings**, you can design tools where end users interact only with Excel via buttons, menus, formulas, while the underlying computation runs in Python. This lowers the barrier for adoption in organizations that rely heavily on Excel.

End-to-end Excel automation

xlwings goes beyond file manipulation. It can do the following:

- Automate worksheet buttons to trigger actions.
- Run VBA macros programmatically.
- Apply filters to tables and ranges in real-time.
- Adjust zoom levels
- Move or resize charts and shapes dynamically within the workbook

This makes it ideal for building robust, interactive Excel tools, not just data pipelines.

Limitations of xlwings

We have explored the advantages of using **xlwings**. Now it is equally important to consider its limitations to make informed decisions about the usage of the same. Here is a list of considerations:

- **Performance considerations: xlwings** can be slower than pure file-based libraries like **openpyxl** or **xlsxwriter** while handling large-scale data exports or batch operations. It is best suited for scenarios where real-time interaction with Excel is needed, such as dynamic updates, UI control, or workbook automation. *In Chapter 13, Python Excel Integration Limits and Vision,* we will discuss performance optimization strategies.

- **Platform dependency: `xlwings`** (open-source) requires an installation of Excel and therefore only works on Windows and macOS. Note that macOS currently does not support UDFs. There are limited Linux compatible features available through xlwings PRO (commercial version). So, if you are working in a **headless or server-side Linux environment**, it is better to use libraries like **`openpyxl`**, **`xlsxwriter`**, or **`pyxlsb`** for file-based operations
- **Excel installation: `xlwings`** requires Excel to be installed, unlike file-based libraries that can manipulate Excel files on a server without Excel. Hence, it is not supported by Google Colab or other cloud-based or headless environments where Excel is not available. Libraries like **`openpyxl`**, **`xlsxwriter`**, or **`pyxlsb`** are more appropriate for such setups.

Comparative insights:

Here is a clear comparison table to help you decide when to use **`xlwings`** versus other popular Excel-related Python libraries like **`openpyxl`**, **`xlsxwriter`**, and **`pandas`**:

Scenario	xlwings	Other libraries
To interact with a live Excel file	Yes	No
To use VBA macros	Yes	Limited or no support
To read/write cell values dynamically	Yes, real-time updates in Excel	Yes, it is only via file I/O
To embed Python logic in Excel	Yes, it is via UDFs and **`RunPython`**	Not supported
To create styled reports or charts	Basic styling supported	**`xlsxwriter`** excels at formatting and charts
Cross-platform compatibility	Windows and macOS only	Most libraries are cross-platform
No Excel installation is available	Requires Excel to be installed	Works without Excel

Table 10.1*: Scenario-based evaluation of Excel automation libraries*

In short, we can say:

- Use **`xlwings`** when you need **live interaction**, **automation**, or **integration with the native features** of Excel.
- Use **`openpyxl`**, **`xlsxwriter`**, or **`pandas`** when working with **offline files**, **large datasets**, or **complex formatting** without needing Excel to be open.

Writing data with xlwings

While writing data using **openpyxl** and **xlsxwriter**, we needed to save or close workbook and open it in excel every time we made a small change to the code. As **xlwings** works directly with Excel object, we can modify the workbook and see those changes live in Excel and save only when we want.

To understand writing data using **xlwings**, let us start simple.

Creating Excel files and sheets

The following code creates a new workbook via **xlwings** and prints the name of the workbook:

```
import xlwings as xw
wb = xw.Book()
wb.name
```

By default, it has one sheet called **Sheet1**. You can verify the same by running **wb.sheets** and **wb.sheet_names.** As you might have guessed already, **wb.sheets[0]** or **wb.sheets['Sheet1']** allow you to access the sheet by its index or name. You can also rename the sheet using **name** method and save the workbook using **save()** method:

```
ws1 = wb.sheets['Sheet1']
ws1.name = 'Scores'
wb.save('gaming.xlsx')
```

It is so convenient to see the changes happening live in the Excel workbook.

Note: **Any modifications you will do will reflect in the Excel workbook opened but changes will save only when you run save() method programmatically or save it manually the way you do with Excel file.**

Writing data

Similar to other libraries you have learnt so far, you can access individual cell by A1-style notation or supplying index in **sheet.range()** method. Both **ws1.range('A1')** and **ws1.range(1, 1)** accesses A1 cell of the sheet and returns a range object. In addition, there are alternative ways to fetch individual cells, which we will discuss soon.

To read from or write to a range, whether it is a single cell, a row, a column, or a block, you can use the **value** property of a range object:

```
# Using cell notation
ws1.range('A1').value = 'PlayerA'
```

```
# or Using index (B1: row1, col2)
ws1.range(1, 2).value = 'PlayerB'
```

This writes data in single cell at a time. To write data in a row, you can use one-dimensional data such as a Python list:

```
players = ["PlayerC", "PlayerD", "PlayerE"]
ws1.range('C1').value = players   # writes across C1:E1
```

By default, it writes data in row. You can use nested list or **option(transpose=True)** for column-wise orientation:

```
# Option 1: converting scoreA to a list of lists (each inner list = row)

scoreA = [105, 90, 98, 69, 85]
ws1.range('A2').value = [[v] for v in scoreA]  # writes down A2:A6

# Option 2: use .options(transpose=True)

scoreB = [75, 59, 38, 79, 26]
ws1.range('B2').options(transpose=True).value = scoreB
```

Let us supply nested list directly:

```
scores = [
    [110, 96, 83, 79, 86],
    [97, 99, 94, 89, 104],
    [120, 98, 102, 87, 118],
    ]

ws1.range('c2').options(transpose=True).value = scores # writes a block C2:E6
```

Data created so far can be seen in the following figure:

	A	B	C	D	E
1	PlayerA	PlayerB	PlayerC	PlayerD	PlayerE
2	105	75	110	97	120
3	90	59	96	99	98
4	98	38	83	94	102
5	69	79	79	89	87
6	85	26	86	104	118
7					

Scores

***Figure 10.1**: Sample data created by xlwings*

For performance and efficiency, it is generally recommended to write data to Excel using a **numpy** array or a **pandas** DataFrame. This approach is faster because it transfers the entire block of data in one operation, rather than writing individual cells, rows or columns.

When working with **xlwings**, it is important to manage Excel–Python interactions thoughtfully to avoid unnecessary overhead. We will demonstrate how to write a **pandas** DataFrame to Excel, but the same technique applies equally to **pandas** Series and **numpy** arrays.

Let us create another sheet by **add()** method:

```
ws2 = wb.sheets.add(name='Ranks', after=wb.sheets['Scores'])
```

By default, the **add()** method, adds a sheet before existing sheet. You can choose to add it before or after a specific sheet and give it a name. Let us write data using **pandas** DataFrame:

```
leaderboard = pd.DataFrame([
    ["PlayerA", 12500],
    ["PlayerB", 11840],
    ["PlayerC", 11010],
],
    columns = ["Player", "TotalScore"],
    index = ['Rank1', 'Rank2', 'Rank3'])

ws2.range('A1').value = leaderboard
wb.save('gaming.xlsx')
```

If you want to write data without headers and index, you can use **options(header=False, index=False)**. To save the file, **wb.save('gaming.xlsx')** is used. You can also export data to binary, legacy **xls**, macro-enabled or PDF file.

Named ranges

You can also assign named ranges for easy reference:

```
ws1.range('A2').name = 'A_score2'
ws2.range('A1:C4').name = 'top_players'
```

This creates named ranges as desired, and the following figure shows the same in the name manager of Excel:

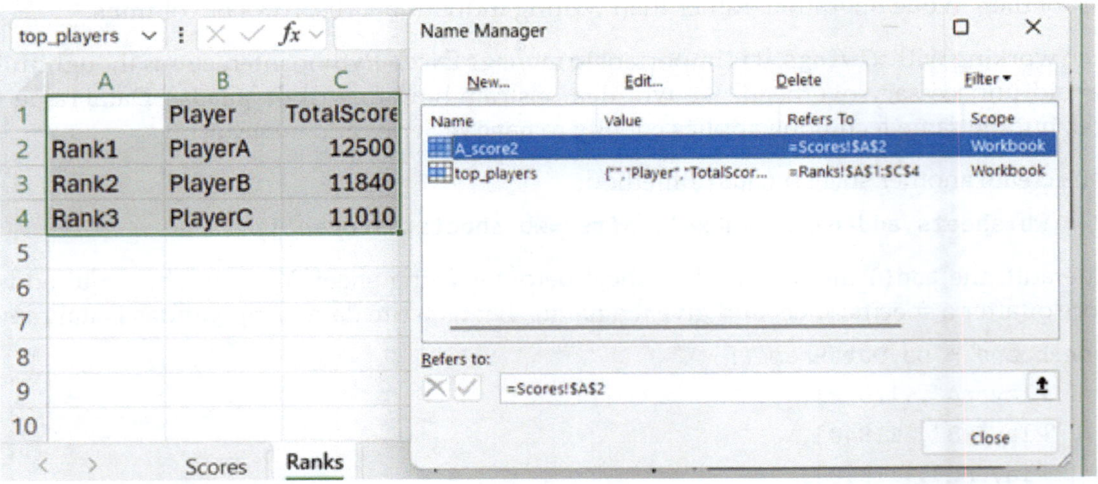

***Figure 10.2**: Named ranges created by xlwings*

To get a list of all named ranges defined in the workbook, you can use **wb.names**:

```
wb.names
# [<Name 'A_score2': =Scores!$A$2>, <Name 'top_players': =Ranks!$A$1:$C$4>]
```

To read values using named range:

```
named_range = wb.names['top_players'].refers_to_range
named_range.value
```

Expand() method

In previous example, we have manually selected a range of cells (A1 to C4), this can be done programmatically using **expand()** method. It is like selecting data in Excel with *Ctr* + *Shift* + *arrow-keys*

```
ws2['A1'].expand()  # Expand in all directions to cover the data block

ws2['A1'].expand('down')  # Expand downward to include filled cells below

ws2['A1'].expand('right')   # Expand rightward to include filled cells across
```

By default, it expands both horizontally and vertically, encompassing the entire table of data connected to the starting cell. You can specify if you want to expand it only downwards or to the right. Close the workbook when finished by calling **wb.close()**. In the next section, we will load the file **gaming.xlsx** again to read its data.

Reading data using xlwings

You have already used **xw.Book()** to create and write workbooks; same function can be used to open an existing file for reading and we can access the sheet(s) as discussed earlier:

```
import xlwings as xw
wb = xw.Book('gaming.xlsx')
ws1 = wb.sheets[0]
```

To read data from **xlwings**, we need to first discuss various ways to access cells and ranges. We have already seen **range()** method, however there are other ways also to access cells and ranges.

Accessing cells and ranges

As discussed earlier, **range()** method creates **xlwings** range object that allows us to read, write or do more with individual cell, row, column or a block of cells. Some examples are mentioned hereafter. VBA users can see similarities in VBA and **xlwings** code:

```
ws1.range('A1')
ws1.range(1, 1)    # 1-based index
ws1.range('A1:E5') # Excel-Style Reference
```

You can also fetch ranges by supplying indices for starting or ending cell, keeping in mind, it takes one-based indexing:

```
ws1.range((2, 2), (3, 4)) # B2:D3
```

Here, starting cell is row 2, column 2, i.e., B2 and ending cell is row 3, column 4, i.e., D3. These range objects can be sliced further using square brackets. You will find more examples in the code file.

You can also fetch ranges directly from the sheet without using **range** method explicitly:

```
# Using cell notation (without range method)
ws1['A1']
ws1['A1:E5']
```

It can also be done by using indices (zero-based index):

```
# Using index (without range method) -------
ws1[0, 0] # 0-based index
ws1[1:3, 1:4] # B2:D3
# rows 2 to 3 (Python index 1 and 2) and columns B to D (Python index 1, 2, 3)
```

As you have seen there are multiple ways of accessing cell(s) or range(s). For example, **ws['A1']** is quick and readable for hardcoded cell references in scripts while **ws.range('A1')** is used when you need options, converters or more control (to be discussed soon).

Note: While accessing cell(s) or range(s) with indices, the square bracket indexer ws[row, col] uses zerobased indices, while round brackets ws.range(row, col) uses onebased indices consistent with Excel and VBA.

Reading data

You can use **value()** method over any **xlwings** Range object to read the value of the same. Hence, **ws.range('A1').value** will simply print the content of cell A1 as expected. This is a scalar value. You can read values from a column or a row by supplying range:

```
ws1.range('A1:A7').value
# ['PlayerA', 105.0, 90.0, 98.0, 69.0, 85.0, None]

ws1.range('A1:E1').value
# ['PlayerA', 'PlayerB', 'PlayerC', 'PlayerD', 'PlayerE']
```

You might have noticed that it reads a blank cell as **None** and you can replace it with any placeholder like **'unknown'** using option method:

```
ws1.range('A1:A7').options(empty = 'Unknown').value
# ['PlayerA', 105.0, 90.0, 98.0, 69.0, 85.0, 'Unknown']
```

By looking at the output, we cannot really differentiate if it is a row or a column in Excel because output is a list in both cases. You can use **options** method to configure the output to be a two-dimensional list:

```
ws1.range('A1:A7').options(ndim=2).value
# [['PlayerA'], [105.0], [90.0], [98.0], [69.0], [85.0], [None]]
```

It provides a nested list with seven elements (or inner lists). Inner list(s) stands for row(s), so basically, we are reading seven rows of that column. And for reading seven columns of a row:

```
ws1.range('A1:E1').options(ndim=2).value
# [['PlayerA', 'PlayerB', 'PlayerC', 'PlayerD', 'PlayerE']]
```

In **options()** method, **ndim=2** returns nested lists and preserves row or column orientation, so use it when the shape or direction of the data matters while **ndim=1** (default) forces a flat list, which is useful for simple processing and to avoid single cells becoming scalars.

Additionally, **xlwings v0.33.19** (Dec 19, 2025) added support for **ndim='natural'**. This returns scalars for single cells, 1D lists for horizontal ranges, and 2D lists for vertical or multi-row ranges.

Converters and options

We have seen using **options()** method with different arguments such as **transpose**, **header**, **index**, **ndim** while writing or reading data. Some of the default settings are:

- Single cells are read in as floats in case the Excel cell holds a number, as unicode in case it holds text, as datetime if it contains a date and as **None** in case it is empty.
- Columns or rows are read in as lists.
- Two-dimensional ranges are read in as list of lists.

You can explore more arguments such as **numbers**, **dates**, **empty**, **err_to_str** and **chunksize** to change these settings. Read document **https://docs.xlwings.org/en/latest/converters.html#converters** for more details.

You can also use different converters in **options()** method such as **dict**, **np.array**, **pd.Series** or **pd.DataFrame**. Converters define how Excel ranges and their values are converted both during **reading** and **writing** operations.

For example, to get output as a **numpy** array instead of list or nested list, we can use **numpy** array converter:

```
ws1.range('A1').options(np.array).value          # 0-D numpy array
ws1.range('A1:A7').options(np.array).value       # 1-D numpy array
ws1.range('A1:A7').options(np.array, ndim = 2).value  #2-D numpy array
```

Similarly, we can use **pandas** DataFrame converter to display the result as a DataFrame:

```
ws1.range('A1:E6').options(pd.DataFrame, index = False).value
# Or verbose
ws1.range('A1:E6').options('df', index = False).value
```

The output is a **pandas** DataFrame:

```
   PlayerA  PlayerB  PlayerC  PlayerD  PlayerE
0    105.0     75.0    110.0     97.0    120.0
1     90.0     59.0     96.0     99.0     98.0
2     98.0     38.0     83.0     94.0    102.0
3     69.0     79.0     79.0     89.0     87.0
4     85.0     26.0     86.0    104.0    118.0
```

The **dict** converter is ideal when your Excel range represents key-value pairs like a lookup table, or a configuration map. Your range must be either two columns wide or two rows tall. When writing, **xlwings** will automatically apply the correct converter (if available) according to the type of object that is being written to Excel. Advanced users can also create their own custom converter.

Automating charts with xlwings

To add a chart, **charts.add()** method can be used. The following code adds a column chart to Ranks sheet of **gaming.xlsx**:

```
bar_chart = ws2.charts.add(top = ws2.range('E2').top,
                           left = ws2.range('E2').left)
bar_chart.chart_type = 'column_clustered'
bar_chart.set_source_data(ws2.range('B1').expand())
```

This simple code inserts a column chart in E2 cell of Ranks sheet, as shown in the following figure:

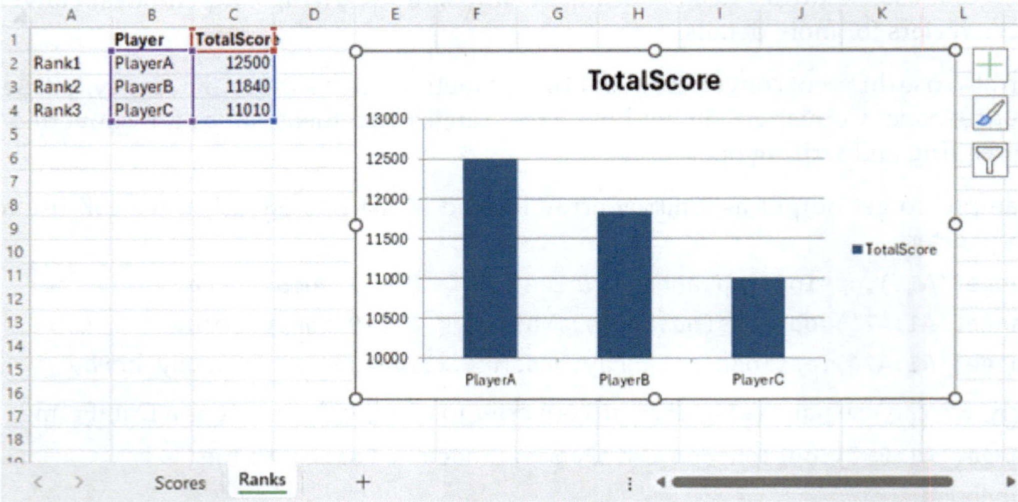

***Figure 10.3:** Column chart generated by xlwings*

You can also export chart or range to **pdf** or **png** format by using **to_pdf()** or **to_png()** methods:

```
bar_chart.to_pdf('ExportedByxlwings.pdf')
ws2.range('B1').expand().to_pdf('ChartDataExported.pdf')
ws2.range('B1').expand().to_png('ChartDataExported.png')
```

You can add **matplotlib**, **seaborn**, **plotly** static charts as an image:

```
df = ws2.range('A1').expand('table').options(pd.DataFrame).value

# matplotlib
ax = df.plot(x = 'Player', y = 'TotalScore', kind = 'bar')
fig = ax.get_figure()
ws2.pictures.add(fig, top = ws2.range('E18').top,
                 left = ws2.range('E18').left)

# plotly static chart
```

```
fig = px.bar(df, x = 'Player', y = 'TotalScore')
ws2.pictures.add(fig, top = ws2.range('N2').top,
                      left = ws2.range('N2').left)
```

Method **pictures.add()** can be used to insert any picture to Excel sheet. It accepts every picture format that your Excel version supports.

```
image = r'path/to/image.png'          # Replace with your actual image path


ws2.pictures.add(
    image= image,
    left=ws2.range('A19').left,
    top=ws2.range('A19').top,
    width=200,                               # Optional: resize image
    height=100
)

# Close file once done
Wb.close()
```

If you want to save these changes, you can use **wb.save('xlwings_chart.xlsx')**, it saves the workbook to the specified path. Using **wb.save()** writes changes to the workbook's existing file. **wb.close()** closes without saving, while **wb.close(save=True)** saves first and then closes.

Working with Excel formula

To insert a formula, you can use **formula()** method:

```
# SUM formulas in single cell ----
ws1.range('F2').formula = '=SUM(A2:E2)'


# Using f-strings to create dynamic formulas for each cell in F col
for i in range(3, 7):
    ws1.range(f'F{i}').formula = f'=SUM(A{i}:E{i})'


for i in range(2, 7):
    ws1.range(f'G{i}').formula = f'=AVERAGE(A{i}:E{i})'
```

The output file shown, hereafter, displays these formula:

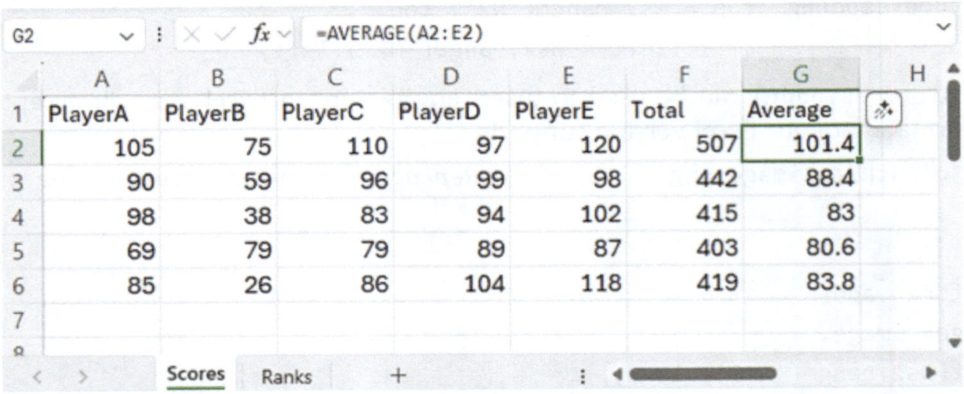

Figure 10.4: Excel formula using xlwings

You can introduce dynamic array formula using **`formula2()`** method. Even if you are using older Excel version, you can see it displays the result spilled to adjacent cells:

```
# values from the row, which are greater than 100
ws1.range('I2').formula2 = '=FILTER(A2:E2, A2:E2 > 100)'

# BYROW - Average each row
ws1['M2'].formula2 = '=BYROW(A2:E6, LAMBDA(row, AVERAGE(row)))'
# BYCOL - Average each col
ws1['A8'].formula2 = '=BYCOL(A2:E6, LAMBDA(row, AVERAGE(row)))'

# LAMBDA - Classify scores
ws1['O2'].formula2 = '''=MAP(A2:E6,
    LAMBDA(x, IF(x>=100, "High", IF(x>=80, "Medium", "Low"))))'''

Wb.close()
```

Formatting ranges

Basic formatting such as font, color, number format, highlight cell etc. can be done smoothly. Run the following code to generate a new Excel file with formatted input, as shown in *Figure 10.5*.

```
import xlwings as xw
from datetime import datetime
```

```
# Create workbook
wb = xw.Book()
ws = wb.sheets['Sheet1']
ws.name = 'Scores'

# Sample data to be written
data = [
    ['Player', 'Score', 'Level', 'Last Login', 'Status'],
    ['Alex', 9200, 12, datetime(2025, 9, 10), 'Active'],
    ['Blake', None, 8, datetime(2025, 9, 5), 'Inactive'],
    ['Casey', 7800, 10, 'ERROR', 'Active'],
    ['Dana', 10200, 15, datetime(2025, 9, 12), 'Active']
]

ws.range('A1').value = data

# Column Autofit
ws.range('A1').expand().columns.autofit()

# Format header row
header = ws.range('A1').expand('right')
header.font.bold = True
header.font.size = 12
header.color = (251, 226, 213)

# Format columns (Number & date formats)
ws.range('B2').expand('down').number_format = '#,##0'  # Score with comma
ws.range('D2').expand('down').number_format = 'dd-mmm-yyyy'  # Date format

# Font styling
ws.range('A2').expand('down').font.italic = True  # Player names italic

# Highlight error cells (Login column)
for cell in ws.range('D2').expand('down'):
    if isinstance(cell.value, str) and cell.value.upper() == 'ERROR':
        cell.color = (255, 0, 0)  # Red fill
        cell.font.color = (255, 255, 255)  # White text
```

The output file is shown as follows:

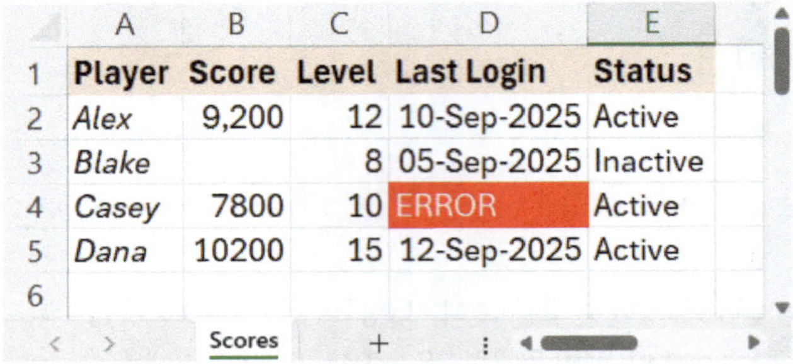

***Figure 10.5**: Formatted data*

You can also create and style Excel table(s):

```
ws.tables.add(ws.range('A1').expand(),
                    name = 'MyTable',
                    table_style_name='TableStyleLight1')

wb.close()
```

For advanced formatting options not directly exposed in the main **`xlwings`** API, you can access the underlying native object using the **`.api`** property. This gives you full access to the Excel object model. If you are using **`xlwings pro`** (paid), you can also enjoy Markdown formatting. It offers an easy and intuitive way of styling text components in your cells and shapes.

Managing sheets in xlwings

To control the contents and layout of Excel sheets using **`xlwings`**, you can use these key methods:

- **Copy a sheet**: Use **`copy()`** to duplicate a sheet within the same workbook or into another workbook.
- **Clear cell contents (but keep formatting)**: Use **`clear_contents()`** to remove all values and formulas while preserving formatting, column widths, and named ranges.
- **Fully reset a sheet**: Use **`.clear()`** to wipe everything such as values, formatting, comments, conditional formatting, etc.
- **Delete a sheet**: Use **`delete()`** to remove a sheet entirely from the workbook.

Sample code:

```
# To copy sheet
ws2.copy(name='CopyRanks')
```

```
# Clear cell contents (but keep formatting)
ws3.clear_contents()

# Clear cell contents and formatting
wb.sheets['CopyRanks'].clear()

# To delete sheet
ws3.delete()
```

Note: xlwings does not hook into the native undo stack of Excel, so the change is immediate and irreversible unless you have manually backed up the data beforehand. You can simulate undo by capturing the state before the operation as done in code file.

Running VBA macro with xlwings

You can also run VBA macro directly from Python using **`xlwings`**. If you do not use legacy Excel files with VBA macro, you can skip this section. However, here we are showing a minimal VBA code, that you might still understand. In the **`game_macro.xlsm`** file, you can press *Alt+F11* to open VBA application, which contains the following code in Module1:

```
Sub GreetPlayer(playerName As String)
    MsgBox "Welcome to the game, " & playerName & "!", vbInforma-
tion, "Game Greeting"
End Sub

Function DoubleScore(score As Double) As Double
    DoubleScore = score * 2
End Function
```

In VBA, **`Sub`** is short for **Subroutine**. It performs an action like showing a message or updating a cell but does not return a value. So, here, **`GreetPlayer`** is a Subroutine that pops up a welcome message with the name of the player.

Also, in VBA, **`Function`** is used when you want to calculate something and return a result. Here, **`DoubleScore`** takes a number (the score) and returns double its value.

You can run this VBA from Excel, but to run it using Python, you need to first grab these macro(s) in **`xlwings`** and then run it:

```
import xlwings as xw

# Open the macro-enabled workbook
vba_book = xw.Book("game_macro.xlsm")
```

```
# Grab the macros
greet = vba_book.macro("Module1.GreetPlayer")
double_score = vba_book.macro("Module1.DoubleScore")

# Call the Sub (shows message box in Excel)
greet("Python Leaners!")
```

The following figure shows message box that opens in Excel:

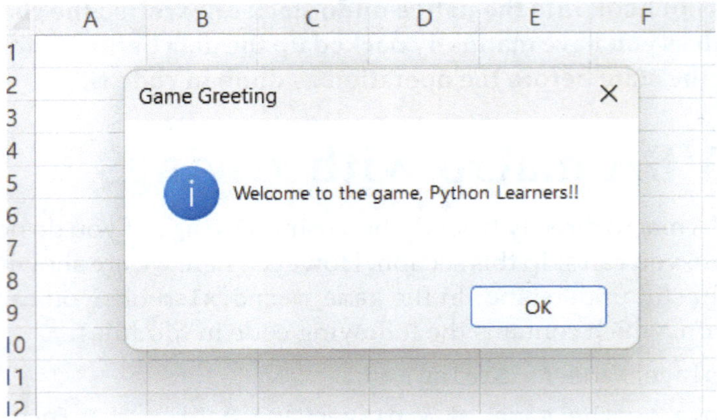

Figure 10.6: Running VBA macro from Python using xlwings

You will need to close the MessageBox by clicking on **OK**. Similarly, you can run **double_score** function with some input:

```
# Call the Function (returns a value to Python)
new_score = double_score(150)
print("New doubled score:", new_score)

# Close the workbook
vba_book.close()
```

VBA module placement

When working with **xlwings**, it is important to understand where your VBA code lives inside the Excel project, because Python interacts with VBA modules a bit differently than Excel does.

The following points outline the appropriate use and scope of standard modules, sheet modules, and workbook modules in VBA:

- **Standard modules (Module1, Module2, ...)**
  - This is the recommended place for functions and subs if you want to call them from Python.
  - Functions in standard modules can return values to Python correctly as we have seen.
- **Sheet modules (e.g., Sheet1) or ThisWorkbook module**
  - VBA code stored here can be called from Python only as a Sub (i.e., procedures that do not return values). For example, a Sub **`ShowMessage()`** in **`Sheet1`** or **`ThisWorkbook`** can be executed from Python using:

```
# From Sheet1 Module
greet_sheet = wb.macro("Sheet1.GreetPlayerSheet")
greet_sheet("Maya")                    #  Shows message box

# From ThisWorkbook Module
greet_wb = wb.macro("ThisWorkbook.GreetPlayerWB")
greet_wb("Sam")                        #  Shows message box
```

  - However, Python cannot read the return value of a function if it is inside **`Sheet1`** or **`ThisWorkbook`**.
  - That is because **`xlwings`** uses COM interface of Excel, which does not expose function return values from these modules.
- **Best practice with legacy VBA projects**
  - If you already have old VBA code in **`Sheet1`** or **`ThisWorkbook`**, you can either:
    - Move functions into a standard module (it might be messy or risky), or
    - Create a wrapper function in a standard module that calls the legacy function and then call the wrapper from Python.
    - For Subs: you can call them as it is.

After learning to use **`xlwings`** for reading and writing excel files, running VBA macro and doing basic stuff with it, it is time to introduce **Excel object model** and an **Excel instance.** Once you understand **`Excel objects`** and **`app`**, you will appreciate the fact that **`xlwings`** is not just another file-based library, but a live Excel controller.

Excel object model

If you have done VBA programming, you might be aware that Excel VBA supports object-based programming, which works on the idea of Encapsulation and stores the state (data) and operation (functions) inside the object. Excel objects are arranged in a hierarchy that governs the excel object. Every element in Excel is represented by an object in VBA.

In Excel object model, we can have the following objects:

- **App:** The actual Excel application instance.
- **Book:** Workbook object(s)
- **Sheet:** Worksheet object(s) in workbook.
- **Range**: A range of cells such as A1:E6.
- **Cell:** Inside range or worksheet object, we can have cell object(s).

We can also have other objects such as charts, images, tables etc.

The following figure shows a sample Excel object model:

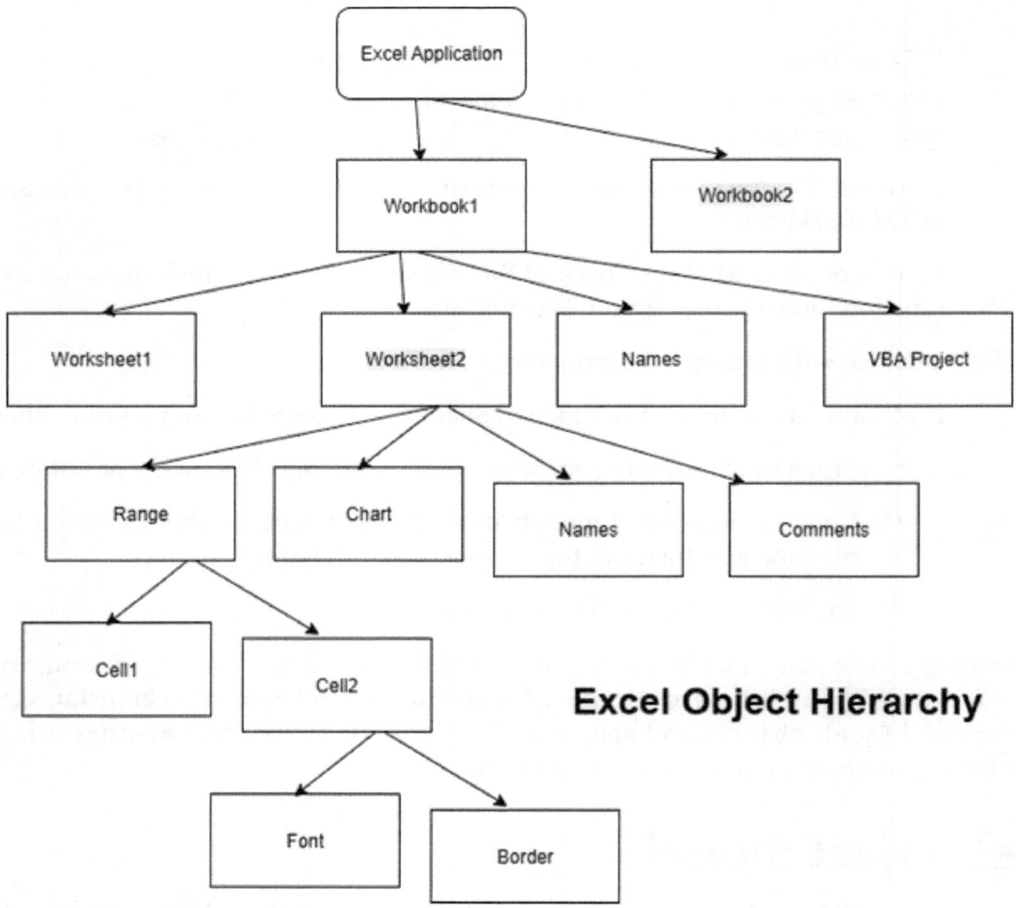

Figure 10.7: *Excel object model*

You can see the hierarchy of these objects. Even if you are reading the term **Excel object model** for the first time, you are still familiar with the pyramid.

```
import xlwings as xw
Book = xw.Book()

Sheet = Book.sheets['Sheet1']
Range = Sheet.range('A1:E6')
Book # <Book [Book1]>
Sheet # <Sheet [Book1]Sheet1>
Range # <Range [Book1]Sheet1!$A$1:$E$6>

# Alternately
xw.Book().sheets['Sheet1'].range('A1:E6')
# <Range [Book2]Sheet1!$A$1:$E$6>
```

You might have realized this code is quite similar to VBA with some natural differences such as indexing and casing.

You can also navigate up in the hierarchy:

```
Range.sheet # <Sheet [Book1]Sheet1>
Range.sheet.book # <Book [Book1]>
```

There is no reason to not be able to see the actual Excel application instance by stepping one more step up:

```
Range.sheet.book.app # <App [excel] 16696>
# same as
Book.app # <App [excel] 16696>
```

The output represents the **Excel application object**, which is the top-level container in the Excel object model. The number 16696 is the **process ID (PID)** of the Excel instance running on our system, as shown in the following figure:

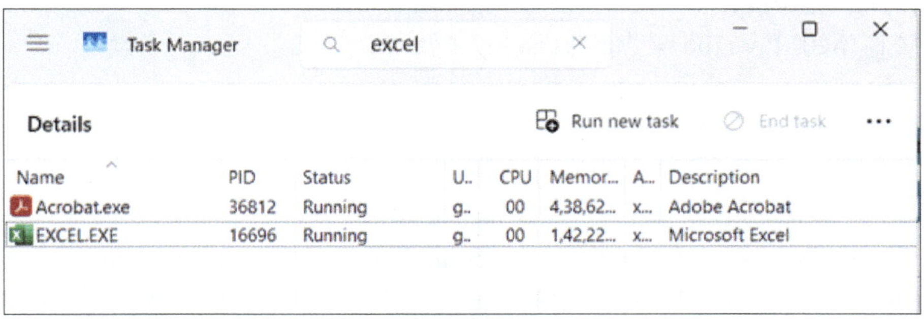

Figure 10.8: PID of Excel instance on our machine

You might have understood that PID will be different on your machine. To view process ID(s), you can go to **Task Manager** (*Ctrl* + *Shift* +*Esc* on windows) or **Activity Monitor** (on MacOS) and check details of Excel.

Alternately, you can run **`xw.apps.keys()`** to list keys of active **`xlwings App`** objects and **`xw.apps.active.pid`** to get the PID of the currently active **`xlwings App`**.

By default, opening several workbooks (whether from Explorer, Excel UI, or via **`xw.Book()`**) will place them in the same Excel process; you will see one **`Excel.exe`** in Task Manager.

Understanding Excel instance helps you in controlling Excel application. Let us see a few applications in next sections.

Interacting with Excel in hidden mode

Sometimes you want Python to work on an Excel file quietly in the background, without popping open Excel or disturbing the things that you are doing. That is where the app object helps. You can tell Python to open Excel in hidden mode.

It is useful for two reasons:

- You can run Python script to work on a file in the background while continuing to work on other Excel files manually or via Python scripts, all at the same time.
- It helps in automation tasks like updating data, generating reports, or cleaning sheets, without interrupting your flow.

Here is the code example, which shows running Excel in background:

```
import xlwings as xw

# Start Excel in hidden mode
app = xw.App(visible=False)
wb = app.books.open('gaming.xlsx')

# Do something quietly
wb.sheets[0]['A20'].value = 'Updated by Python'

# Save and close
wb.save()
app.quit()
```

Whenever you want to specify using a particular Excel instance (for example, here the app in hidden mode), you cannot use **`xw.Book`**, you need to use **`app.books`**, where app is that particular Excel instance.

It is recommended that if Python is working on **gaming.xlsx** in hidden mode, avoid opening that same file manually until the script finishes to prevent file locking issues or conflict between Excel instances.

You might have realized that you can use **xw.App()** to create multiple Excel instances that enable simultaneous processing. Let us see that in practice.

Working with multiple Excel instances

Working with multiple Excel instances allows multitasking that helps in automating parallel workflows, isolating tasks across workbooks, and avoiding UI conflicts during complex operations.

xlwings makes this straightforward by allowing explicit instance creation with **xw.App()** and opening workbooks in the desired app for controlled isolation and parallelism.

Each instance (visible or hidden) runs in its own process and will appear as a separate Excel.exe (having its own PID) in **Task Manager**, as shown in the following figure:

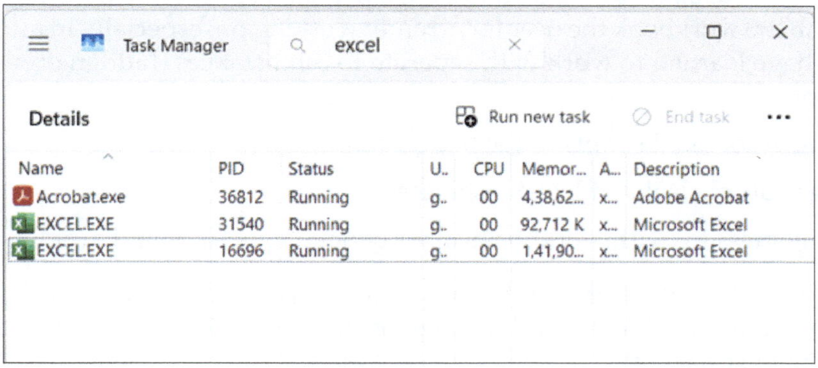

***Figure 10.9**: Process ID (PID) of multiple Excel instances on our machine*

The following code demonstrates how to run tasks in parallel Excel windows for better performance or isolation:

```
import xlwings as xw

# First Excel instance
app1 = xw.App(visible=True)
wb1 = app1.books.open('C:/path/to/file1.xlsx')
wb1.sheets[0]['A1'].value = 'Updated by Instance 1'

# Second Excel instance
app2 = xw.App(visible=True)
```

```
wb2 = app2.books.open('C:/path/to/file2.xlsx')
wb2.sheets[0]['A1'].value = 'Updated by Instance 2'

# process IDs
xw.apps.keys()          # List of running Excel instances
app1.pid                # Process ID of first Excel instance
app2.pid                # Process ID of second Excel instance
xw.apps.active.pid      # PID of the currently active Excel instance

# Save and close both
wb1.save()
wb2.save()
app1.quit()
app2.quit()
```

As you have seen **xw.books.active** displays the currently active workbook. It is handy when you want to grab the workbook the user is currently working on, especially in multi-workbook scenarios. You have learned to work with separate Excel instances (hidden or visible modes). This is useful for:

- Running automated scripts in the background.
- Having multiple isolated Excel instances.
- Avoiding messing with workbooks already open in your main Excel.

Here, we would like to address the confusion of most **xlwings** beginners which is the need to close Excel (App) and/or just the workbook. Let us discuss Book vs. App, when to close what, in **xlwings** in the next section.

Best practices for closing Excel with xlwings

Whenever you use **xw.Book()**, you are just opening or attaching to a workbook inside your normal Excel. In this case, the rule is simple, close only the workbook you opened using **wb.close()**.

It closes only that workbook; it does not quit the Excel application. So, if you have other open workbooks, the Excel process stays running.

If you run **wb.app.quit()** after **wb.close()**, you will get a COM since you closed the workbook object, so **wb** no longer has a valid reference.

Running **wb.app.quit()** directly (**without wb.close()**) will close Excel instance but it is not recommended usually because that would close the entire Excel application, including the following:

- The workbook you opened with **`xlwings`**
- Any other workbooks you had open manually

This means if you had an unsaved file open, Excel would prompt to save (or in silent mode, it may just discard).

When you use **`xw.App()`**, you are starting a brand-new Excel application instance which is separate from your normal Excel instance (sometimes hidden, sometimes visible). Since you created it, you must also close it when you are done to free up system resources and avoid leaving hidden Excel instances running in the background.

If you do not close it, Excel will remain open in the background (invisible). You will see it in Task Manager as EXCEL.EXE. and too many left-open instances can lead to memory leaks, strange behavior.

The safe way is **`app.quit()`**.

Additionally, **`xlwings`** also supports context managers, which means you can use a **`with`** block which closes Excel automatically.

```
import xlwings as xw

with xw.App() as app:       # Excel starts here
    wb = app.books.open(r"Path\to\YourFile.xlsx")
    # Do stuff...

# At this point, Excel is closed automatically
```

Note: **Using context managers (at app level with `xw.App()` or at workbook level with `wb.Book()`) guarantees automatic closing but can prevent you from seeing live updates because the workbook is closed when the block exits.**

For interactive inspection, create the App/Book manually and control `wb.save()`,`wb.close()`, and `app.quit()` yourself so the Excel instance remains open for debugging or further work.

If Excel freezes badly, you can use **`app.kill()`**, but that is only for emergencies. This is a hard kill of the Excel process (like ending task in Task Manager). This should be used only if Excel is unresponsive, e.g. a macro is stuck, or Excel froze.

Best practice recap

Outlined below are recommended usage patterns for working with Excel at the application (**`xw.App()`**) and workbook (**`xw.Book()`**) levels to ensure reliable and maintainable Excel automation:

- **Book level (xw.Book())**:
    - Use when you do not need multiple instances of Excel.
    - Only `wb.close()` what you open.
    - Do not call `wb.app.quit()`, unless you really want to kill all of Excel.
- **App level (xw.App())**:
    - Use when you want multiple instances (visible or hidden sessions) or automation.
    - Always call `app.quit()`.
    - Can use `with xw.App()` block for short, selfcontained automation to guarantee resources are released.

In short, If you create Excel using `xw.App()`, you must close it. If you connect to Excel using `xw.Book()`, close only what you have opened, and do not shut down the whole Excel session of the user.

Conclusion

In this chapter, we have learned to get started with xlwings for reading, writing, formatting, charts, formulas, running VBA macros, tracing Excel object model and interactive with Excel application for multi-instance Excel automation.

Some of these tasks, we had done with openpyxl or xlsxwriter in previous chapters. In the current chapter, you have seen some advantages of xlwings over other libraries. You do not need to save Excel file to see the changes, you can see file manipulates live, VBA macros can be run from Python directly, and you can directly control Excel application, which is great for parallel automation and performance reasons.

There are many more powerful things you can do with xlwings like calling Python by clicking a button in Excel using xlwings add-in or calling a **user-defined function** (**UDF**). We will discuss such deeper xlwings Excel integration in the next chapter. In *Chapter 13, Python Excel Integration Limits and Vision*, we will discuss performance optimization strategies for xlwings.

Try it yourself

1. **Manufacturing (Production report):** You are preparing a daily production report for a factory. Write the following table into Excel starting at A1:

Machine	Units produced	Defects	Efficiency
M1	1200	12	0.98
M2	950	20	0.95
M3	1500	10	0.99

Table 10.2: *Production data*

Format it so that:

- The header row is bold, dark blue background (or any colour of your choice), white font.
- Efficiency column shows as a percentage with 2 decimals.
- Autofit all columns.

The output Excel should look like the following:

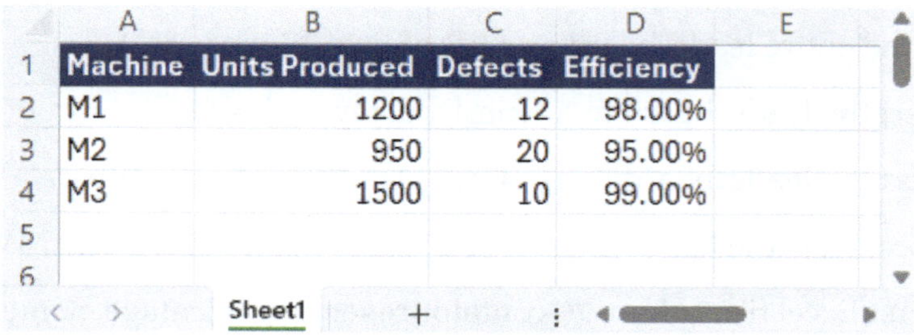

***Figure 10.10**: Expected output*

2. **Web testing (Bug report)**: Write a bug report into Excel with the following data and format as mentioned.

Bug ID	Description	Status	Priority
B101	Login button not working	Open	High
B102	Page loads slowly	Closed	Medium
B103	Dropdown missing option	Open	Low

***Table 10.3**: Web testing data*

Formatting requirements:

- Highlight Open rows in yellow.
- Make Priority = High red font, bold.

The output Excel file should look like this:

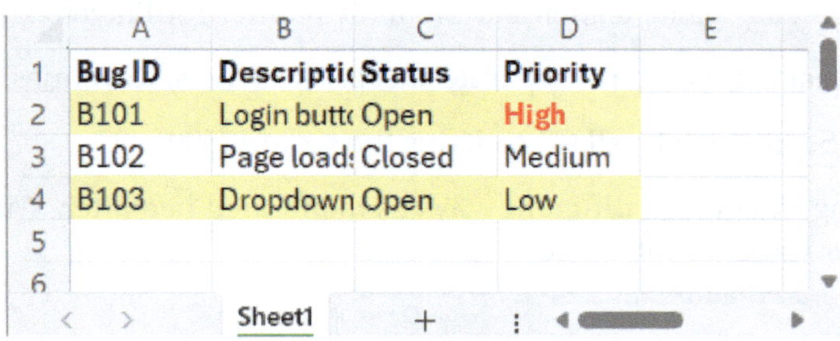

***Figure 10.11**: Expected output format*

- Also, add a Timestamp column and display as dd-mmm-yyyy hh:mm.

Concept check

1. You have a leaderboard with 100 players. You want to write it into Excel using xlwings. Here are four possible approaches:
   - Write each cell one by one in a for loop.
   - Write the entire leaderboard as a list of lists (block write).
   - Convert the leaderboard to a NumPy array and write it.
   - Convert the leaderboard to a pandas DataFrame and write it.

   Which approach is the least efficient, and which are most efficient? Why?
2. Imagine in an Excel file, column A contains revenue percentage. Some are missing, and one cell has #DIV/0!.
   - How will Python see the missing cells?
   - How will Python see the error cell?
3. You are trying to call a VBA macro from Excel using xlwings with this code:

```
import xlwings as xw
wb = xw.Book(r"Path\to\Macro-enabled file.xlsm")
# Trying to call a VBA macro
MyMacro()
```

   Here, `MyMacro` is just the name of your VBA Subroutine or Function. Why will this code fail? What is missing? How should it be corrected?
4. Match the following real-world scenarios to the correct Excel object:
   - The entire Excel program is running in the background, even before you open a file.
   - You save your game leaderboard in a file named TopPlayers.xlsm.
   - Inside that file, you have separate sheets like Scores, Revenues, and Ranks.
   - On the Scores sheet, cell C5 contains the score 12500.
5. You are using xlwings in different ways as mentioned hereafter. Without running the code, answer the questions that follow:

Scenario A: You run

```
wb = xw.Book("Report.xlsx")
```

Then you edit a few cells, finally you run **`wb.close()`**.

Scenario B: You run

```
app = xw.App(visible=False)
wb = app.books.open("Data.xlsx")
wb.close()
```

You forget to run **`app.quit()`**.

Scenario C: You run

```
app = xw.App(visible=True)
wb1 = app.books.open("File1.xlsx")
wb2 = app.books.open("File2.xlsx")
app.quit()
```

- After Scenario A, what happens to Excel?
- After Scenario B, what happens to Excel?
- After Scenario C, what happens to both workbooks?
- Which scenario(s) might leave hidden Excel processes running in Task Manager?

Join our Discord space

Join our Discord workspace for latest updates, offers, tech happenings around the world, new releases, and sessions with the authors:

https://discord.bpbonline.com

CHAPTER 11
Running Python Code from Excel

Introduction

One of xlwings' most powerful features is its ability to run Python code directly from Excel, bridging the gap between traditional spreadsheet workflows and Python's advanced capabilities. This chapter explores multiple ways to integrate and execute Python scripts within Excel, catering to different levels of flexibility and automation needs.

Readers will learn how to use xlwings add-in, VBA integration, and standalone Python scripts to automate tasks efficiently. We will compare various approaches, discuss their pros and cons, and provide step-by-step guidance on setting up each method. By the end of this chapter, readers will be equipped with the knowledge to choose and implement the best approach based on their workflow requirements. They will also learn to deploy xlwings for end users.

This chapter lays the foundation for even more advanced Excel-Python integration, with the next chapter diving into **user-defined functions** (**UDFs**) for executing Python code dynamically within Excel formulas.

Structure

In this chapter, we will discuss the following topics:

- Introduction to xlwings add-in in Excel
- Understanding ways to run Python from Excel
- Running Python via the Run main button
- Using the RunPython function in VBA
- Quickstart command
- Workbook-specific settings in xlwings
- Running Python code without installing add-in
- Deployment options for xlwings

Introduction to xlwings add-in in Excel

Whether you are in engineering, finance, quality assurance, human resources, sales, or data science, you might have used or at least seen some Excel add-ins that can transform your workflow. For example, Power Query to connect and transform external data from various sources, Analysis ToolPack, or MegaStat add-in to develop complex statistical or engineering analyses.

Imagine if you could use an add-in that allows you to run Python just by clicking a button. With the **`xlwings add-in`**, this vision becomes reality. It seamlessly bridges the gap between Excel and Python, empowering users to harness the full potential of Python's capabilities within the familiar interface of Excel.

It is an optional but powerful extension that enhances this integration by exposing Python functions directly in Excel. It supports both Excel automation (read / write cells, format sheets, analysis, etc.) and custom Excel functions written in Python.

Upon completion of this chapter and the subsequent one, you will gain a deeper understanding of the advantages offered by the **`xlwings add-in`** and its practical applications within Excel-Python integration.

System requirements for xlwings add-in

A local Python installation is generally required to utilize the **`xlwings add-in`** and its features fully. However, there are workarounds if Python is not installed on your end-users' machines (Refer to section *Deployment options for xlwings*).

If you are using anaconda or miniconda, you need at least **`conda 4.6`**.

As you already know, **`xlwings`** (open-source package) requires the installation of Excel and therefore only works on Windows and MacOS.

The ribbon of the add-in is compatible with Excel >= 2007 on Windows and >= 2016 on macOS. On MacOS, all UDF-related functionality is not available.

In short, **`xlwings add-in`** (open source) typically requires Excel installation and Python with **`xlwings`** package. The add-in needs to be the same version as the **`xlwings`** package. It means, if you upgrade the **`xlwings`** package in the future, you need to install **`xlwings add-in`** again, which is a quick task.

Installing xlwings add-in

The simplest and recommended way is to (Windows machine) open Anaconda Prompt or command prompt, if Python or Conda commands are recognized. On a Mac machine, open the Terminal and run the following code:

```
xlwings addin install
```

After restarting Excel, you will see a new **`xlwings`** tab in the ribbon with buttons such as Run main, Import Functions, Restart UDF Server, and add-in version info etc., as shown in the following figure:

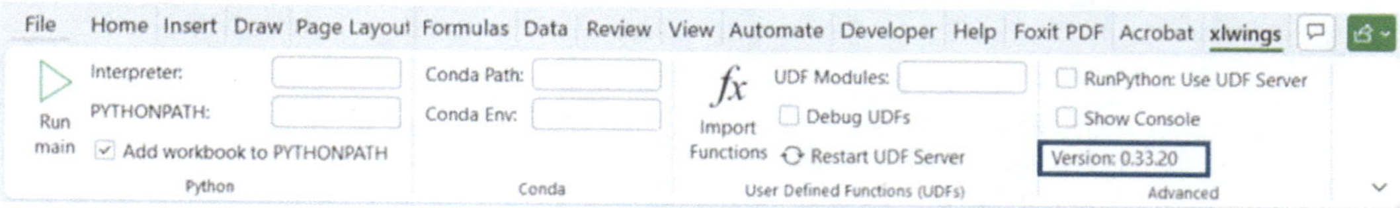

***Figure 11.1**: xlwings ribbon*

Note: On MacOS, all UDF-related functionality is not available. Also, on MacOS, the ribbon does not show a section for Conda. The Conda Env is configured as Interpreter in the Python group if you are on a Mac machine. Do not worry, we will talk about the configuration soon.

Underlying installation workflow

When you run installation code, behind the scenes, it copies **`xlwings.xlam`** from the directory of the Python package into Excel's XLSTART folder. Excel opens all files that are in this folder every time you start Excel.

It means, if you have **`xlwings.xlam`** (from your Python installation or otherwise) file, you can also install the add-in directly from Excel, the way you do for other add-ins:

`File | Options | Add-ins | Manage: Excel Add-ins | Go | Click OK`

Figure 11.2 shows how to search for Excel add-ins:

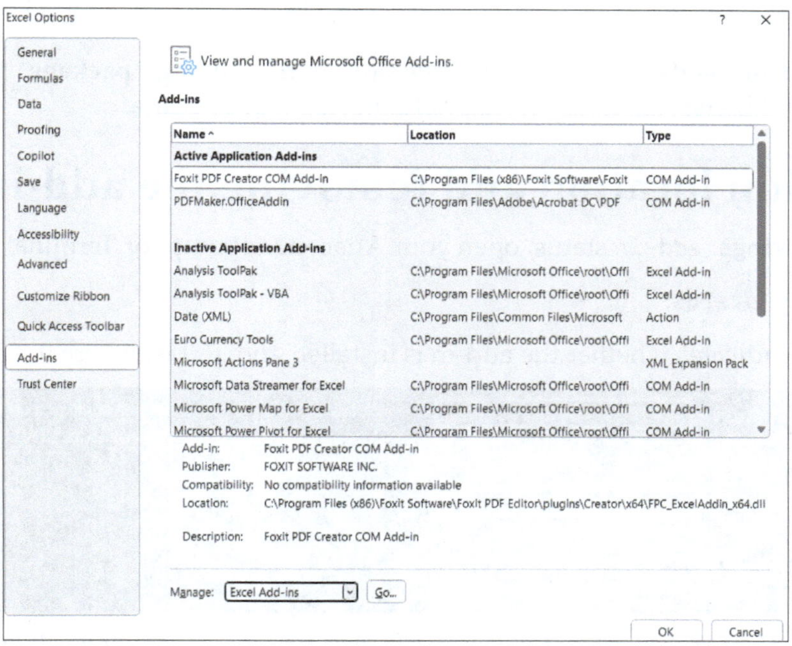

***Figure 11.2**: Searching for Excel add-ins*

You will see available add-ins. Scroll and select the **`xlwings add-in | Click OK.`** Refer to *Figure 11.3*:

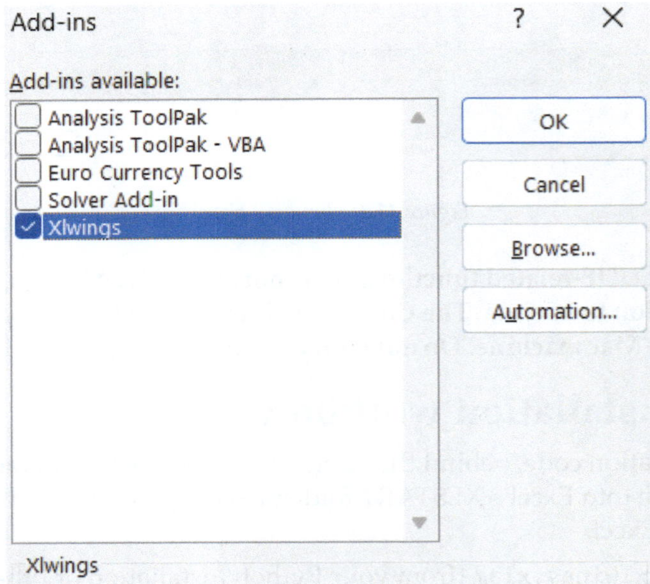

***Figure 11.3:** Installing xlwings add-in*

Usually, the **`.xlam`** file lives under the **`xlwings`** package directory in a subfolder, often called addin or similar.

Note: The add-in needs to be the same version as the xlwings package. Make sure to run xlwings add install again if you upgrade the xlwings package.

Installation location and removing the add-in

To check the **`xlwings add-in`** status, open your Anaconda Prompt or Terminal and type

```
xlwings add-in status.
```

This command indicates whether the add-in is installed and, if it is, where it is located.

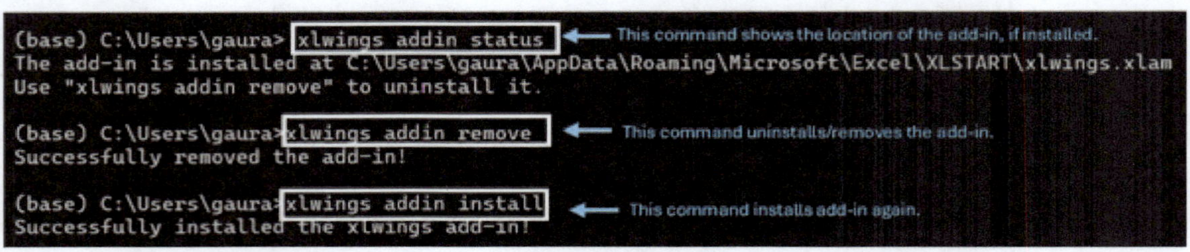

***Figure 11.4:** Checking add-in status, uninstalling and installing again via Anaconda Prompt*

You can also verify its installation by opening Excel and looking for the **xlwings** tab in the ribbon. And to find the location of the add-in installation, you can open the VBA editor (*Alt* + *F11*) in Excel, and then in the **Immediate Window** (*Ctrl* + *G*), running **?Application.StartupPath.**

It gives you the path of Excel's startup folder, where Excel looks for **add-ins** (such as **xlwings.xlam**) and startup files when it is launched. Refer to *Figure 11.5:*

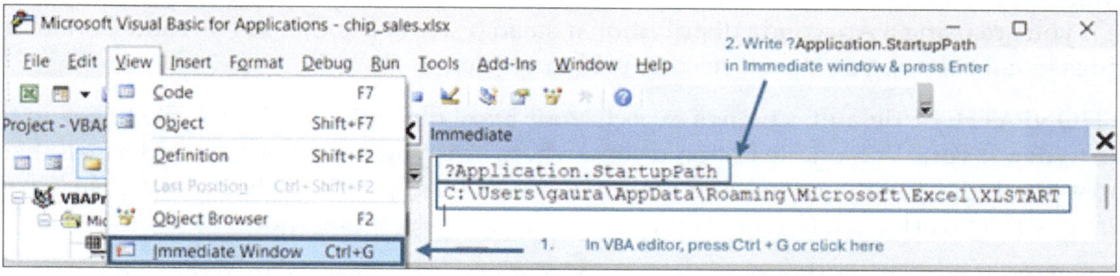

Figure 11.5: *The path of Excel's startup folder*

If you choose to remove or uninstall the **xlwings add-in**, you can run **xlwings addin remove** in Anaconda Prompt (Windows) or Terminal (MacOS). Refer to *Figure 11.4* again.

Also, simply running **xlwings** on Anaconda Prompt or Terminal shows **xlwings** version and its quick usages via the help menu, such as commands for installing the Excel add-in, launching the quickstart template, enabling the REST API server, and more, as shown in the following figure:

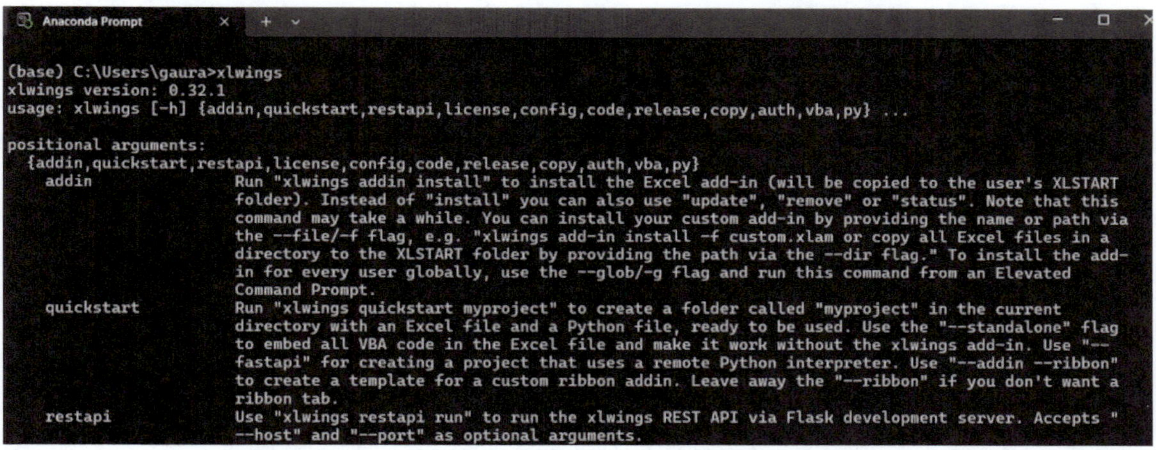

Figure 11.6: *xlwings CLI by typing xlwings on an Anaconda Prompt*

Configuration of xlwings add-in

The configuration you do in the **xlwings** ribbon (Interpreter, Conda Path, Conda Env, PYTHONPATH) is a one-time setup. These settings are stored globally and apply to all Excel workbooks that use **xlwings add-in** on your computer. Once you set them correctly, you do not need to repeat the process every time you open or create a new file. If needed, you can still override them later at the workbook level.

Let us understand Python and Conda settings in **xlwings** ribbon as follows:

Interpreter: This is the path to the Python interpreter (python.exe on Windows, or Python3 on MacOS). If you are using a plain Python installation (not Anaconda), then you need to set this. If you are using a Anaconda distribution instead (refer to the Conda Path and Conda Env settings given below), you do not need to set Interpreter.

PYTHONPATH: By default, **xlwings** expects your Excel file and your Python file to live in the same folder. If your Python file is stored somewhere else, you can enter that folder path here. It must point to the folder containing your module, not the .py file itself. For example, *C:\my D Drive\scripts* works, but *C:\my D Drive\scripts\chip_sales.py* does not.

Conda Path: If you are on Windows and use Anaconda or Miniconda, then type here the path to your installation, e.g. *C:\Users\Username\Miniconda3* or *C:\Users\Username\anaconda3*

Basically, this tells **xlwings** where your Conda installation lives. If you are using plain Python instead, you can leave it empty. You also need to set Conda Env, see next point.

Conda Env: This is the name of the Conda Env you want to use. For example, *base* or *excel_python* (**You need to use this**), the environment created for the book.

These configuration settings are not stored just in Excel, but they are also written in a *config* file that can also be manipulated externally. Refer to *Figure 11.7:*

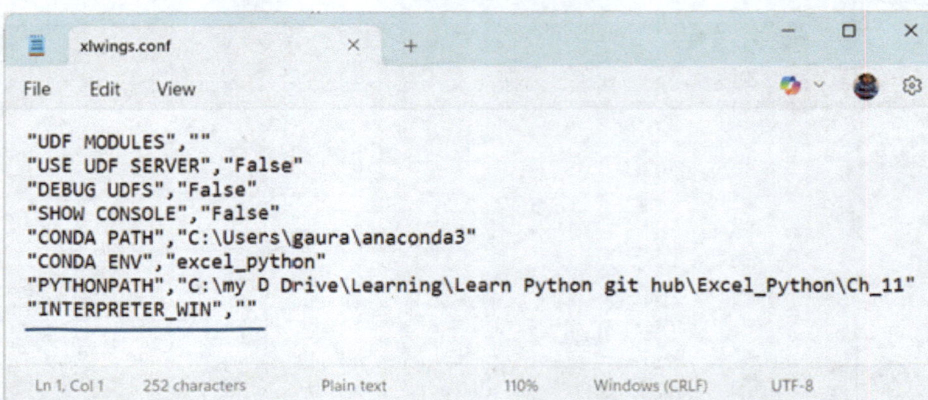

Figure 11.7: *The xlwings config file*

Note that Interpreter setting is stored as **Interpreter_Win** or **Interpreter_Mac**, depending open the operating system.

The location of this file is usually *.xlwings\xlwings.conf* in your user folder for Windows users, and for Mac users, it is *~/Library/Containers/com.microsoft.Excel/Data/xlwings.conf*

You can also set workbook-specific settings, which will override global (Ribbon) settings. We will discuss this later. (Refer to section *Workbook-specific settings in xlwings*). In case your antivirus is blocking **`xlwings add-in`**, you need to whitelist the add-in folder and the Python interpreter used by **`xlwings.`**

So we have installed **`xlwings add-in`** and set up things. Now, let us see how we can run Python scripts from Excel.

Understanding ways to run Python from Excel

There are multiple ways to run a Python script from Excel, which we will explore in the current and subsequent chapters. Each method is suited to different purposes and levels of automation.

Let us see what those methods are and what they offer:

- **Method 1:** Running Python via the **`Run main`** button in the add-in (Requires add-in)
- **Method 2:** Using the **`RunPython`** function in VBA (Requires add-in)
- **Method 3:** Running Python with standalone workbooks (No add-in required)
- **Method 4:** Calling Python directly from Excel cells as user-defined functions (to be covered in the next chapter)

Comparing each method

The most straightforward approach is using the **`Run main`** button available in the **`xlwings add-in`**. This method executes the **`main()`** function defined in your Python script and is ideal for quick testing, refreshing data, or applying formatting repeatedly. It requires the **`xlwings add-in`** to be installed and configured, but involves no coding in VBA, making it beginner-friendly.

A more flexible approach is using the **`RunPython`** function in VBA. Here, a short VBA macro calls your Python function (for example, **`RunPython("import script; script.function()")`**). This method allows you to link Python code to buttons or automate workflows. It still relies on the add-in but provides more control over how and when Python runs.

When you need to share your Excel-Python solution with others who may not have the **`xlwings add-in`**, the standalone workbook approach is recommended. This setup is created using the **`xlwings quickstart command`**, which generates a ready-to-use Excel file containing all required VBA code. End users can open the workbook and run Python without separately installing the **`add-in`**, if they have Python and **`xlwings`** installed. This makes it a practical choice for deployment in corporate environments.

Finally, **`xlwings`** also supports **user-defined functions** (**UDFs**), where you can call Python functions directly from Excel cells, like built-in formulas like **`=SUM()`** or **`=AVERAGE()`**. This method is powerful for performing complex calculations within cells, but requires the **xlwings add-in** and some understanding of Python function design. We will discuss UDFs in detail in the next chapter.

In summary, **Run main** and **RunPython** are best suited for development and interactive use, **standalone workbooks** are ideal for sharing or deployment, and **UDFs** enable live, formula-based integration of Python within Excel.

We will start with the simplest approach, where Excel users can just click a button in **xlwings add-in**, and the entire Python script will run automatically, and you can see the updated Excel live with a button click.

Running Python via the Run main button

Let us see how we can run Python scripts from Excel just by clicking a button. For demonstration purposes, we have added an Excel file named **real_estate.xlsx** and a script **real_estate.py**.

You can download these two files to the same folder. Excel files look like the following figure, which has some imaginary data for the real estate industry:

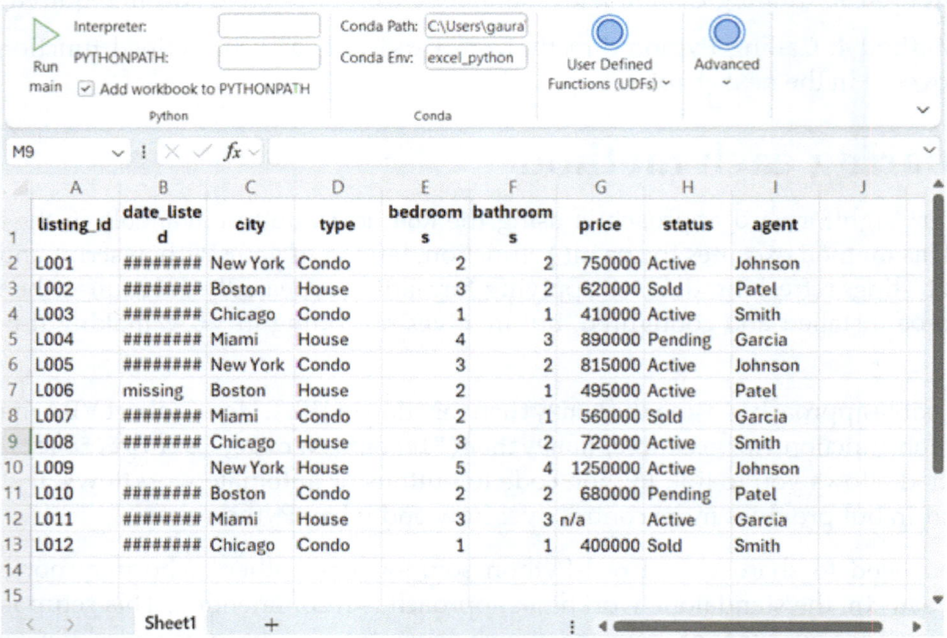

Figure 11.8: Workbook real_estate.xlsx

Simply, click on the **Run main** button and observe what happens to the Excel file. You might need to wait for a few seconds. Do not keep pressing the button repeatedly. You might be amazed to see it highlights rows with missing dates with a light red color and highlights prices above 800k with a light green color, as shown in the following figure:

	A	B	C	D	E	F	G	H	I	J
1	listing_id	date_listed	city	type	bedrooms	bathrooms	price	status	agent	
2	L001	01-03-2024	New York	Condo	2	2	750000	Active	Johnson	
3	L002	02-03-2024	Boston	House	3	2	620000	Sold	Patel	
4	L003	05-03-2024	Chicago	Condo	1	1	410000	Active	Smith	
5	L004	07-03-2024	Miami	House	4	3	890000	Pending	Garcia	
6	L005	09-03-2024	New York	Condo	3	2	815000	Active	Johnson	
7	L006	missing	Boston	House	2	1	495000	Active	Patel	
8	L007	12-03-2024	Miami	Condo	2	1	560000	Sold	Garcia	
9	L008	15-03-2024	Chicago	House	3	2	720000	Active	Smith	
10	L009		New York	House	5	4	1250000	Active	Johnson	
11	L010	19-03-2024	Boston	Condo	2	2	680000	Pending	Patel	
12	L011	21-03-2024	Miami	House	3	3	n/a	Active	Garcia	
13	L012	25-03-2024	Chicago	Condo	1	1	400000	Sold	Smith	
14										

Sheet1 +

***Figure 11.9:** After clicking Run main button*

If you are wondering how Excel has applied this formatting just with one click, it is time to check the Python script named **real_estate.py**:

```
import xlwings as xw
import pandas as pd
def main():
    wb = xw.Book.caller()   # Connect to Excel
    sheet = wb.sheets["Sheet1"]
    # Load data
    df = sheet.range("A1").options(pd.
DataFrame, header=1, index=False, expand="table").value
    # --- Formatting Rules ---
    # Highlight rows with missing dates
    missing_dates = df[df["date_listed"].isna()].index + 2
    for row in missing_dates:
        sheet.range(f"B{row}").color = (255, 200, 200)  # Light red
    # Highlight prices above 800k
    high_price = df[pd.to_numeric(df["price"], errors="coerce") > 800000].
index + 2
    for row in high_price:
        sheet.range(f"G{row}").color = (200, 255, 200)  # Light green
```

Let us check what this script does in the following steps:

1. It imports **pandas** and **xlwings**
2. Defines a function called **main()**. This is required for the **Run main** button; Excel will always call **main()** when you click **Run main** in **xlwings add-in.** This function:
   a. Connects to your workbook (workbook that clicked **Run main** button) using **Book.caller()** and then grabs **Sheet1** where the data lives
   b. Then it reads your table (starting at cell **A1**) into a **pandas** DataFrame, which makes it easy to filter and apply rules.
   c. Next, it applies formatting rules such as finding rows where **date_listed** is missing, to color them light red, and finding rows where **price > 800,000** to color them light green.

Here, we would like to throw light on the difference between **Book.caller()** and **Book()** methods, which might confuse beginners:

- The function, **xw.Book()** opens or attaches to a workbook by name or path. You would use this if running Python directly (outside Excel). For example, if you are launching a Python script from your Terminal or editor, **xw.Book()** helps you connect to the workbook you want to work with. You have already used it in the previous chapter.
- On the other hand, **xw.Book.caller()** is used when your Python code is triggered from inside Excel, typically via the **Run main** button or a VBA call like **RunPython**. It tells Python to connect to the Excel file from where you clicked the **Run main** button. It is like instructing Python, *Hey, connect to the Excel file that just called you.*

  This is essential when your workflow starts from Excel and hands control over to Python.

Additionally, for testing purposes, **xlwings** provides **xw.Book.set_mock_caller().** This is a helper function that simulates what **xw.Book.caller()** would do. This is useful when you are developing or debugging your Python code outside Excel but still want to mimic how it behaves when called from Excel. You can apply **set_mock_caller()** method to your workbook, so your code thinks it was triggered from Excel, even though you are running it manually. You can run this code for any workbook in your directory and observe what it does:

```
import xlwings as xw

# Load the workbook you want to simulate as the caller
wb = xw.Book("Book1.xlsx")

# Set it as the mock caller
wb.set_mock_caller()
```

```
# Now your function can use Book.caller() as if it was triggered from Excel
def main():
    wb = xw.Book.caller()
    sheet = wb.sheets[0]
    sheet.range("A1").value = "Hello from mock_caller!"
# Run the function manually
main()
```

This function makes it easy to switch back and forth between calling the function from Excel and Python.

Understanding the Run main button

When you click on **Run main** button, it automatically runs a Python function called **main()** from a Python script that:

- Has the same name as the Excel workbook
- Is located in the same folder as the Excel workbook

If the Python script and Excel file are not in the same folder, you can configure the PYTHONPATH setting in the **xlwings add-in** to point to the correct script location.

However, if the script is saved with a different name (not matching the workbook) or you want to run different function(s) (not named **main()**), then you *cannot* use the **Run main** button.

In such cases, you must call Python functions explicitly from VBA using **RunPython.** We will discuss this in the next section. For now, let us see when configuring PYTHONPATH becomes necessary.

For demonstration purposes, we have given you a Python script that creates an additional sheet named Summary to store analysis results, such as pivot tables or data summaries. The script named **chip_sales.py** is in the scripts folder, and data **chip_sales.xlsx** is in a different folder.

When you click **Run main** in **chip_sales.xlsx**, it looks for a Python file with the same name **chip_sales.py,** in the same folder and throws an **Error** when it cannot find the file there, as displayed in the following figure:

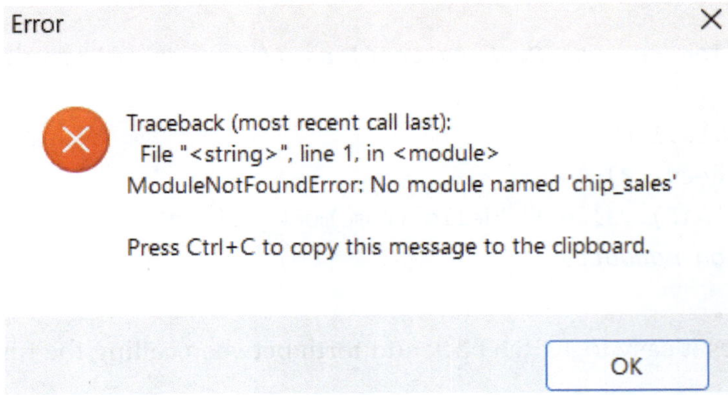

Figure 11.10: *ModuleNotFoundError*

To handle this, you can copy the full path[1] of your Python script and paste it in **PYTHONPATH** before clicking the **`Run main`** button, and it will work. Refer to *Figure 11.11:*

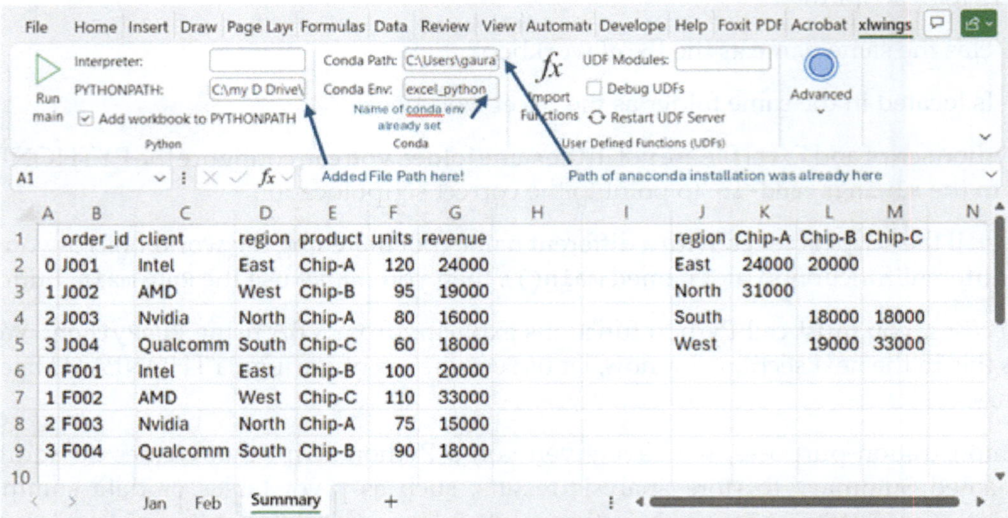

Figure 11.11: *Works after setting PYTHONPATH*

As you can see, just with one click, you have merged data from two different sheets (Jan and Feb), created a pivot table, and put it in a new sheet called Summary.

This approach is extremely powerful for business users who are most comfortable working inside Excel. You can hand them a ready-made Python script, and all they need to do is update the data in Excel and click **`Run main`**. Instantly, the latest analysis or report will be refreshed, no coding required.

[1] In the xlwings add-in settings, the PYTHONPATH must point to the folder containing your module, not the .py file itself. For example, *C:\my D Drive\scripts* works, but *C:\my D Drive\scripts\chip_sales.py* does not.

Troubleshooting

While using the **xlwings add-in** is simple, beginners can sometimes face trivial issues. Let us quickly guide you on common problems and how to fix those without searching on Google or Stack Overflow:

- **Python Not Found:** This error indicates that Excel cannot locate the correct **Python** installation. Refer to *Figure 11.12:*

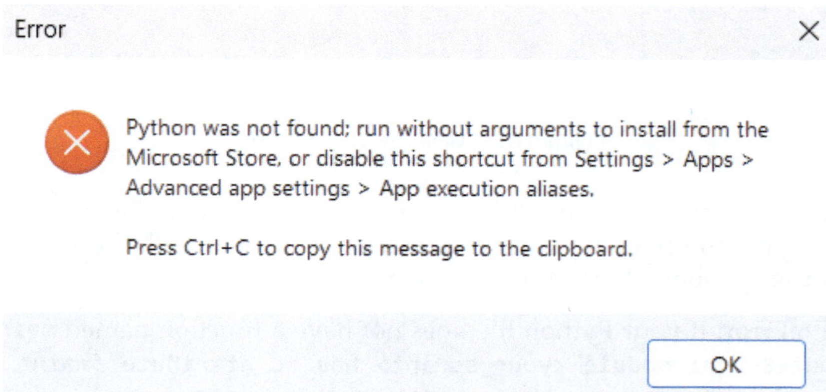

Figure 11.12: *Python Not Found Error*

  A quick fix is to set this configuration in **xlwings** ribbon:

  - In in the **Interpreter** of the add-in, set the full path to your Python interpreter, if you have installed plain Python Or
  - Set Conda Path and Conda Env, if you have installed Python via anaconda or miniconda.

- **No Module Named xlwings:** This error tells you that the Python Env does not have **xlwings** installed. This is possible if you have installed plain Python (not from Anaconda Distribution, which has **xlwings** pre-installed) and forgot to install **xlwings** package.

  To fix this error, you need to install **xlwings** using **pip**, **Conda**, or **Conda-Forge**.

- **ModuleNotFoundError:** This error also shows that your Python file (module) with the same name as the Excel file is not found in the same folder. It means either your Python file (module) name is not the same as the name of the Excel file, or your Python file is saved in a different folder. Refer to *Figure 11.13:*

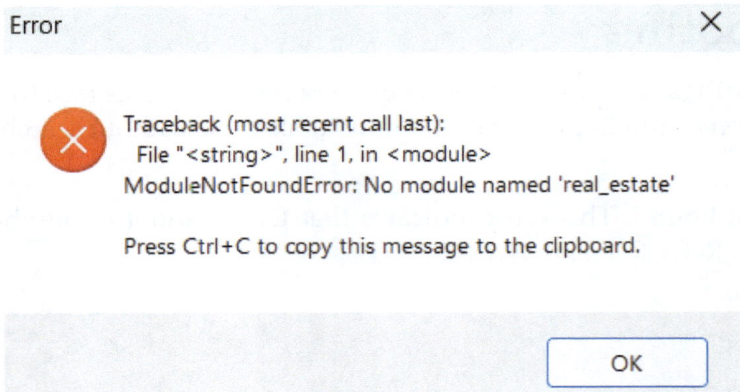

***Figure 11.13**: ModuleNotFoundError*

This can be easily sorted by either renaming one of your files to match names or supplying the full path of your Python script in the PYTHONPATH configuration of the **`xlwings`** ribbon, depending upon what caused this error.

- **AttributeError:** If your Python file does not have a function named **`main()`**, you get **`AttributeError: module <your_script> has no attribute 'main'`** or **`Run main`** fails silently. Refer to *Figure 11.14:*

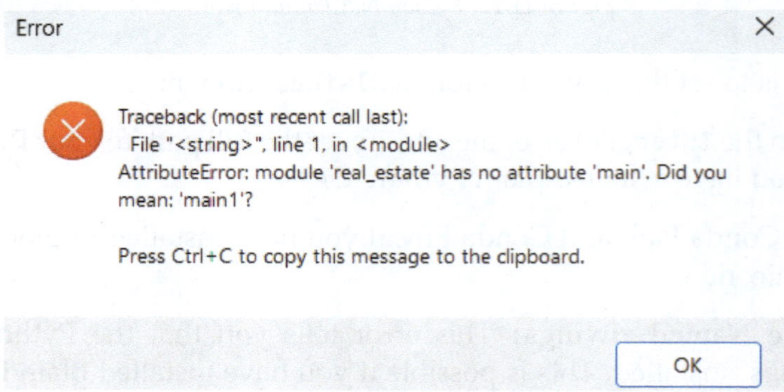

***Figure 11.14:** AttributeError*

Either you need to rename your function as **`main()`** or build a small wrapper called **`main()`** that calls other function(s) in your script.

- **Excel add-in Not Installed or Disabled:** You can uninstall and reinstall the add-in from the Anaconda Prompt or Terminal.
- **Script runs but does not affect the active Excel and opens a new file instead:** It may be because the **`main()`** function in your script does not interact with the Excel workbook. You can handle this by using **`xlwings.Book.caller()`** (maybe you have used **`xlwings.Book()`** by mistake) to reference the workbook that triggered the script. You need to ensure your script modifies or reads from Excel using **`xlwings`** objects.

Using the RunPython function in VBA

You might have enjoyed clicking a button in Excel to run an entire Python script. However, this approach had some limitations:

- Excel file and Python script must be in the same folder (unless PYTHONPATH is set manually, you can do this easily).
- Excel file and Python script should have the same name (still manageable).
- Python script should have a function called **`main()`**, which does not accept any arguments.

If you prefer to keep raw data in Excel and name your scripts meaningfully, or if your script has different functions for different tasks, and you want to choose which function to call in Excel, then you can use **`RunPython`** function in VBA. This will require very limited knowledge of VBA. If you have never written any VBA code before, no issues, we will give you all that you need.

VBA basics

Even if you have never written any VBA code yourself, you were able to run a VBA macro from Python using **`xlwings`** in the previous chapter. There, you have used a macro-enabled Excel file named **`game_macro.xlsm`**, which had VBA code for a Subroutine and a function in Module1. Only that much understanding of a Subroutine is needed for this and the next section. In case you are not confident, let us revise the VBA basics for you.

Execute the following steps to insert a VBA macro:

1. To get started, press *Alt* + *F11* **(Windows)** to open the **VBA Editor** as shown in the following figure:

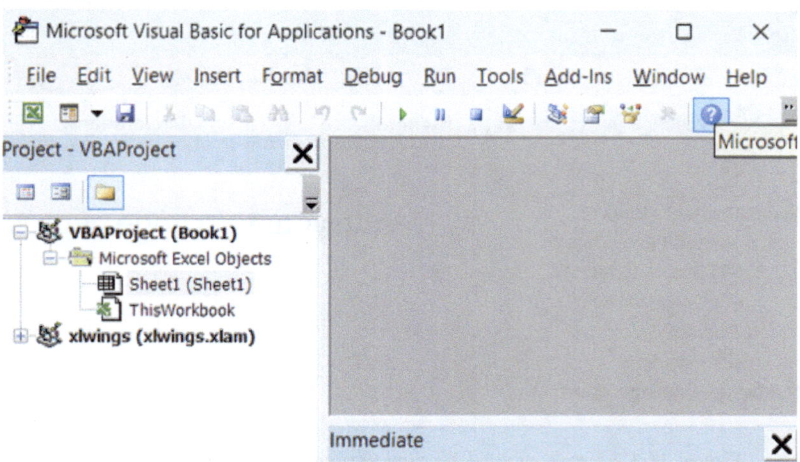

Figure 11.15: *VBA Editor*

2. In the left pane, right-click your workbook name and choose **Insert | Module.** It will add a new blank module where you can write and store your VBA code. Refer to *Figure 11.16:*

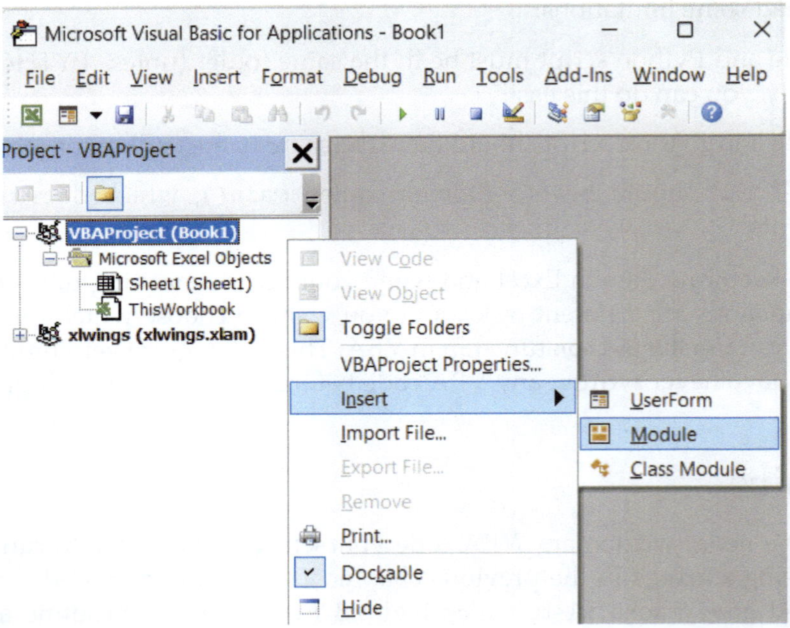

Figure 11.16*: Inserting Module in VBA Editor*

3. Here, you can type or paste your macro code, as shown in the following figure:

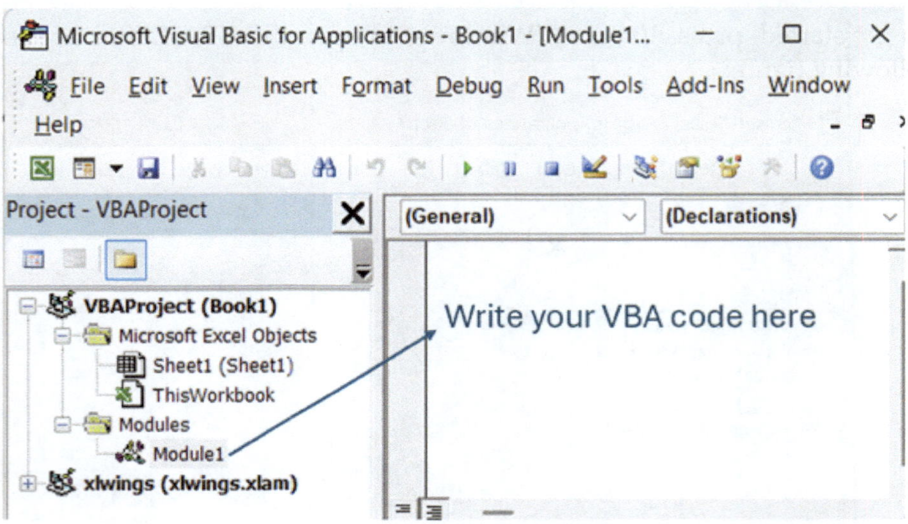

Figure 11.17*: Newly created Module to type or paste your macro code*

Alternatively, in this newly created module, you can click on **Insert | Procedure**, as shown in the following figure:

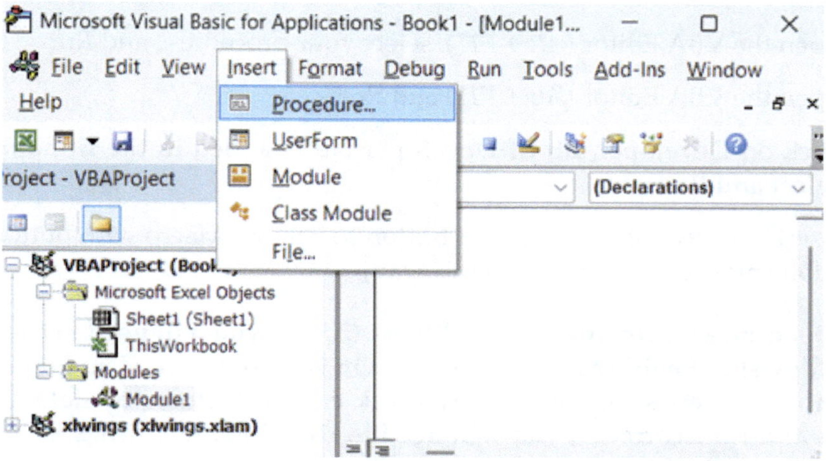

***Figure 11.18**: Inserting a Procedure to help you in typing macro code*

This pops up a window, where you need to add a suitable name to your macro, select Sub, choose Public scope, and click **OK.** This adds a new procedure, where you can type your code. Refer to *Figure 11.19:*

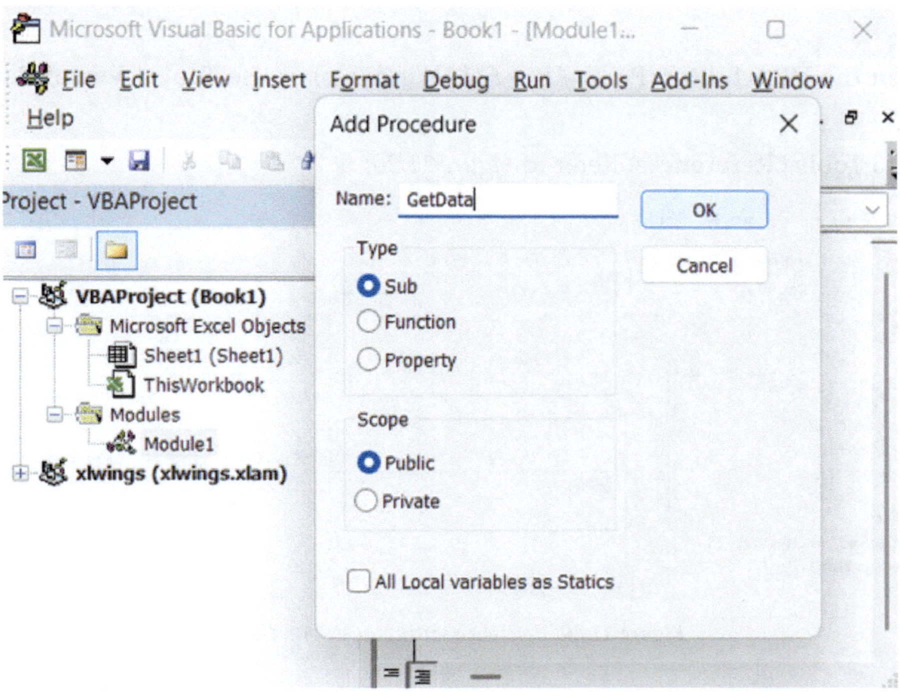

***Figure 11.19**: Inserting a Subroutine Procedure named GetData*

4. Save your file as a macro-enabled file **`(.xlsm)`**

   Once saved, there are several ways to run it:

   a. Open the VBA Editor (*Alt* + *F11*), select your procedure, and Run

   b. Open the VBA Editor (*Alt* + *F11*) and Press *F5*

   c. Click on **Developer tab (if Developer tab is added in the ribbon) | Macros | Select and Run**

   d. Insert and use the form control button to run the Macro with button click (Only Public procedures can be run this way)

Note: While opening a macro-enabled workbook (.xlsm), you will need to click on Enable Content (Windows) or Enable Macros (MacOS). On Windows, for .xlsm files downloaded from the companion repository, Excel may block certain features by default. To ensure the file opens and runs correctly, you will need to click Enable Editing when prompted; otherwise, macros and add-in functionality might not work as expected.

Reference setting

For using the **`RunPython`** function in VBA, one key step is setting the reference to **`xlwings`**. This allows VBA to recognize the **`RunPython`** command. To set the reference, execute the following steps:

1. **Open the VBA Editor**: Press *Alt* + *F11* (Windows) or use **Tools | Visual Basic Editor** (Mac)

2. **Go to Tools | References**. Refer to *Figure 11.20:*

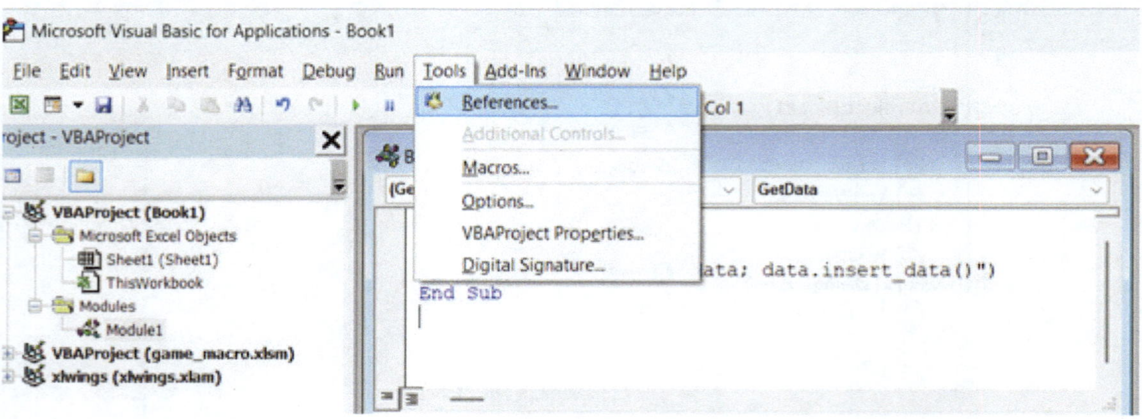

***Figure 11.20**: Reference setting in VBA Editor*

3. **Scroll and check: `xlwings`** and then click **OK** to confirm. Refer to *Figure 11.21:*

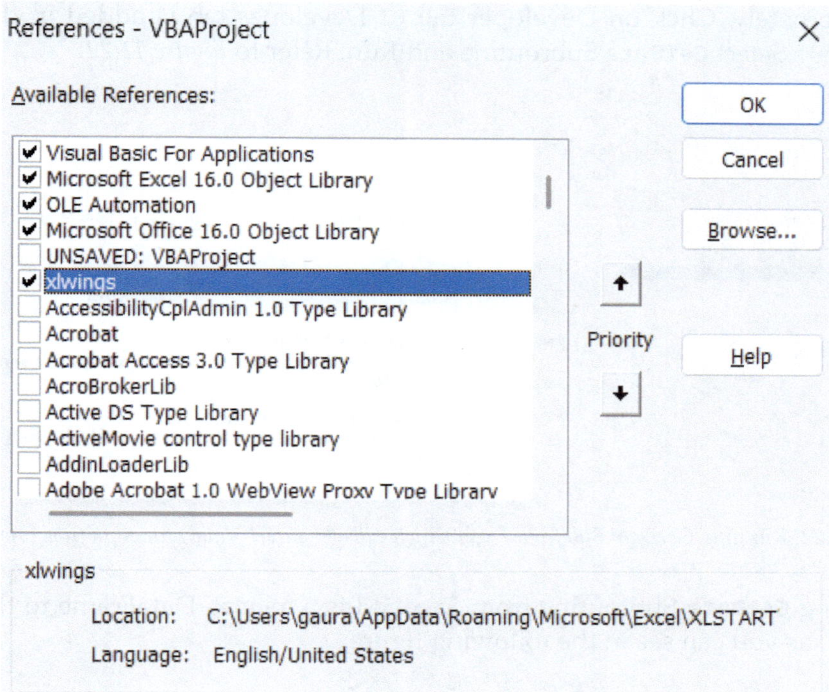

Figure 11.21*: xlwings reference in VBA*

Demonstration

This chapter folder includes one Python file named **`analysis.py`**. The script is a simple Python module with two functions:

- Function **`insert_data()`** inserts a **`pandas`** DataFrame to A1 cell for Sheet1 and
- Function **`analyse_data()`** insert summary of this data in Sheet2.

We are willing to run these Python functions (not named as **`main()`**) in a newly created Excel file (not necessarily named as **`analysis.xlsm`**). For your convenience, we have supplied a macro-enabled Excel file named `RunPythonDemo.xlsm`.

The steps to run these functions in Excel are as follows:

1. Save the **`analysis.py`** module on your machine.
2. Open **`RunPythonDemo.xlsm`**
3. Open the VBA Editor (*Alt + F11*) | Press *F5* | Select GetData Subroutine | Run

Or alternately, Click on Developer tab (if Developer tab is added in the ribbon) | Macros | Select **GetData** Subroutine and Run. Refer to *Figure 11.22:*

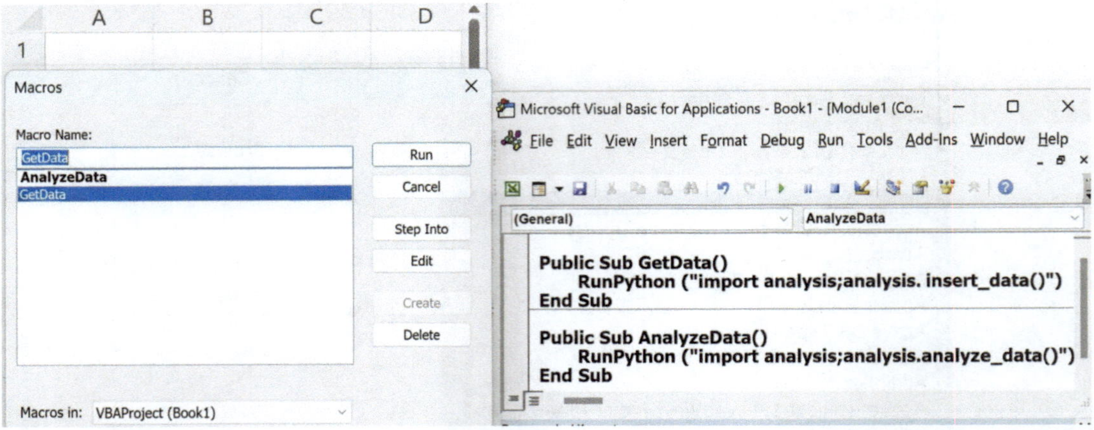

***Figure 11.22**: Running GetData Sub from Excel which calls for insert_data() function from analysis.py*

4. Running **GetData** Subroutine from Excel adds a **pandas** DataFrame to the A1 cell of Sheet1, as you can see in the following figure:

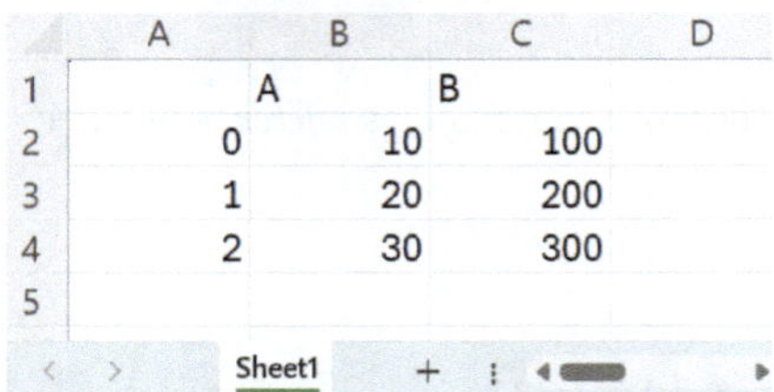

***Figure 11.23**: pandas DataFrame inserted by running GetData Sub from Excel*

5. Similarly, you can run **AnalyzeData** Sub, which calls for **analyze_data()** from module **analysis.py**, as shown in the following figure:

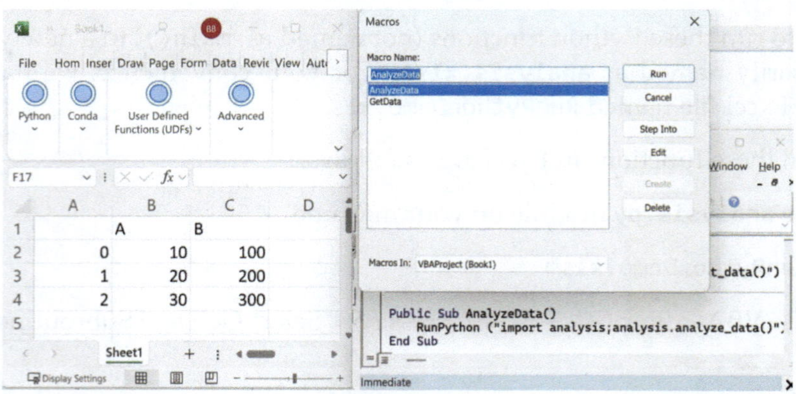

***Figure 11.24**: Running AnalyzeData Sub from Excel*

This action inserts a data summary in the newly created sheet, as shown in the following figure:

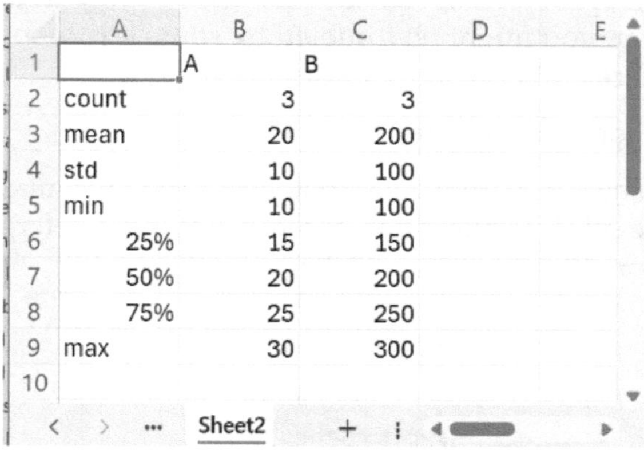

	A	B	C	D	E
1		A	B		
2	count	3	3		
3	mean	20	200		
4	std	10	100		
5	min	10	100		
6	25%	15	150		
7	50%	20	200		
8	75%	25	250		
9	max	30	300		
10					

Sheet2

***Figure 11.25**: Data summary inserted in newly created sheet*

Alternatively, you can create your own Excel file and write a Subroutine that uses the **`RunPython`** function to import the module named **`analysis`** and call any function from that module the way you do in Python. You can use semicolons or triple quotes to write multi-line code inside the **`RunPython`** function. The **`RunPython`** function is available because you have added a reference to **`xlwings`** in VBA (Tools | Reference | xlwings), and this function accepts Python code as a string.

As you must have noticed, the VBA macros used in `analysis.xlsm` are very simple, like:

```
Public Sub GetData()
    RunPython ("import analysis;analysis.insert_data()")
End Sub

Public Sub AnalyzeData()
    RunPython ("import analysis;analysis.analyze_data()")
End Sub
```

These macros tell Excel to:

- Use Python (via **`RunPython`**, typically from the **`xlwings add-in`**)
- Import a Python module named analysis (basically analysis.py)
- Call the function **`insert_data()`** or **`analyze_data()`** from that module

You can modify this as per your requirement.

Troubleshooting

Using **RunPython** from VBA process is simple and flexible as compared to the **Run main** button discussed earlier. However, you might be troubled by some errors sometimes. Let us discuss common errors you can face and how to fix those.

Some common troubleshooting errors are:

1. **Compile error:** This error indicates that you probably missed adding a reference to **xlwings** in the VBA application. Without adding a reference, it cannot find the **RunPython** function. Refer to *Figure 11.26:*

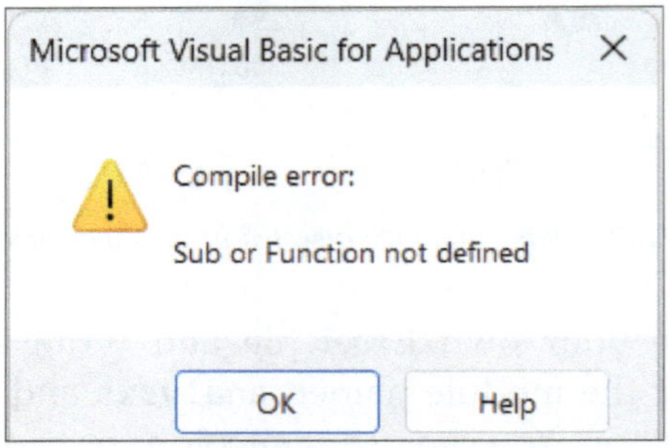

Figure 11.26: Compile error

To fix this issue, you need to add references to **xlwings** in the VBA editor as we had discussed in the reference setting section (**Developer | Visual Basic | Tools | References | Check xlwings | Click on OK**).

Another reason for a Compile error can be forgetting to type quotation marks before and after the Python command (Refer to *Figure 11.27*). **RunPython** expects Python commands as a string; otherwise, VBA would not be able to understand the code.

To fix this issue, simply put your Python code as a string wrapped in quotation marks.

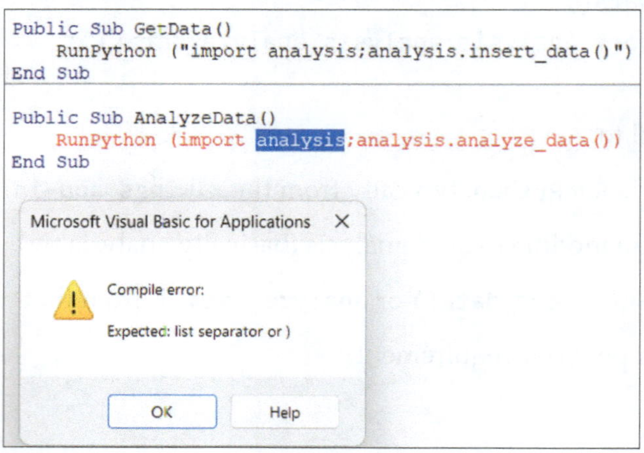

Figure 11.27: Another Compile error

2. **ModuleNotFoundError:** This might be because you mistyped the module name (spelling is wrong) or PYTHONPATH is not set when your module is in a different folder than your Excel file. You need to set PYTHONPATH and correct typos, if any, to fix this issue. Refer to *Figure 11.28:*

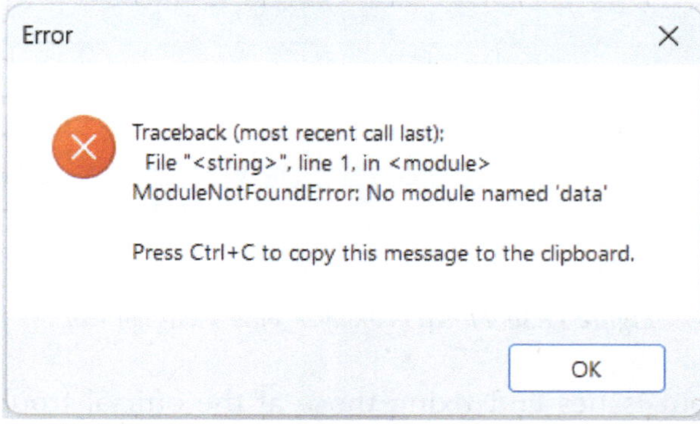

***Figure 11.28**: ModuleNotFoundError*

3. **Attribute Error:** If you have mistyped name of the Python function, then you might get an **`Attribute Error`**, as shown in *Figure 11.29*. To fix this error, just check and correct name of the Python function used in the module.

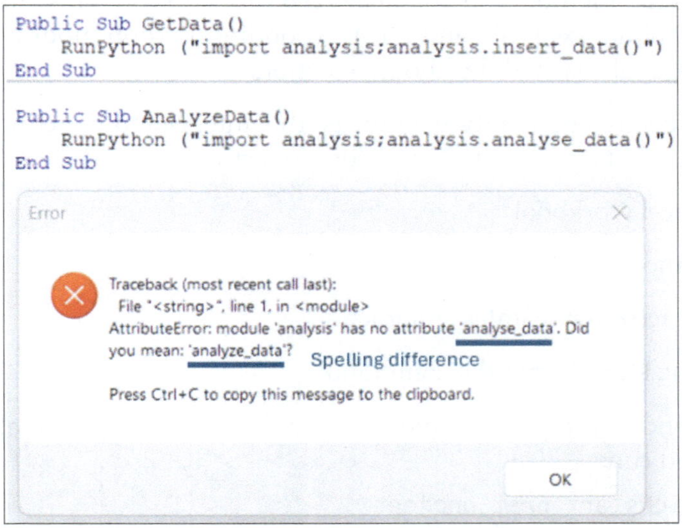

***Figure 11.29**: AttributeError*

4. **Function not working but no error:** Another issue can be if you forget to use parenthesis after function call (Refer to *Figure 11.30*), it will not show any error message, but function will not be called. Do not forget to use a parenthesis after function call as you always do in a Python script.

```
Public Sub GetData()
    RunPython ("import analysis;analysis.insert_data()")
End Sub

Public Sub AnalyzeData()
    RunPython ("import analysis;analysis.analyze_data")
End Sub
```

No parenthesis here

***Figure 11.30**: Function analyze_data() will not run*

You can read more about issues and fixing those at the official troubleshooting document (**https://docs.xlwings.org/en/stable/troubleshooting.html**)

Quickstart command

In the previous two sections, we have discussed two different methods to integrate Excel with Python: the **Run main** method and the **RunPython** function in VBA. In both sections, we demonstrated creating an Excel file and a corresponding Python module to automate tasks like data generation, analysis, and dashboard creation.

Another quick and beginner-friendly way to see this integration in action is to use **xlwings quickstart** command. It sets up a ready-to-run project with:

- A sample Excel workbook
- A linked Python script
- Pre-wired macros for seamless interaction

Execute the following steps to run the command:

1. Open Anaconda Prompt (Windows) or Terminal (MacOS), navigate to your working directory, and run:

   ```
   xlwings quickstart first_project
   ```

2. This will create a folder called **first_project** in your current working directory. This folder contains one macro-enabled Excel file named **first_project.xlsm** and one Python module named **first_project.py.**

3. Now, open the Excel file and notice that it has an additional sheet **named _xlwings.** conf. We will talk in detail about this sheet later (refer to section Workbook-specific settings in **xlwings**)

Revisiting the Run main button

In the Excel file, click on the **Run main** button. It will write **Hello xlwings!** into cell A1 of the first sheet. Click the button again, and it will change to **Bye xlwings!** In the same cell.

To understand it better, you can look at the Python script **first_project.py**. It has a function called **main()** which gets triggered with a click on the **Run main** button:

```
def main():
    wb = xw.Book.caller()
    sheet = wb.sheets[0]
    if sheet["A1"].value == "Hello xlwings!":
        sheet["A1"].value = "Bye xlwings!"
    else:
        sheet["A1"].value = "Hello xlwings!"
```

This function creates a connection to the active Excel workbook that triggered the Python code (via **xw.Book.caller()**), accesses the first sheet, and toggles the value in cell A1 between **Hello xlwings!** and **Bye xlwings!** each time it runs.

Revisiting RunPython in VBA

For **RunPython** in VBA, you can run **SampleCall()** Subroutine in **first_project.xlsm**. It will import the module and call **first_project.main()** function. Hence, it will also perform the same job, printing **Hello xlwings!** or **Bye xlwings!** into cell A1.

To understand better, you can open the VBA editor in **first_project.xlsm** and look at the macro:

```
Sub SampleCall()
    mymodule = Left(ThisWorkbook.Name, (InStrRev(ThisWorkbook.
Name, ".", -1, vbTextCompare) - 1))
    RunPython "import " & mymodule & ";" & mymodule & ".main()"
End Sub
```

Let us understand this. The Subroutine **SampleCall()** is a VBA macro designed to dynamically import and run a Python module based on the name of the Excel workbook. The first line extracts the module name without extension from the current Excel workbook. For example, if your workbook is named **first_project.xlsm**, it sets **mymodule = "first_project".**

RunPython, which is provided by the **xlwings add-in**, accepts a string with Python code. And usually, we import some Python module and run one of the functions defined in it. Here, **"import " & mymodule & ";" & mymodule &**

".main()" constructs a Python command like:

```
import first_project; first_project.main()
```

Now, you understand that when you run this macro, it inserts **`Hello xlwings!`** or **`Bye xlwings!`** into cell A1.

Workbook-specific settings in xlwings

We had discussed that **`xlwings add-in`** configuration settings are not stored just in Excel, but they are also written in a config file that can also be manipulated externally. Additionally, **`xlwings`** allows you to override global settings (like those set via the Ribbon or config files) by embedding workbook-specific settings directly into the Excel file itself.

This is useful if:

- You want different Excel files to use different Python enviornments.
- You want to share your workbook with others, so it runs correctly without them needing to adjust their global settings.

Note: The ribbon always shows global values, even if a workbook has its own overrides. Do not be misled, the overrides still work when you run Python from that workbook.

Overriding the global configuration

`xlwings` allows each Excel file to override global addin settings by using a special worksheet named **`xlwings.conf`**. This sheet acts as a local configuration file for that workbook.

Here are the steps to create workbook-specific settings:

1. Open your Excel workbook, for example, **`chip_sales.xlsx`**.
2. Insert a new sheet and rename it exactly as **`xlwings.conf`** (all lowercase, no extra spaces)
3. In that sheet, create a 2-column table. Refer to the following table:

Key	Value
Interpreter	C:\Users\YourName\anaconda3\envs\excel_python\python.exe
PYTHONPATH	C:\Path\To\Your\Scripts

***Table 11.1**: xlwings add-in configration*

   Make sure that the key and value are exactly spelled like that in the add-in.

4. Save and close the workbook.

Since the ribbon still shows your global settings, you might think nothing happened. However, you can test it by reopening it, then clicking the **`Run main`** button. For this to work, you need to keep a Python file with the same name as the Excel file, and that Python file must contain a function named main. This function will be executed when you click **`Run main.`**

If you apply a leading underscore in the sheet name (**_xlwings.conf**), add-in ignores this sheet and falls back to global setting. By convention, developers use underscore (_) prefix to indicate *do not use this*.

If you are sharing your workbook with colleagues, always include an **_xlwings.conf** sheet. They will need to update it to reflect their own setup and activate it by removing the underscore from the sheet name. This makes it easy to toggle workbooklevel configuration on or off without deleting anything, just by renaming the sheet.

Configuration hierarchy

To understand how this extra sheet overrides add-in's global setting, let us discuss where does **xlwings** look for settings. It searches for settings in the following locations and order:

1. **Workbook configuration:** First, **xlwings** looks for a sheet called **xlwings.conf**.
2. **Directory configuration:** Next, **xlwings** looks for a file called **xlwings.conf** in the same directory as your Excel workbook.
3. **User configuration:** Finally, **xlwings** looks for a file called **xlwings.conf** in the **.xlwings** folder in the user's home directory. Normally, you do not edit this file directly. Instead, it is created and edited by the add-in whenever you change the setting.

Running Python code without installing add-in

Using **xlwings add-in** made it super easy to run Python code either using **Run main** button or using **RunPython** function in VBA. Another powerful feature in **xlwings** is to write a Python function and call it directly from an Excel cell, just like native Excel formulas, but powered by Python's full capabilities. We will discuss this in the next chapter. All these methods require you to have **xlwings add-in** installed.

There is one more way to run Python code from Excel without needing to install **xlwings add-in.** For Excel users, a convenient and recommended way to install an add-in; however, it helps to see how to set up a standalone workbook, which does not need the add-in.

To demonstrate this, let us first remove the **xlwings add-in** by running **xlwings add-in remove** in Anaconda Prompt or Terminal.

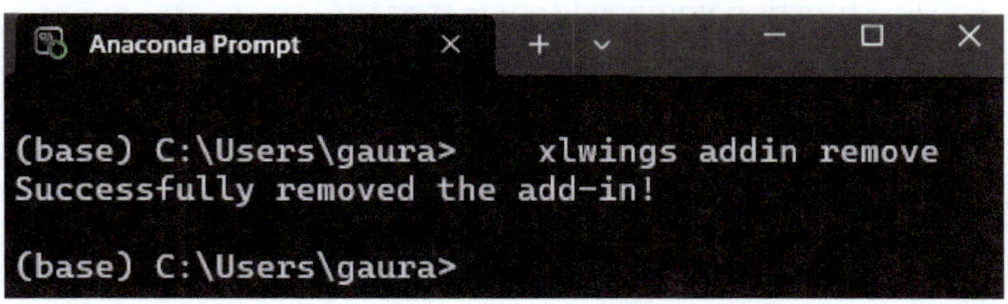

***Figure 11.31:** Removing xlwings add-in*

As we have seen earlier, using the **quickstart** command makes it easy to get started. You can open Anaconda Prompt or Terminal, navigate to your working directory, and run:

```
xlwings quickstart second_project -standalone
```

This will create a folder named `second_project` in that location, which contains a Python script named **second_project.py** and a macro-enabled file named **second_project.xlsm.**

For now, understand the function **main()** (You can give it other names too). It is the same function that we have seen in **first_project.py**.

Open the Excel file, go to VBA editor, and you can notice that in addition to Module 1, it has the **xlwings** module and the Dictionary class module that are required in place of the add-in.

Module 1 has the same **SampleCall()** macro that dynamically determines which Python module to import based on the name of the Excel workbook.

You can call this macro, and it will work the same way as before, but without needing **xlwings add-in**. This is possible because this Excel has the **xlwings** module and the Dictionary class module that are required in place of the add-in.

It serves as a user-friendly workbook and accompanying Python module. However, it has the same limitations as we have seen in **Run main** button of **xlwings add-in:**

- It works only when the workbook name matches the Python file name. As of now, both have the same name, **second_project.xlsm** and **second_project.py**
- The Python file must be in a folder listed in your PYTHONPATH.
- The Python file must define a **main()** function. As of now, **second_project.py** has a function named **main().**

In more realistic scenarios, your Excel file might be stored in a data folder, while your Python scripts live in a separate scripts folder. Your Python module may also contain multiple functions, not necessarily named **main().**

To handle such setups, you can modify both the Python code and the VBA macro to suit your folder structure and function names. This gives you the flexibility to:

- Import the correct Python module from its actual location
- Call any specific function you need (not just **main()**)
- Organize your project in a modular, maintainable way

For example, you can update your VBA macro to reference the correct function:

```
RunPython "import mymodule; mymodule.generate_dashboard()"
```

You can adjust your Python script to ensure the function is defined correctly and accessible. This approach lets you scale your automation beyond simple tasks, ideal for production-grade workflows or client-specific setups.

Demonstration

Let us open the VBA editor in **`second_project.xlsm`** and change the macro code in Module 1 as mentioned in the following figure:

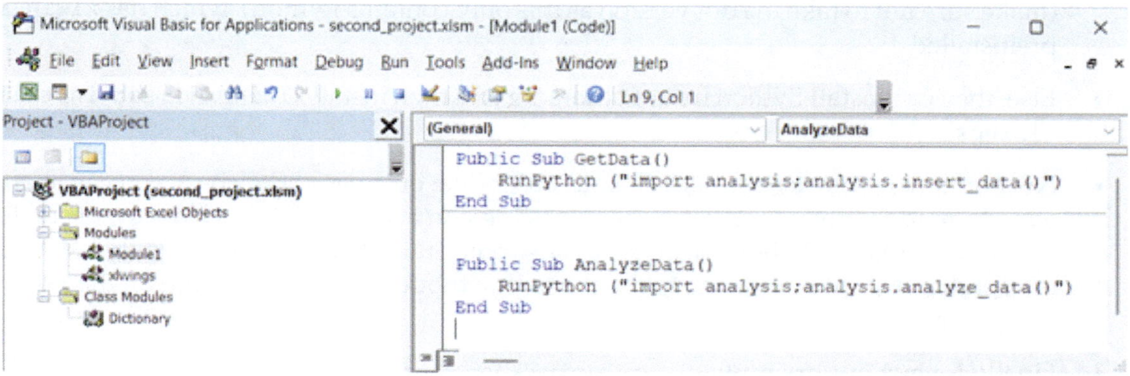

Figure 11.32: *Updated macro code in second_project.xlsm*

Now, you can still run the Subroutine **`GetData()`** and **`AnalyzeData()`** from module analysis.py without needing **`xlwings add-in`** after setting PYTHONPATH.

In this section, we have discussed using standalone workbooks (No add-in required) to run Python code using a VBA macro. So far, we have looked at different ways of running Python from Excel, both with and without the **`xlwings add-in`**. However, when it comes to sharing your workbooks with others, especially colleagues who may not have Python installed, you need to think about deployment. Let us now explore the different deployment options available with **`xlwings`**.

Deployment options for xlwings

As you are unlocking new powers with **`xlwings`** to automate your Excel workflows, it is time to think a step ahead, beyond just making things work for yourself. Imagine handing that power to someone else, seamlessly. That is where deployment comes in, turning your smart solution into something others can use.

This can be useful when you want your boss, teammate, or client to use your **`xlwings`**-powered Excel file. For that, you need to understand the strategies for distributing **`xlwings`** to end users.

Deployment means getting a tool or app ready for others to use. In simple words, before deployment, your **`xlwings`**-powered workbook lives only on your computer, and only you can use it. After deployment, others can open the file, click a button, and everything works without them needing to set up the code manually.

To run **xlwings**, Python must always be available somewhere. If your colleagues do not already have Python installed, you (as the developer) have a few ways to make it easier for them. You can opt for one of these ways:

- The most straightforward option is to ask them to install a full distribution like Anaconda, It comes with **xlwings** preinstalled. Windows users can also use Winconda (make sure **not** to take the dot version as this only contains Python), which has **xlwings** preinstalled.
- Else, they can install Python from python.org and then install **xlwings** via **pip install xlwings**
- Next option, if your team uses a shared folder (like on a network drive), you can share a ready-made Python installation with **xlwings** on a shared drive. This way, users do not need to install Python locally; they just point the **xlwings add-in** to that shared interpreter. It allows everyone to use the tool without installing anything on their own computer.
- Finally, for maximum simplicity, you can package your Python tool as a frozen executable (e.g., with tools like **PyInstaller**), which bundles Python and all dependencies into a single **.exe** file so users do not even need to know Python is involved. Note, however, that frozen executables cannot be used for UDFs (Python functions as Excel formulas), but can be used only for scripts run via **Run main** or **RunPython**.
- Alternate options include **xlwings Lite add-in** (free), which is cross platform compatible and does not require Python to be installed.
- Additionally, **xlwings PRO** (paid) offers a simple way to deploy your **xlwings** tools to your end users. They do not need to know anything about Python as they only need to:
    - o Run an installer (one installer can power many different Excel workbooks)
    - o Use the Excel workbook as if it was a normal macro-enabled workbook
- Also, **xlwings Server** (paid) adds Python support to Microsoft Excel and Google Sheets without the need of a local Python installation.

Conclusion

In the previous chapter, we learned to get started with xlwings for common tasks. In this chapter, we have learned about different ways to run a Python script from Excel, such as using Run main button or RunPython function in a VBA Subroutine. These approaches allowed us to run Python code and relied on xlwings add-in.

We have also discussed using standalone workbooks for the task where no add-in installation is required. We have also included an introductory overview of VBA, a practical troubleshooting guide, and actionable tips to support early-stage learning and implementation. Finally, we have discussed deployment strategies for xlwings.

Furthermore, xlwings also offers the capability to create user-defined functions in Python that you can call in Excel. We will discuss this in the next chapter.

Try it yourself

1. In the last chapter exercises, you have created a manufacturing data set and used xlwings package to format the same. Now, repeat the same task, but this time run it from inside Excel using the Run main button in the xlwings add-in ribbon

   Refer to the following data in *Table 11.3*:

Machine	Units Produced	Defects	Efficiency
M1	1200	12	0.98
M2	950	20	0.95
M3	1500	10	0.99

***Table 11.3**: Daily production report for a factory*

   The formatting rules are as follows:

   - The header row is bold, dark blue background (or any colour of your choice), white font.
   - Efficiency column shows as a percentage with two decimals.
   - Autofit all columns.

   The output Excel should look like this:

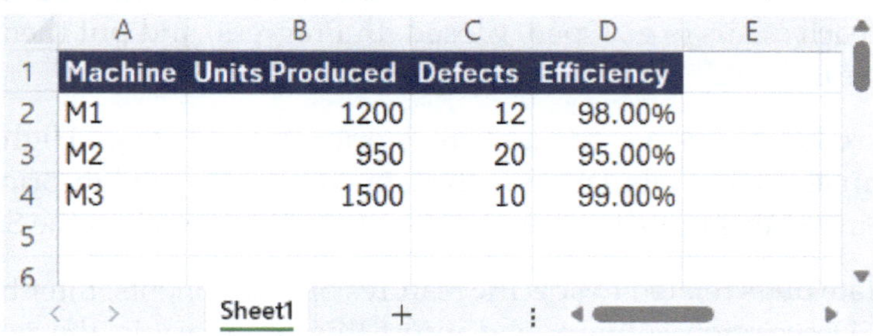

***Figure 11.33**: Formatted daily production report*

2. In the last chapter exercises, you have also created a web testing bug report.

Data sample:

Bug ID	Description	Status	Priority
B101	Login button not working	Open	High
B102	Page loads slowly	Closed	Medium
B103	Dropdown missing option	Open	Low

***Table 11.4**: Web testing data*

Now, use Excel VBA RunPython function (which requires the xlwings add-in) for the following tasks:

a. Format data as per these formatting requirements:

    i. Highlight Open rows in yellow.

    ii. Make Priority = High red font, bold.

The output Excel file should look like this:

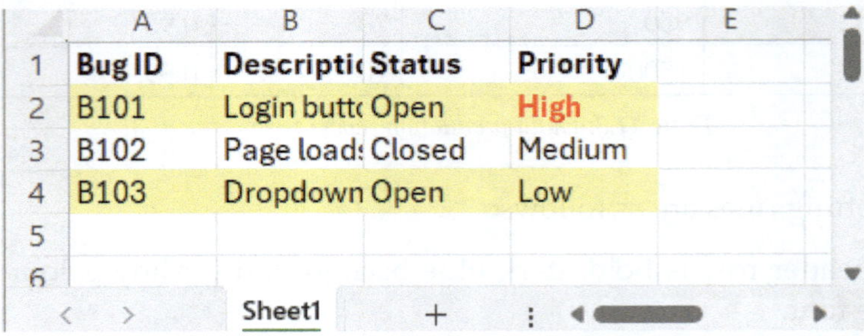

***Figure 11.34**: Formatted web testing data*

b. Insert a new sheet named Summary

c. To get a quick overview of your bug resolution pipeline, count how many bugs are in each status (e.g., Open, Closed, In Progress) and put them in cell A1 of the Summary sheet.

d. Analyze how bugs are spread across priority levels (e.g., High, Medium, Low). You can also cross tabulation with status to see which high-priority bugs are still open. Insert this priority distribution into a suitable cell in the Summary sheet.

e. To isolate bugs related to specific features or components, filter bugs by keywords in the Description column, and insert this summary in the relevant sheet. It is useful for tracking recurring issues or modules.

Concept check

1. You have used xlwings Python package, but when you open Excel, you do not see the xlwings ribbon. How do you install the add-in properly? Where is the .xlam file stored on Windows by default?

2. Suppose you want to remove xlwings from Excel or reinstall it. How can you remove the add-in?

3. You created the following functions in summary.py:

```
import xlwings as xw
import pandas as pd

def result():
    wb = xw.Book.caller()
    ws = wb.sheets["Sheet1"]

    df = ws.range("A1").expand().options(pd.
DataFrame, header=True, index=False).value

    summary = df.describe()

    out_sheet = wb.sheets.add("Summary", after=sheet)
    out_sheet.range("A1").value = summary
```

   You want to run the function result() via the xlwings add-in ribbon Run main button. What change do you need?

   How can you make your code idempotent? Idempotent code means the code that can be repeated multiple times without altering the result beyond the initial execution.

   What if you want to run this analysis on another Excel file?

4. Your manager does not want to install the xlwings add-in on their Excel. Can he/she still run Python code from Excel? How?

CHAPTER 12
Advanced Automation with xlwings

Introduction

After mastering the fundamentals of xlwings, it is time to unlock its true potential by diving deeper into **user-defined functions** (**UDFs**) and advanced automation techniques. UDFs allow users to call Python functions directly from Excel cells, making complex calculations, data retrieval, and **application programming interface** (**API**) integrations seamless. This chapter will provide a structured approach to writing, testing, and optimizing UDFs, ensuring Excel professionals can extend Excel's functionality beyond built-in formulas.

To bring everything together, we will conclude with a real-world case study that demonstrates how xlwings can be used in an Excel-driven workflow to automate reporting, process large datasets, or enhance decision-making. By the end of this chapter, readers will have the knowledge to build powerful, custom automation workflows that integrate Python and Excel efficiently.

This chapter ensures practical, hands-on learning, while keeping it simple and relevant to Excel users with no prior programming experience.

Structure

In this chapter, we will discuss the following topics:

- Introduction to UDFs in xlwings
- Writing and testing Python-based UDFs
- Troubleshooting
- Advanced UDF techniques
- Case study

Introduction to UDFs in xlwings

Python offers exceptional capabilities when it comes to analysing, merging, and visualizing Excel data. In *Chapter 11, Running Python Code from Excel*, we explored how to run Python scripts directly from Excel, an important step in bridging the gap between automation and accessibility.

We will work on the possibility of making Python functions available inside Excel cells, just like native formulas.

We are not referring to the `=PY()` function introduced in Excel 365. Instead, our focus is on a powerful feature of the **`xlwings`** library, which enables writing custom functions in Python and using those in Excel. It is compatible with older Excel versions as well.

With **`xlwings`** UDFs, we can define custom logic in Python and expose it as Excel formulas, making it possible to harness Python's full power without leaving the spreadsheet interface. This opens a new dimension for Excel users who want to combine Python's flexibility with Excel's familiarity.

Note: UDFs are currently supported only on Windows. For writing and using UDFs, you need the xlwings add-in installed, reference setting done, and Trust access to the Visual Basic for Applications (VBA) project object mode enabled in Excel, as discussed next.

Setting Excel for UDFs

For writing and using UDFs, the user needs these settings:

- The **`xlwings add-in`** needs to be installed, as has been done in the previous chapter.
- Set the reference to **`xlwings`** in the VBA editor (as done in the previous **`chapter _ Developer| Visual Basic |Tools | References | Check xlwings | Click on OK`**), refer to *Figure 12.1*:

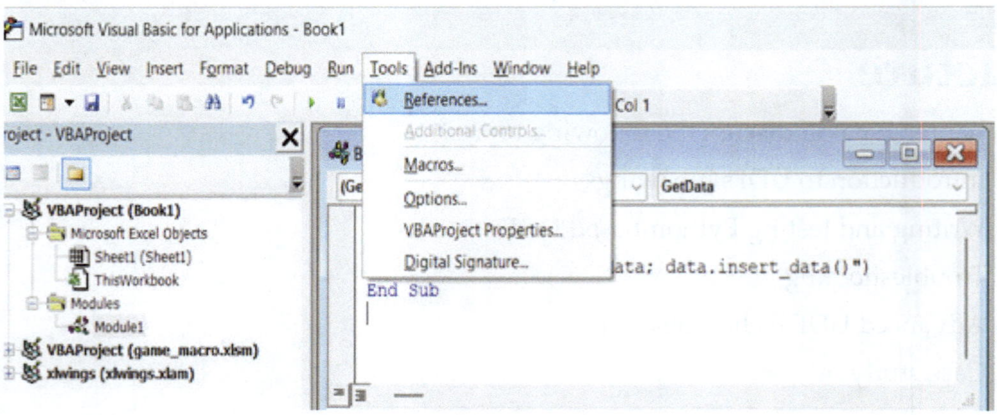

***Figure 12.1**: Reference setting in VBA editor*

- The Trust Center setting in Excel is a small one-time setting that allows the user to use UDFs. **Go to File | Options | Trust Center | click on Trust Center Settings.** Refer to *Figure 12.2*:

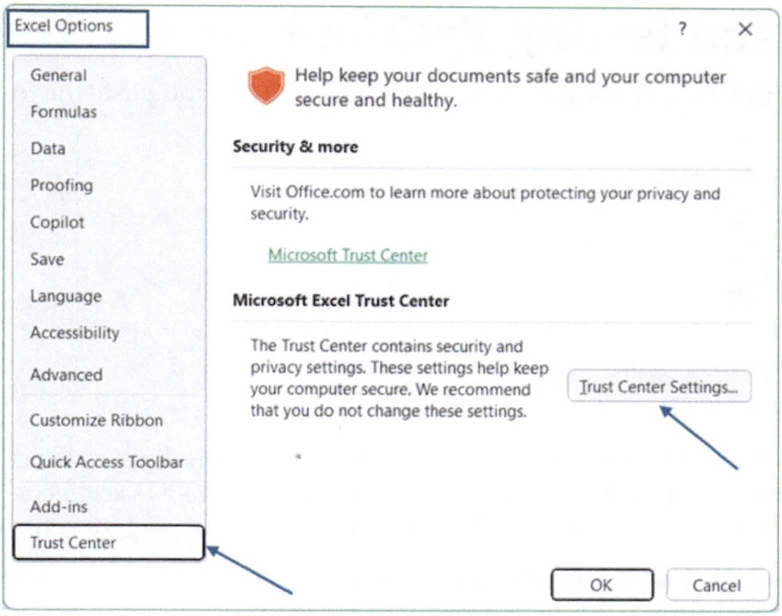

***Figure 12.2:** Trust Center settings in Excel*

- Next, go to **Macro Settings** and activate the checkbox to **Trust access to the VBA project object model**, as displayed in the following figure:

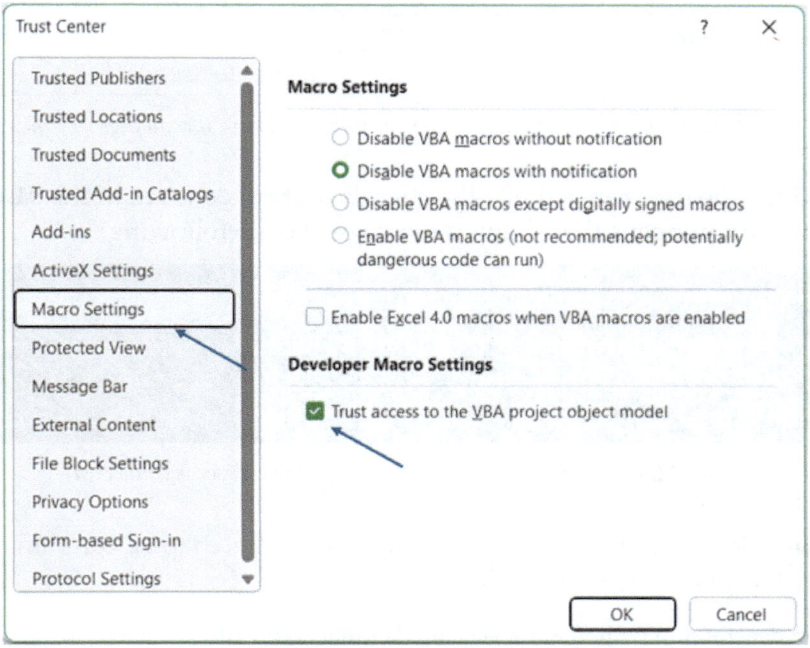

***Figure 12.3:** Trust access to VBA project object model*

Writing and testing Python-based UDFs

To get started with UDFs, create a Python file named **udf1.py** and paste the following code in the same:

```
import xlwings as xw
@xw.func
def add_ten(a):
    return a + 10
@xw.func
def my_sum(a, b):
    return a + b
```

This code imports the **xlwings** library and defines two simple Python functions. Adding **@xw.func** decorator[1] on top of the function registers these functions as Excel-accessible functions. The **@xw.func** decorator is essential, without it, Excel would not recognize the function.

Create a macro-enabled Excel file with the same name udf1.xlsm in the same folder. Then, in the **xlwings** ribbon add-in, click the **Import Functions** button. If no error is seen, it means Excel has imported functions marked with the **@xw.func** decorator from the modules with the same name (i.e., **udf1.py**). The **Import Functions** option is displayed in the following figure:

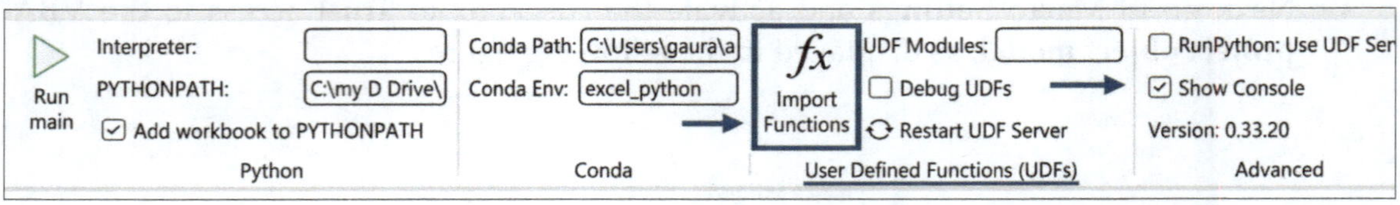

Figure 12.4: Import Functions and Show Console option in the xlwings ribbon

To ensure the same, the user can activate the checkbox **Show Console** in the **xlwings** ribbon, and a command prompt opens that shows a message like the following:

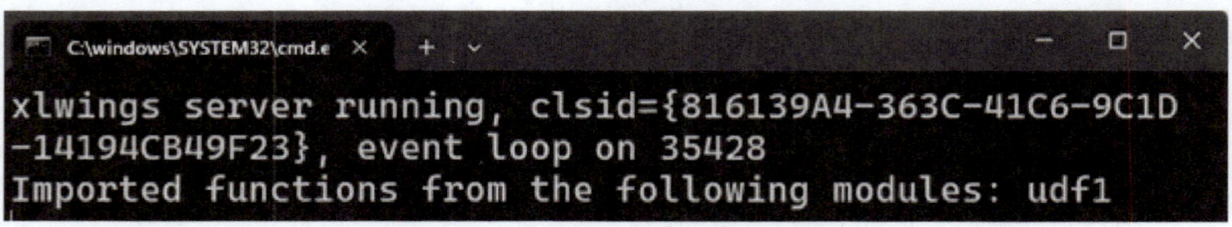

Figure 12.5: Command Prompt shows the xlwings server is connected

You can also directly use **udf1.py** and **udf1.xlsm** from the chapter companion repository. Download these two files to the same folder.

[1] In simple terms, a decorator in Python is a special marker that adds extra behaviour to a function. When we use `@xw.func`, it tells Excel to recognize that function as a custom formula so that it can be called directly from a cell, just like `=SUM()` or `=IF()`.

To test this, observe the following steps:

1. Enter a value such as 5 in cell **`A2`**.
2. In cell **`B2`**, call the function **`=add_ten(A2)`**. This will pass the value from **`A2`** to the Python function and return the result.
3. In cell **`C2`**, try **`=my_sum(A2, B2)`** to combine both values using another Python-defined function.

If everything is configured correctly, the functions will execute seamlessly within Excel. Change the input in cell **`A2`**, and the formulas are recalculated automatically.

Congratulations, you have successfully called a Python function from an Excel cell, as displayed in the following figure:

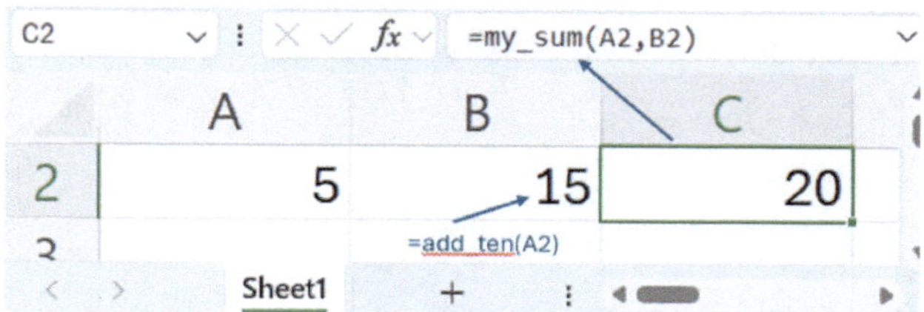

***Figure 12.6:** Using Python functions in Excel*

Let us briefly discuss the internal workflow and execution to see how it works.

Internal UDF integration workflow

To understand how functions written in a Python module work in Excel, you can open the VBA editor (*Alt+F11*) and find a new module named **`xlwings_udfs`**, as shown in *Figure 12.7*:

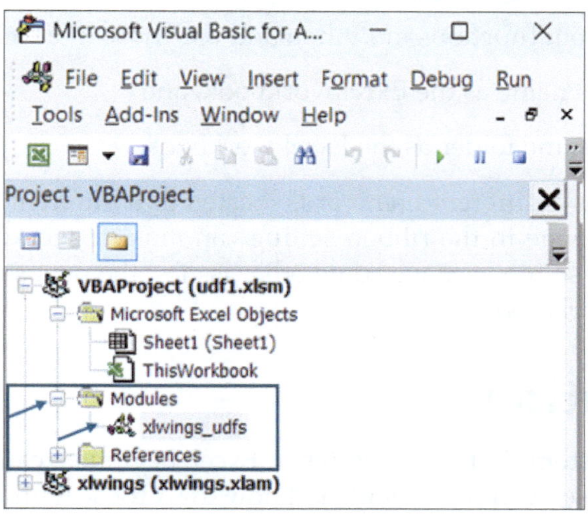

***Figure 12.7:** xlwings_udfs module*

This module has autogenerated code by **xlwings** for each function defined in **udf1.py** and marked with the **@xw.func** decorator. You are not supposed to change anything here, and you can ignore these details.

It was to show you that when you click Import Function in the **xlwings add-in**, **xlwings** automatically creates a module **xlwings_udfs** in your Excel workbook. It includes VBA code, which serves as a wrapper for Python functions that were imported. For example, the VBA code for **udf1.py**, is shown in the following figure:

```
'Autogenerated code by xlwings - changes will be lost with next import!
#Const App = "Microsoft Excel" 'Adjust when using outside of Excel
Function add_ten(a)
    #If App = "Microsoft Excel" Then
        If TypeOf Application.Caller Is Range Then On Error GoTo failed
        add_ten = XLPy.CallUDF("udf1", "add_ten", Array(a), ThisWorkbook, Application.Caller)
        Exit Function
    #Else
        add_ten = XLPy.CallUDF("udf1", "add_ten", Array(a))
        Exit Function
    #End If
failed:
    add_ten = Err.Description
End Function

Function my_sum(a, b)
    #If App = "Microsoft Excel" Then
        If TypeOf Application.Caller Is Range Then On Error GoTo failed
        my_sum = XLPy.CallUDF("udf1", "my_sum", Array(a, b), ThisWorkbook, Application.Caller)
        Exit Function
    #Else
        my_sum = XLPy.CallUDF("udf1", "my_sum", Array(a, b))
        Exit Function
    #End If
failed:
    my_sum = Err.Description
End Function
```

Figure 12.8: *Autogenerated VBA code by xlwings*

Now, you can write custom functions in Python and use those in Excel from a Python script:

- that has the same name as the Excel workbook, and
- is located in the same folder as the Excel workbook

If your Python script has a different name or is located in a different folder, you might have guessed that a slight change in the ribbon setting can make it work. If you want to import functions from multiple scripts or have some other issues, the next section, Troubleshooting, will help in finding a workaround.

Troubleshooting

While it is fun to call custom Python functions in Excel, beginners can sometimes face issues. Let us quickly guide you on common issues and how to fix those without searching on Google or Stack Overflow:

1. **ModuleNotFoundError or FileNotFoundError:** This error indicates that your Python file (module) with the same name as the Excel file is not found in the same folder. It means either your Python file (module) name is not the same as the name of the Excel file, or it is saved in a different folder.

   To replicate this error, you can rename **`udf1.py`** to **`udf2.py`** or simply put **`udf1.py`** in some other folder.

   When you refresh Excel (double-click on **`B2`**), you see a **`ModuleNotFoundError message in all the cells that include`** imported functions, as shown in the following figure:

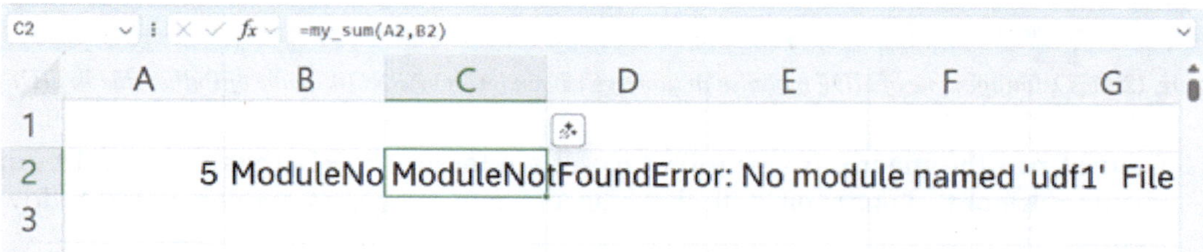

Figure 12.9: ModuleNotFoundError-1

   Or, if you click on Import Function again, it fails to import. Console shows a message: **`ModuleNotFoundError: No module named 'udf1'`**

   A new Error window pops up. The following is a cropped screenshot showing the error:

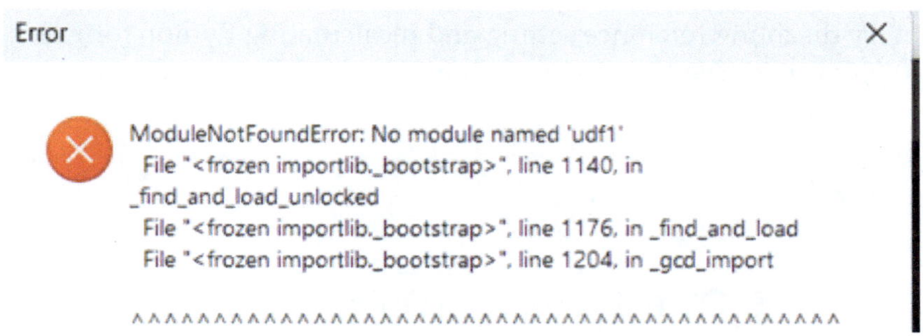

Figure 12.10: ModuleNotFoundError-2

   To fix this error, you can try one of the following, depending on what caused this error:

   - Supplying the full path of your Python script in the **`PYTHONPATH`** configuration of the **`xlwings`** ribbon,
   - Rename one of your files to match the names (if that makes sense), else
   - Write the name of your Python file in the UDF modules in the **`xlwings`** ribbon as displayed in *Figure 12.11*.

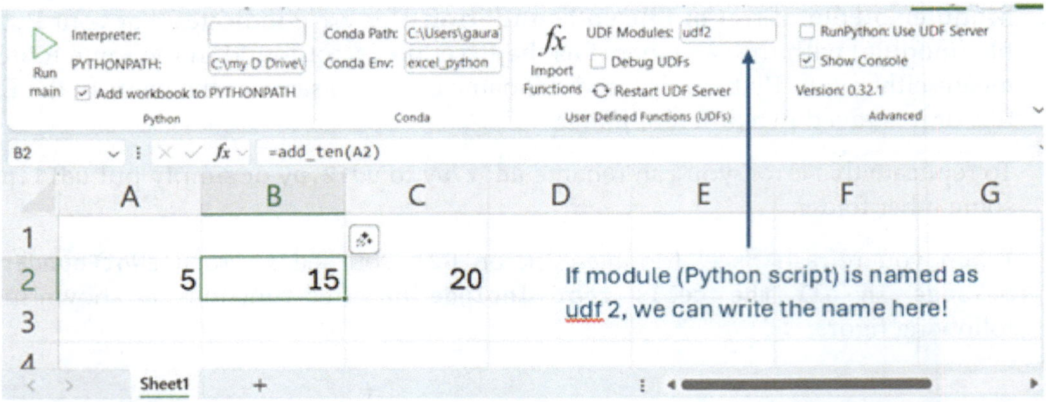

Figure 12.11: Defining name of UDF modules in xlwings ribbon [ADD ARROW name of Python file in UDF]

2. **Cannot run the macro**: If you forgot to set a reference to **`xlwings`** in the VBA editor, clicking **`Import Function`** will show an error message, as shown in the following figure:

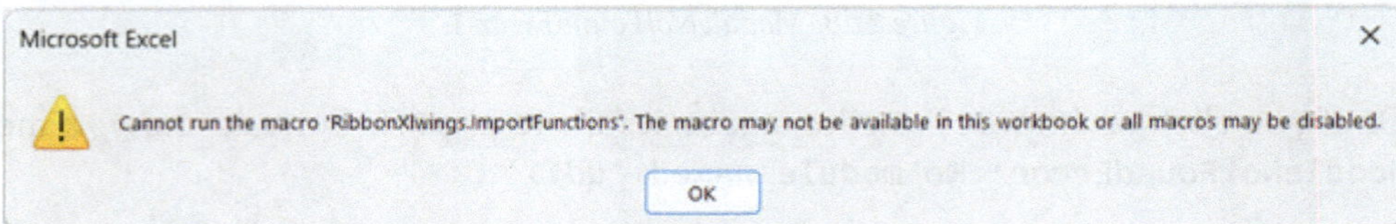

Figure 12.12: Cannot run the macro error message

You can try disabling reference setting and recalculating Python formulas in Excel and get an **`Object required`** message, as shown in the following figure:

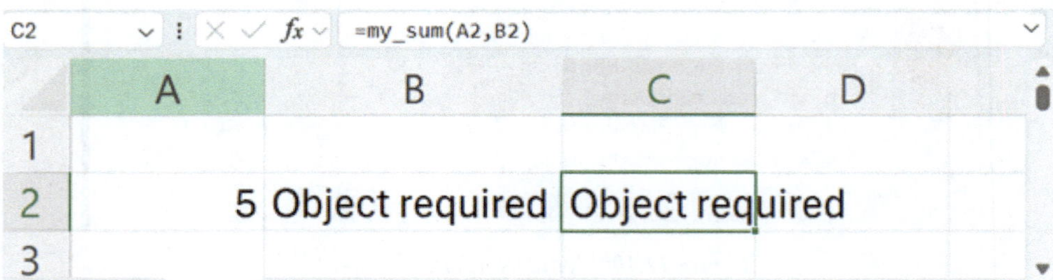

Figure 12.13: Object required error message

To fix this, you need to add a reference to **`xlwings`** in the VBA editor. Press *Alt + F11* | **Go to Tools | Reference | check: xlwings | Click OK**

3. **Run-time error '1004'**: If you did not enable the Trust Center setting in Excel, you might get the following error:

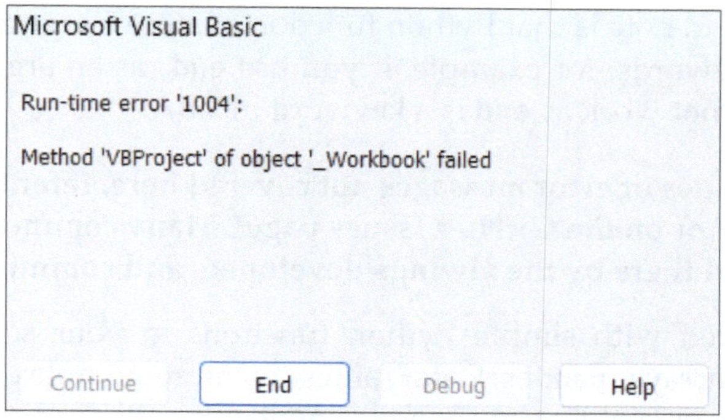

Figure 12.14: *Run-time error '1004'*

To fix this issue, **Go to File | Options | Trust Center | Trust Center Settings | Go to Macro Settings | activate the checkbox to Trust access to the VBA project object model**

4. **Run-time error '1'**: If you have used the wrong Conda Environment (the one that does not exist or the one that does not have the **`xlwings`** package installed) or **`your xlwings add-in`** version is not same as **`xlwings`** package version, you can get the error message similar to what is shown in the following figure:

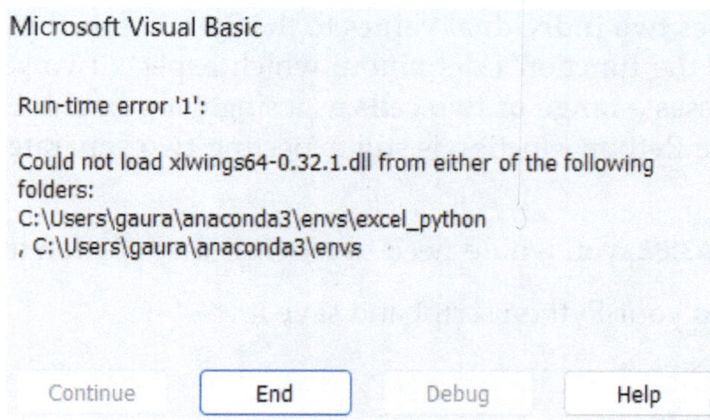

Figure 12.15: *Run-time error '1'*

To fix this, choose the right conda environment that has the **`xlwings`** package installed. You already understand the common settings of Conda Path and Conda Environment in the **`xlwings`** ribbon, as discussed in the previous chapter.

And ensure that you are using the same version of **`xlwings add-in`** as that of **`xlwings`** package. If you have upgraded your **`xlwings`** package, you can install in re-install the add-in to match versions.

Apart from these configuration-related issues, you can also get Python errors such as **`Attribute Error`**, **`Type Error`**, **`Index Error`**, **`Syntax Error`**, etc. To fix those issues, you need to debug your Python code and make changes in the script accordingly.

One more thing to note is that Python function names or argument names should not be any VBA keywords; for example, if you use **end** as an argument in your Python function, it will not work as **end** is a keyword in VBA.

Note: For any other issues or error messages not covered here, refer to the official xlwings Troubleshooting page[2] or on the GitHub Issues page[3]. Many common problems and their solutions are discussed there by the xlwings developers and community.

So far, you have worked with simple Python functions in your scripts. However, when you start using **numpy** arrays, **pandas** DataFrames, or more complex functions that require advanced data handling or custom error management, you will need a deeper understanding of how **xlwings** manages data conversion and error handling between Excel and Python. We will explore these advanced topics in the next section.

Advanced UDF techniques

To extend UDF workflows for complex logic, richer functionalities, or data integration, we need to understand how to implement such functions in Python. Let us start by enhancing the **my_sum()** function.

You might have noticed that **my_sum(A2, B2)** works but **=my_sum(A3:B3)** fails. This is because **=my_sum(A2, B2)** passes **two individual values** to the Python function, one from **A2** and one from **B2**. This matches the function's definition, which expects two separate inputs (a and b). **=my_sum(A3:B3)** passes a **range of two cells** as a single argument. Excel treats this as one array-like input, but the Python function is still expecting **two separate arguments**, not a list or range.

To support ranges like **A3:B3**, you would need to redefine the function to accept a list or array.

Add another function to your Python script and save it[4]:

```
@xw.func
def my_sum_range(values):
    return sum(values)
```

It will accept ranges like **A3:B3** (row) or **B2:B3** (column). The following figure displays calling this new function with range of values as input:

[2] **(https://docs.xlwings.org/en/stable/troubleshooting.html)**

[3] **(github.com/xlwings/xlwings/issues)**

[4] You must save changes to the Python script and click on Import Function or Restart UDF Server again to access this function in Excel.

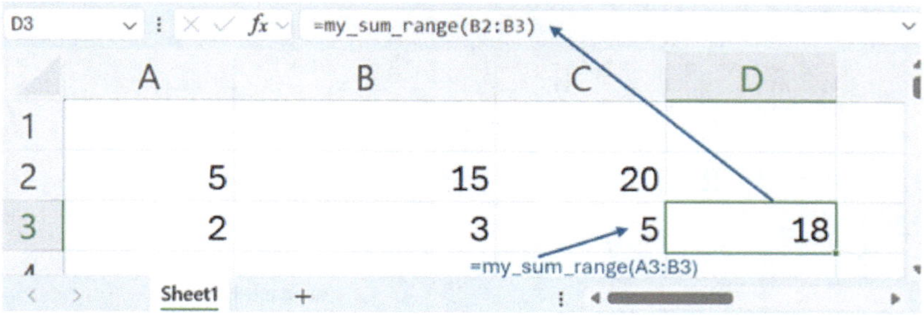

***Figure 12.16**: Function my_sum_range() accepts range of cells*

However, if you try to call the function on a two-dimensional range, such as **A2:B3**, you get a Python error such as **TypeError: unsupported operand type(s) for +: 'int' and 'list'**

This happens because **xlwings** passes Excel ranges to Python as nested lists, in this case, a 2D list like **[[5, 15], [2, 3]]**. However, Python's built-in **sum()** function expects a flat iterable of numbers, not a list of lists. Let us see how to fix this using the **xlwings** argument decorator.

xlwings argument decorator

You can modify your function to flatten the input before summing but this function should always get a two-dimensional data structure. To ensure this, we can use the **xlwings** argument decorator **@xw.arg("values", ndim = 2)**. This decorator tells **xlwings** to convert the Excel input values into a 2-dimensional **numpy** array (even if it is only one element, or a single row or a column).

Behind the scenes, this works similarly to using **sheet.range().options(ndim=2).value** to ensure that Excel data is always passed to Python as a 2-dimensional **numpy** array.

Let us add another function in the same Python script and save it:

```
@xw.func
@xw.arg("data", ndim = 2)
def my_sum_range2(data):
    return sum([sum(row) for row in data])
```

This function takes a 2D Excel range, whether it is a single cell, a row, a column, or a two-dimensional range (such as **A2:B3**) and returns the sum of all the numeric values within that range. Restart the server and test this function in Excel. The following figure displays this function in action:

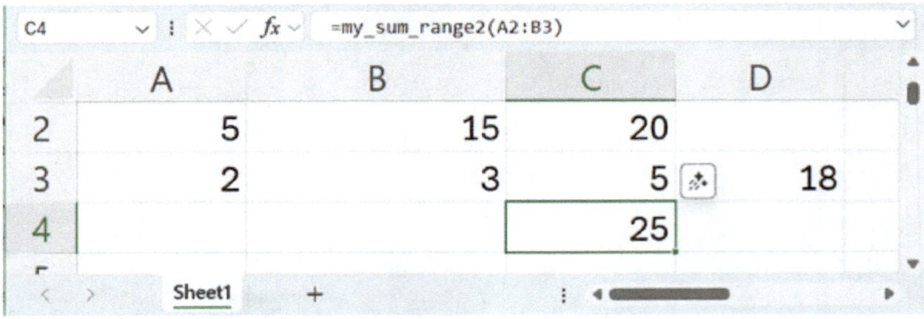

Figure 12.17: *Function with xlwings argument decorator*

You can also use **`ndim='natural'`** in the **`xlwings`** argument decorator and change the function slightly, to make it work for both 1-dimensional and 2-dimensional ranges as shown in the code file.

Alternatively, you can use a simpler solution to read the data as a **`numpy`** array and apply the **`sum()`** method on the same, which we will be discussing next.

NumPy operations in xlwings UDF

You can use the **`xlwings`** argument decorator **`@xw.arg("data", np.array)`** to enable **`numpy`** workflow in **`xlwings`** UDFs. This **`numpy`** converter decorator tells **`xlwings`** to convert the Excel input into a NumPy array before passing it to the Python function.

In other words, the argument decorator in a UDF works just like the **`.options()`** method on a **`range`** object, for example, **`sheet.range().options(np.array).value`**

Let us add another function to the same Python script and save the file:

```
@xw.func
@xw.arg("data", np.array)
def my_sum_array(data):
    return data.sum()
```

Now, re-import it into Excel and test the new function, as shown in *Figure 12.18:*

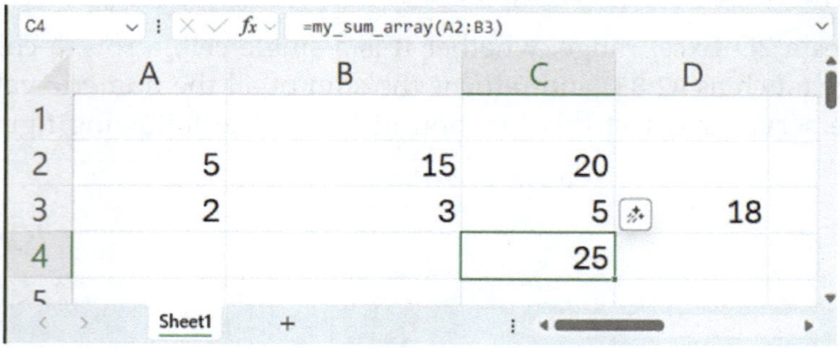

Figure 12.18: *UDF with numpy array converter*

UDF and array formulas

If your UDF returns an array-like object that should spill over adjacent cells, newer versions of Excel provide dynamic array support for the same. In case you are using an older version of Excel, you would generally do the following:

1. Select the range of cells where you want the array formula to display its results.
2. Enter the UDF formula.
3. Press *Ctrl-Shift-Enter* to confirm the formula as an array formula. This will enclose the formula in curly braces {}.

This approach works but has some issues. If you change the input and the output range needs to be adjusted, you must first delete the entire array by selecting the full range, then reselect the suitable output range, re-enter the new formula, and press *Ctrl-Shift-Enter*. This is a lengthy procedure.

Suppose you are querying an API or database to retrieve data of variable length via a user-defined function. In that case, you usually do not know the dimensions of the array prior to execution.

Dynamic arrays represent a significant enhancement in newer versions of Excel. However, for users operating on older versions of Excel, **`xlwings`** offers a practical workaround to simulate dynamic array behaviour. When you are on an older version of Excel, which does not support dynamic arrays, you can use the **`@xw.ret(expand='table')`** decorator on the UDF that can return arrays to Excel, functioning as array formulas. Basically, this decorator automatically resizes the legacy array for you:

```
@xw.func
@xw.ret(expand='table')
def dynamic_array(r, c):
    return np.random.randn(int(r), int(c))
```

Importing and running this function in Excel returns an **`r × c`** table of random numbers to Excel, as shown in *Figure 12.19*:

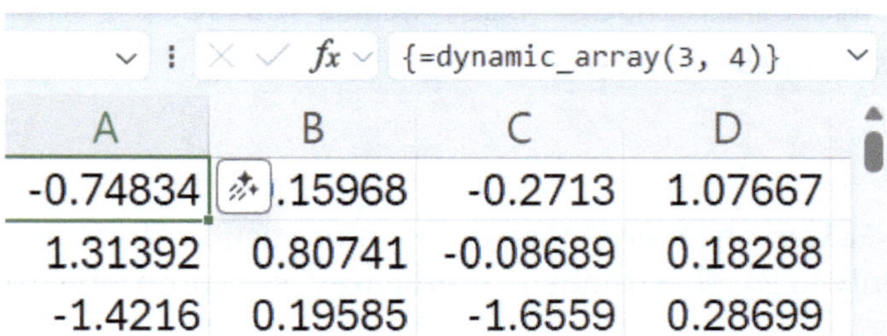

***Figure 12.19**: Dynamic array with xlwings UDF*

Pandas-powered xlwings UDF

To enable **pandas** within **xlwings** UDFs, you can use the **@xw.arg('df', pd.DataFrame)** decorator to tell **xlwings** to convert the Excel input into a **pandas** DataFrame.

To understand this, add the following function to your Python script:

```
@xw.func
@xw.arg('df', pd.DataFrame, index=False, header=False)
def describe(df):
    return df.describe()
```

Here, the decorator **@xw.arg('df', pd.DataFrame, index=False, header=False)** ensures that the data selected in Excel is passed to Python as a **pandas** DataFrame without treating the first row or column as headers or index. The function then calls **df.describe()** to return key summary statistics. The following figure shows the output of this function in Excel:

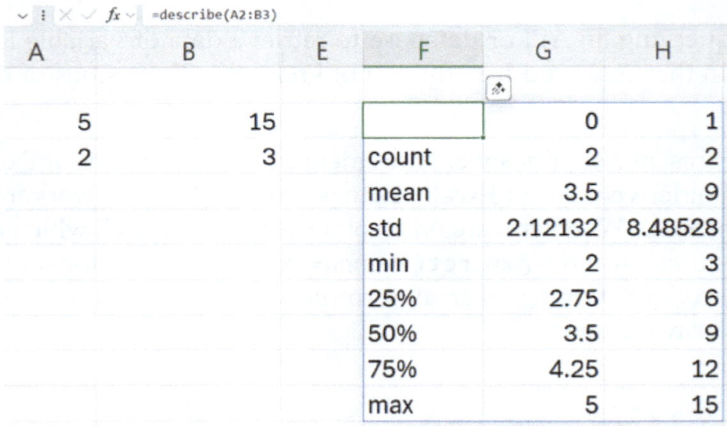

Figure 12.20: *UDF with pandas DataFrame converter*

When your Python function returns a DataFrame or array, you can control how it appears in Excel using the **@xw.ret()** decorator. For instance:

```
@xw.arg('df', pd.DataFrame, index=False, header=False)
@xw.ret(index=False, header=False)
def correlation(df):
    return df.corr()
```

The **@xw.ret(index=False, header=False)** decorator ensures that the resulting correlation matrix is written cleanly to Excel, without including row or column labels from the DataFrame.

As you have seen, various **xlwings** UDF decorators let you control how Excel inputs and outputs are interpreted and formatted, enabling seamless data conversion with **@xw.arg** and **@xw.ret**. Specifically, **pandas** UDFs in **xlwings** empower Excel users to run sophisticated data analysis within familiar spreadsheets, while seamlessly leveraging Python's full analytical capabilities in the background.

Volatile UDFs

In Excel, some functions, such as **RAND()**, **TODAY()**, and **NOW()**, recalculate every time the worksheet is refreshed. These are called volatile functions. If you need to create a UDF that is volatile, you can add **@xw.func(volatile=True)** decorator to your function. This allows your function to recalculate with every refresh, even if the input is not changed. Let us add this function to the script:

```
@xw.func(volatile = True)
def volatile_function(n=10):
    return np.random.randint(n)
```

When called in Excel, this volatile user-defined function returns a new random integer between **0** and **n-1** (default 0–9) every time the worksheet recalculates.

Case study

As you have learned to use **xlwings** UDFs, it is time to create a real-world Excel workflow with **xlwings**. Let us explore a case in the healthcare domain. Hospital management wants to understand key drivers of healthcare costs and patient outcomes. They provided you with data for patients, encounters, and providers, and want you to analyse pertinent questions such as:

- Which departments are associated with higher treatment costs or frequent readmissions?
- Are certain providers or departments performing better in terms of patient outcomes and cost efficiency?
- Who are the top N providers by number of encounters with columns, and what are the encounter count and average treatment cost?
- Fetch a small table summarizing any patient's encounters, which includes the number of total encounters, last encounter date, total and treatment cost, and average cost, etc.

Data is provided in an Excel file named **healthcare_data.xlsx**. The goal is to practice **xlwings** UDFs for exploring and analyzing data that can help hospital management in data-driven decision-making.

We recommend you apply your learnings from the chapter to answer these simple business questions by using **xlwings** UDFs on your own before looking at the Python script.

Project files (available in the companion repository): You need to download **healthcare.xlsm**, which contains data in three sheets, namely, patients, encounters, and providers. The sheet named **UDF Applications** demonstrates the use of Python functions imported into Excel.

The corresponding Python script, named **`healthcare.py`**, contains code for Python functions that are used as UDFs in Excel. Save data and the Python module in the same folder.

Project walkthrough: You need to configure the **`xlwings add-in`**, if not already done, by setting the Interpreter, Conda Environment, and adding the required reference. Click **`Import Functions`** to proceed, and Excel will load the module accordingly.

You can now use the UDFs as native Excel functions, modify inputs to test them, or define additional UDFs in the script as needed.

Limitations and best practices: The following points outline key limitations and recommended practices:

- **Synthetic data**: The data presented is fictitious, results may not reflect real-world scenarios.
- **Performance**: UDFs called on many cells can be slow. We will discuss performance improvement tips in the next chapter.
- **Security**: Only run trusted UDF modules and workbooks. Running code from unknown sources can be risky.

Conclusion

In this chapter, we learned to work with user-refined functions in xlwings, which opens the door for advanced automation. Using UDFs with suitable decorators discussed in the chapter allows Excel users to perform advanced data analysis directly inside Excel, while keeping the full analytical power of Python behind the scenes.

However, performance can sometimes become a concern when working with xlwings, especially with UDFs. Since xlwings communicates with Excel through the **Component Object Model** (**COM**) interface, this can introduce some overhead during data exchange.

In the next chapter, we will explore practical strategies and best practices to make your xlwings solutions more efficient, along with limitations and challenges for using Python in Excel.

Try it yourself

1. You maintain an Excel sheet containing monthly sales figures from different regions. You want to create a formula in Excel that automatically identifies which regions exceeded the target sales (for example, ₹1,00,00). Write a simple xlwings UDF sales_performance() and use it in Excel.

   The sample data and output are shown in the following figure:

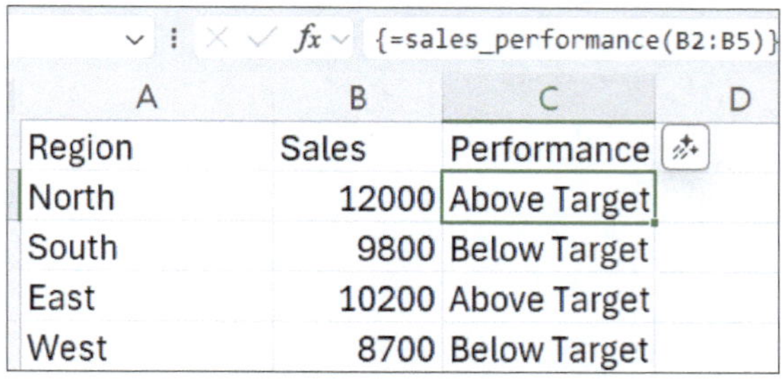

Figure 12.21: *sales_performance UDF*

2. Your company tracks inventory data in Excel. Build a UDF that uses pandas to summarize Excel data, computing average stock levels per category. The sample data and output are shown in the following figure:

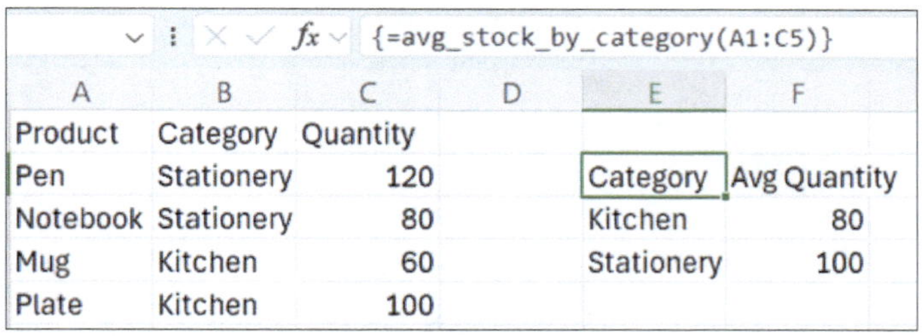

Figure 12.22: *Inventory UDF*

3. In this chapter, we have discussed a healthcare project that uses pandas UDFs to analyse data in Excel. Enhance the given Python script to answer more meaningful business questions that can be answered using the provided data.

Concept check

1. You are building an Excel dashboard for a hospital's outpatient department. Doctors want to enter patient vitals (height, weight, BP, sugar levels) into Excel and immediately see the health risk score auto-calculated in the next column.

   The management team, however, wants to click a button once a week to generate a department summary report, which includes average risk scores, patient counts by category, etc.

   Should you use xlwings UDFs or Run Main for each requirement? Why?

2. An analyst created a workbook using several xlwings UDFs to connect to an internal clinic database. On their computer, everything works fine. When they share the file with a colleague, Excel shows #VALUE! errors for all UDFs. The colleague has the xlwings add-in installed, but does not have Python or the same folder paths. What might be causing the issue, and how can you make the workbook portable for others?

CHAPTER 13
Python Excel Integration Limits and Vision

Introduction

Python-Excel integration can save your time and effort by automating your tasks or helping you create in-depth reports, if you follow the best practices to make automation workflows more reliable and efficient.

This chapter highlights the key takeaways from the book, best practices of using Python for Excel automation, and provides insights about when to favor native Excel tools.

We will also briefly explore Microsoft 365's evolving capabilities, such as Python in Excel and Copilot or Claude integration, to help readers understand how Excel automation is evolving beyond traditional **Visual Basic for Applications** (**VBA**) and moving towards Python-based solutions and generative AI capabilities. This will allow professionals to make informed decisions about the best tools for their specific needs.

By the end of this chapter, readers will have a clear understanding of best practices for Python-Excel integration, the boundaries of its effectiveness, and future trends in Excel automation.

Structure

In this chapter, we will discuss the following topics:

- Efficiency-driven optimization practice
- Strategic automation with Python and Excel
- Evolving landscape of Excel automation
- xlwings Lite as an alternative to PIE

Efficiency-driven optimization practice

You have learnt about powerful libraries such as **`pandas`**, **`openpyxl`**, **`xlsxwriter`**, and xlwings, and you are now comfortable making a choice between these tools. Next, you should learn about ways to improve the performance of these tools while working with large data sets. Let us discuss some strategies to optimize the performance of each of these libraries.

While working with pandas

In *Chapter 7, Smart Tools for Faster Analysis,* we have discussed strategies to optimize performance with **pandas** such as using efficient datatypes, loading less data, chunking, vectorization, using **query()** function instead of boolean indexing methods, etc.

Additionally, **pandas** supports reading or writing Parquet format, which provides optimal on-disk performance. Parquet is a modern file (**.parquet** file) format designed for storing large datasets efficiently. Unlike Excel, which saves data row by row, Parquet uses a columnar structure. This format reduces memory usage by applying compression and encoding techniques that shrink the size of the data stored. It is also languageagnostic, meaning developers can read and write Parquet files using many different programming languages including Python, and R. In practice, this makes Parquet both efficient and flexible, allowing large datasets to be handled more easily across diverse tools and environments.

While working with openpyxl

As discussed in *Chapter 8, Unlocking Excel with openpyxl,* the primary performance bottleneck in **openpyxl** arises due to inefficient iteration patterns such as, cell-by-cell access. It is recommended to use iterators like **insert_rows()**, **insert_cols()**, **iter_rows()**, **iter_cols()**, **ws.append()** or generator like **ws.values** as applicable. Iterators are fast and avoid loading the entire file into memory at once.

Also, for read-intensive operations on large datasets, read-only mode enables lazy loading. Similarly, write-only mode is ideal for generating large reports efficiently without excessive memory consumption.

Additionally, you should store intermediate data in variables rather than calling the same functions repeatedly and avoid unnecessary formatting when speed is the priority. As complex cell styles and formatting can slow down performance.

You already understand that using **pandas** for heavy data analysis tasks and combining it with **openpyxl** for specific formatting requirements is more efficient than manipulating data in **openpyxl** itself.

While working with xlsxwriter

Although **xlsxwriter** is significantly faster than **openpyxl** for writing large datasets, it is still possible to run out of memory when creating large files. This memory usage can be reduced almost completely by using **constant_memory** property of the **Workbook** as shown here:

```
workbook = xlsxwriter.Workbook(filename, {'constant_memory': True})
```

In **constantmemory** mode, Excel writes one row to the file and immediately clears it from memory when the next row arrives. That means the workbook never has to hold more than a single row at a time.

Another reason constantmemory mode is efficient is that Excel bypasses the use of the shared string table. Instead of storing all text values in a central list and referencing them, each string is written directly into the cell as inline text. This approach eliminates the need to maintain a large string table in memory, thereby reducing overall memory consumption. It is a documented Excel feature and is fully supported by most spreadsheet applications, ensuring compatibility while optimizing performance.

In **`constantmemory`** mode, each new row replaces the previous one, so the data must be written in **strict toptobottom order** as shown:

```
# Writing data in row-by-row, in column order.
for row in range(0, row_max):
    for col in range(0, col_max):
        worksheet.write(row, col, some_data)
```

If you loop columnfirst and write cells in the order (row, col) with **`constantmemory`** mode, you are no longer writing rows sequentially, so this pattern does not follow the toptobottom requirement needed for constantmemory mode:

```
# writes columnbycolumn, not rowbyrow. It breaks constantmemory order
for col in range(0, col_max):
    for row in range(0, row_max):
        worksheet.write(row, col, some_data)
```

Currently, the **`add_table()`** method does not work in this mode.

While working with xlwings

Library **`xlwings`** makes real-time interaction between Excel and Python easy. However, this convenience sometimes comes at the expense of performance, particularly for large data sets or complex calculations.

This is because **`xlwings`** abstracts platform-native automation, COM technology on Windows, and AppleScript on macOS, into a unified Python interface.

When you write large amounts of data to Excel from Python and perform calculations, the two biggest performance traps are:

- Frequent COM calls
- Unnecessary recalculation or screen updates

If you are facing performance issues, you need to look at performance optimization strategies as mentioned here.

Use bulk operations over individual calls

Library **xlwings** can be slower in handling large-scale data exports or batch operations. For read-write tasks, instead of looping over rows or writing each cell individually, you should read or write an entire Excel range as **pandas** DataFrame or **numpy** array. This minimizes the number of calls to COM or AppleScript. Each inter-application communication is an overhead.

To benchmark, we have created a DataFrame of modest size (a few thousand rows):

```
n = 30_000
df = pd.DataFrame({
    "A": np.random.randn(n),
    "B": np.random.randn(n),
    "C": np.random.randint(0,100, size=n)
})
```

Use **df.iterrows()** to iterate over the rows for writing it to Excel, and timed our code using the magic command **%%time**[1]:

```
%%time

for idx, row in df.iterrows():
    sheet.range(f"A{idx + 1}").value = row["A"]
    sheet.range(f"B{idx + 1}").value = row["B"]
    sheet.range(f"C{idx + 1}").value = row["C"]
```

After clearing the sheet, we have written the data again, this time using a **pandas** DataFrame:

```
sheet.clear()                    # clear previous write

%%time
sheet.range("A1").options(index=False).value = df
```

On our machine, the second approach is over 1,300× improvement in CPU time and more than 1,500× faster in wall time compared to the first one.

Since excel-refresh is the expensive part, doing heavy lifting in Python with efficient data structures, **pandas**, or **numpy** is smart. For example, read a large table, filter, pivot, summarize in **pandas**, then write a smaller result table to Excel.

---

[1] When placed at the beginning of a code cell, %%time will execute all the code within that cell and then report the "wall time" (the actual elapsed time) and "CPU times" (user and system CPU time) taken for the execution. CPU time is the amount of time the processor is actively executing a program, while wall time is the total elapsed time from when a process starts to when it finishes.

Use array formulas or spill behaviour for UDFs

Although **`xlwings`** allows you to use many **user-defined functions** (**UDFs**), it is still wise to avoid writing one formula per cell and instead have one UDF that returns a 2D array (table) and let Excel spill it. This reduces the number of calls from Excel to Python.

For example, the function to return projected sales based on last year's sales and the growth rate, you can write an inefficient UDF as:

```
# Inefficient Way
@xw.func
def sales_year(last_year, growth_rate, period = 0):
    return last_year * ((1 + growth_rate) ** period)
```

In Excel, you can call this formula in a single cell, and then drag it to the entire range (say, **`C6:G6`** in *Figure 13.1*). This works, but it is not the best way to use custom functions as it requires frequent interaction between Excel and Python. Instead, you can use an array formula, which accepts data as a **numpy** array and returns an array of values that spills into adjacent cells.

```
# Array-Formula (Efficient)
@xw.func
@xw.arg("period", np.array)
@xw.ret(expand='down')
def sales_growth(last_year, growth_rate, period):
    """Returns 5 years of projected sales"""
    return last_year * ((1 + growth_rate) ** period)
```

The following Excel screenshot (*Figure 13.1*) displays the use of both approaches. For larger datasets, using array-based UDF might show significant improvement in performance.

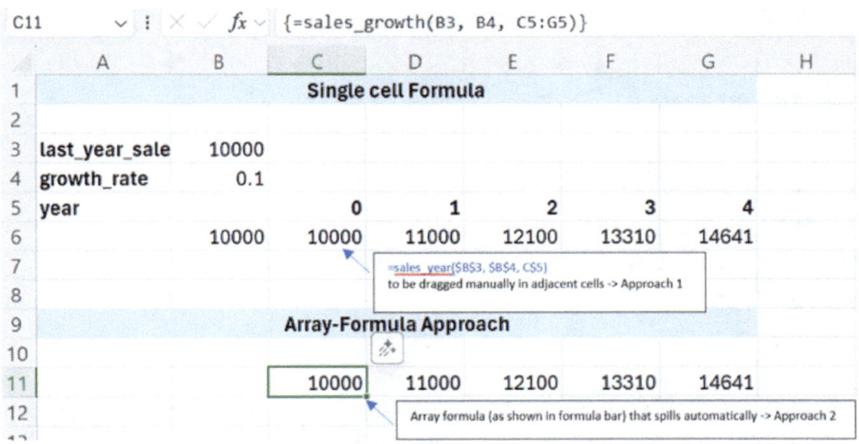

***Figure 13.1**: Single-cell formula vs. array-based UDF*

Disable Excel auto-calculation

Large writes can trigger Excel's automatic recalculation or screen updates, which slows things down. Do not use volatile UDFs unless you need them. Also, you can reduce overhead by temporarily changing Excel application settings, such as turning off screen refreshes, setting calculation to manual so Excel does not recalculate after each write, and suppressing DisplayAlerts prompts during automated runs as shown:

```
import xlwings as xw
wb = xw.Book()
app = wb.app

# --- Turn OFF expensive Excel features ---
app.screen_updating = False
app.calculation = 'manual'
app.display_alerts = False
app.enable_events = False
```

Always restore the original settings at the end of your Python script.

Result caching for faster repeated execution

If your script includes a slow function, such as large **pandas** calculations or heavy loops, you can cache the results. Caching refers to the practice of storing the result of a function's initial computation so that subsequent calls with the same inputs can return the precomputed result instantly, bypassing redundant processing.

Cache heavy results in Python avoid repeating expensive work, which can significantly improve performance for functions used many times in Excel. You can use **@cache** decorator[2] from **functools** library, also known as **memorize**.

```
import time
from functools import cache

# Simulating a slow function
def slow_double(x):
    """Pretend this is slow (e.g., heavy pandas calculation)."""
    time.sleep(2)
    return x * 2
```

[2] For older Python versions (< 3.9), you can use @lru_cache decorator from functools library, which stores up to the maxsize (default 128) most recent calls. You can set maxsize to None, and the cache will grow without bound.

```
# Calling twice: It' slow both times
print(slow_double(10))   # waits 2 sec
print(slow_double(10))   # waits 2 sec again

# Caching the result (fast after first call)
@cache
def slow_double_cached(x):
    """Same function, but cached."""
    time.sleep(2)      # Simulate heavy work
    return x * 2

# Calling twice: It' slow only first time
print(slow_double_cached(10)) # First call is slow (2 sec)
print(slow_double_cached(10)) # Second call is Instant!
```

Preventing defunct process states

In programming, a defunct process refers to a process that is dead but not buried; it means a process that has completed execution but still has an entry in the process table because its parent has not yet read its exit status.

If you open a new Excel instance using **xlwings** and close Excel, you might still see the Excel application running in Task Manager (Windows). In *Chapter 10, Transitioning to xlwings for Excel Automation,* we have discussed the best practices for closing Excel with **xlwings**.

Practical checklist for Excel users: In summary, the following points, taken together, offer a practical guide for optimizing performance with **xlwings**:

- Keep your data write range as contiguous as possible (e.g., one DataFrame write rather than cell-loops).
- If using UDFs over large ranges, design one UDF that returns a block (2D array) rather than many per-cell UDF calls.
- For heavy data processing, do it in Python (**pandas**), then write back only the result table.
- Temporarily disable Excel screen updates/auto-calc if you notice slowness.
- If the dataset grows huge (hundreds of thousands of rows), ask if the user really need all rows in Excel, or would a summary suffice?

Strategic automation with Python and Excel

The journey through this book has taken you from foundational Python concepts to a broad understanding of how multiple libraries interact with Excel's ecosystem. As you transition from individual chapters to real-world use, the next step is to integrate these tools and techniques into a coherent and efficient workflow.

The core value of Python-Excel automation lies in its flexibility. Throughout this book, you have worked with libraries such as **`pandas`**, **`openpyxl`**, **`xlsxwriter`**, **`pyxlsb`**, and **`xlwings`**, each offering unique capabilities. By viewing each library as part of a broader toolkit, rather than as isolated options, you gain the ability to construct workflows that are streamlined and aligned with your specific objectives.

Python is especially well-suited for operations that require repetitive logic, structured data manipulation, integration with external systems, or multi-step transformations. Excel complements this by providing an accessible interface for analysis, modeling, and presentation. When combined strategically, Python handles the heavy lifting while Excel becomes the flexible reporting layer. This blend allows you to reduce manual effort without removing the familiarity and accessibility that make Excel a dominant tool in business environments.

Choosing the right library for the task, separating logic from presentation, using clear folder structures, consistent naming conventions, modular Python scripts, and version-controlled code supports long-term sustainability. Likewise, minimizing unnecessary interactions with Excel, especially when using COM-based tools, can dramatically improve performance and reduce the risk of locking or instability. These are not just technical optimizations; they are core principles of professional-grade automation.

By consolidating your understanding of the tools, patterns, and decision-making frameworks explored throughout this book, you now possess the foundation to tailor solutions to a wide range of real-world contexts.

Notable highlights

Let us outline the principal lessons and insights derived from the book. If you are using Python for Excel automation, understand the strengths and limitations of each tool and choose the best one as per you need:

- Use **`pandas`** for data wrangling and analysis.
- Use **`openpyxl`** or **`xlsxwriter`** for formatting, charts, and formulas.
- Use **`xlwings`** when you need to interact with a live Excel instance.
- Use **`pyxlsb`** only when reading **`.xlsb`** files is essential.

Also, keep data processing (**`pandas`**) separate from Excel formatting (**`openpyxl`** or **`xlsxwriter`**). You should not embed your calculations or decisions directly inside Excel-writing code. For example:

```
# BAD: Mixing logic and Excel formatting
for row in data:
    tax = row['salary'] * 0.2                    # business logic
    worksheet.write(row_num, 4, tax)             # Excel write
```

Mixing calculations of your workflow and writing to cells or formatting is a bad idea, as this approach makes it hard to test the logic independently or reuse it in a web app or API. Instead, you should separate the business logic from Excel-specific code, such as:

```
# Step 1: Business logic (pure function)
def compute_tax(df):
    df['tax'] = df['salary'] * 0.2
    return df
# Step 2: Presentation (Excel formatting)
def write_to_excel(df, filename):
    with pd.ExcelWriter(filename, engine='xlsxwriter') as writer:
        df.to_excel(writer, index=False)
        # Apply formatting here
```

This approach allows you to test **`compute_tax()`** with dummy data, reuse it in a web app, API, or notebook, and swap Excel for CSV, HTML, or database output, as needed. You can also add schema validation to your code. Schema validation means verifying that your data has the expected structure (such as required columns, correct data types, and valid values) before processing it. This structure makes your workflow reliable, maintainable, and efficient.

Using Python for heavy data wrangling, API calls, or web scraping, and complex logic or ML models, and then exporting clean data to Excel for presentation, interactivity, and stakeholder review is an effective strategy. For computations, avoid relying on Excel formulas or macros unless necessary.

Additionally, to make your workflows reproducible, it is recommended to use virtual environments and pin library versions.

You can take it a step further to record what your automation does, when it does it, and what results it produces, so you (or others) can understand, debug, and audit the workflow later. This is called **logging**, and it helps in debugging, auditing, collaboration, and versioning. Logging is like keeping a running diary of what your automation does, step by step. It records actions (like *file loaded* or *10 rows filtered*) so you can trace what happened, spot errors, and explain results later.

To make log steps and outputs for traceability, you can use Python's **`logging`** module (which is available in Python's standard library, so it does not need a separate installation). A simple example is mentioned in the following:

```
import logging
import pandas as pd

# Set up logging to file
logging.basicConfig(
    filename='sales_log.log',
    level=logging.INFO,
    format='%(asctime)s - %(levelname)s - %(message)s'
)

# Step 1: Create sample data
data = {
    'region': ['North', 'South', 'East', 'West'],
    'units_sold': [120, 85, 90, 110],
    'unit_price': [10.0, 12.5, 9.5, 11.0]
}
df = pd.DataFrame(data)
logging.info("Created initial sales DataFrame")

# Step 2: Calculate total sales
df['total_sales'] = df['units_sold'] * df['unit_price']
logging.info("Calculated total_sales column")

# Step 3: Save to Excel
output_file = 'regional_sales.xlsx'
df.to_excel(output_file, index=False)
logging.info(f"Saved processed data to {output_file}")
```

This creates a file called **`sales_log.log`**, which can be opened in any text editor such as notepad. This file logs three messages with timestamps and levels.

Finally, it is important to mention that **Don't use a sledgehammer to crack a nut**, which means that just because you have mastered Python libraries, it does not imply that Python should be applied in every scenario. In certain cases, standard Excel functionality offers a more appropriate and efficient solution.

Situations favoring native Excel tools

As an Excel user, there are scenarios where using Python might be overkill. We recommend not using Python:

- When Excel formulas are easier, quicker, and you do not need to repeat those steps on new data, you can simply use Excel for such basic tasks.
- When your audience needs simplicity and is not comfortable with scripting. If non-technical users need to maintain or tweak the workflow, if required, as a Python coder, you can provide them with workbook powered by **`xlwings`**, where they need to just click to run Python analysis.
- When live Excel interactivity is required, such as dashboards with slicers, pivot tables, or linked charts, and data volume is small, using Excel with power-pivot would be enough.
- If there are any deployment constraints, such as no Python environment available or allowed in your machine due to corporate IT restrictions, and Excel is the only approved tool for sharing or collaboration and Excel add-ins are restricted too. You can use cloud-based environments such as Google Colab, which is useful for experimentation, learning, and prototyping but it is generally unsuitable for production workflows or enterprise collaboration.

Evolving landscape of Excel automation

Recent developments in Excel show a significant transformation, inspired by Python's simplicity and power. This includes native **Python integration**, **Copilot** support and recent **Claude** integration, marking a shift toward AI-enhanced productivity and more flexible analytical workflows.

Anticipating technological trends helps you position your skills effectively and use each tool to its fullest potential. Given today's automation landscape, VBA is no longer a strategic investment, as organizations shift toward more scalable alternatives.

Python in Excel

Python in Excel (**PIE**) is available in **Microsoft 365** (subscription version). *Figure 13.2* displays the Python in Excel option available in the **`Formulas`** tab of Excel 365. The core libraries available with Python in Excel by default are **`numpy`**, **`pandas`**, **`matplotlib`**, **`seaborn`**, and **`statsmodel`**. By selecting Formulas | Initialization in the Excel ribbon, you can verify the same.

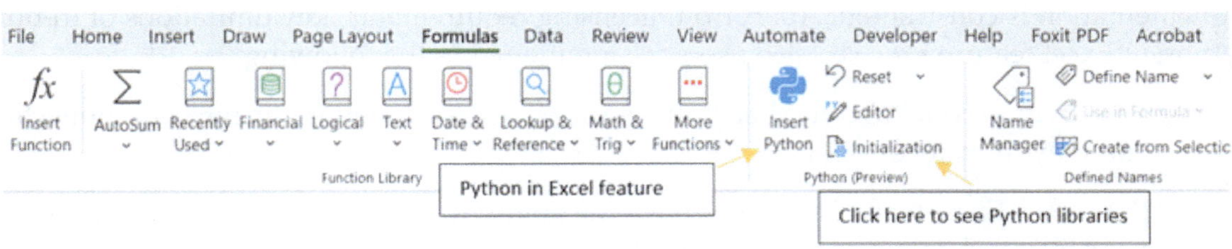

***Figure 13.2**: Python in Excel 365*

This feature allows you to type Python directly into a cell using **`=PY()`** function or by clicking at **`Insert Python`**. To explore, just type a simple one liner code in the Python cell and hit *Ctr + Enter* to see the output:

```
df = pd.DataFrame({'a':[1,2,3]}); df['a'].sum()
```

It runs Python calculations on the Microsoft cloud, and your results are returned to the worksheet. You can also the Python Editor pane from formulas tab to write multi-line code. The following figure shows the use of Python in Excel feature in cells I2, I4, and I14 along with Editor displaying Python code used:

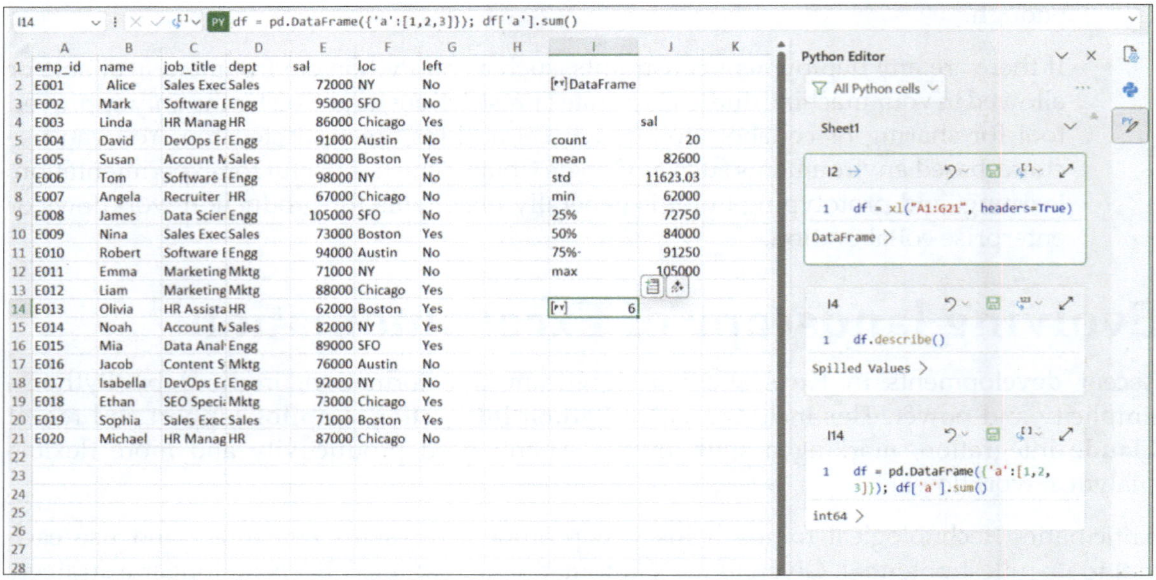

Figure 13.3: *Using Python in Excel feature (Excel 365)*

Python fundamentals, **`numpy`**, **`pandas`**, and other concepts and skills you have learned in this book remain fully relevant and can be directly applied within Python in Excel (Excel 365).

Limitations of Python in Excel feature of Excel 365

While the capabilities of Python in Excel (365) streamline certain tasks, its current implementation is constrained. Apart from licensing requirements, key limitations of in-built Python in Excel feature for Excel 365 users are mentioned in the following:

- Your Python code runs on Microsoft's Azure cloud, so it requires an internet connection and may introduce latency.
- Python in Excel feature does not have the ability to make network requests or access your files and data on your local machine.

- Python code returns output to your workbooks through the **`=PY()`** Excel function, which displays the result of the Python code in the cell where the function is entered. It requires manual adjustment to view complete results and careful handling to avoid overwriting existing data.
- Python functions cannot return other object types like macros, VBA code, or other formulas.
- The Python code does not have access to other properties in the workbook, such as formulas, charts, PivotTables, macros, or VBA code.
- Writing and debugging Python code within Excel cells is less intuitive and flexible compared to working in standalone Python scripts, which offer a more robust development environment.

Python inside Excel works well for exploratory analysis and small experiments; however, you cannot replace all external automation with Python-in-Excel formulas. External Python, as covered throughout this book, offers full-scale automation, integration with files and APIs, scheduled workflows, and production-grade data handling. If you are looking for a simple alternative to Python in Excel feature, you can also explore **`xlwings Lite`** (to be discussed in the next section, *xlwings Lite as an alternative*).

Copilot in Excel

Artificial intelligence, particularly through tools like Copilot, is becoming more deeply integrated into Office applications. Copilot in Excel can only be used with Excel files (**`.xlsx`**, **`.xlsb`**, or **`.xlsm`**) that have been saved to OneDrive or SharePoint locations with **`AutoSave`** turned on.

AI is increasingly capable of generating formulas, suggesting transformations, or interpreting data. However, AI still relies heavily on well-structured worksheets, clear logic, and accurate data sources. To effectively use Copilot as an assistant, you also need to learn the art of prompting.

Additionally, its responses may contain incorrect or suboptimal codes, errors or inconsistencies, especially when performing complex logic operations.

Claude in Excel

Claude in Excel is an add-in (currently in beta) that brings Anthropic's Claude (Opus 4.5) into Excel via a sidebar. Microsoft documents that Agent Mode in Excel now supports selecting Claude models from the Copilot model switcher.

However, using Claude in Excel is currently available to customers on the Claude Pro, Max, Team and Enterprise plans (Commercial plan).

Additionally, Claude does not have advanced Excel capabilities, including data tables, macros and VBA.

As a beta feature, Claude in Excel is **not recommended** for final client deliverables without human review and models containing highly sensitive or regulated data without proper controls.

The techniques you have learned in Python, such as cleaning data, structuring workflows, thinking step-by-step, directly enhance your ability to use AI tools effectively. Instead of replacing your skills, AI amplifies them when you understand the underlying mechanics.

Most importantly, the future of Excel automation is not about choosing between Excel, Python, AI, or cloud tools. It is about developing the judgment to match each task with the most appropriate approach. Some workflows will remain Excel-centric, others will shift to Python or cloud platforms; still others will combine methods. Your knowledge now spans multiple layers of this ecosystem, enabling you to work more flexibly and design solutions that endure as technology continues to advance.

These ongoing developments reinforce the fact that Python-Excel automation is a foundational capability for the modern data workplace. As tools evolve, professionals who understand both Excel's interface and the programmatic power of Python will be uniquely positioned to lead, guide, and build the next generation of automated workflows.

xlwings Lite as an alternative to PIE

For basic Excel automation, you can also use `xlwings Lite`, which does not require a local Python installation and stores the Python code inside Excel for easy distribution. So, the only requirement is to have the `xlwings Lite add-in` installed. This is free to install for both personal and commercial use with no usage limit.

Using `xlwings Lite` instead of PIE feature allows you to run Python code locally instead of Microsoft's server. It also gives you access to the Excel object model, which means you can insert new sheets and format data as an Excel table. Another great thing about `xlwings` Lite is that it allows web API requests.

Unlike `Python in Excel` feature, `xlwings Lite` only requires a network connection for loading the add-in. Once loaded, `xlwings Lite` works offline. `xlwings Lite` has some limitations such as control over package versions, database connectivity, memory limit and unavailability of debugger. You can read more about the same at official page (**https://lite.xlwings.org/**).

Conclusion

In this chapter, we discussed best practices for performance optimization while working with large files in Python-Excel landscape, the strategies to automate your workflow by integrating Excel and required Python tools.

We have also talked about recent developments in Microsoft Excel, and xlwings Lite as another lightweight alternative within the broader Python–Excel ecosystem.

Some additional useful topics are included in the appendix for further learning.

Concept check

1. Your task is to generate a monthly report Excel file with 12 sheets, clean formatting, conditional formatting, and charts. The report must be created from scratch every month and shared with stakeholders. No one needs to edit formulas after creation.

   Which tool(s) would you choose and why?

2. You are processing a 200,000-row dataset and exporting it to Excel with formatting. Your current workflow is slow and sometimes crashes. You are using Python, but you are unsure whether the bottleneck is in data processing or Excel writing.

   What are three practical optimization decisions you should make, and how do they relate to the tools covered in this book?

3. Python in Excel (Microsoft 365) is a new capability. However, it is not designed to replace Python–Excel workflow covered in this book.

   Based on what you have learned so far, what are the key limitations of Python in Excel that requires external Python automation using tools such as pandas, openpyxl, xlsxwriter, or xlwings?

Closing remarks

This is the end of the book. We have achieved meaningful growth, starting with learning Python basics to exploring various libraries for Excel automation. All packages used in the book are open source.

Furthermore, you can explore topics like connecting Python to databases, fetching data from APIs or websites, unit testing, logging, scheduling Python scripts, automatic email sending with Python, etc. Each of these tasks can be accomplished using specialized Python libraries purpose-built for efficient and targeted functionality, such as requests, sqlite3, unittest, pytest, logging, schedule, and smtplib, etc.

This additional learning will equip you with powerful automation to streamline data access, automate routine tasks, and build scalable workflows that reduce manual effort and enhance productivity across tools and platforms.

Thank you for your interest in the book, and wish you all the best!

Appendix: Python Charts for Business Analysis

Matplotlib and Seaborn in practice

Earlier chapters used **pandas** and other libraries to create or export charts to Excel. Here, we are introducing **matplotlib** and **seaborn**, the two libraries most Python users rely on for professional-quality visualizations.

Matplotlib is the core data visualization library in Python, which supports a wide range of charts such as line, bar, scatter, histogram, area, 3D, polar, etc. This library offers **fine-grained control** over almost every visual element, say, figure size, axes, ticks, labels, colors, annotations, layouts, and export settings. It is because of this flexibility that matplotlib acts as the foundation for most Python plotting libraries, such as seaborn, plotly, and more.

Seaborn is a high-level (built on top of **matplotlib**) Python library that focuses on creating statistical and distribution-focused charts with minimal code. It provides better default styling, automatic handling of categories, and direct integration with **pandas** DataFrames. This makes **seaborn** especially useful for exploratory data analysis and comparison of distributions.

While **seaborn** simplifies chart creation, it does not replace **matplotlib**. If you need more control over titles, annotations, axes, or layout, you can further customize **seaborn** charts using **matplotlib** functions.

In practice, both libraries are often used together in the same script:

- **Seaborn** to quickly create meaningful statistical charts
- **Matplotlib** to refine and customize them as required

For example, the chart shown in the following figure is created using both plotting libraries:

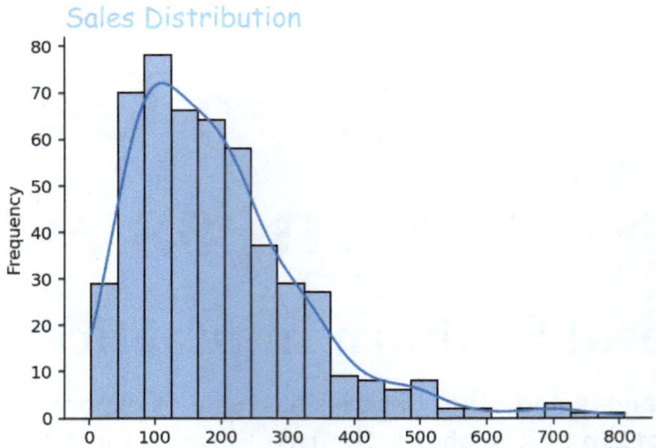

***Figure A.1**: Histogram plus density plot with customized header (font, size, color, position)*

Using the familiar **plotting_data.csv** to generate the above-mentioned plot:

```
df = pd.read_csv('plotting_data.csv')

# Seaborn for distribution
sns.histplot(data=df, x='Sales', bins=20, kde=True)

# Matplotlib for customization
plt.title("Sales Distribution", loc='left',
          fontdict = {'fontsize': 16, 'fontname': 'Comic Sans MS',
                      'color': 'skyblue'})
plt.xlabel("")
plt.ylabel("Frequency")
```

We can see seaborn makes plotting effortless and matplotlib low-level customization possible. This is why most Python data-visualization workflows use **both libraries side by side**, rather than choosing one over the other.

Irrespective of the tool we use for plotting, we must first understand which chart is suitable for your requirements. Many times, there are multiple charts available and technically feasible for the same data. You need to look at the objective (that includes the number and type of variables to plot), your audience, context, and sometimes design or other limitations to pick the appropriate chart for your requirement.

A rapid checklist (not covering details of chart selection guideline) is to use bar chart (known as column chart) for categorical data, histogram, box plot, violin plot, or density plot (also known as KDE plot) for understanding distribution of a numerical variable (maybe for different categories), line chart for trend over time, scatterplot for relationship between numerical variables, and heatmap for encoding intensity and variation of values in a numeric table, making patterns, clusters, and anomalies easier to spot.

Charts for categorical data

To answer business questions such as which category or region perform better in terms of sales or profit, you can create bar chart as follows:

```
sns.barplot(data = df, x='Region', y='Sales')

# Alternately you can use sns.catplot()
sns.catplot(data=df, x='Region', y='Sales', kind='bar')

# Stacked Bar Chart_ Sales by Region and Category
sns.catplot(data = df, x='Region', y='Sales',
            hue='Category', kind = 'bar')
```

Seaborn provides two functions for column charts. The function **sns.barplot()** is a lowlevel function, draws a single bar chart (optionally with hue for grouped/ stackedstyle bars). And **sns.catplot()** is a highlevel function which also supports **faceting** to split into multiple subplots automatically. Faceting means splitting the graph into several subplots (multiple rows or columns).

To make comparisons across categories easier, let us apply column wise faceting:

```
sns.catplot(data=df, x='Region', y='Sales', col='Category', kind='bar')
```

You can customize title, axis labels, subtitle, etc. and produce chart, as shown in the following figure:

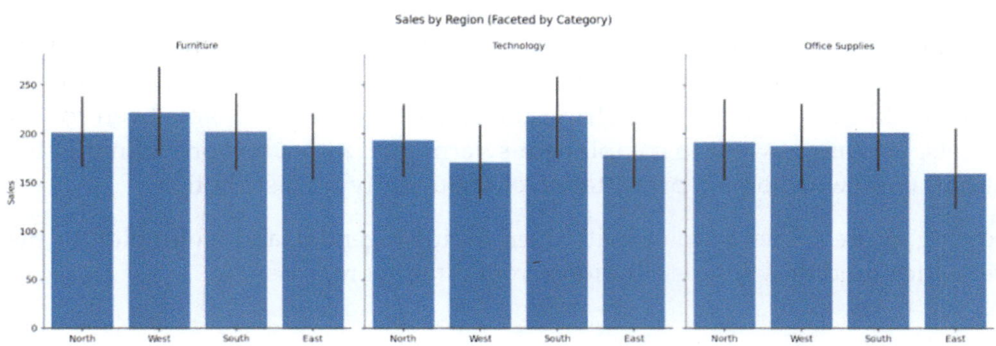

Figure A.2: Facetted Chart _ One chart per Category

Seaborn makes to convenient to visualize multi-variable relationships using faceting as we have done for sales, region and category.

Charts for numerical distribution

To understand the distribution of sales or profit, seaborn provides multiple chart options. It is also convenient to see how numbers are spread across regions or categories. You have already seen **sns.histplot()** for histogram. Simple code for other charts is as follows:

```
# Boxplot _Sales Distribution
sns.boxplot(df, y = df['Sales'])

# Boxplot _Sales Distribution for different regions
sns.boxplot(df, y = df['Sales'],
            hue = df['Region'], gap = 0.5, fill = False)

# Violin plot _Sales Distribution for different regions
sns.violinplot(data=df, hue='Region', y='Sales', inner='quartile')
plt.tight_layout() # auto-adjust spacing to prevent overlap

# Swarmp plot
sns.swarmplot(df, x='Region', y='Sales')
```

As you may have noticed, in a few places columns have been referenced using expressions like **df['Sales']** and **df['Region']**. While this works, it is not necessary when using **seaborn**. When a DataFrame is passed using the data parameter, **seaborn** allows columns to be referred to directly by their names (e.g., **'Sales'**, **'Region'**), making the syntex simpler and cleaner.

You need to choose suitable chart as per your requirements and you should also play with chart designs to understand what works best for your data and objective. For example, here **plt.tight_layout()** is used to auto-adjust spacing to quicky fit the legend, else you can customize it in detail.

Another example is, while exploring with different data sets and different plot functions, you might notice that using a swarm plot for large data set is not a good idea as it tries to place every point without overlapping, so strip plot might be a better choice. Even for medium size data sets, you might want to compliment swarm plot with a box or violin plot to see all observations along with some representation of the underlying distribution.

The following figure shows boxplot (with overlapping legends), and violin plot for the same objective, understanding sales distribution across different regions:

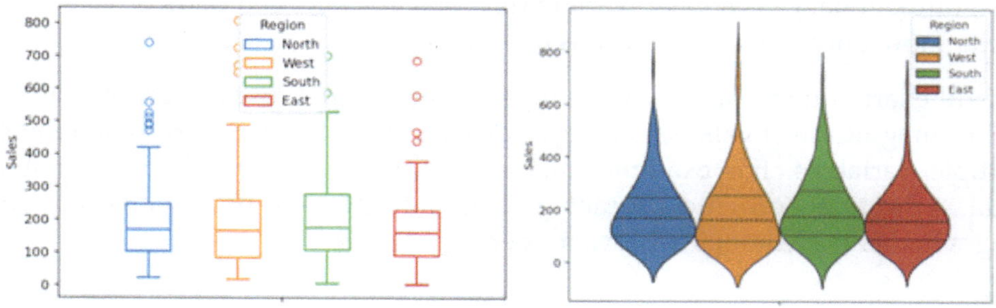

***Figure A.3**: Boxplot with overlapping legends (left) and Violin plot (right)*

Charts for relationship

To explore how numerical variables such as sales and profit move together, we can create scatterplot. Additional parameters like hue, and size can display the impact of some grouping variable(s).

```
sns.scatterplot(df, x = 'Sales', y = 'Profit', hue='Region', alpha = 0.5)
```

Usually, the data sets have too many numerical variables, to visualize pair-wise relationships between each or selected variables, you can simply use **`sns.pairplot()`**. It creates a grid of plots, as shown in the following figure:

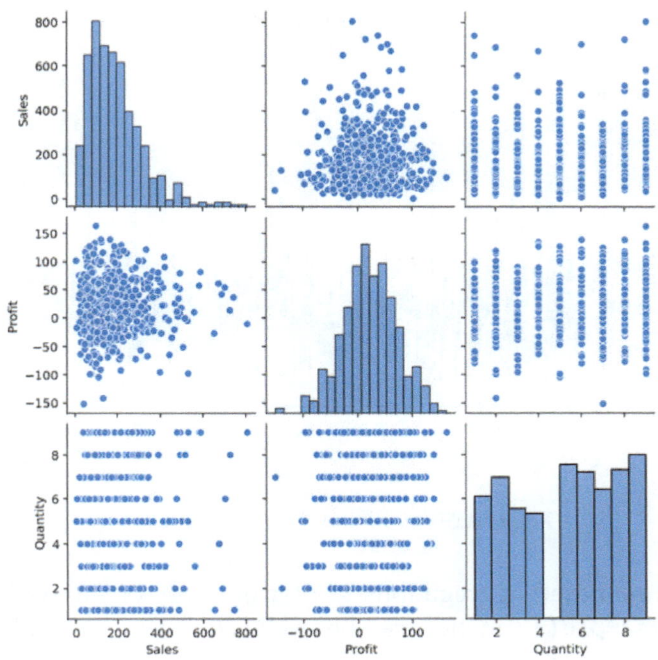

***Figure A.4**: Seaborn pairplot illustrating variable relationships and individual distributions*

In this chart, offdiagonal cells show bivariate relationships between pairs of variables, while diagonal cells show univariate distributions of each variable.

Another useful chart you might want to explore is a heatmap. It uses color intensity to show the strength or magnitude of values, making it ideal for identifying patterns and relationships across multiple variables. For example, manually scanning a large correlation matrix is not practical. A heatmap provides instant insights into positive or negative relationships, highlighting whether correlations are low, moderate, or high.

Charts for trend

To visualize how numbers change over time, often line chart is used. Let us create a simple line chart to visualize daily sales pattern.

```
sns.lineplot(data = df, x = 'Date', y = 'Sales')
plt.xticks(rotation=45) # rotate x-axis labels for readability
plt.title('Sales Pattern')
plt.xlabel("")
plt.ylabel("")
sns.despine()
```

The resultant chart is shown in the following figure:

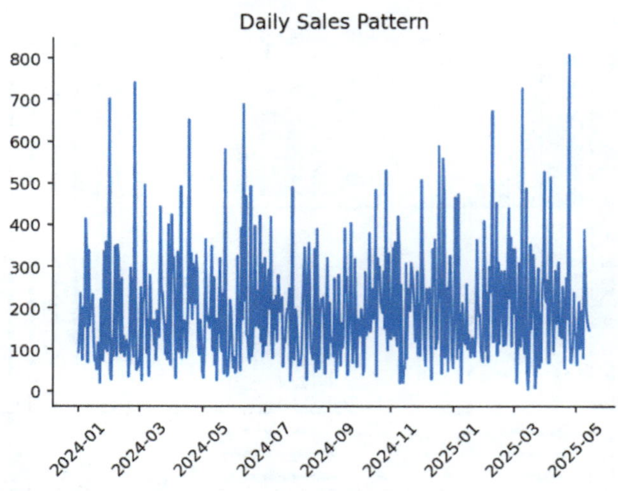

Figure A.5*: Sales Trend (Daily Frequency)*

You can also create time-based aggregations to plot monthly or quarterly trends. For time-based aggregation, **`resample()`** function can be used with frequency rules such as seconds, minutes, hours, days, weeks, months, quarters, or years.

```
monthly_sales = (
    df
    .set_index('Date')
    .resample('ME')['Sales']
    .sum()
    .reset_index()
)
```

The first few rows of **monthly_sales** data are shown in the following figure:

Index	Date	Sales
0	2024-01-31 00:00:00	5654.97
1	2024-02-29 00:00:00	4754.92
2	2024-03-31 00:00:00	5700.73
3	2024-04-30 00:00:00	6653.12
4	2024-05-31 00:00:00	4966.49
5	2024-06-30 00:00:00	6370.28

***Figure A.6**: Glimpse of Sales figures aggregated monthly*

If you replace **.resample('ME')** in the above code with **.resample('QE')**, you get data down sampled to quarterly frequency.

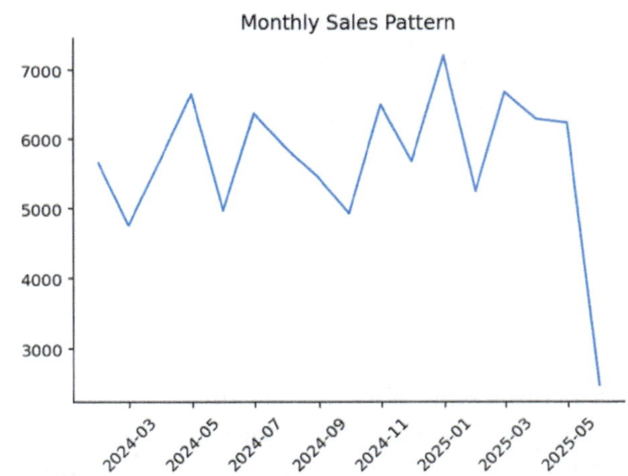

***Figure A.7**: Sales Trend (Monthly Frequency)*

Figure A.7 displays monthly sales trend. To capture raw sales alongside the moving average for clearer insights, you can use **.rolling()** method of pandas, which allows you to compute moving averages with ease.

```
# Calculate 7-day moving average
df['Sales_MA7'] = df['Sales'].rolling(window=7).mean()

# Plot raw sales vs moving average
plt.figure(figsize=(12,6))
plt.plot(df['Date'], df['Sales'], label='Daily Sales', alpha=0.5)
plt.plot(df['Date'], df['Sales_MA7'], label='7-
Day Moving Average', color='red')
plt.title("Sales with 7-Day Moving Average")
plt.xlabel("Date")
plt.ylabel("Sales")
plt.legend()
```

The resultant chart is shown in the following figure:

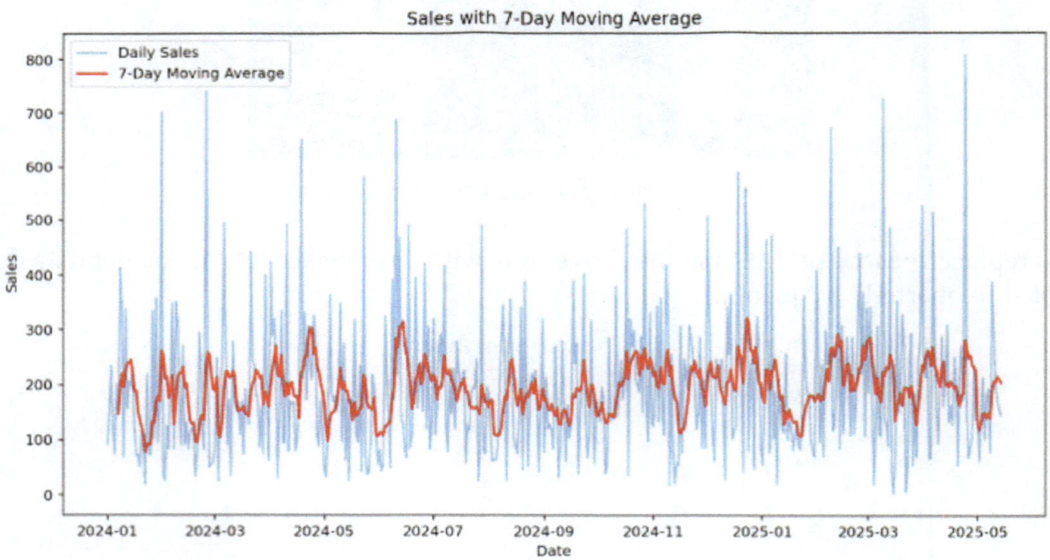

***Figure A.8**: Plotting sales with moving average*

In time series data, to reveal recurring patterns (such as holiday sales spikes, or summer slowdowns), contextual benchmarking, anomaly spotting (for example, sudden drop in one year's Q4) or plotting year on year growth (for example, to understand whether performance improved or declined for the same calendar window), basic pandas functions along with seaborn or matplotlib plots comes handy.

To find year-on-year comparison of monthly sales:

```
df['Year'] = df['Date'].dt.year
df['Month'] = df['Date'].dt.month

sns.lineplot(data=df, x='Month', y='Sales', hue='Year')
```

While our data set is relatively small, it is sufficient to illustrate a year-on-year comparison of sales in the following figure:

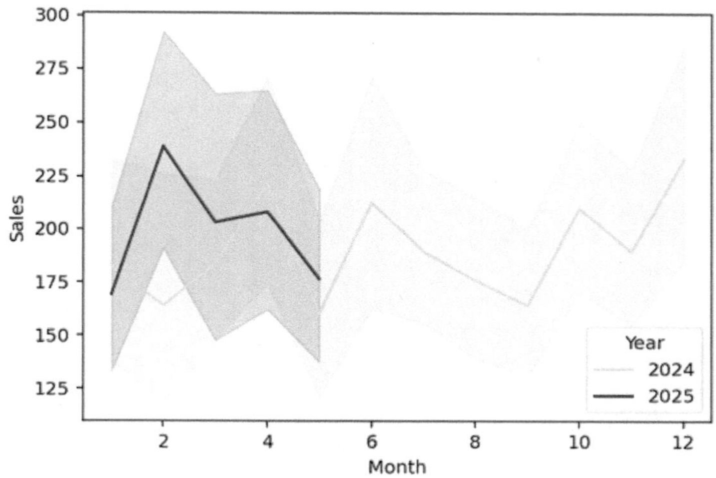

Figure A.9: Year-on-year comparison of sales

You have seen that date-based analysis that requires multiple helper columns and manual steps in Excel, can often be done in Python with simple code. A lot more customizations can be done in these basic charts for better exploration of hidden information in the data or effectively communicating results.

Furthermore, **matplotlib** allows precise layout management using subplots, flexible placement of annotations, arrows, and text, and supports advanced visuals such as 3D and polar plots. It also offers strong control over axes, ticks, spacing, and export settings (DPI, file formats), making it ideal for publication-quality and highly customized visuals.

Charts created with **matplotlib** or **seaborn** are exported to Excel as static images. This is why we have focused on libraries such as **openpyxl**, **xlsxwriter**, and **xlwings** that allow embedding charts linked to data in their specific chapters. However, learning **matplotlib** and **seaborn** provides you an advantage because they are available by default in Excel 365 with Python integration. This enables users to generate dynamic, data-aware charts directly within Excel by writing Python code. You can check these libraries official documentations for details of different plots and customizations.

Index

Symbols

A

B

C

D

E

N

O

P

Q

R

S

T

U

V

W

X

Y